An Incurable Case of Love

1

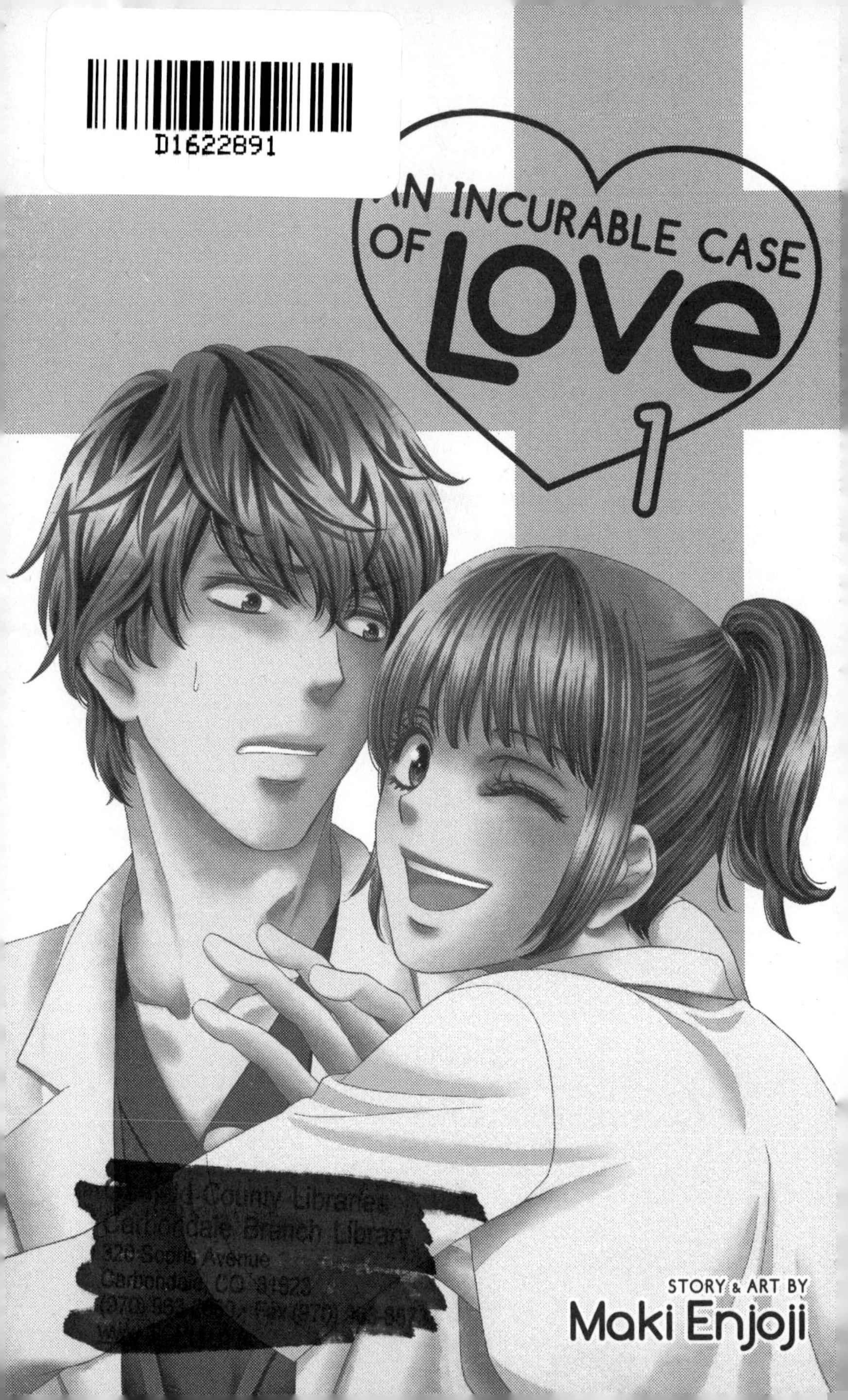

STORY & ART BY

Maki Enjoji

CONTENTS

First Love
Love Is Blind ... But I Don't Believe That! (3)

Second Love
Love Is a Showdown. It Really Is! (45)

Third Love
Love Always Strikes Unexpectedly. (80)
It's Rather Frustrating!

Fourth Love
Love Is One Big Contradiction. (117)
I Know That, But...!

Fifth Love
Gravity Doesn't Make People Fall in Love. (152)
I Already Know That!

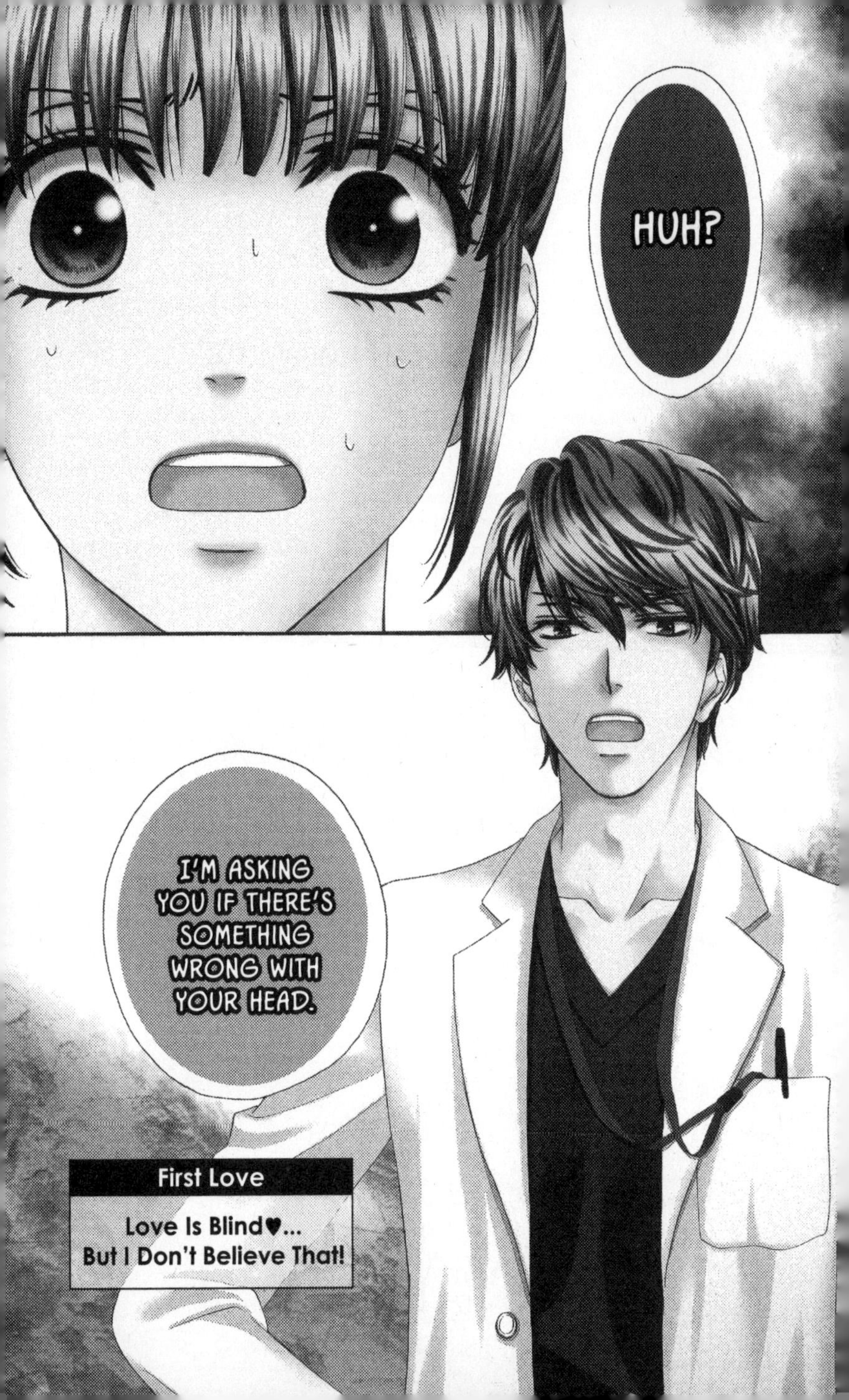
HUH?
I'M ASKING YOU IF THERE'S SOMETHING WRONG WITH YOUR HEAD.
First Love
Love Is Blind♥... But I Don't Believe That!

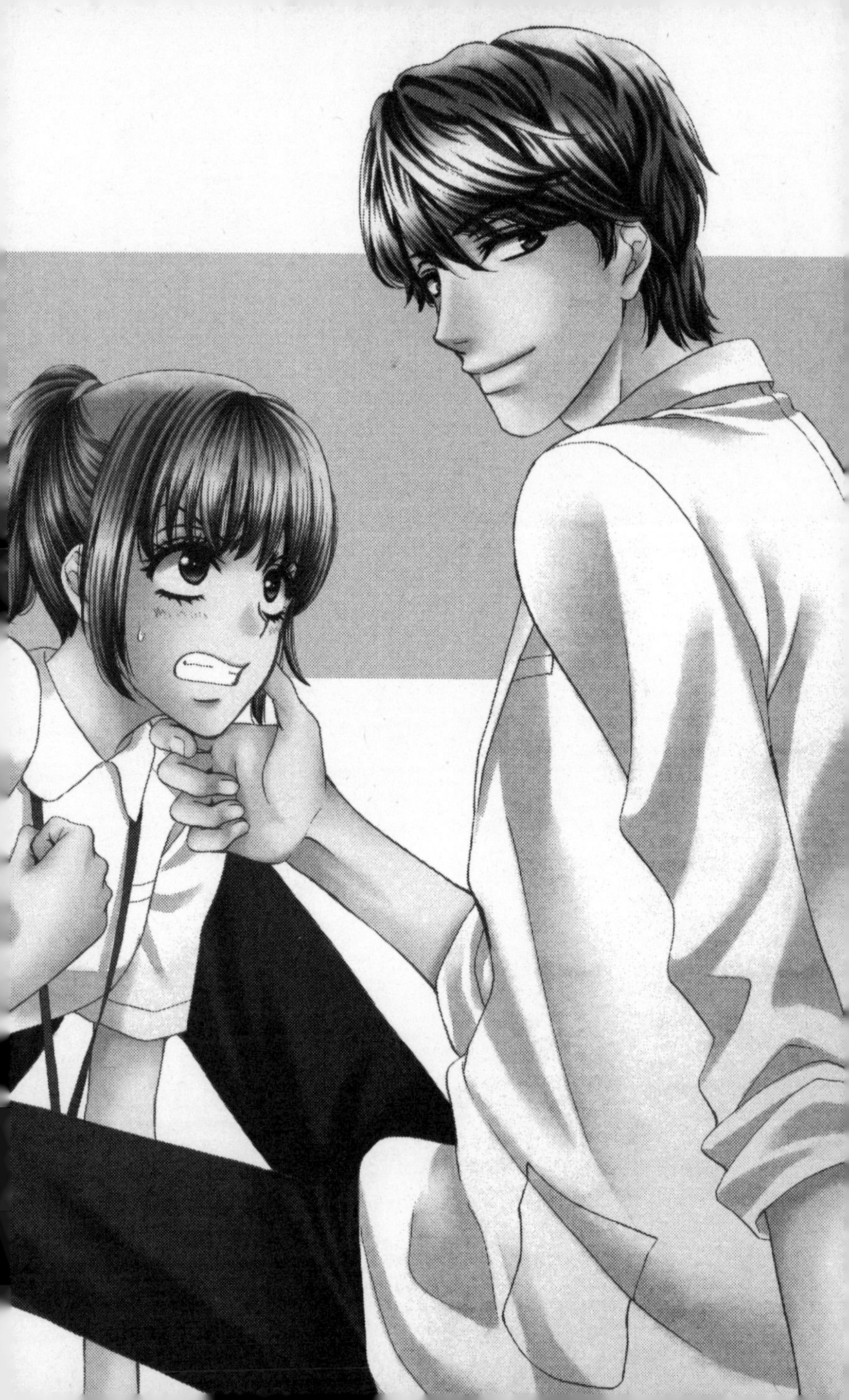

First Love

Love Is Blind♥... But I Don't Believe That!

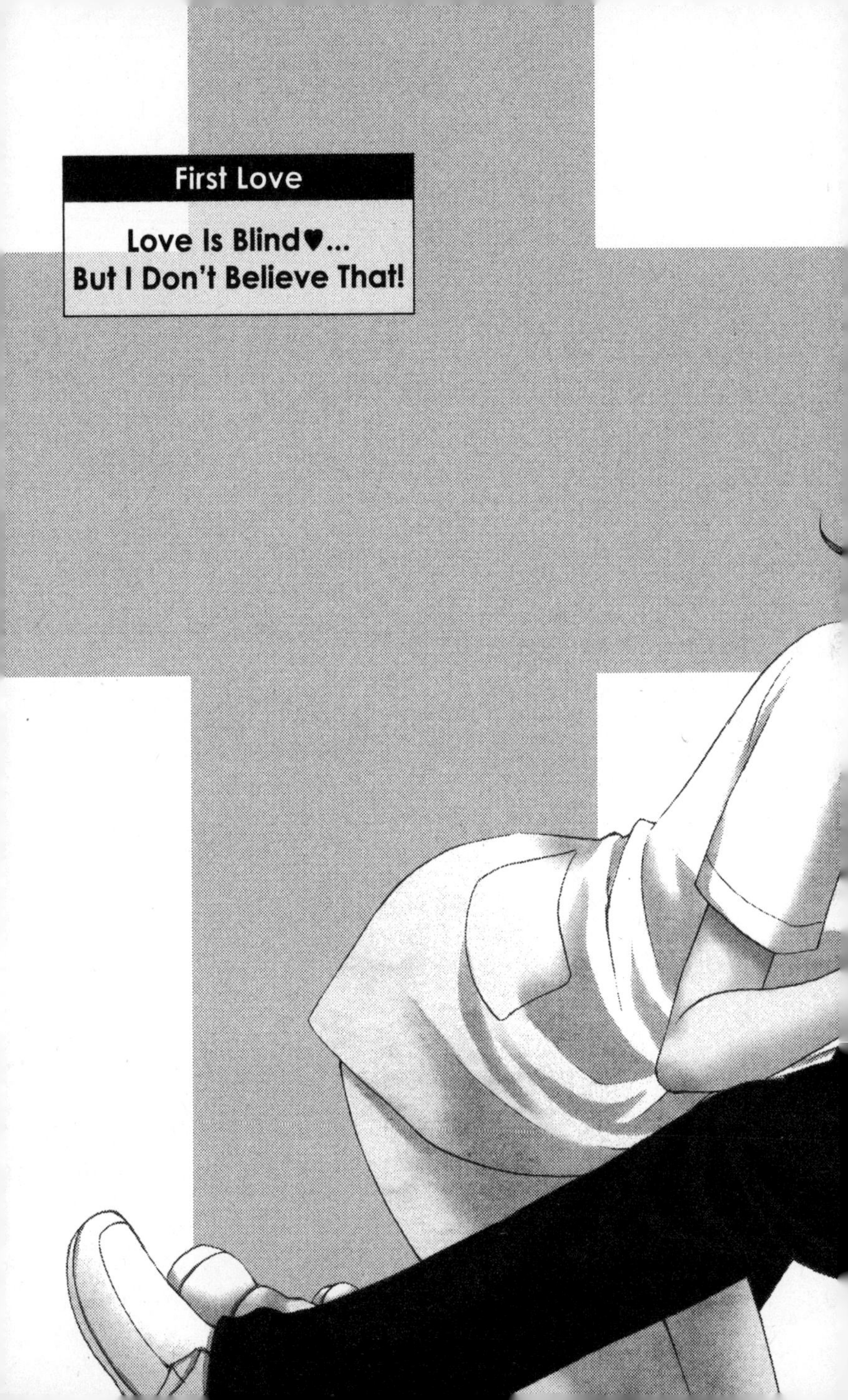

AN INCURABLE CASE OF LOVE

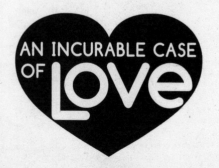

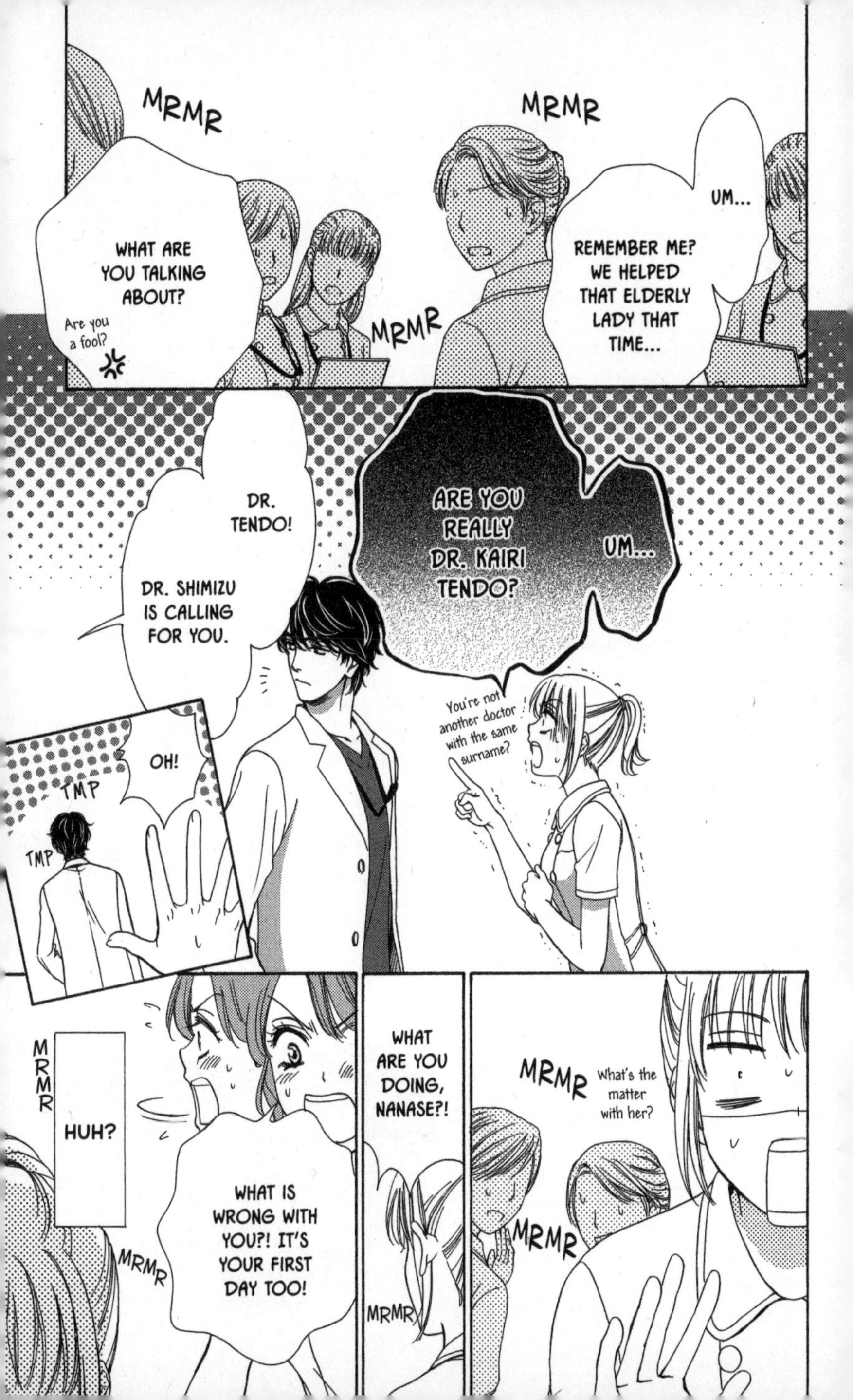
MRMR
UM...
REMEMBER ME? WE HELPED THAT ELDERLY LADY THAT TIME...
MRMR
MRMR
WHAT ARE YOU TALKING ABOUT?
Are you a fool?
UM...
ARE YOU REALLY DR. KAIRI TENDO?
You're not another doctor with the same surname?
DR. TENDO!
DR. SHIMIZU IS CALLING FOR YOU.
OH!
TMP
TMP
MRMR
What's the matter with her?
MRMR
WHAT ARE YOU DOING, NANASE?!
MRMR
MRMR
HUH?
WHAT IS WRONG WITH YOU?! IT'S YOUR FIRST DAY TOO!
MRMR

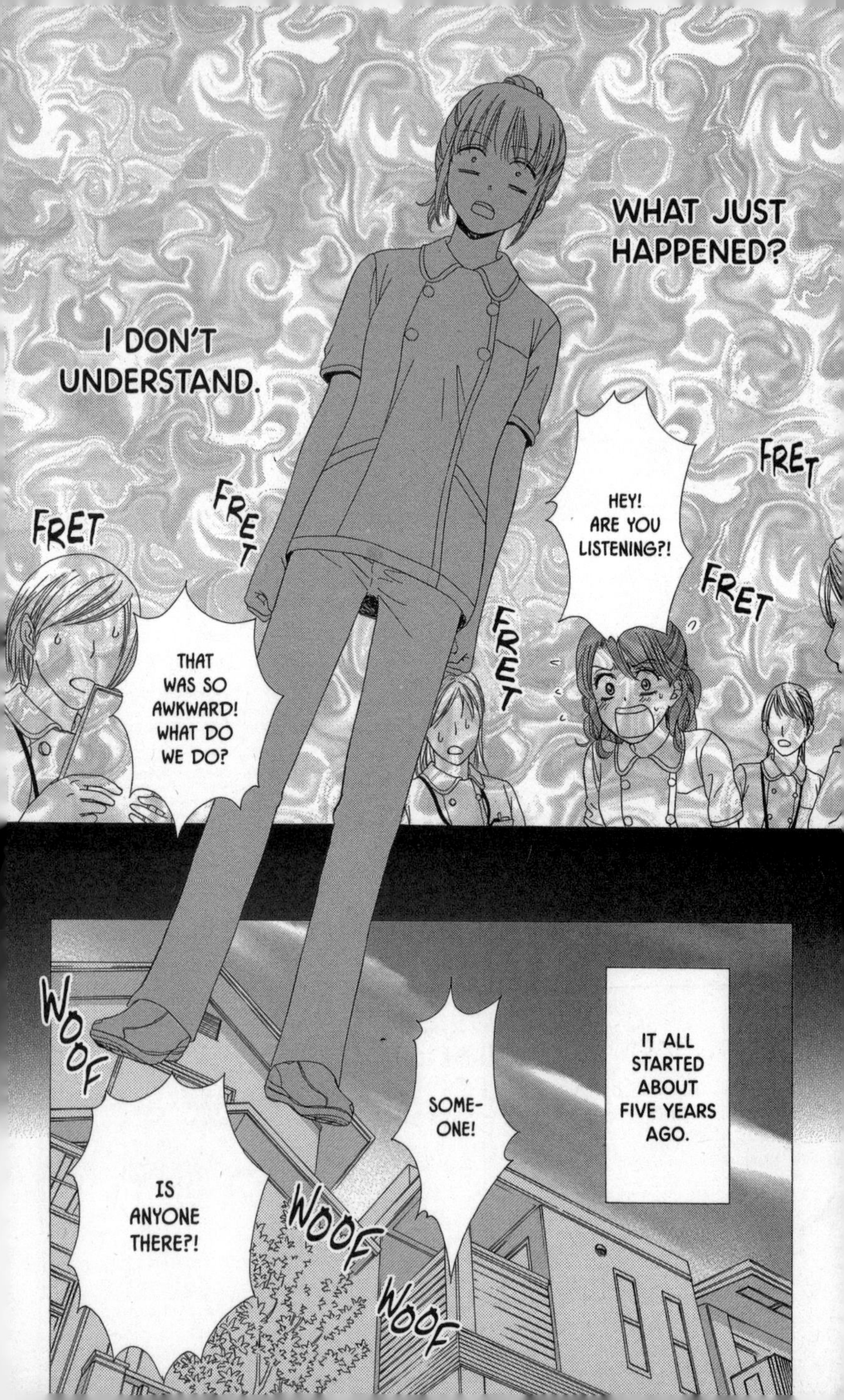
WHAT JUST HAPPENED?
I DON'T UNDERSTAND.
FRET
HEY! ARE YOU LISTENING?!
FRET
FRET
FRET
THAT WAS SO AWKWARD! WHAT DO WE DO?
FRET
IT ALL STARTED ABOUT FIVE YEARS AGO.
SOME-ONE!
WOOF
WOOF
IS ANYONE THERE?!
WOOF

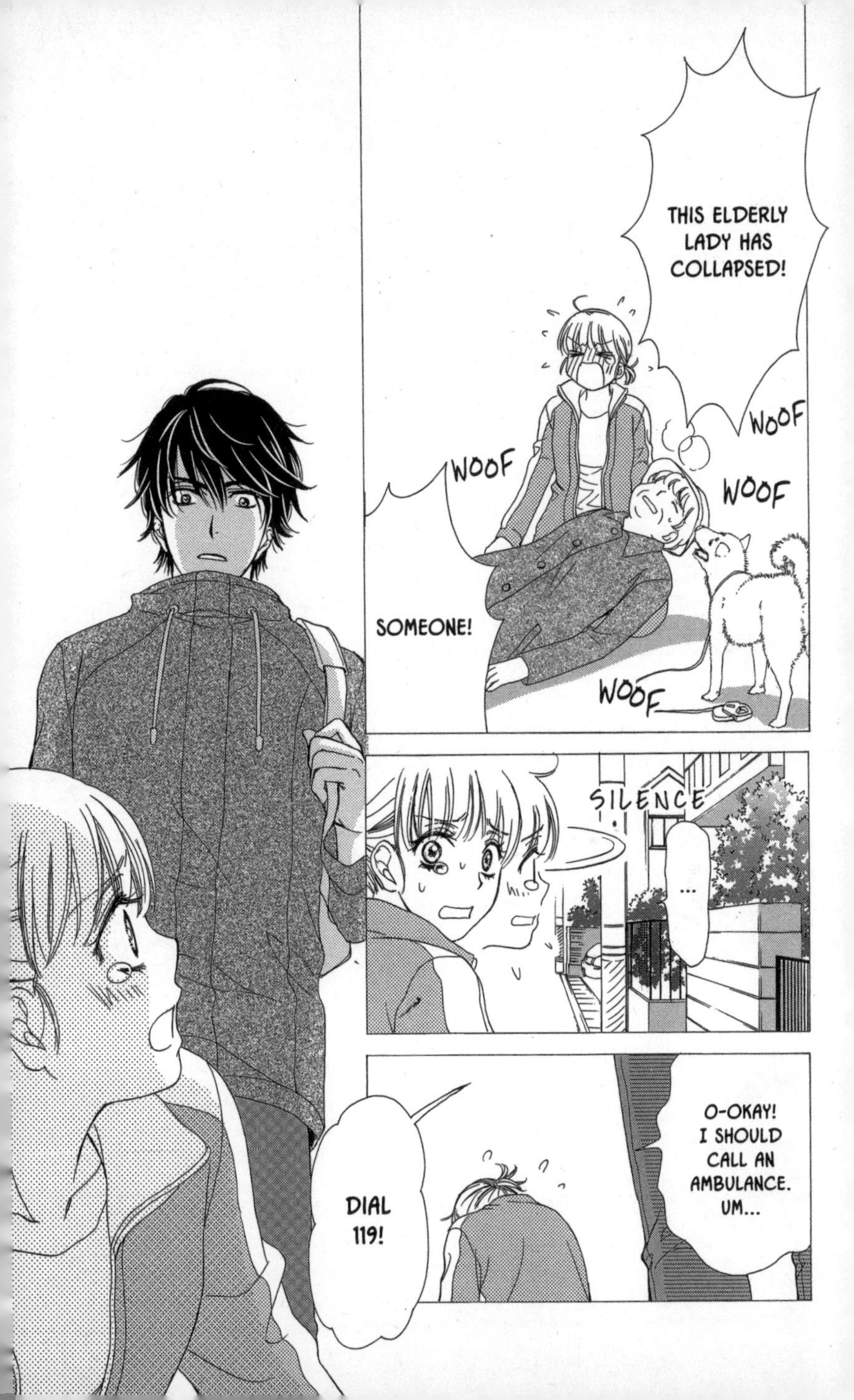
THIS ELDERLY LADY HAS COLLAPSED!
WOOF
WOOF
WOOF
SOMEONE!
WOOF
SILENCE
...
O-OKAY! I SHOULD CALL AN AMBULANCE. UM...
DIAL 119!

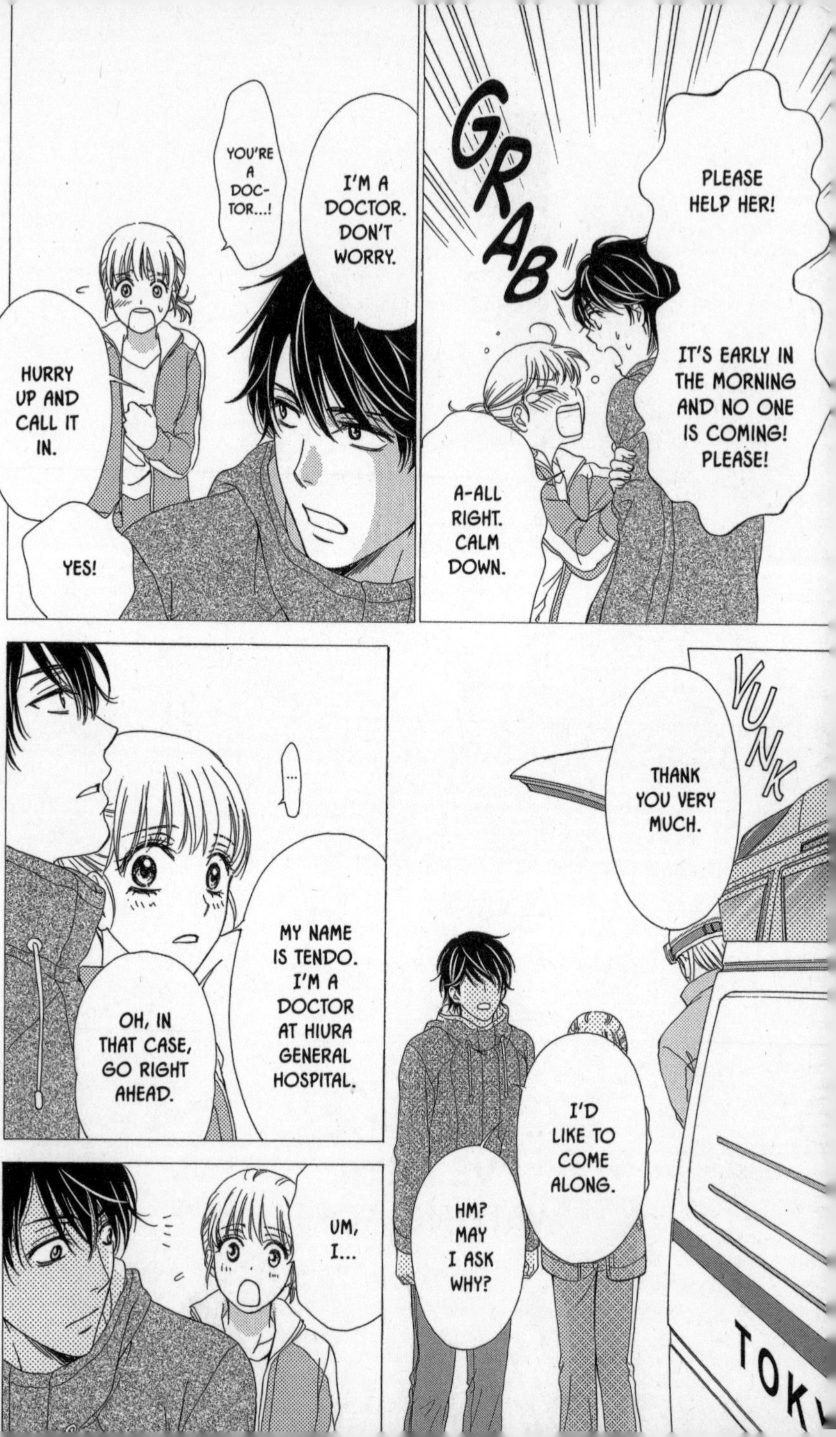
GRAB
PLEASE HELP HER!
IT'S EARLY IN THE MORNING AND NO ONE IS COMING! PLEASE!
A-ALL RIGHT. CALM DOWN.
I'M A DOCTOR. DON'T WORRY.
YOU'RE A DOC-TOR...!
HURRY UP AND CALL IT IN.
YES!
YUNK
THANK YOU VERY MUCH.
I'D LIKE TO COME ALONG.
HM? MAY I ASK WHY?
...
MY NAME IS TENDO. I'M A DOCTOR AT HIURA GENERAL HOSPITAL.
OH, IN THAT CASE, GO RIGHT AHEAD.
UM, I...

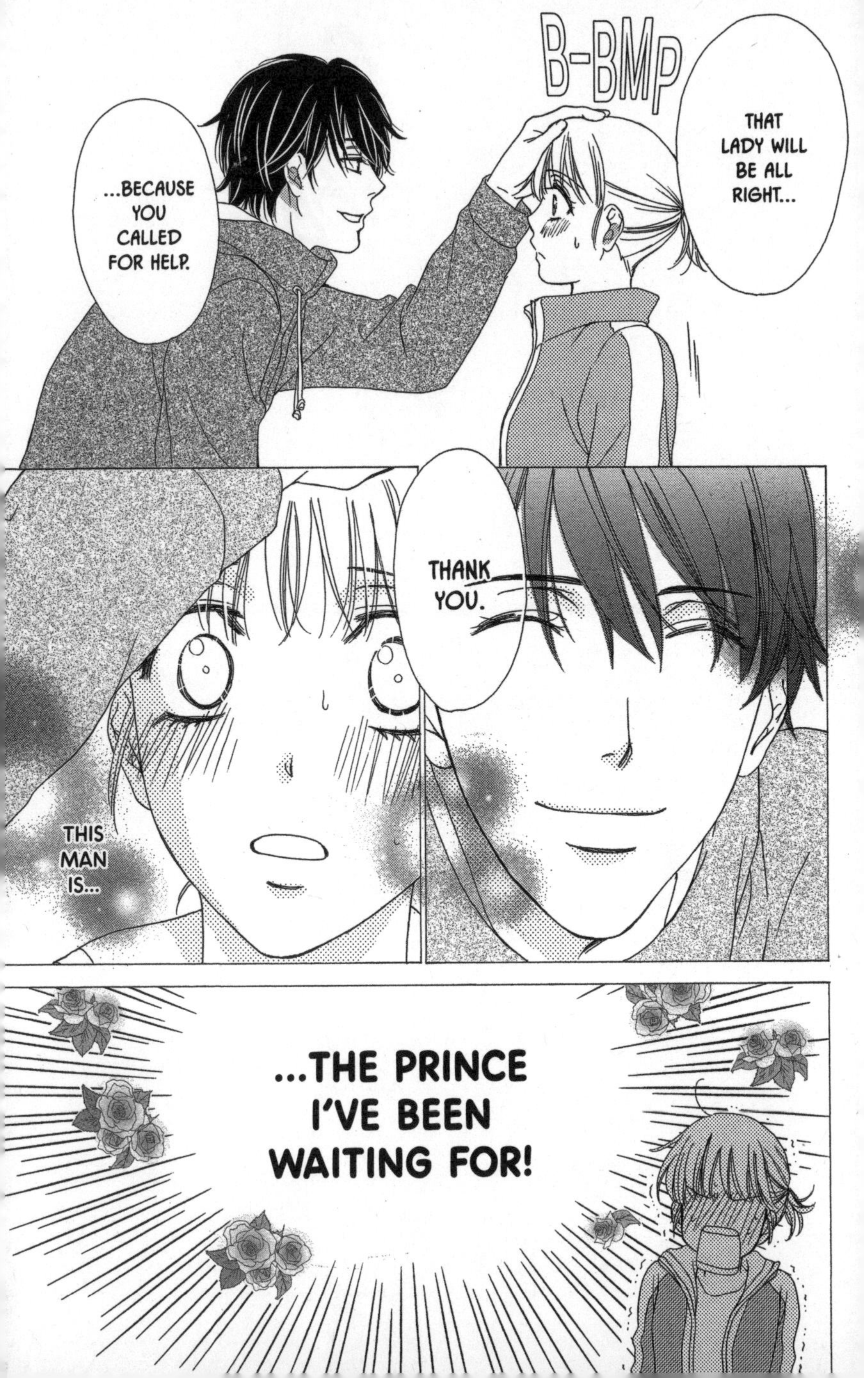
B-BMP
THAT LADY WILL BE ALL RIGHT...
...BECAUSE YOU CALLED FOR HELP.
THANK YOU.
THIS MAN IS...
...THE PRINCE I'VE BEEN WAITING FOR!

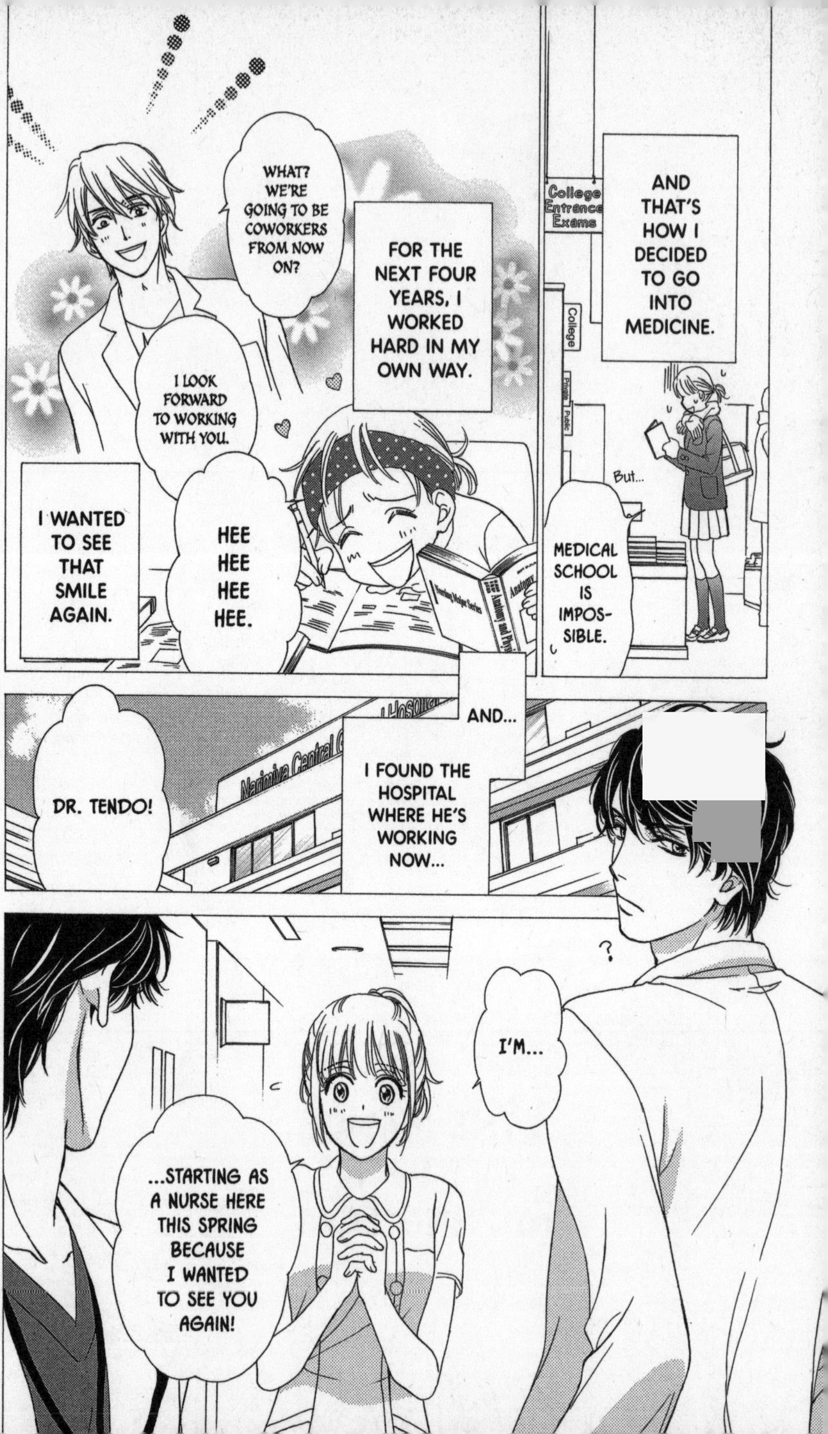
AND THAT'S HOW I DECIDED TO GO INTO MEDICINE.
College Entrance Exams
College
But...
MEDICAL SCHOOL IS IMPOSSIBLE.
FOR THE NEXT FOUR YEARS, I WORKED HARD IN MY OWN WAY.
WHAT? WE'RE GOING TO BE COWORKERS FROM NOW ON?
I LOOK FORWARD TO WORKING WITH YOU.
HEE HEE HEE HEE.
I WANTED TO SEE THAT SMILE AGAIN.
AND...
I FOUND THE HOSPITAL WHERE HE'S WORKING NOW...
DR. TENDO!
?
I'M...
...STARTING AS A NURSE HERE THIS SPRING BECAUSE I WANTED TO SEE YOU AGAIN!

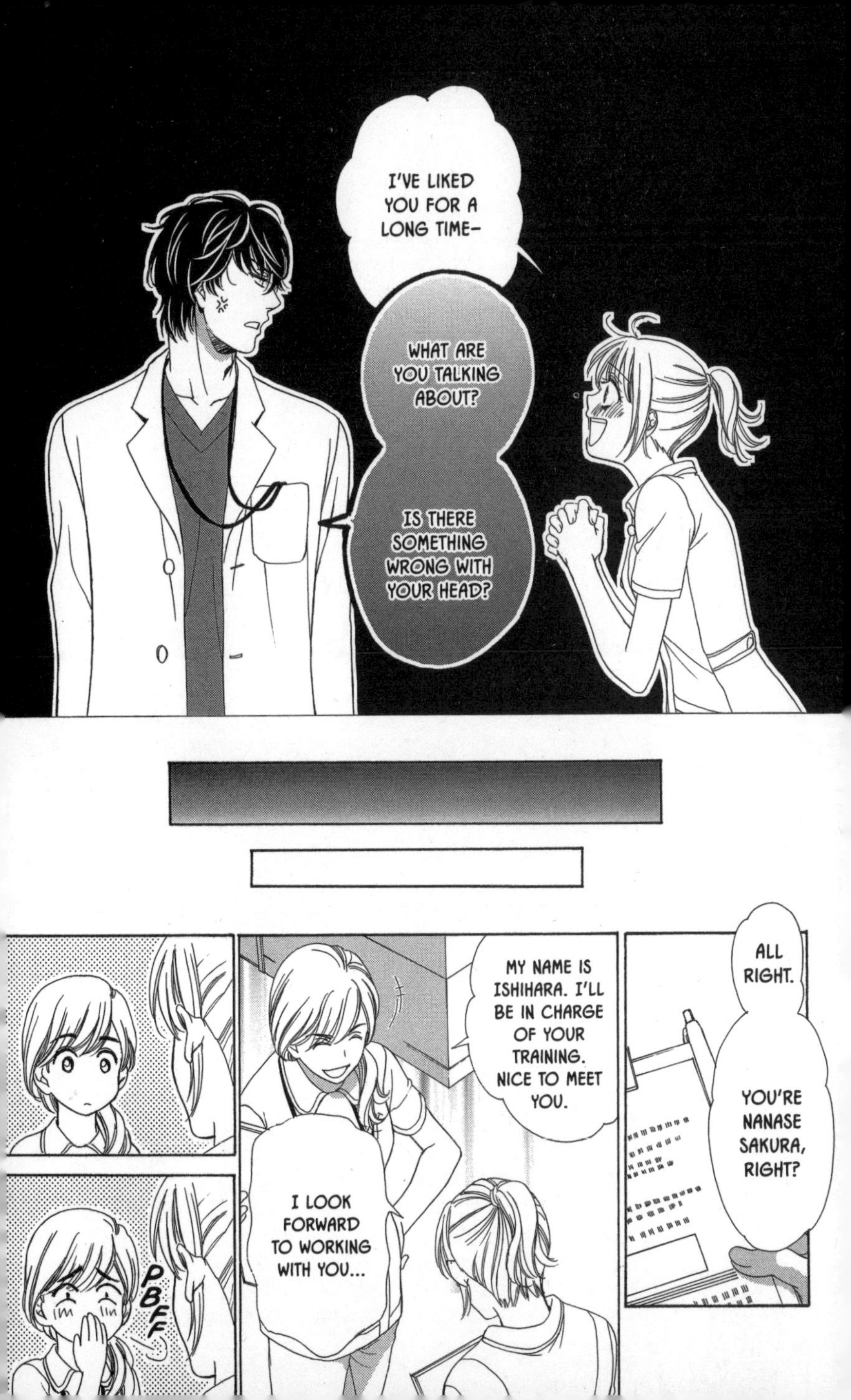
I'VE LIKED YOU FOR A LONG TIME–
WHAT ARE YOU TALKING ABOUT?
IS THERE SOMETHING WRONG WITH YOUR HEAD?
ALL RIGHT.
YOU'RE NANASE SAKURA, RIGHT?
MY NAME IS ISHIHARA. I'LL BE IN CHARGE OF YOUR TRAINING. NICE TO MEET YOU.
I LOOK FORWARD TO WORKING WITH YOU...
PBFF

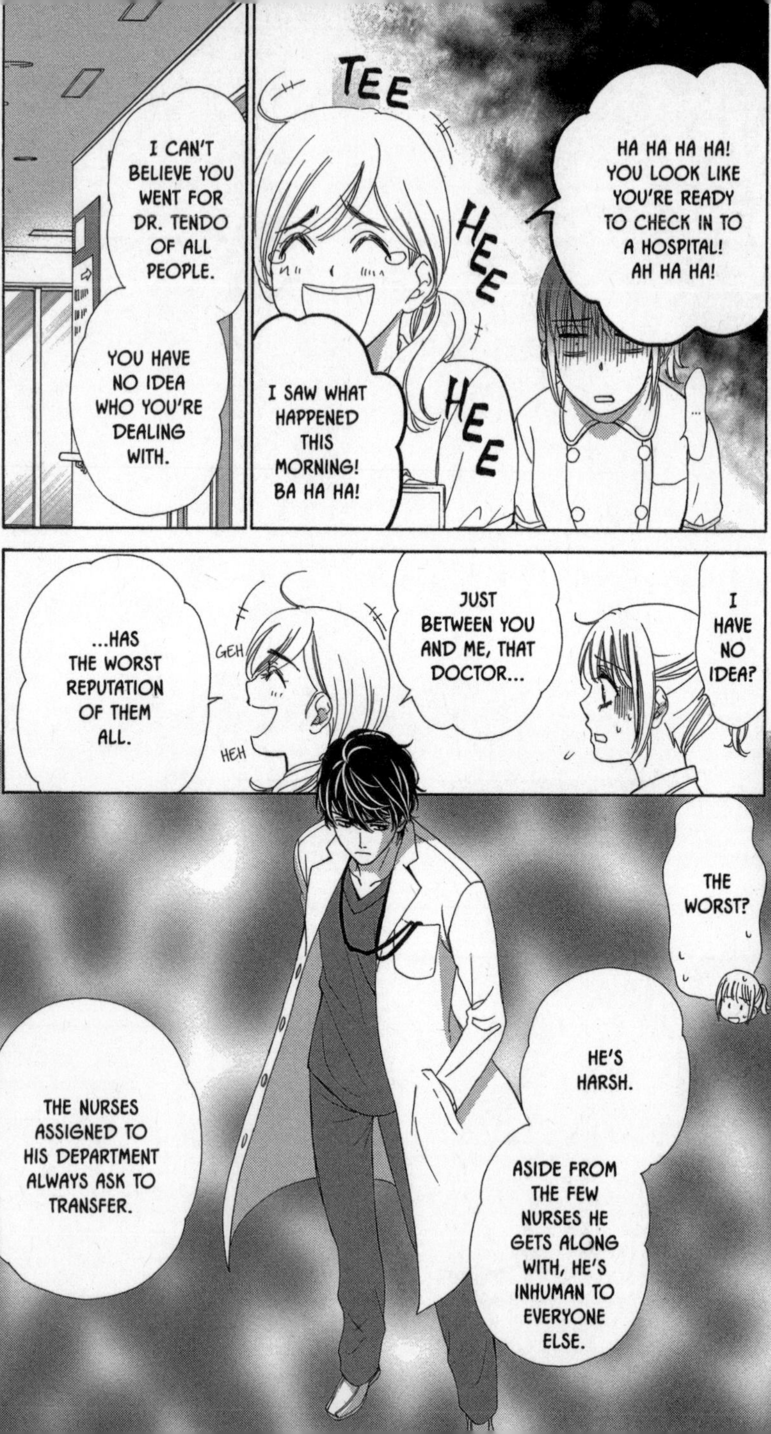
HA HA HA HA! YOU LOOK LIKE YOU'RE READY TO CHECK IN TO A HOSPITAL! AH HA HA!
TEE HEE HEE
...
I SAW WHAT HAPPENED THIS MORNING! BA HA HA!
I CAN'T BELIEVE YOU WENT FOR DR. TENDO OF ALL PEOPLE.
YOU HAVE NO IDEA WHO YOU'RE DEALING WITH.
I HAVE NO IDEA?
JUST BETWEEN YOU AND ME, THAT DOCTOR...
GEH
HEH
...HAS THE WORST REPUTATION OF THEM ALL.
THE WORST?
HE'S HARSH.
ASIDE FROM THE FEW NURSES HE GETS ALONG WITH, HE'S INHUMAN TO EVERYONE ELSE.
THE NURSES ASSIGNED TO HIS DEPARTMENT ALWAYS ASK TO TRANSFER.

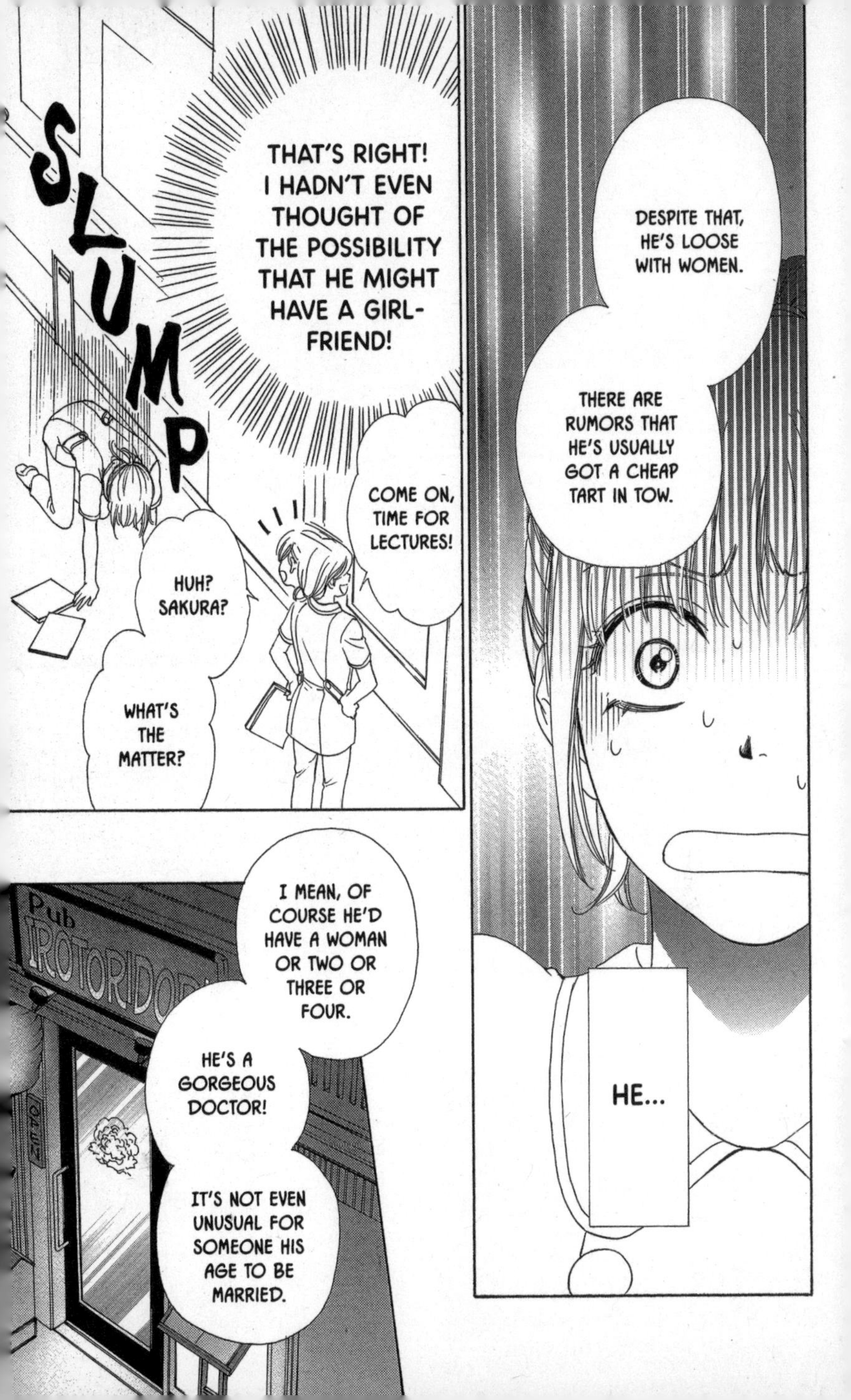
DESPITE THAT, HE'S LOOSE WITH WOMEN.
THERE ARE RUMORS THAT HE'S USUALLY GOT A CHEAP TART IN TOW.
HE...
THAT'S RIGHT! I HADN'T EVEN THOUGHT OF THE POSSIBILITY THAT HE MIGHT HAVE A GIRL-FRIEND!
SLUMP
COME ON, TIME FOR LECTURES!
HUH? SAKURA?
WHAT'S THE MATTER?
I MEAN, OF COURSE HE'D HAVE A WOMAN OR TWO OR THREE OR FOUR.
HE'S A GORGEOUS DOCTOR!
IT'S NOT EVEN UNUSUAL FOR SOMEONE HIS AGE TO BE MARRIED.
Pub
IROTORIDO
OPEN

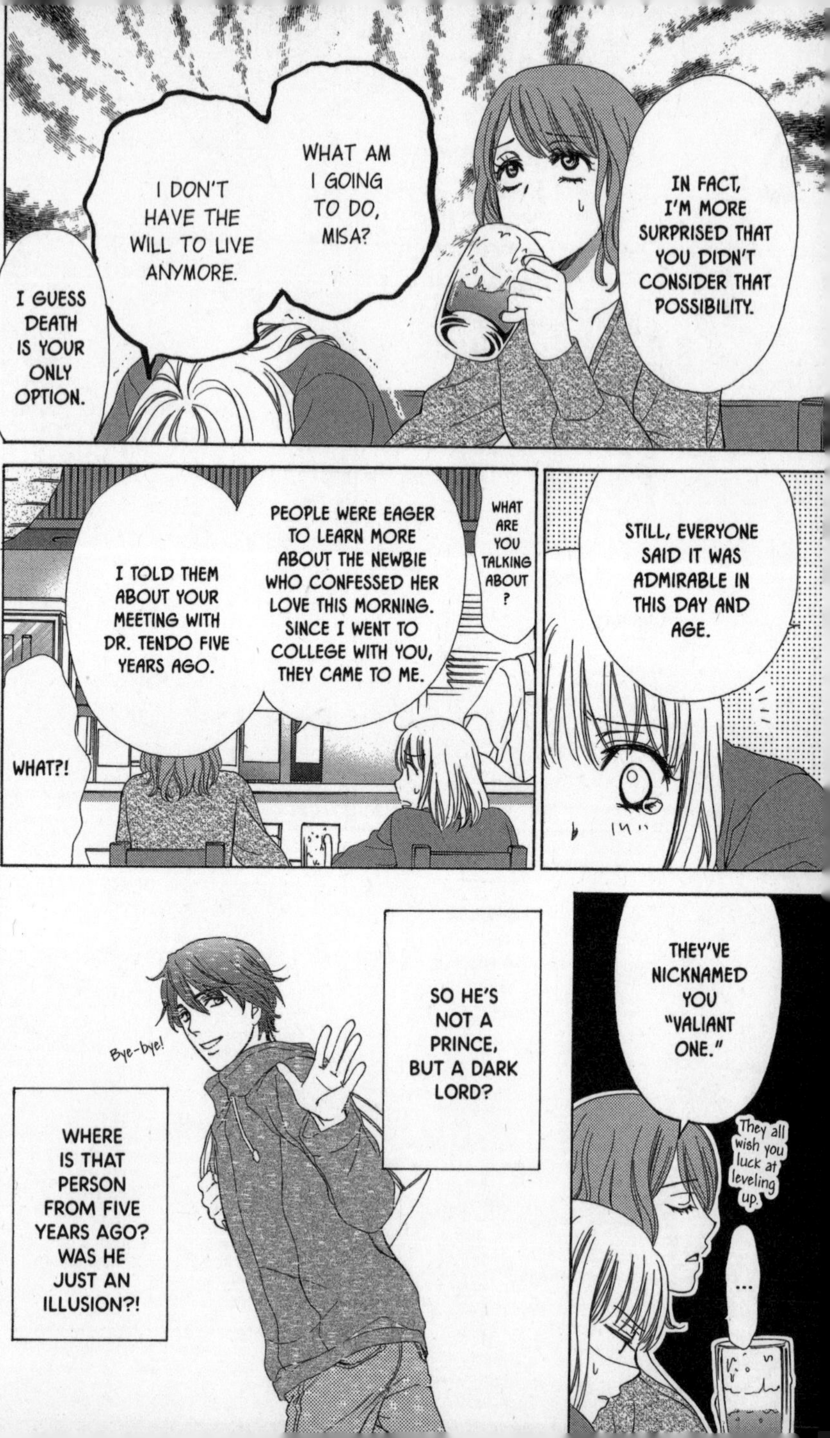
WHAT AM I GOING TO DO, MISA?
I DON'T HAVE THE WILL TO LIVE ANYMORE.
I GUESS DEATH IS YOUR ONLY OPTION.
IN FACT, I'M MORE SURPRISED THAT YOU DIDN'T CONSIDER THAT POSSIBILITY.
STILL, EVERYONE SAID IT WAS ADMIRABLE IN THIS DAY AND AGE.
WHAT ARE YOU TALKING ABOUT?
PEOPLE WERE EAGER TO LEARN MORE ABOUT THE NEWBIE WHO CONFESSED HER LOVE THIS MORNING. SINCE I WENT TO COLLEGE WITH YOU, THEY CAME TO ME.
I TOLD THEM ABOUT YOUR MEETING WITH DR. TENDO FIVE YEARS AGO.
WHAT?!
THEY'VE NICKNAMED YOU "VALIANT ONE."
They all wish you luck at leveling up.
...
SO HE'S NOT A PRINCE, BUT A DARK LORD?
Bye-bye!
WHERE IS THAT PERSON FROM FIVE YEARS AGO? WAS HE JUST AN ILLUSION?!

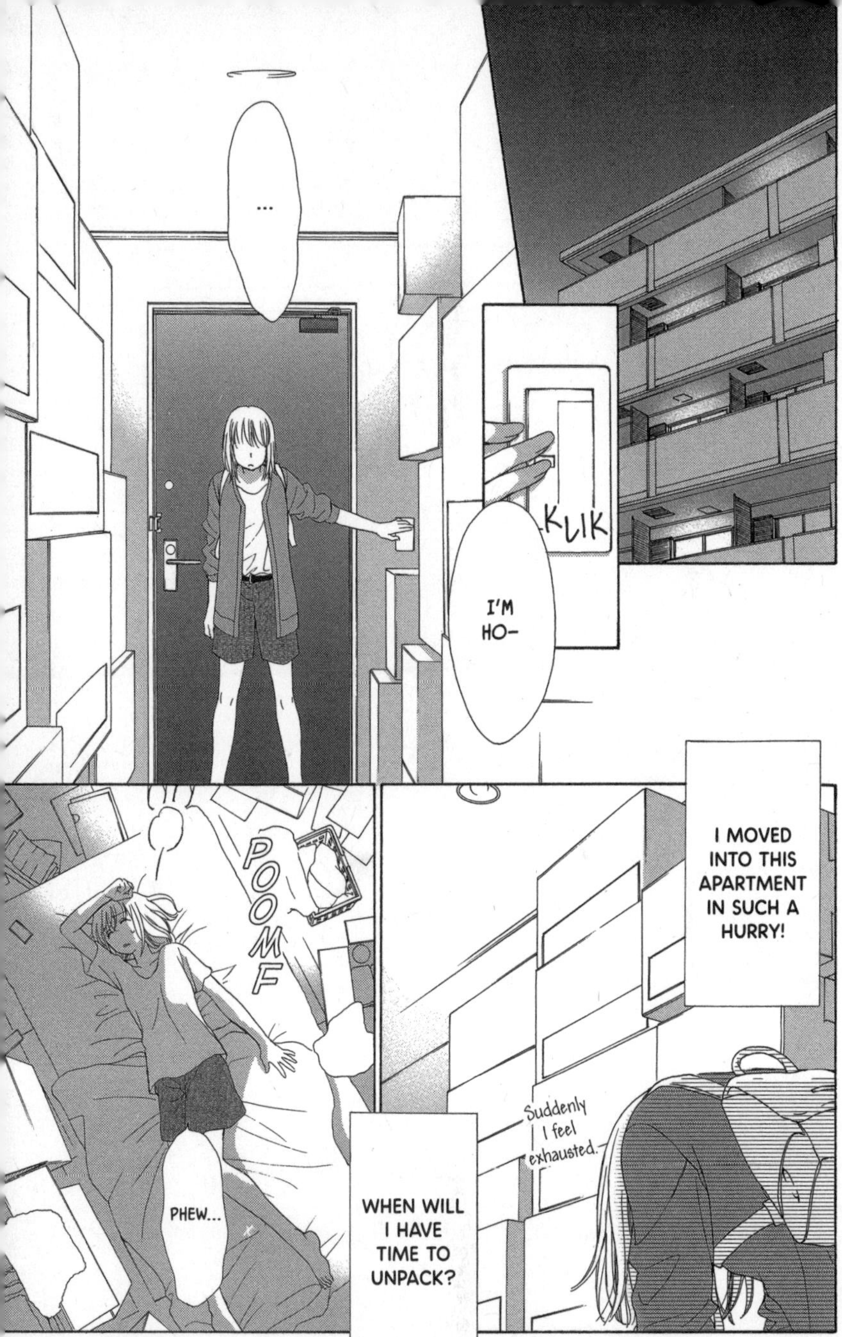
KLIK
I'M HO-
...
I MOVED INTO THIS APARTMENT IN SUCH A HURRY!
Suddenly I feel exhausted.
WHEN WILL I HAVE TIME TO UNPACK?
POOMF
PHEW...

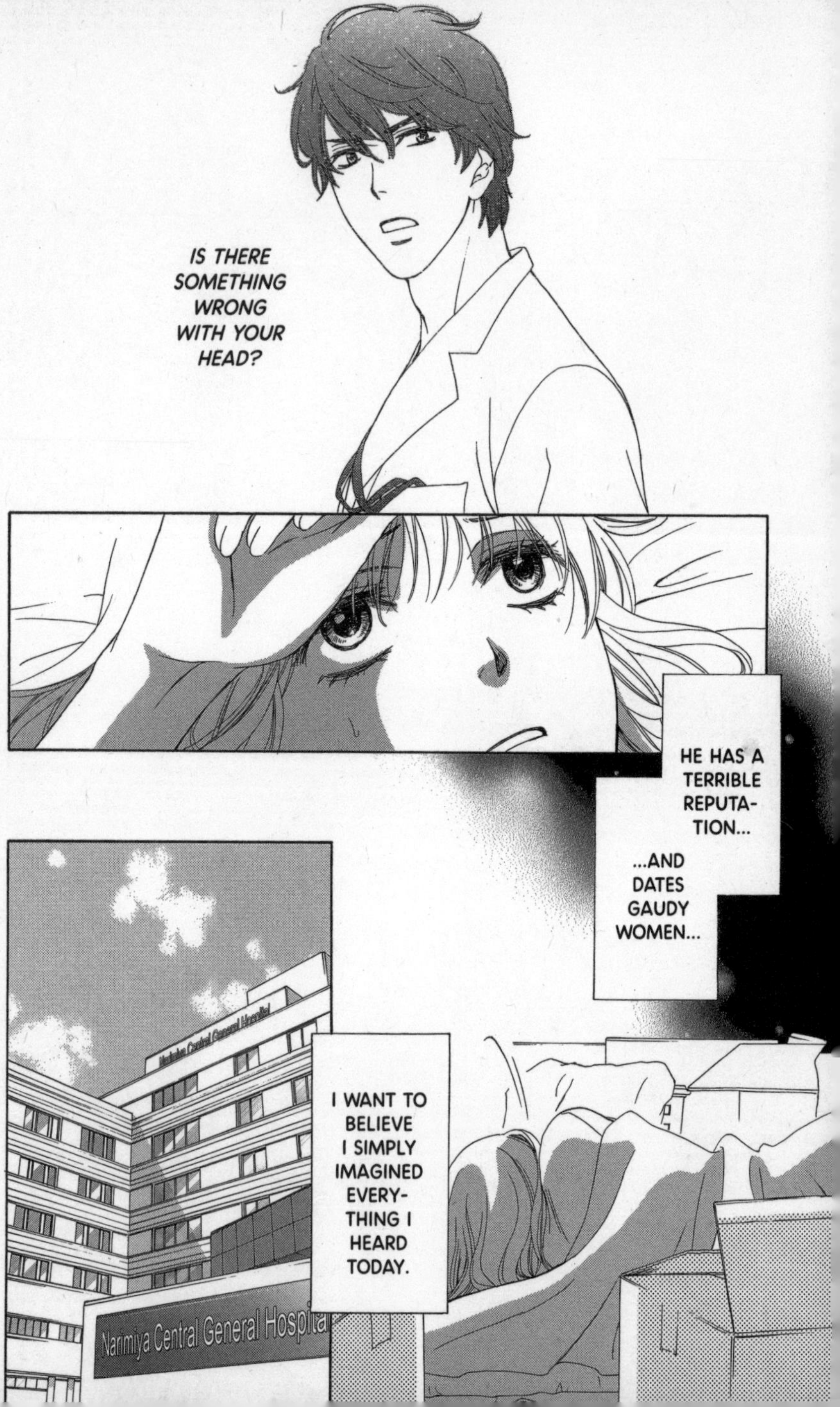
IS THERE SOMETHING WRONG WITH YOUR HEAD?
HE HAS A TERRIBLE REPUTA-TION...
...AND DATES GAUDY WOMEN...
I WANT TO BELIEVE I SIMPLY IMAGINED EVERY-THING I HEARD TODAY.
Narimiya Central General Hospita

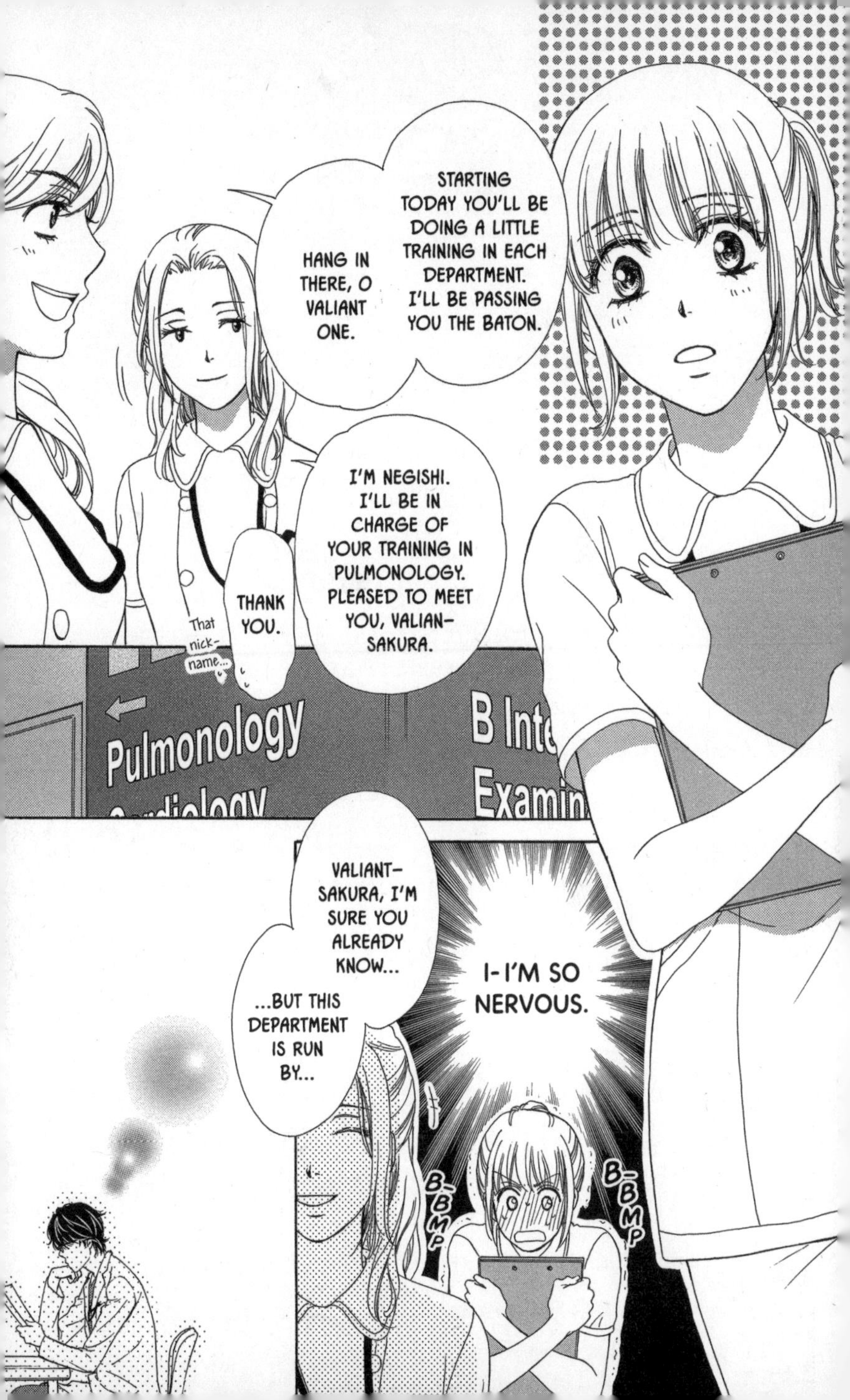
STARTING TODAY YOU'LL BE DOING A LITTLE TRAINING IN EACH DEPARTMENT. I'LL BE PASSING YOU THE BATON.
HANG IN THERE, O VALIANT ONE.
I'M NEGISHI. I'LL BE IN CHARGE OF YOUR TRAINING IN PULMONOLOGY. PLEASED TO MEET YOU, VALIAN-SAKURA.
THANK YOU.
That nick-name...
Pulmonology
VALIANT-SAKURA, I'M SURE YOU ALREADY KNOW...
...BUT THIS DEPARTMENT IS RUN BY...
I-I'M SO NERVOUS.
B-BMP
B-BMP

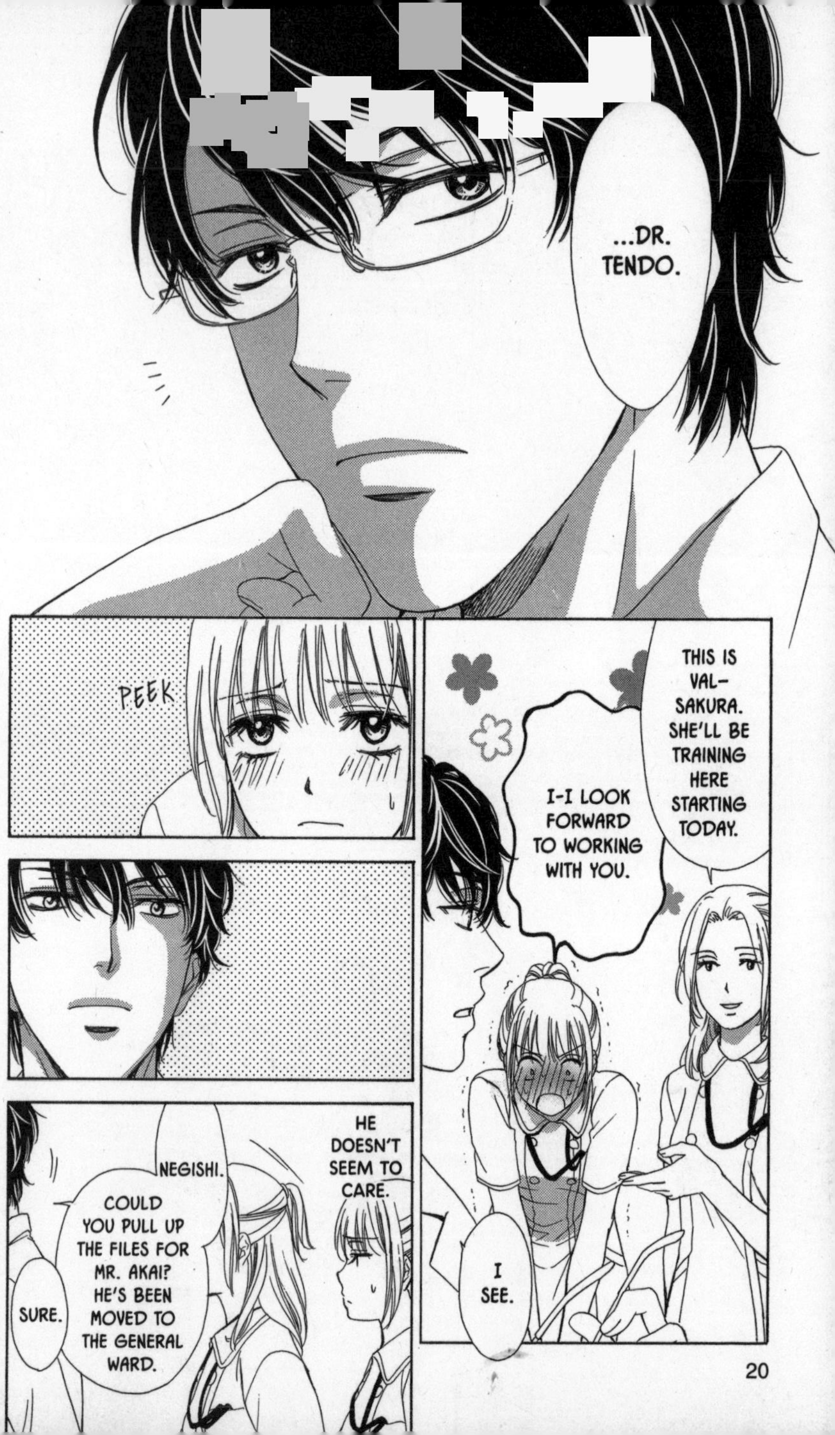
...DR. TENDO.
THIS IS VAL-SAKURA. SHE'LL BE TRAINING HERE STARTING TODAY.
I-I LOOK FORWARD TO WORKING WITH YOU.
I SEE.
PEEK
HE DOESN'T SEEM TO CARE.
NEGISHI.
COULD YOU PULL UP THE FILES FOR MR. AKAI? HE'S BEEN MOVED TO THE GENERAL WARD.
SURE.

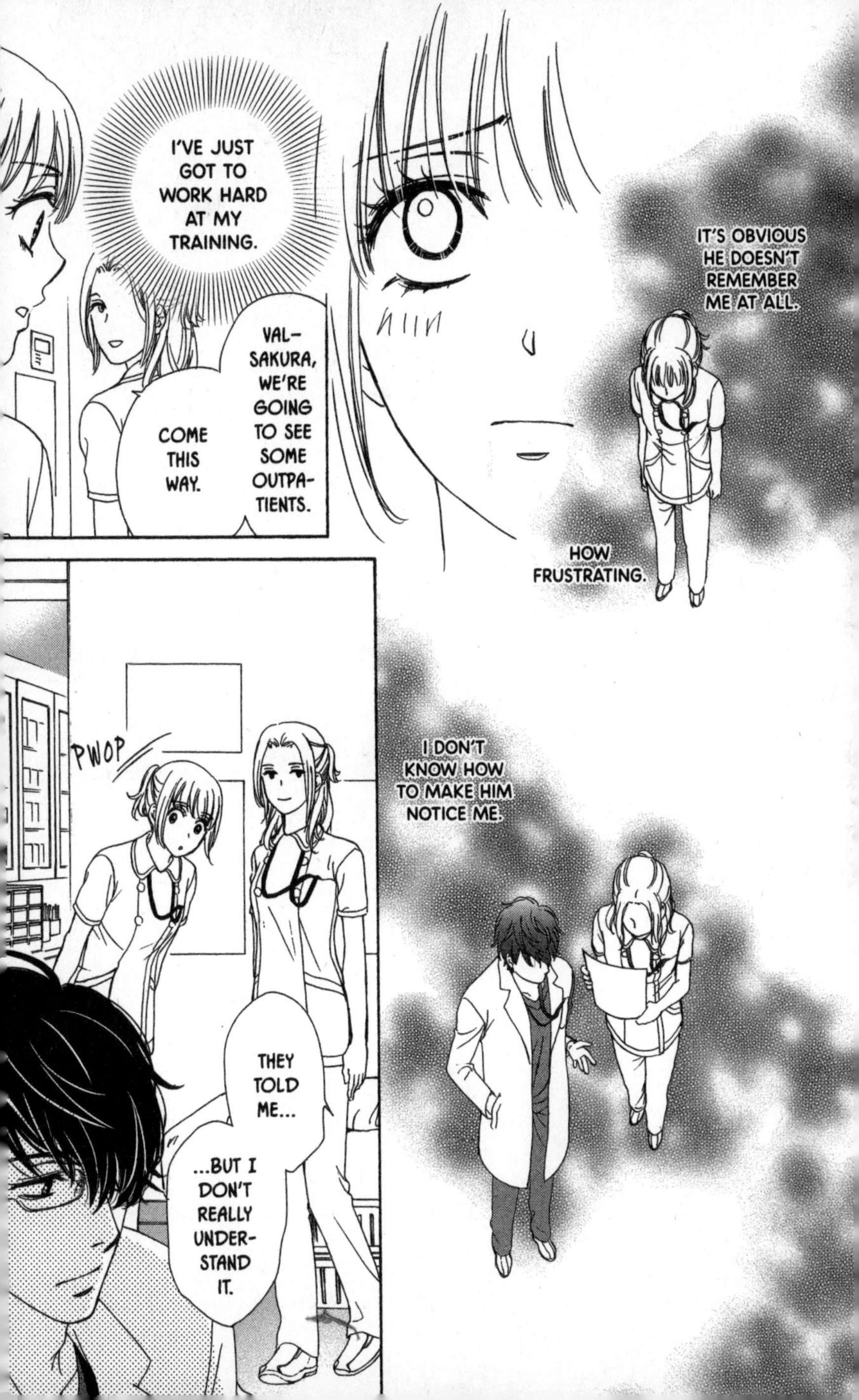
IT'S OBVIOUS HE DOESN'T REMEMBER ME AT ALL.
HOW FRUSTRATING.
I DON'T KNOW HOW TO MAKE HIM NOTICE ME.
I'VE JUST GOT TO WORK HARD AT MY TRAINING.
VAL-SAKURA, WE'RE GOING TO SEE SOME OUTPATIENTS.
COME THIS WAY.
PWOP
THEY TOLD ME...
...BUT I DON'T REALLY UNDERSTAND IT.

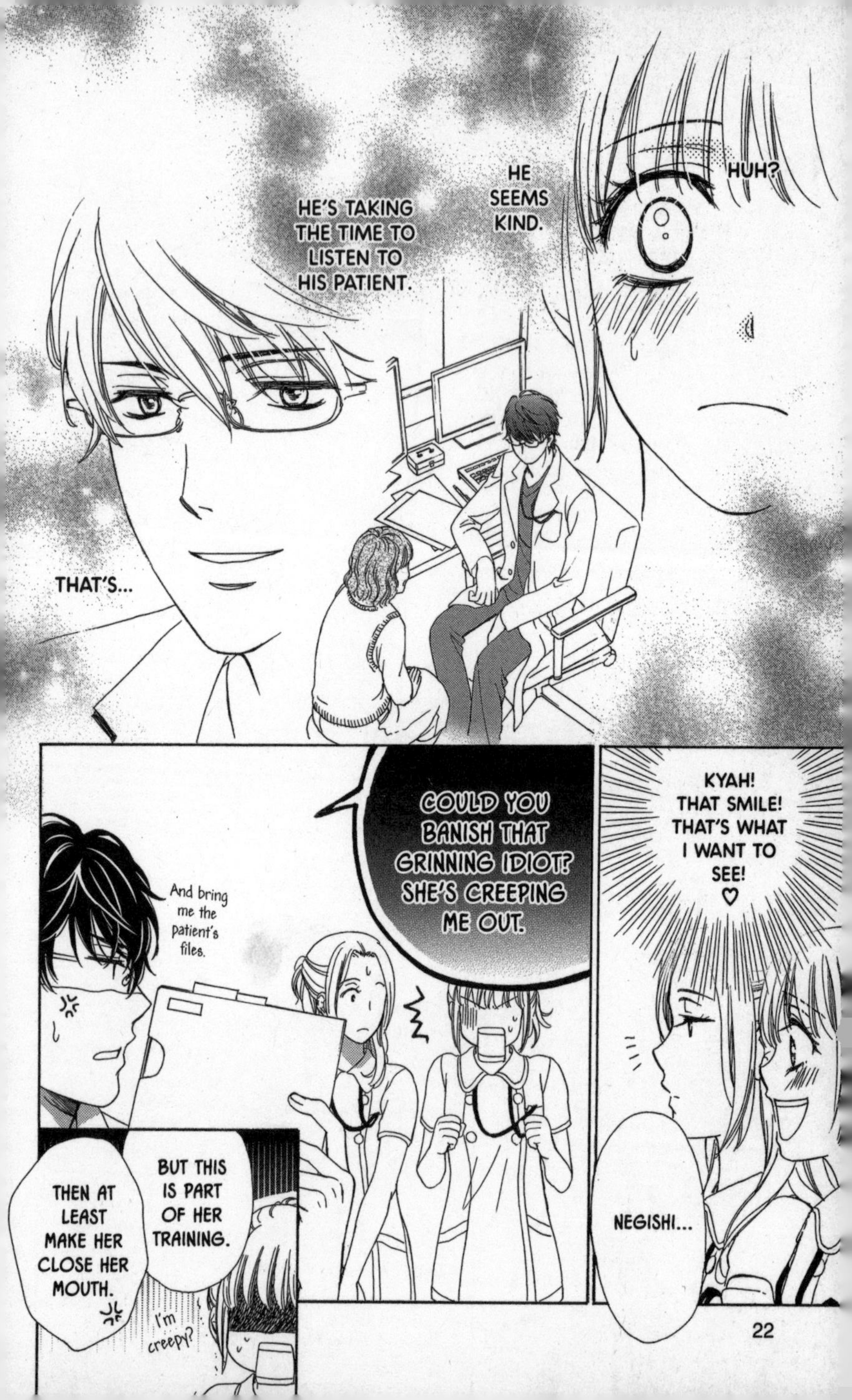

HUH?
HE SEEMS KIND.
HE'S TAKING THE TIME TO LISTEN TO HIS PATIENT.
THAT'S...
KYAH! THAT SMILE! THAT'S WHAT I WANT TO SEE! ♡
NEGISHI...
COULD YOU BANISH THAT GRINNING IDIOT? SHE'S CREEPING ME OUT.
And bring me the patient's files.
BUT THIS IS PART OF HER TRAINING.
THEN AT LEAST MAKE HER CLOSE HER MOUTH.
I'm creepy?

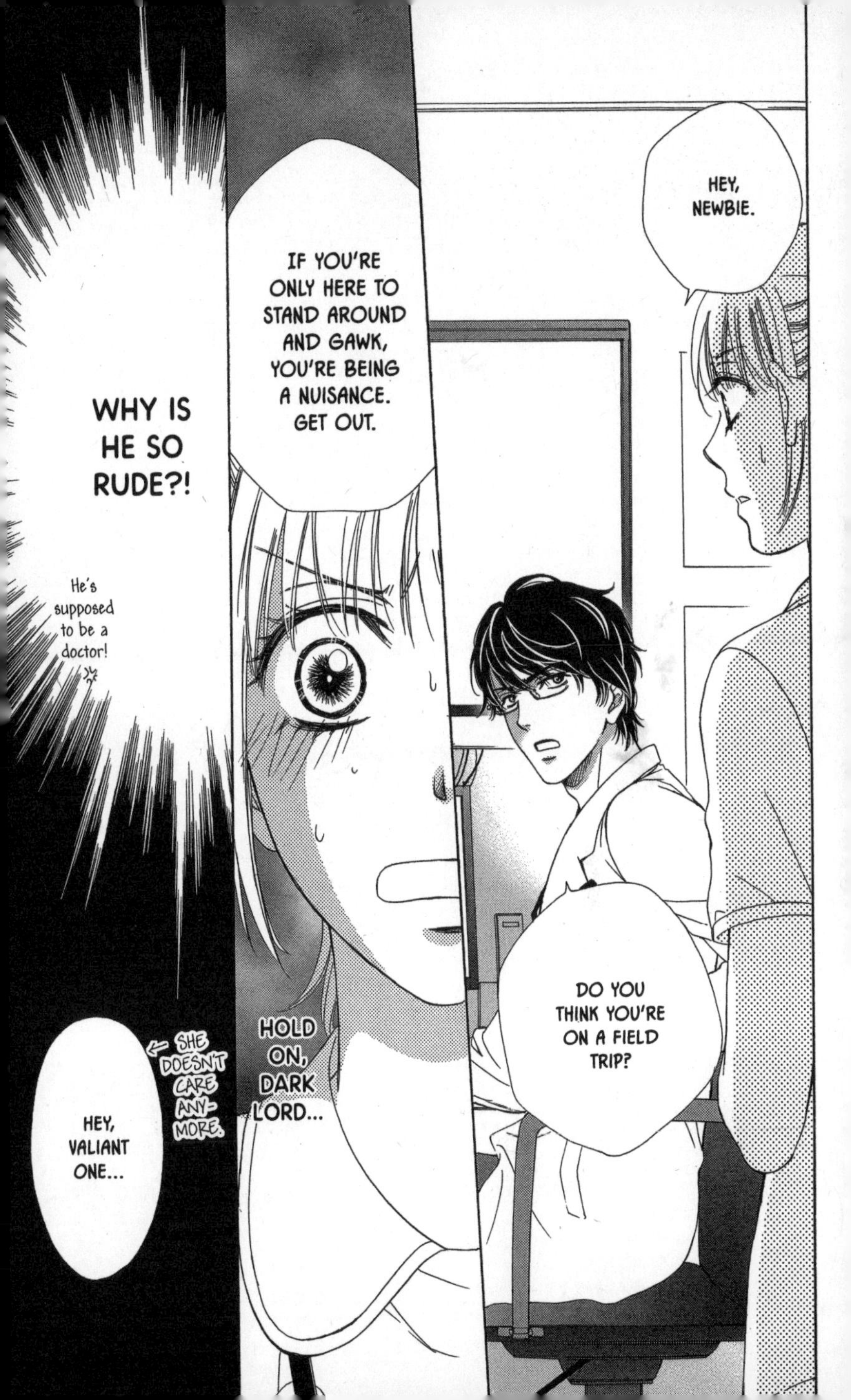
HEY, NEWBIE.
DO YOU THINK YOU'RE ON A FIELD TRIP?
IF YOU'RE ONLY HERE TO STAND AROUND AND GAWK, YOU'RE BEING A NUISANCE. GET OUT.
HOLD ON, DARK LORD...
WHY IS HE SO RUDE?!
He's supposed to be a doctor!
SHE DOESN'T CARE ANYMORE.
HEY, VALIANT ONE...

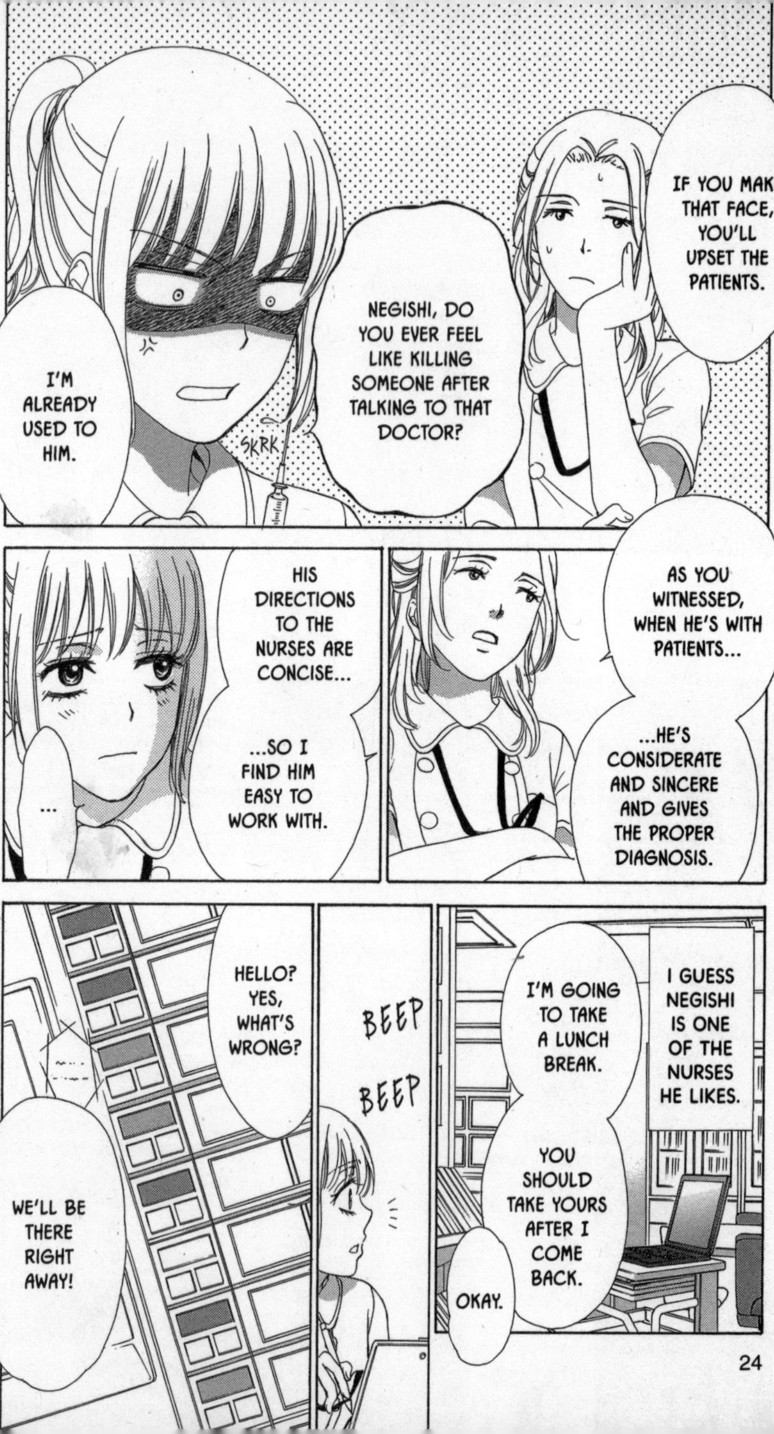

IF YOU MAKE THAT FACE, YOU'LL UPSET THE PATIENTS.
NEGISHI, DO YOU EVER FEEL LIKE KILLING SOMEONE AFTER TALKING TO THAT DOCTOR?
SKRK
I'M ALREADY USED TO HIM.
AS YOU WITNESSED, WHEN HE'S WITH PATIENTS...
...HE'S CONSIDERATE AND SINCERE AND GIVES THE PROPER DIAGNOSIS.
HIS DIRECTIONS TO THE NURSES ARE CONCISE...
...SO I FIND HIM EASY TO WORK WITH.
...
I GUESS NEGISHI IS ONE OF THE NURSES HE LIKES.
I'M GOING TO TAKE A LUNCH BREAK.
YOU SHOULD TAKE YOURS AFTER I COME BACK.
OKAY.
BEEP
BEEP
HELLO? YES, WHAT'S WRONG?
WE'LL BE THERE RIGHT AWAY!

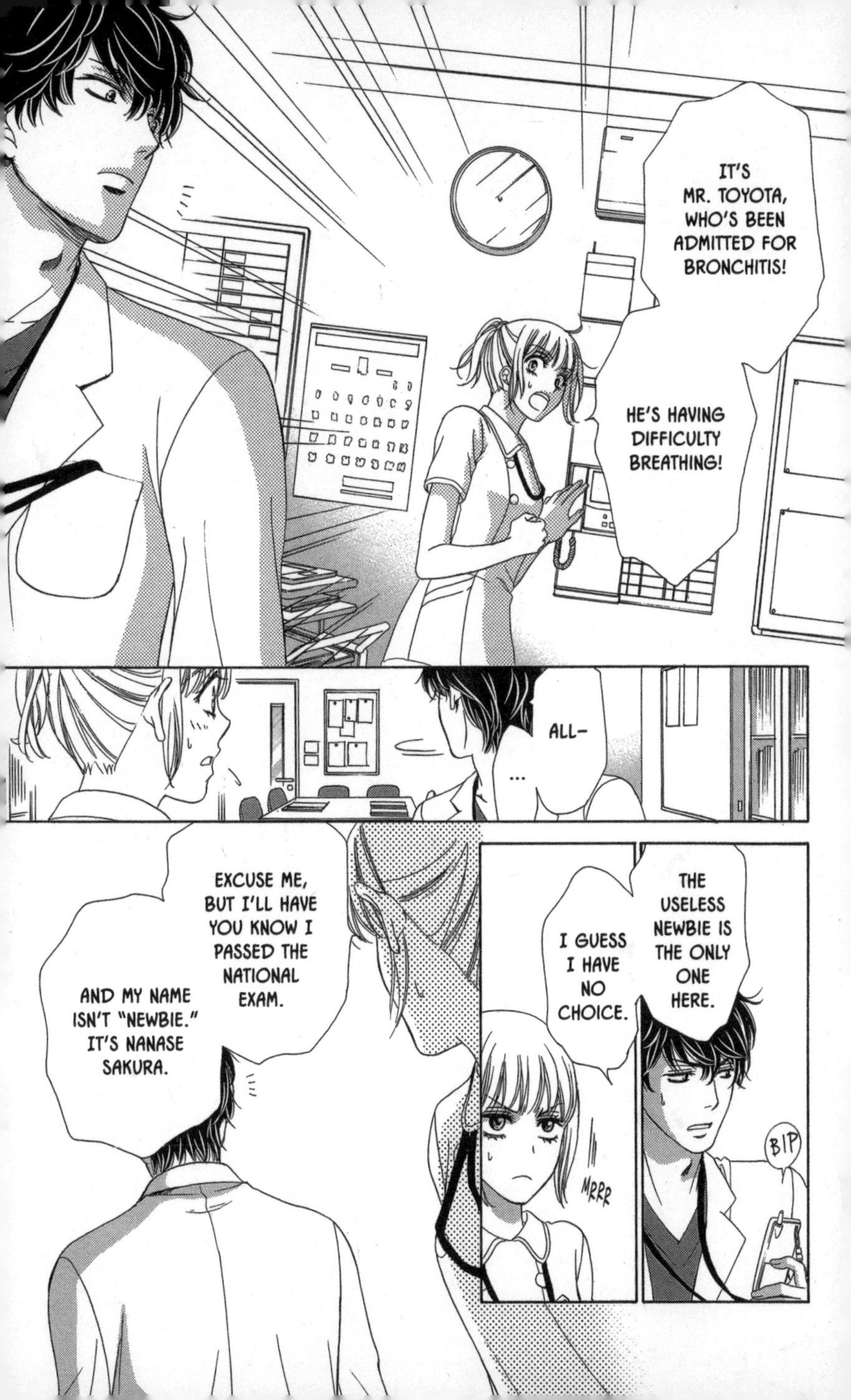
IT'S MR. TOYOTA, WHO'S BEEN ADMITTED FOR BRONCHITIS!
HE'S HAVING DIFFICULTY BREATHING!
ALL—
...
THE USELESS NEWBIE IS THE ONLY ONE HERE.
BIP
I GUESS I HAVE NO CHOICE.
MRRR
EXCUSE ME, BUT I'LL HAVE YOU KNOW I PASSED THE NATIONAL EXAM.
AND MY NAME ISN'T "NEWBIE." IT'S NANASE SAKURA.

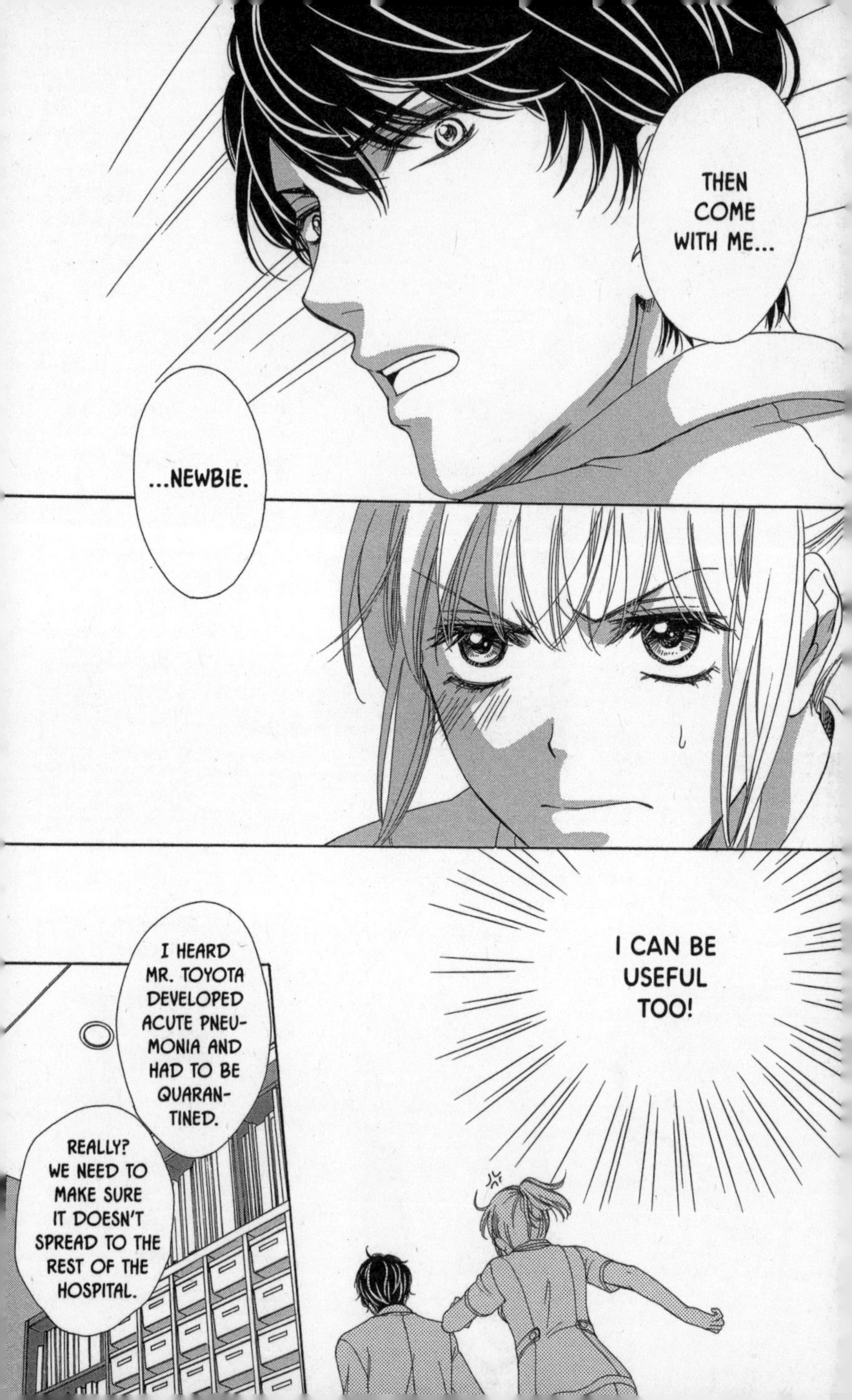
THEN COME WITH ME...
...NEWBIE.
I CAN BE USEFUL TOO!
I HEARD MR. TOYOTA DEVELOPED ACUTE PNEU-MONIA AND HAD TO BE QUARAN-TINED.
REALLY? WE NEED TO MAKE SURE IT DOESN'T SPREAD TO THE REST OF THE HOSPITAL.

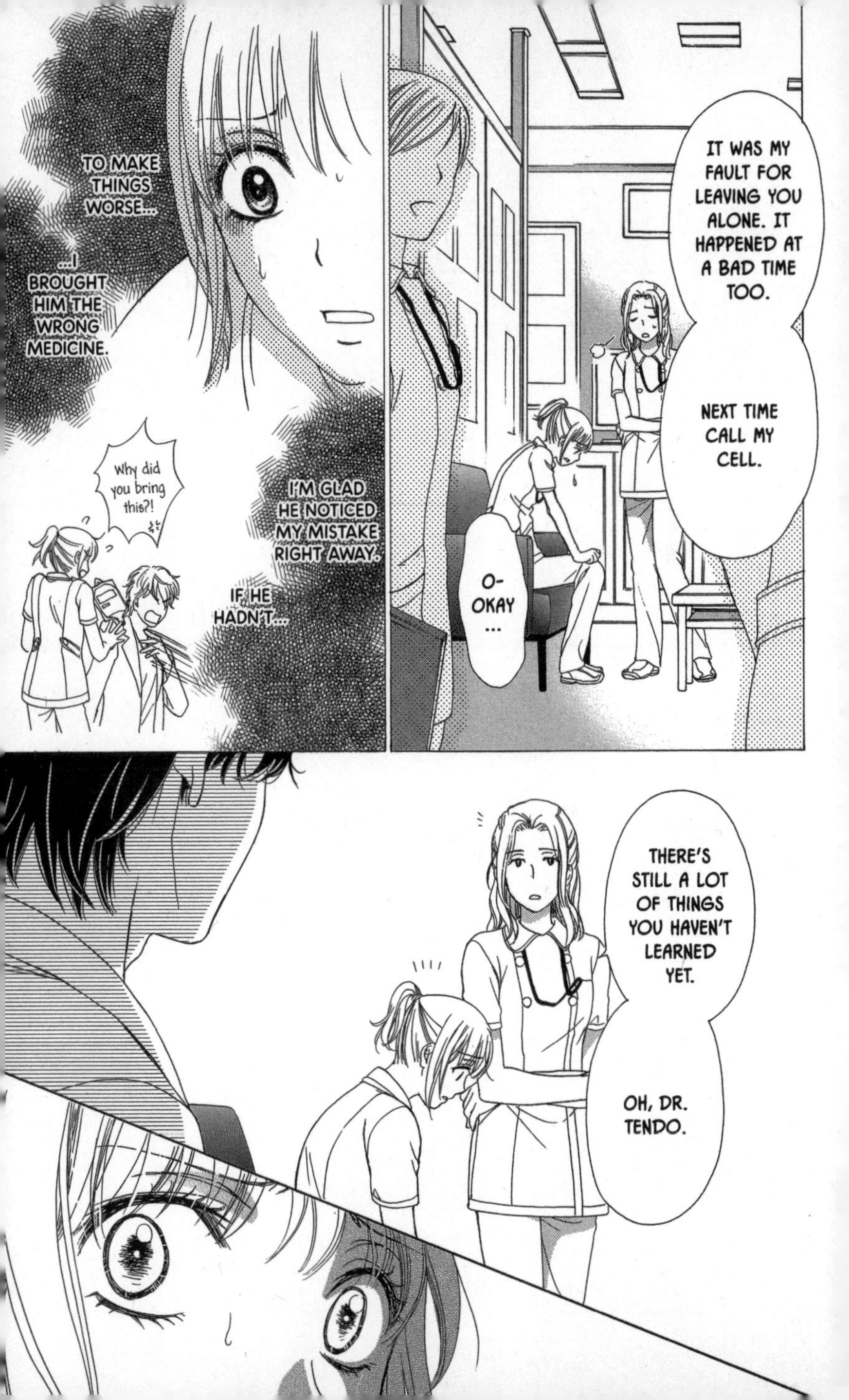
IT WAS MY FAULT FOR LEAVING YOU ALONE. IT HAPPENED AT A BAD TIME TOO.
NEXT TIME CALL MY CELL.
O-OKAY...
TO MAKE THINGS WORSE...
...I BROUGHT HIM THE WRONG MEDICINE.
Why did you bring this?!
I'M GLAD HE NOTICED MY MISTAKE RIGHT AWAY.
IF HE HADN'T...
THERE'S STILL A LOT OF THINGS YOU HAVEN'T LEARNED YET.
OH, DR. TENDO.

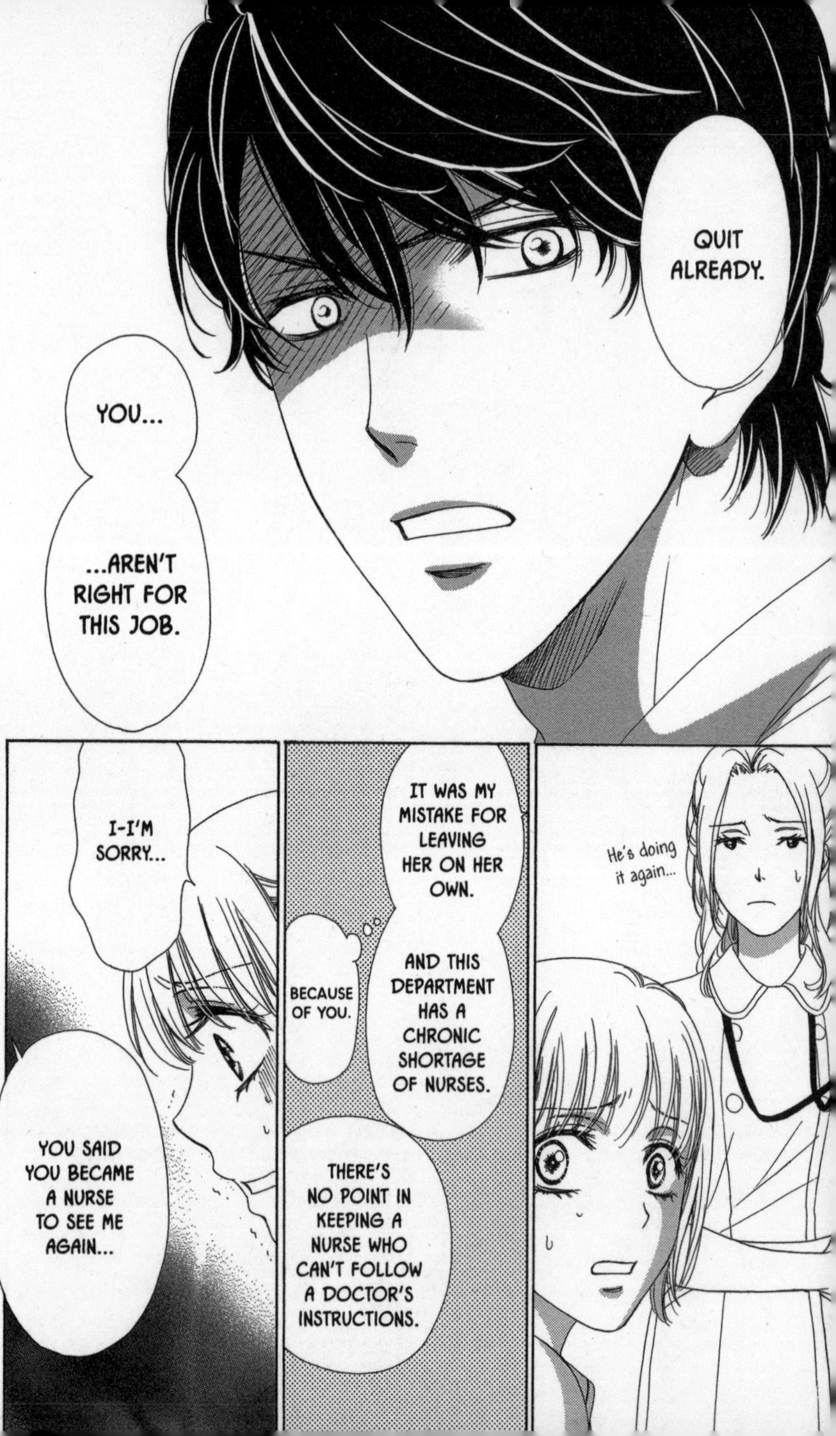
QUIT ALREADY.
YOU... ...AREN'T RIGHT FOR THIS JOB.
He's doing it again...
IT WAS MY MISTAKE FOR LEAVING HER ON HER OWN.
AND THIS DEPARTMENT HAS A CHRONIC SHORTAGE OF NURSES.
BECAUSE OF YOU.
THERE'S NO POINT IN KEEPING A NURSE WHO CAN'T FOLLOW A DOCTOR'S INSTRUCTIONS.
I-I'M SORRY...
YOU SAID YOU BECAME A NURSE TO SEE ME AGAIN...

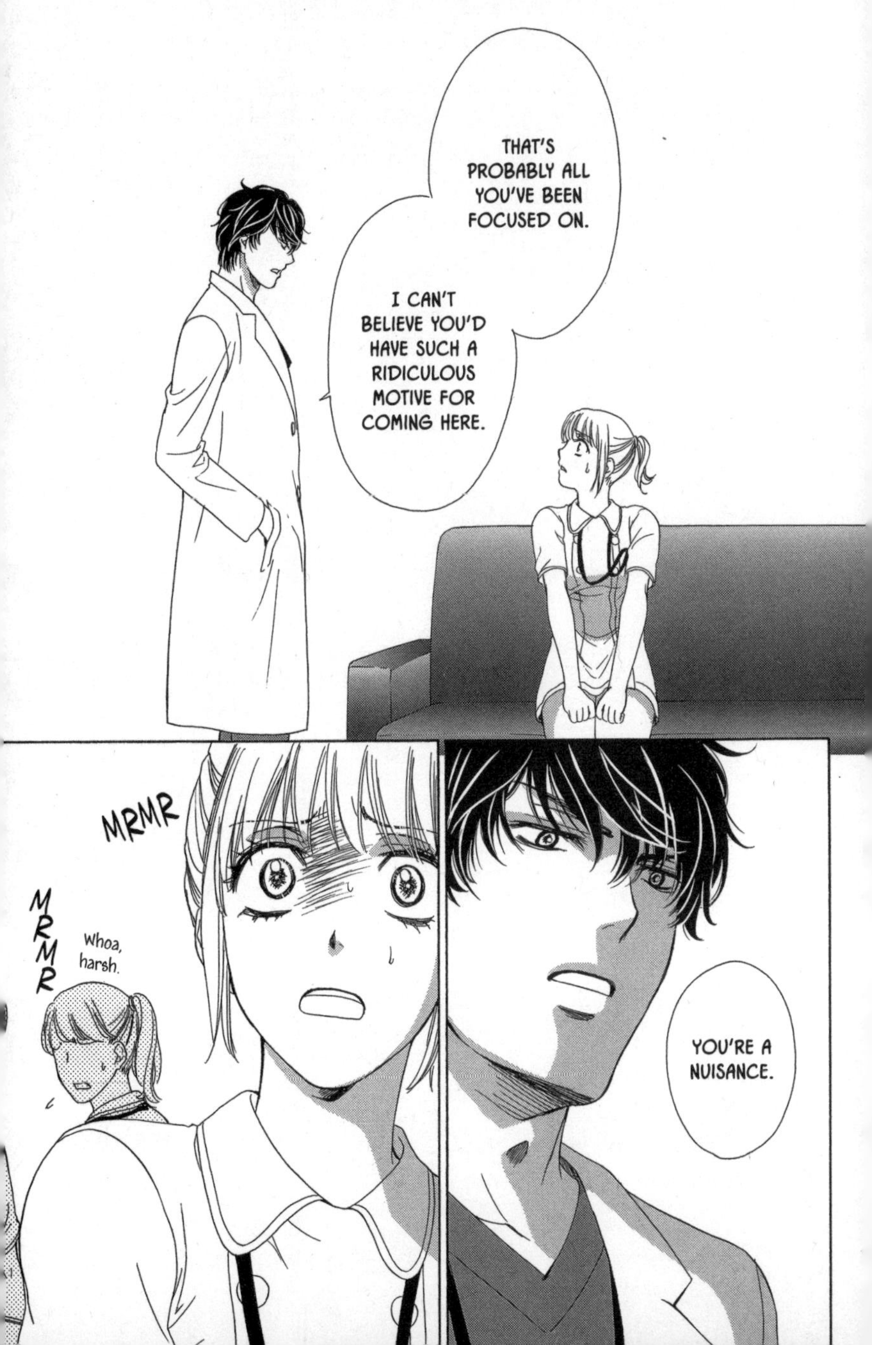
THAT'S PROBABLY ALL YOU'VE BEEN FOCUSED ON.
I CAN'T BELIEVE YOU'D HAVE SUCH A RIDICULOUS MOTIVE FOR COMING HERE.
YOU'RE A NUISANCE.
MRMR
MRMR
Whoa, harsh.

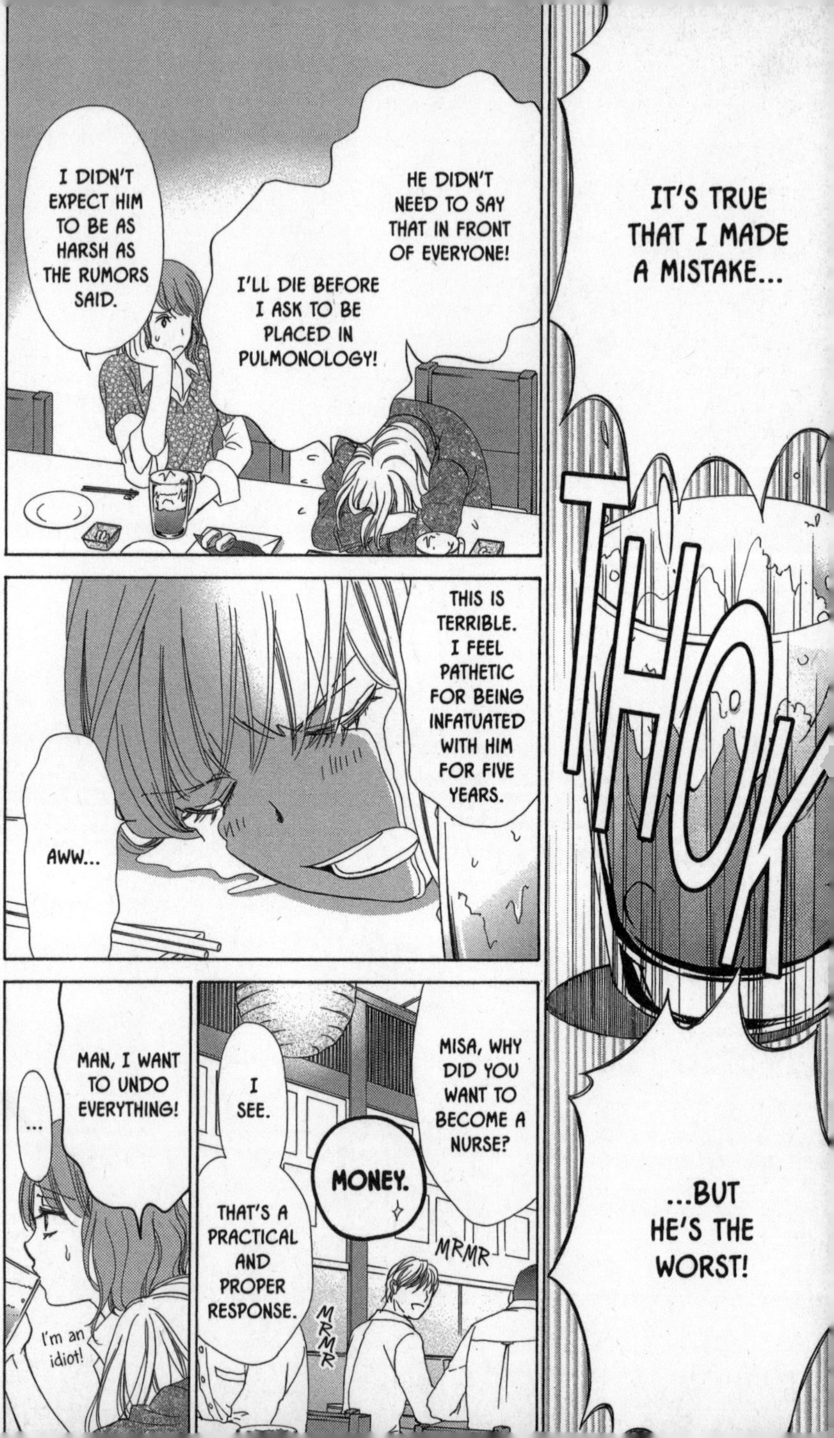
IT'S TRUE THAT I MADE A MISTAKE...
THOK
...BUT HE'S THE WORST!
HE DIDN'T NEED TO SAY THAT IN FRONT OF EVERYONE!
I'LL DIE BEFORE I ASK TO BE PLACED IN PULMONOLOGY!
I DIDN'T EXPECT HIM TO BE AS HARSH AS THE RUMORS SAID.
THIS IS TERRIBLE. I FEEL PATHETIC FOR BEING INFATUATED WITH HIM FOR FIVE YEARS.
AWW...
MISA, WHY DID YOU WANT TO BECOME A NURSE?
MONEY.
MRMR
I SEE.
THAT'S A PRACTICAL AND PROPER RESPONSE.
MRMR
MAN, I WANT TO UNDO EVERYTHING!
...
I'm an idiot!

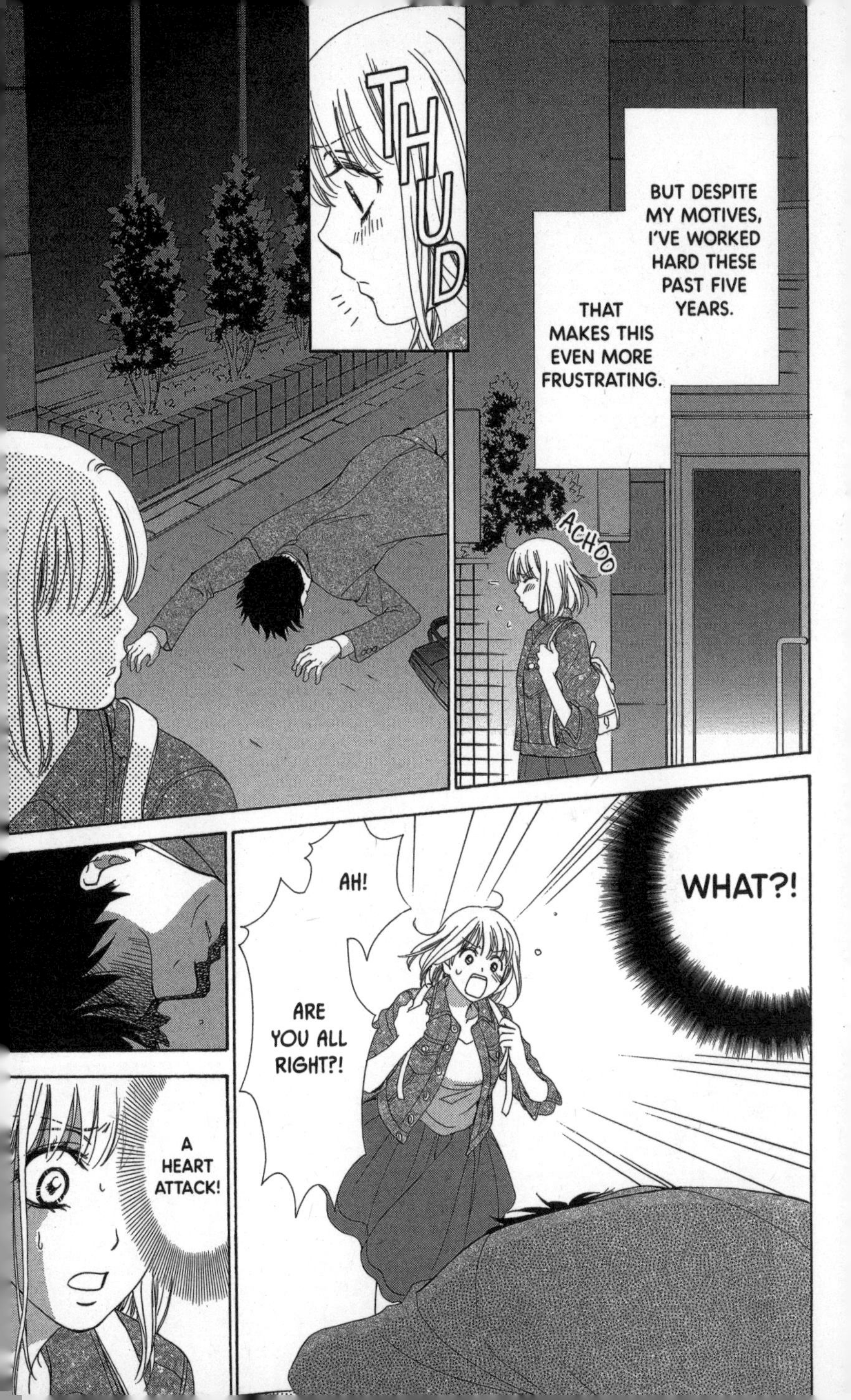
BUT DESPITE MY MOTIVES, I'VE WORKED HARD THESE PAST FIVE YEARS.
THAT MAKES THIS EVEN MORE FRUSTRATING.
ACHOO
THUD
WHAT?!
AH!
ARE YOU ALL RIGHT?!
A HEART ATTACK!

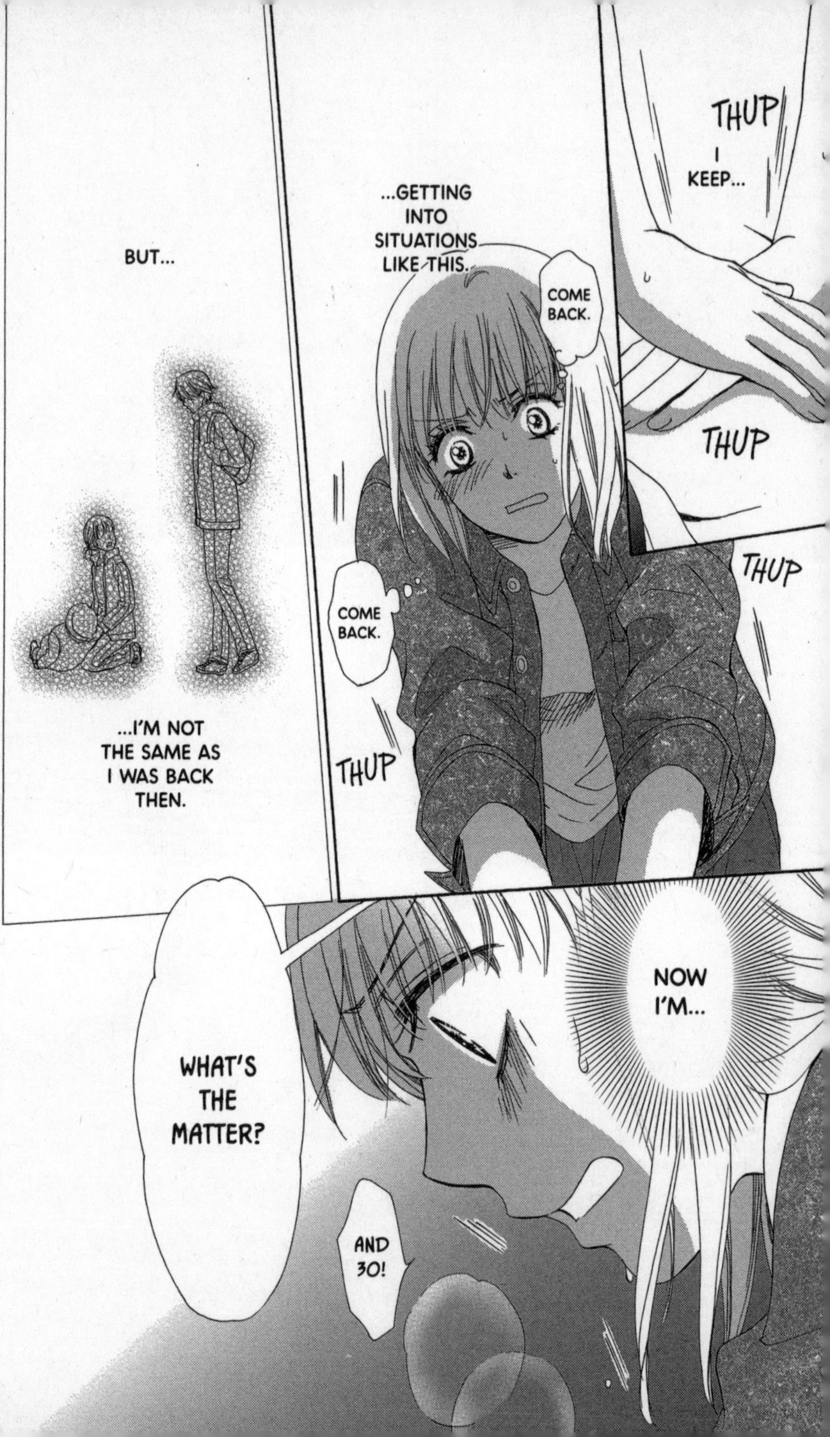
THUP
I KEEP...
THUP
THUP
...GETTING INTO SITUATIONS LIKE THIS.
COME BACK.
COME BACK.
THUP
BUT...
...I'M NOT THE SAME AS I WAS BACK THEN.
NOW I'M...
WHAT'S THE MATTER?
AND SO!

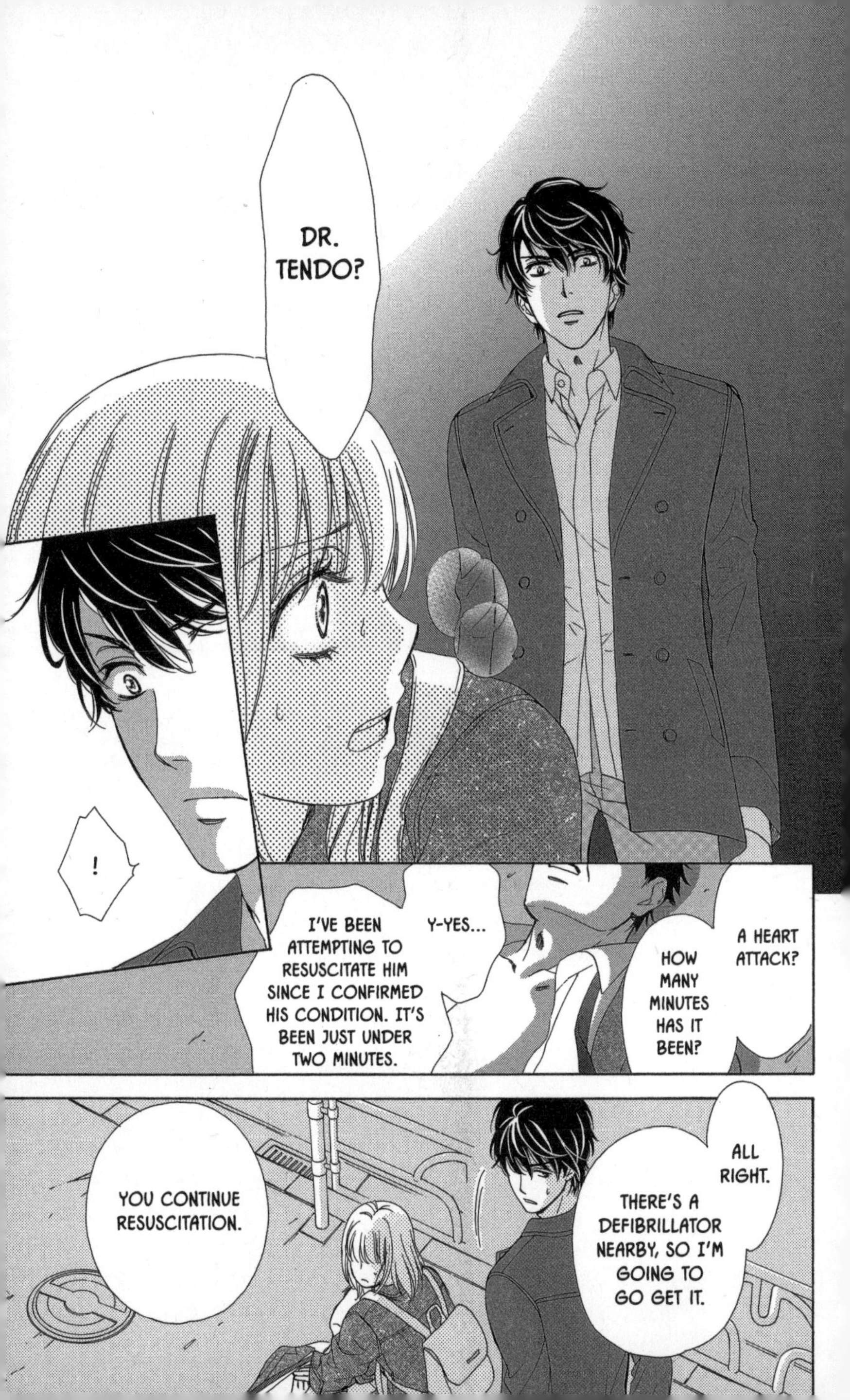

DR. TENDO?
!
A HEART ATTACK?
HOW MANY MINUTES HAS IT BEEN?
Y-YES...
I'VE BEEN ATTEMPTING TO RESUSCITATE HIM SINCE I CONFIRMED HIS CONDITION. IT'S BEEN JUST UNDER TWO MINUTES.
ALL RIGHT.
THERE'S A DEFIBRILLATOR NEARBY, SO I'M GOING TO GO GET IT.
YOU CONTINUE RESUSCITATION.

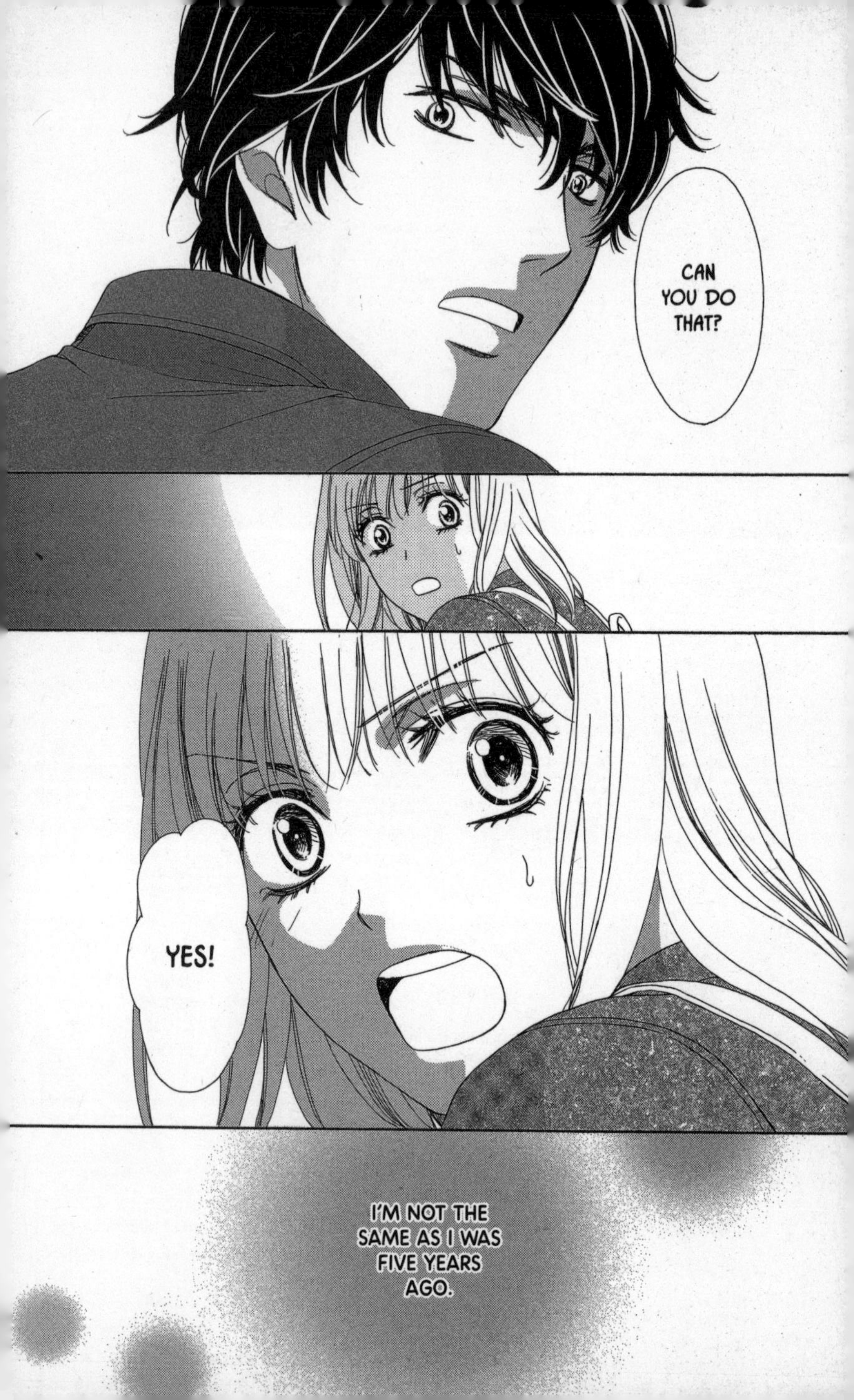
CAN YOU DO THAT?
YES!
I'M NOT THE SAME AS I WAS FIVE YEARS AGO.

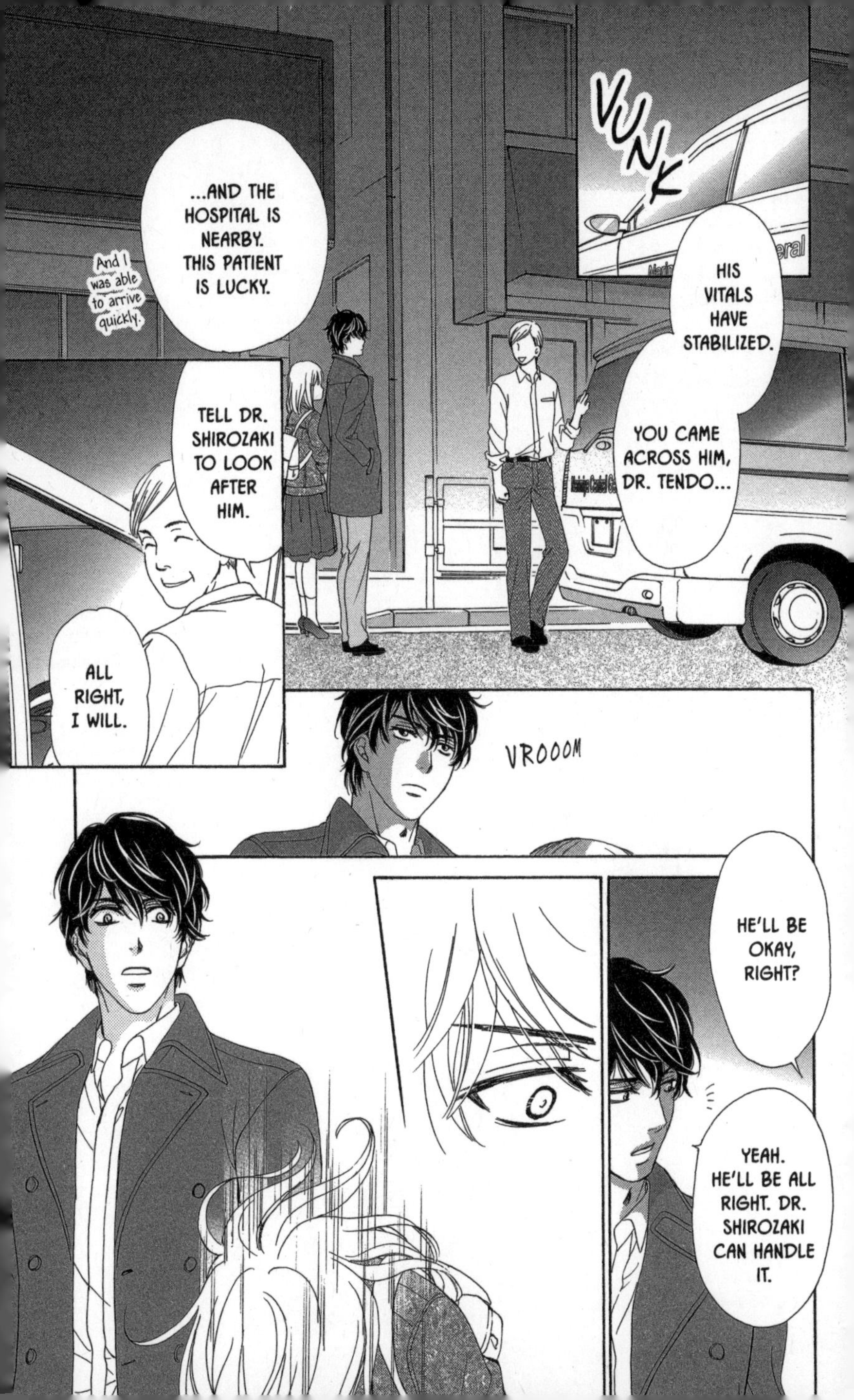
VUNK
HIS VITALS HAVE STABILIZED.
YOU CAME ACROSS HIM, DR. TENDO...
...AND THE HOSPITAL IS NEARBY. THIS PATIENT IS LUCKY.
And I was able to arrive quickly.
TELL DR. SHIROZAKI TO LOOK AFTER HIM.
ALL RIGHT, I WILL.
VROOOM
HE'LL BE OKAY, RIGHT?
YEAH. HE'LL BE ALL RIGHT. DR. SHIROZAKI CAN HANDLE IT.

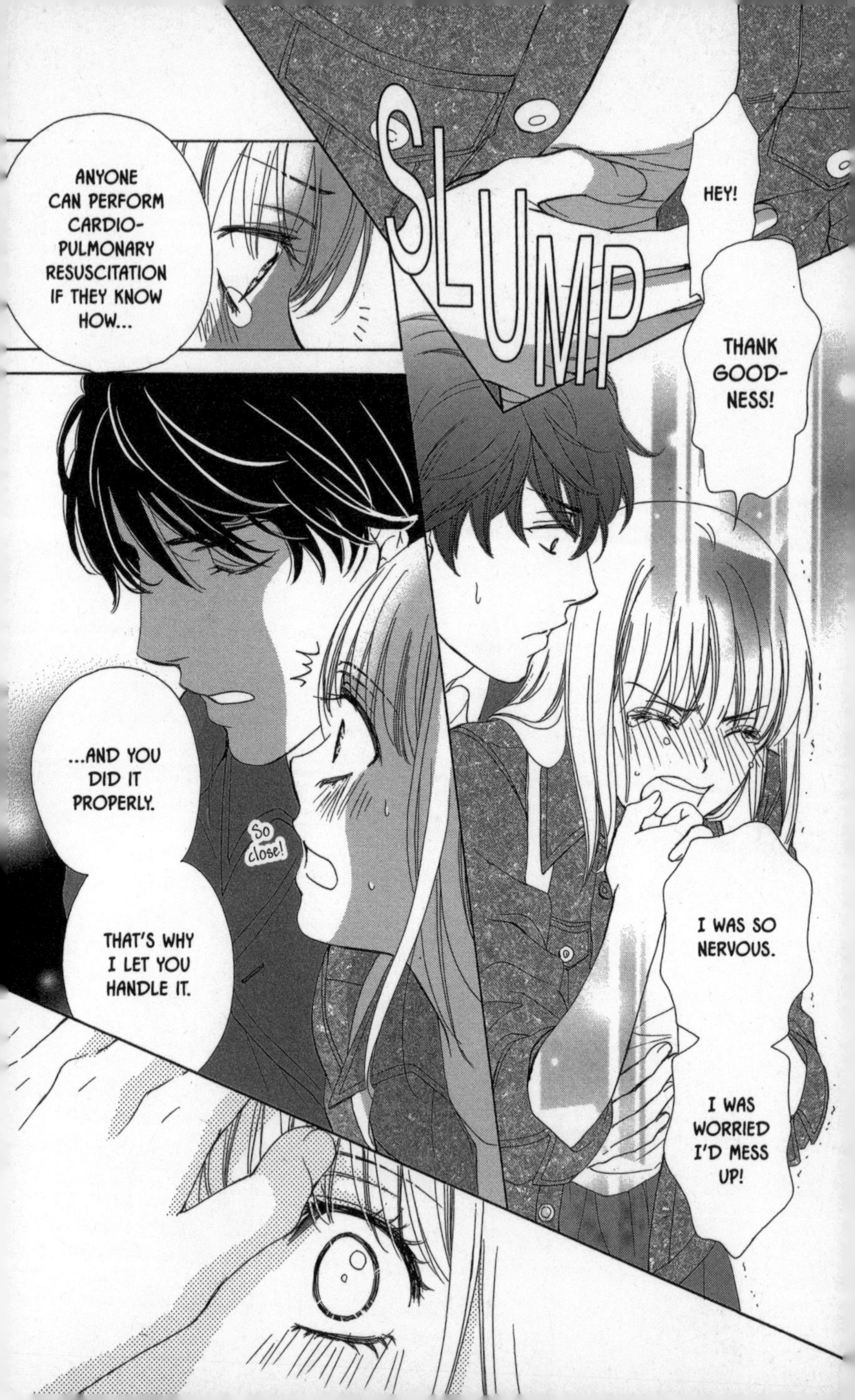
SLUMP
HEY!
THANK GOODNESS!
ANYONE CAN PERFORM CARDIO-PULMONARY RESUSCITATION IF THEY KNOW HOW...
I WAS SO NERVOUS.
I WAS WORRIED I'D MESS UP!
...AND YOU DID IT PROPERLY.
So close!
THAT'S WHY I LET YOU HANDLE IT.

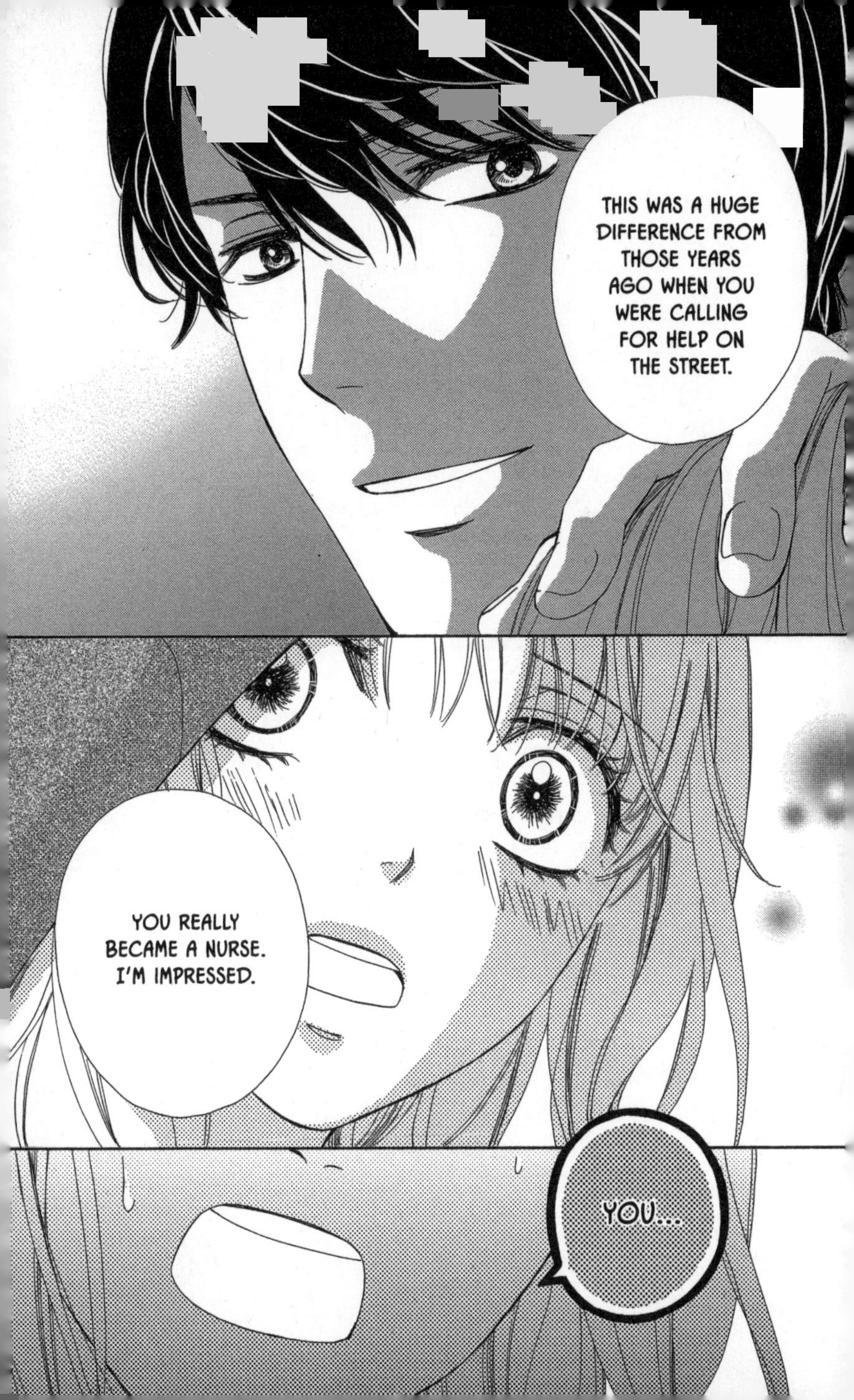
THIS WAS A HUGE DIFFERENCE FROM THOSE YEARS AGO WHEN YOU WERE CALLING FOR HELP ON THE STREET.
YOU REALLY BECAME A NURSE. I'M IMPRESSED.
YOU...

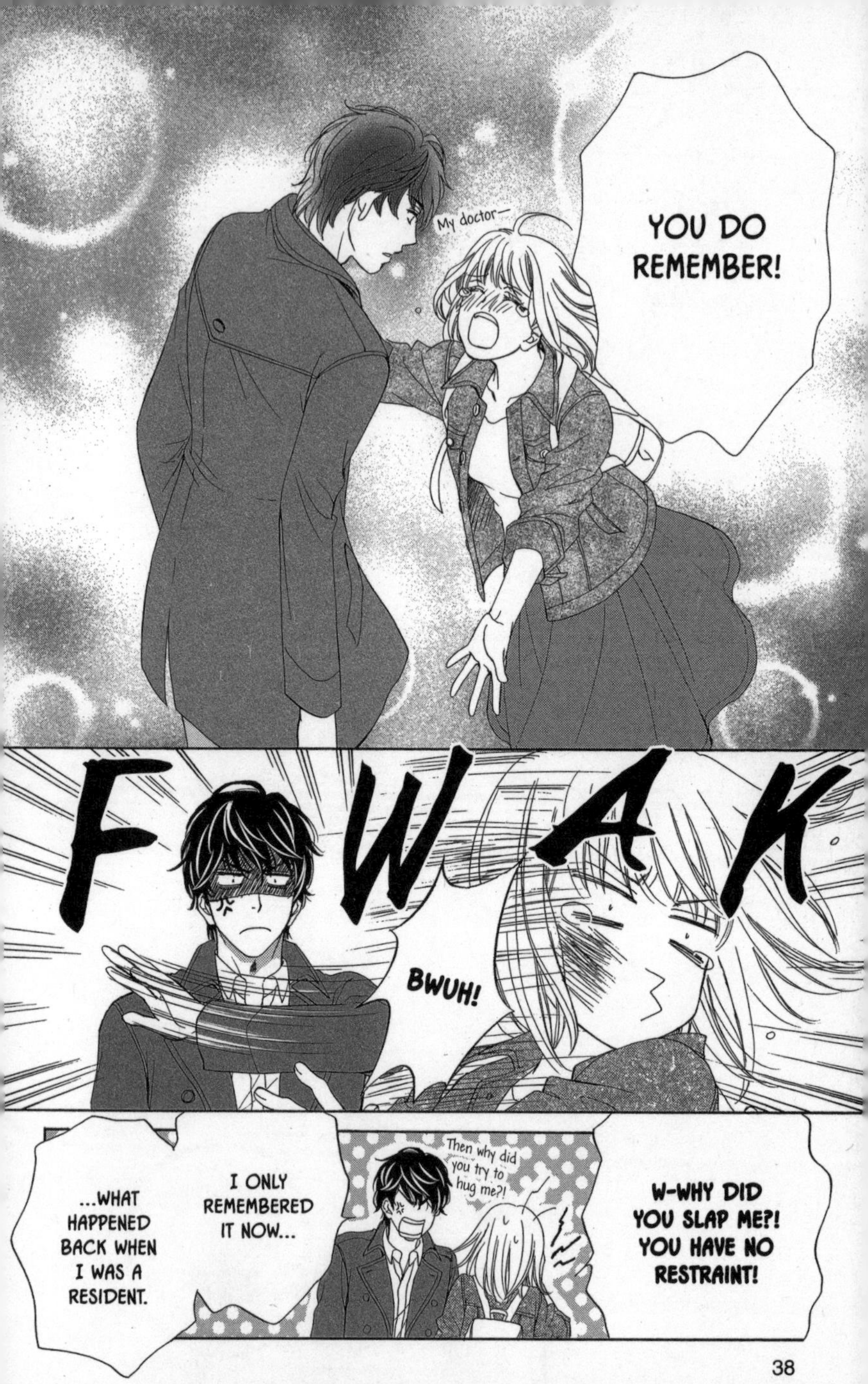

YOU DO REMEMBER!
My doctor—
FWAK
BWUH!
W-WHY DID YOU SLAP ME?! YOU HAVE NO RESTRAINT!
Then why did you try to hug me?!
I ONLY REMEMBERED IT NOW...
...WHAT HAPPENED BACK WHEN I WAS A RESIDENT.

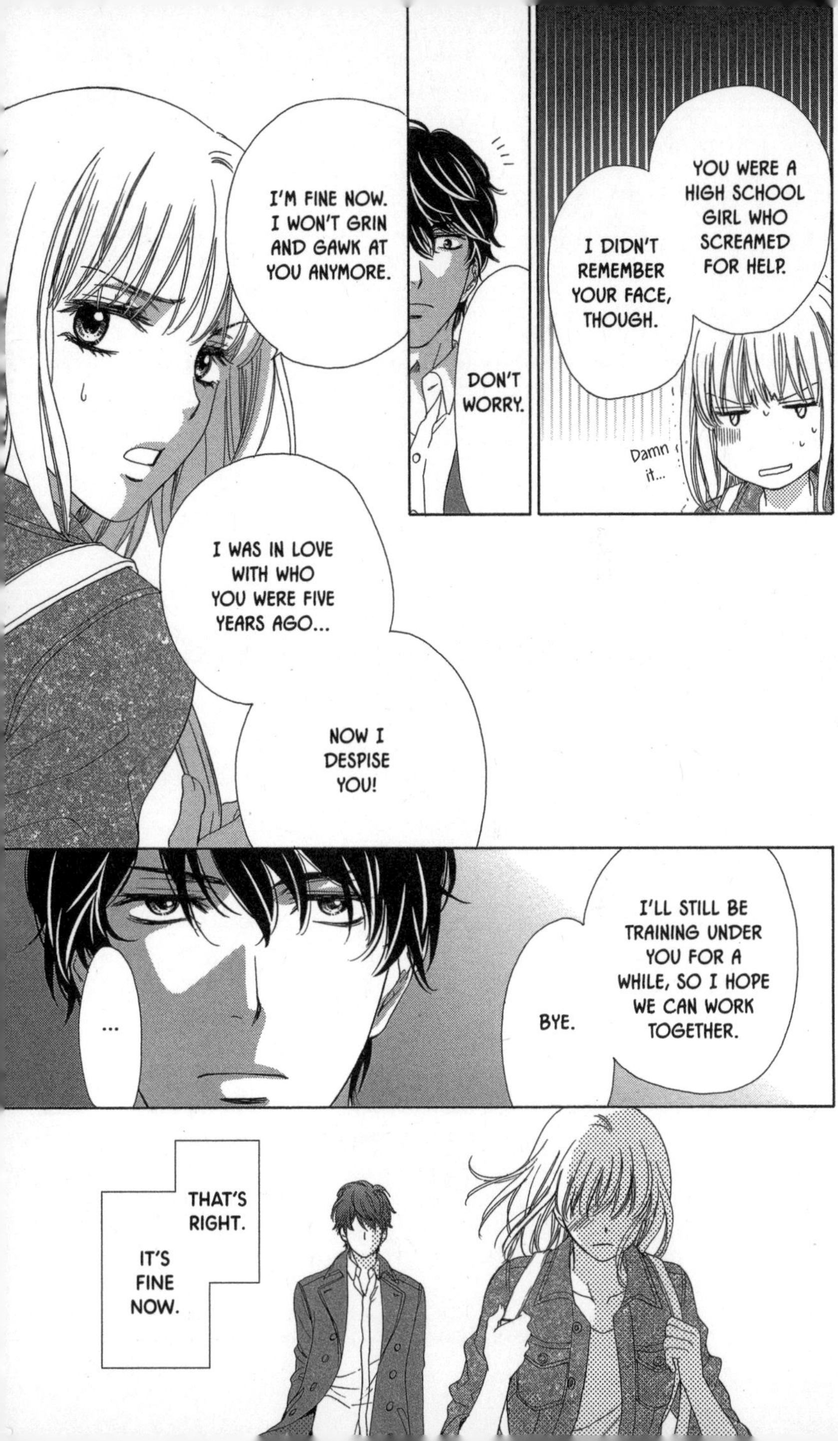
YOU WERE A HIGH SCHOOL GIRL WHO SCREAMED FOR HELP.
I DIDN'T REMEMBER YOUR FACE, THOUGH.
Damn it...
DON'T WORRY.
I'M FINE NOW. I WON'T GRIN AND GAWK AT YOU ANYMORE.
I WAS IN LOVE WITH WHO YOU WERE FIVE YEARS AGO...
NOW I DESPISE YOU!
I'LL STILL BE TRAINING UNDER YOU FOR A WHILE, SO I HOPE WE CAN WORK TOGETHER.
BYE.
...
THAT'S RIGHT.
IT'S FINE NOW.

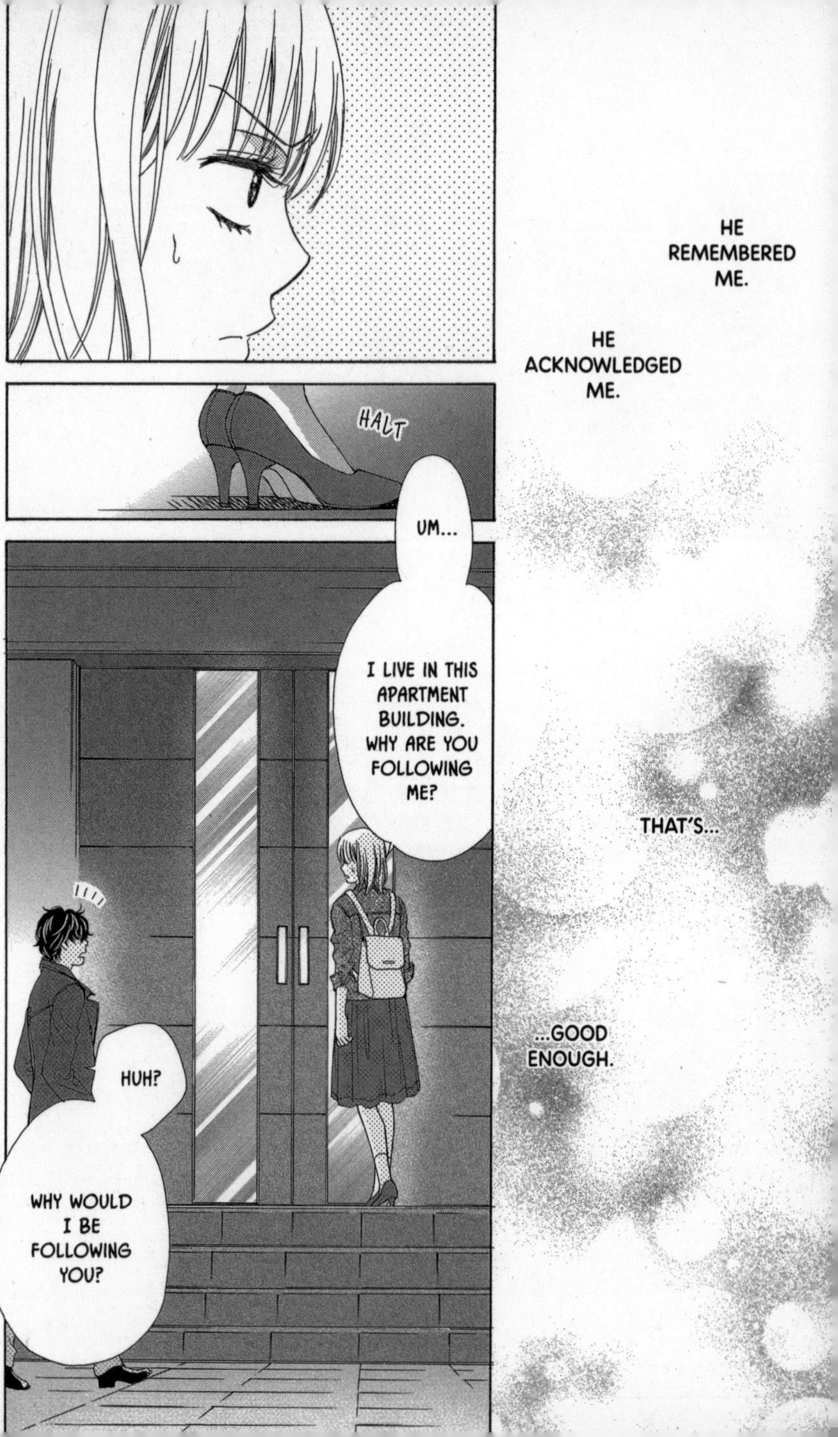
HE REMEMBERED ME.
HE ACKNOWLEDGED ME.
THAT'S...
...GOOD ENOUGH.
HALT
UM...
I LIVE IN THIS APARTMENT BUILDING. WHY ARE YOU FOLLOWING ME?
HUH?
WHY WOULD I BE FOLLOWING YOU?

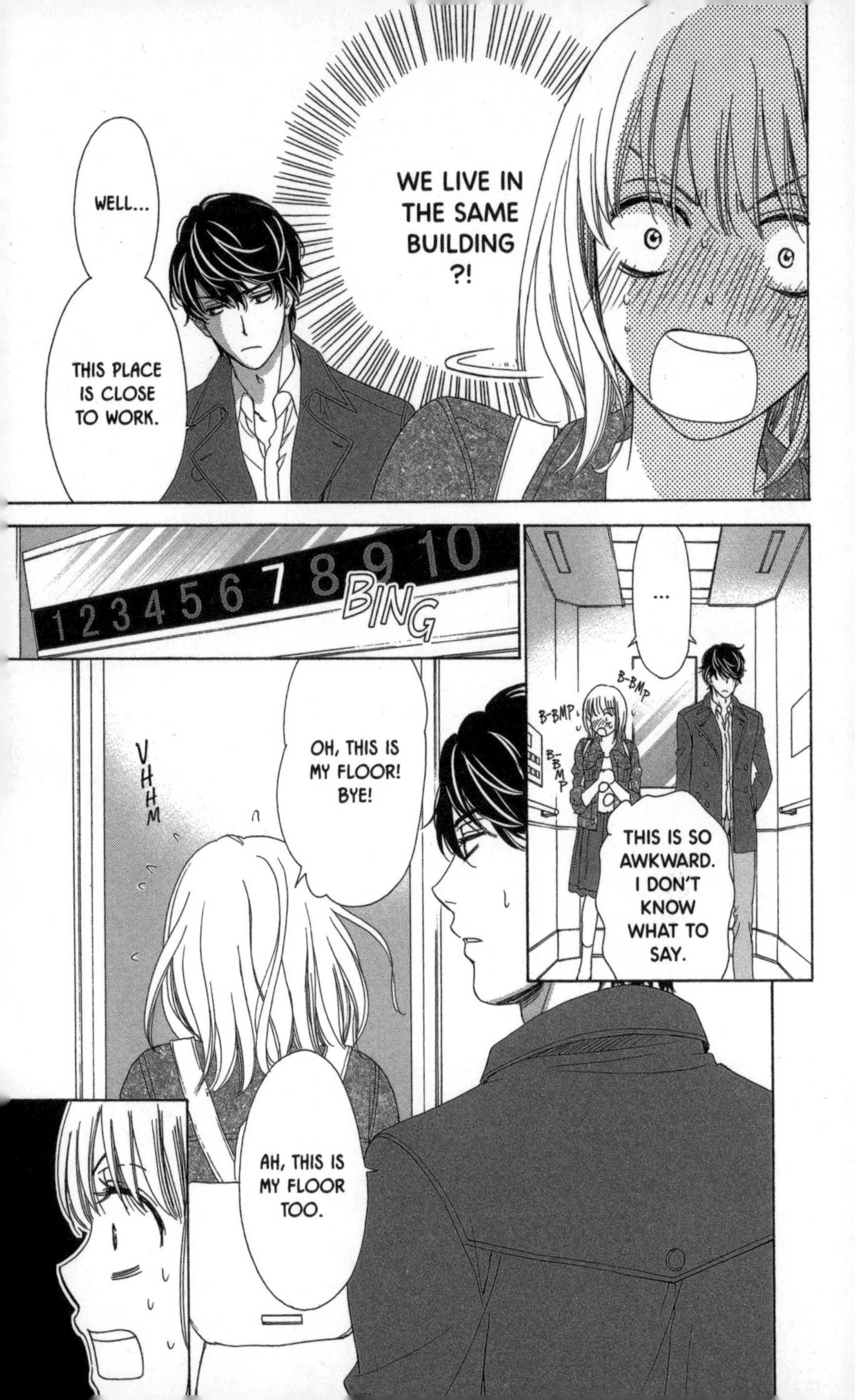
WE LIVE IN THE SAME BUILDING ?!
WELL...
THIS PLACE IS CLOSE TO WORK.
...
B-BMP
B-BMP
B-BMP
THIS IS SO AWKWARD. I DON'T KNOW WHAT TO SAY.
1 2 3 4 5 6 7 8 9 10
BING
OH, THIS IS MY FLOOR! BYE!
VHHM
AH, THIS IS MY FLOOR TOO.

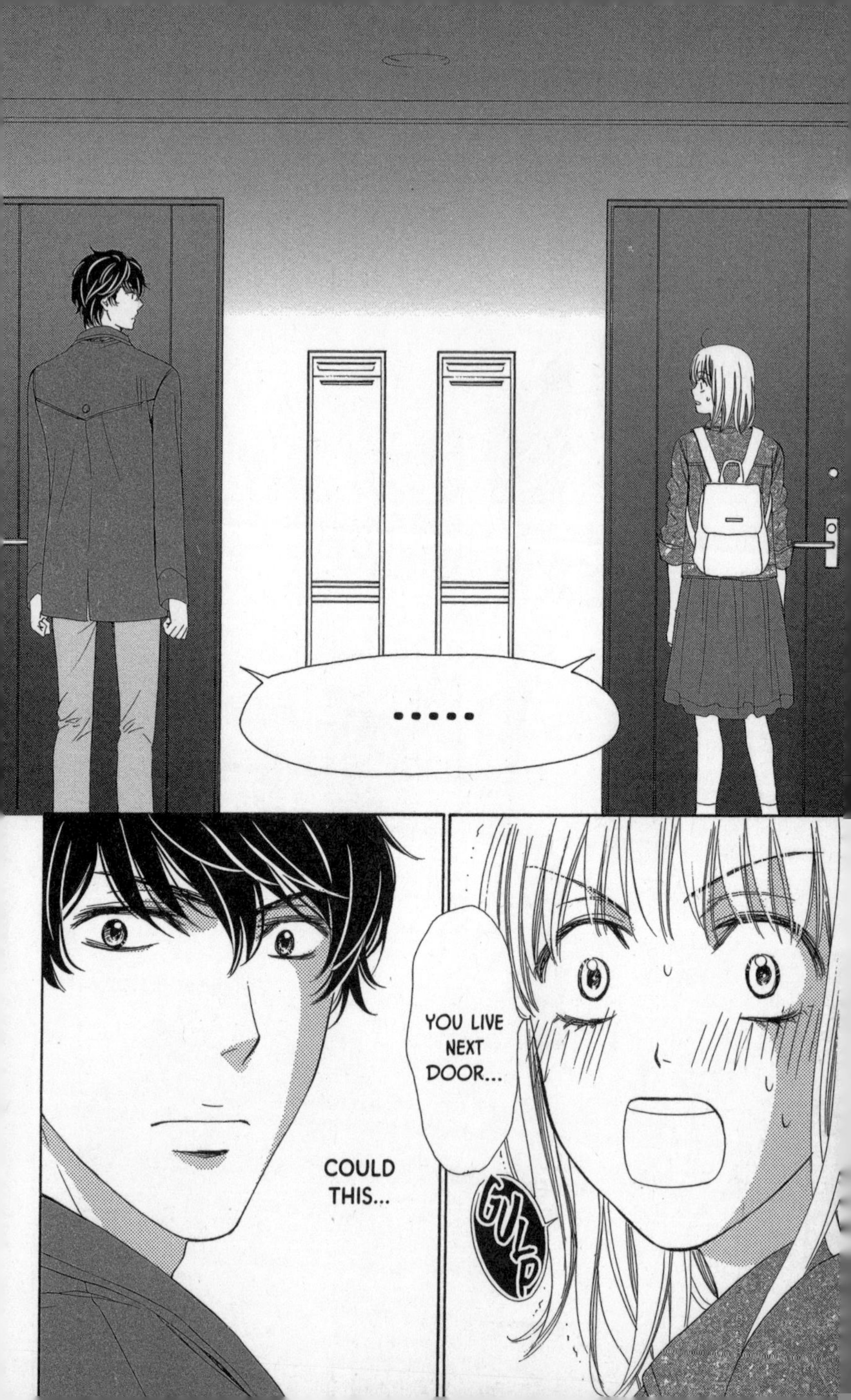
.....
YOU LIVE NEXT DOOR...
GULP
COULD THIS...

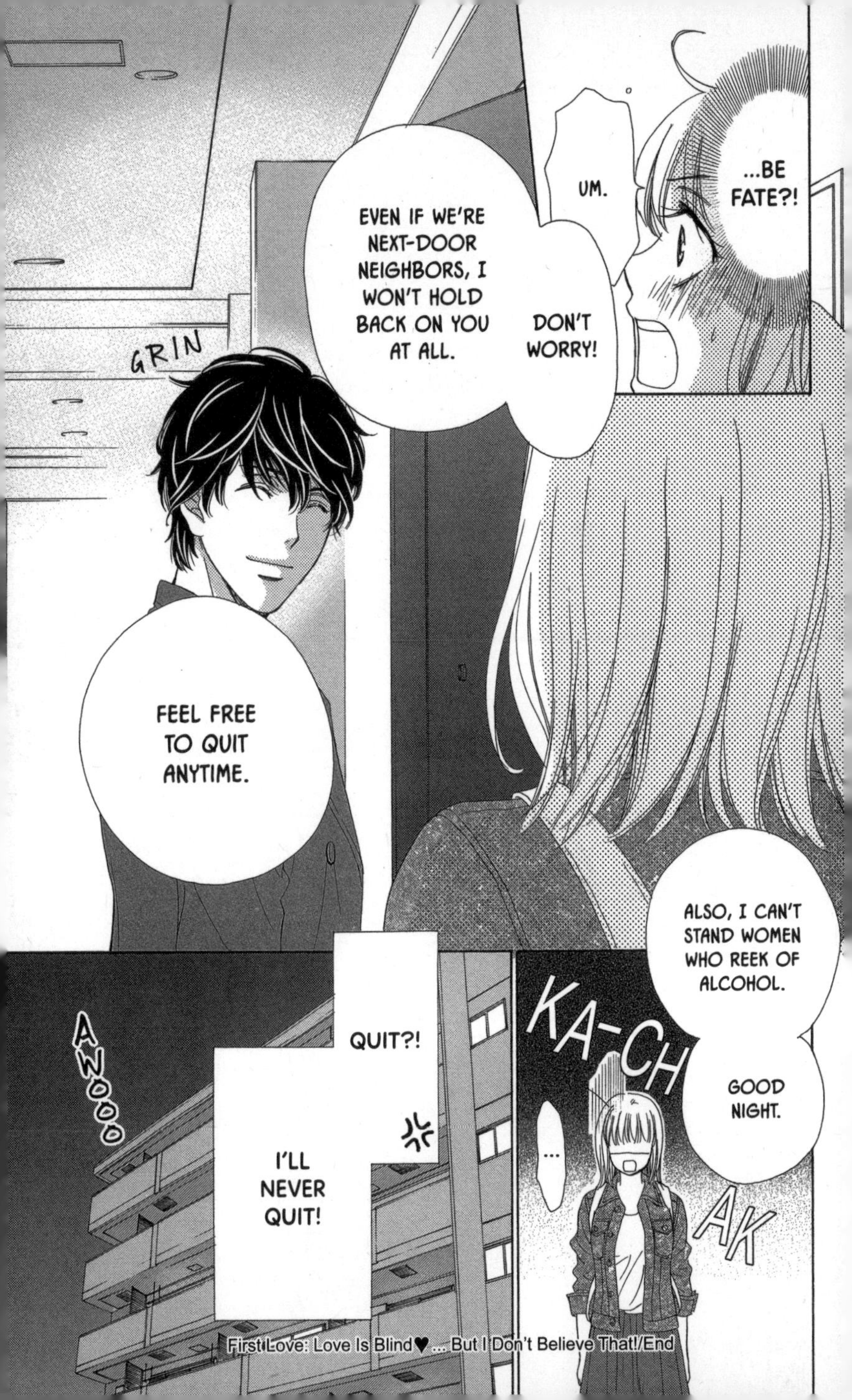
...BE FATE?!
UM.
DON'T WORRY!
EVEN IF WE'RE NEXT-DOOR NEIGHBORS, I WON'T HOLD BACK ON YOU AT ALL.
GRIN
FEEL FREE TO QUIT ANYTIME.
ALSO, I CAN'T STAND WOMEN WHO REEK OF ALCOHOL.
GOOD NIGHT.
KA-CHAK
...
QUIT?!
I'LL NEVER QUIT!
AWOOO

First Love: Love Is Blind♥... But I Don't Believe That!/End

● Long ago, soon after I began my manga career, I drew a manga about a doctor and a nurse. At that time, I drew the nurse uniform as a dress, but it's not common anymore. The pants uniform is certainly easier to work in. The dress uniform is still available and in use, though. I like the dress uniform (am I some old man?), and I don't want it to go away, so I drew Nanase wearing one.

Like this! →

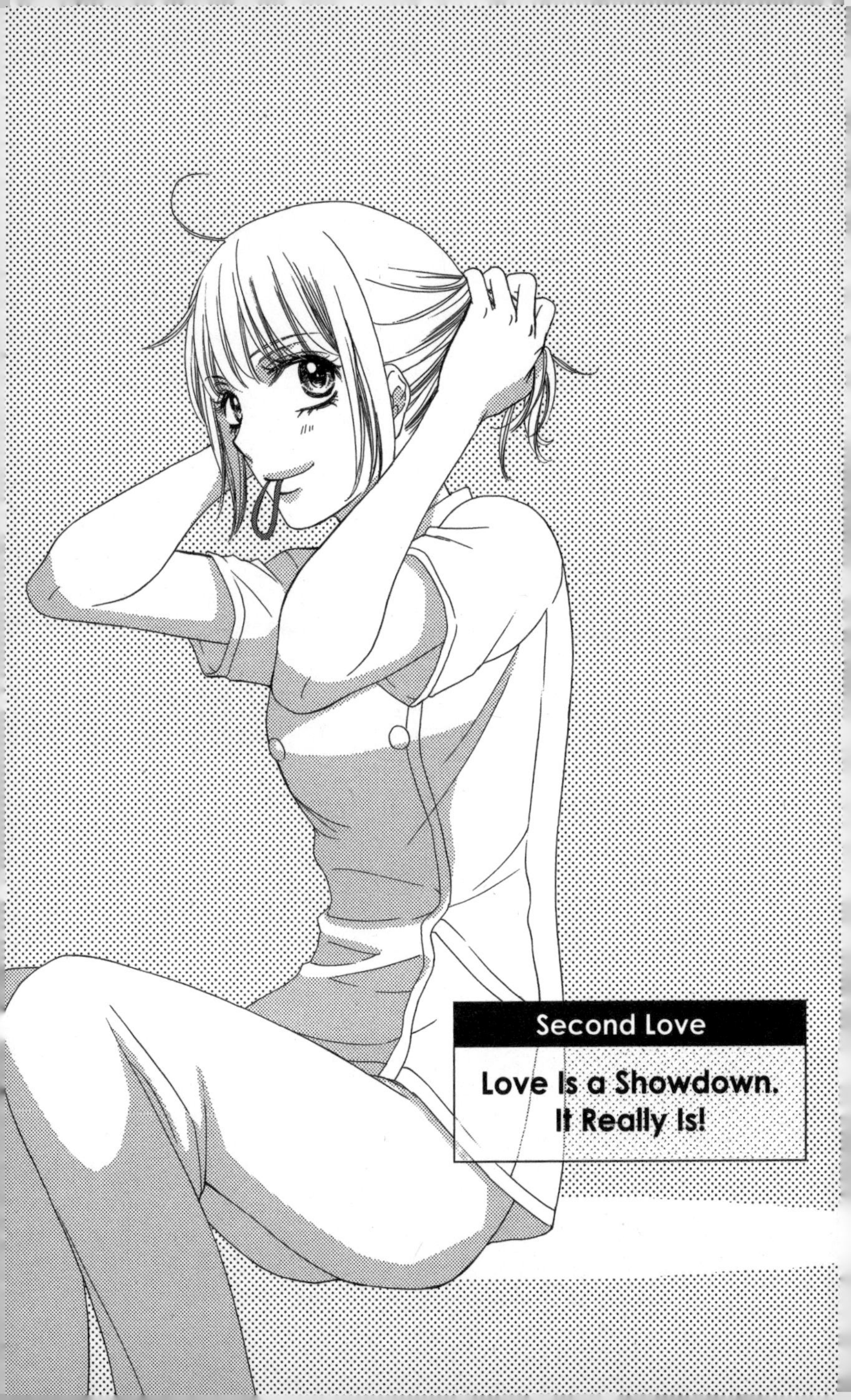
Second Love
Love Is a Showdown.
It Really Is!

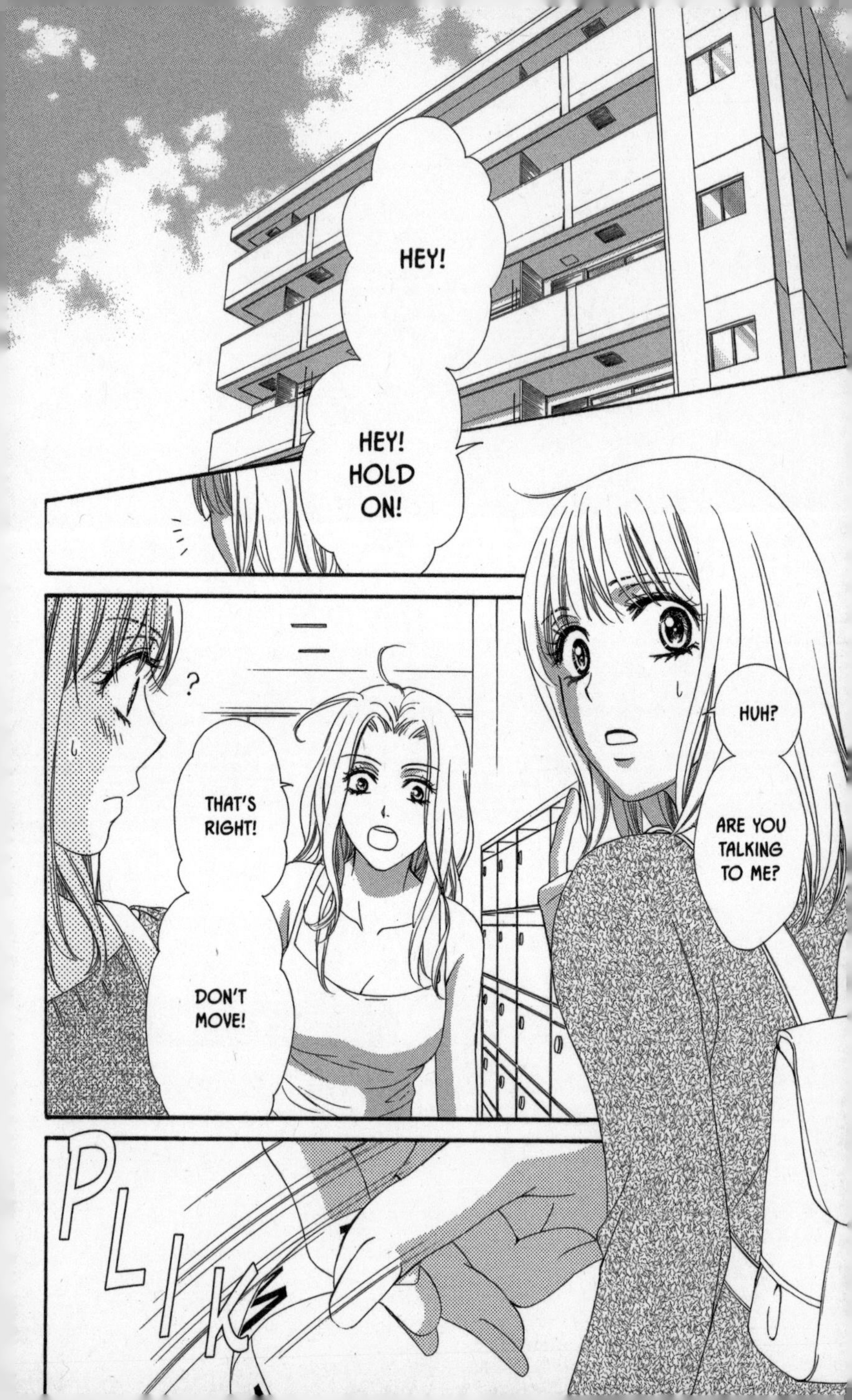
HEY!
HEY! HOLD ON!
HUH?
ARE YOU TALKING TO ME?
?
THAT'S RIGHT!
DON'T MOVE!
PLIK

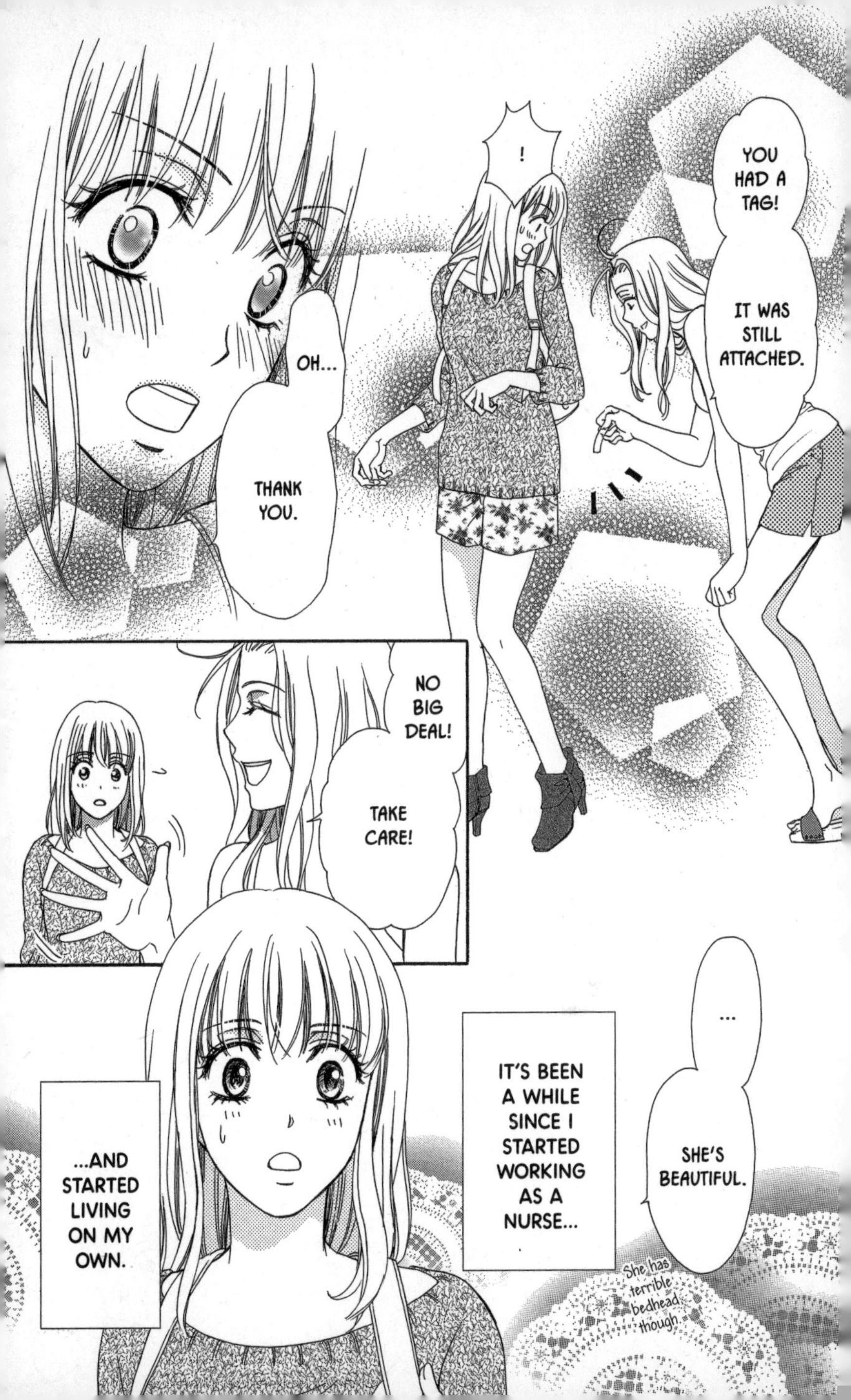
YOU HAD A TAG!
IT WAS STILL ATTACHED.
!
OH...
THANK YOU.
NO BIG DEAL!
TAKE CARE!
...
SHE'S BEAUTIFUL.
She has terrible bedhead though.
IT'S BEEN A WHILE SINCE I STARTED WORKING AS A NURSE...
...AND STARTED LIVING ON MY OWN.

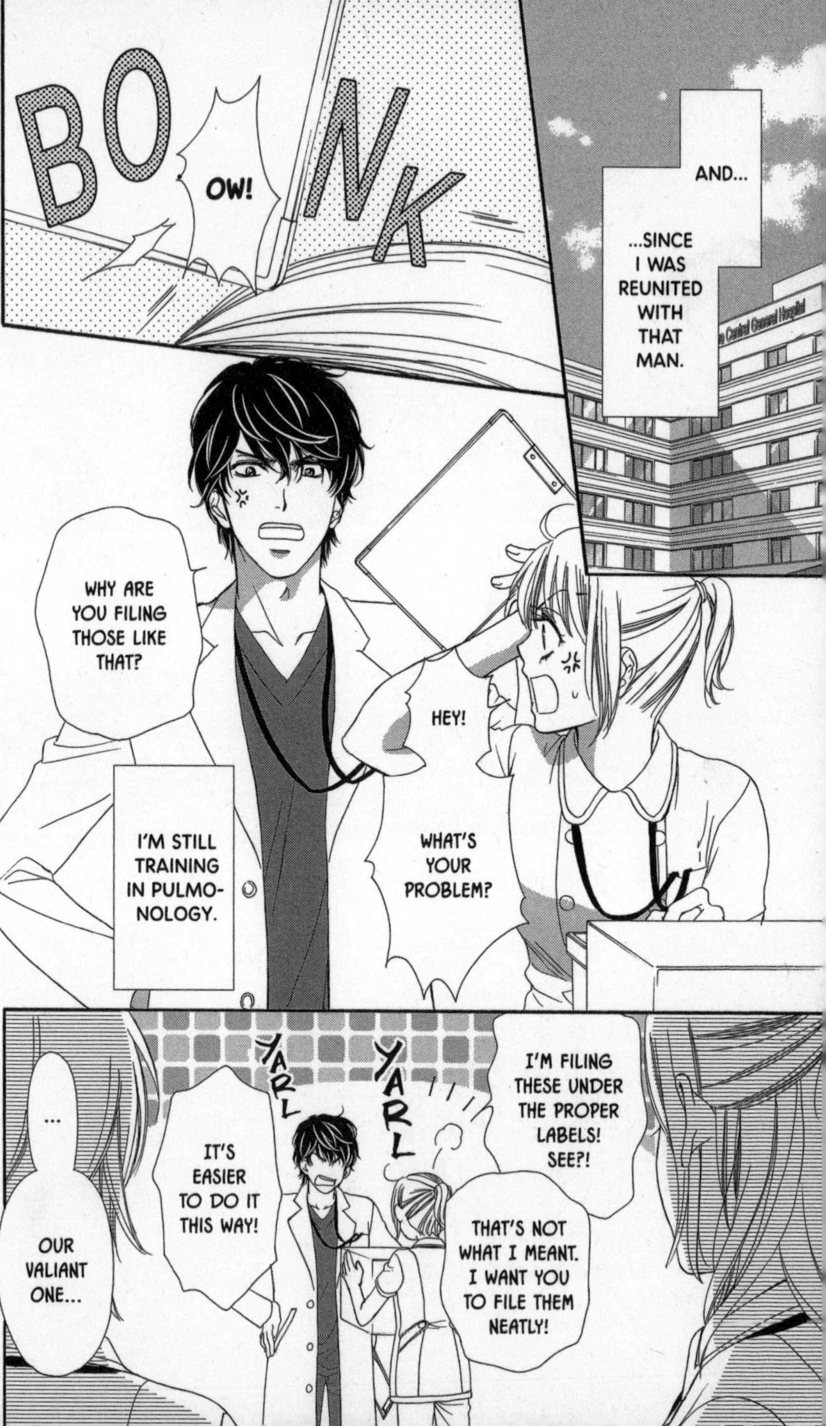
AND...
...SINCE I WAS REUNITED WITH THAT MAN.
Central General Hospital
BONK
OW!
HEY!
WHAT'S YOUR PROBLEM?
WHY ARE YOU FILING THOSE LIKE THAT?
I'M STILL TRAINING IN PULMO-NOLOGY.
I'M FILING THESE UNDER THE PROPER LABELS! SEE?!
YARL YARL
IT'S EASIER TO DO IT THIS WAY!
THAT'S NOT WHAT I MEANT. I WANT YOU TO FILE THEM NEATLY!
...
OUR VALIANT ONE...

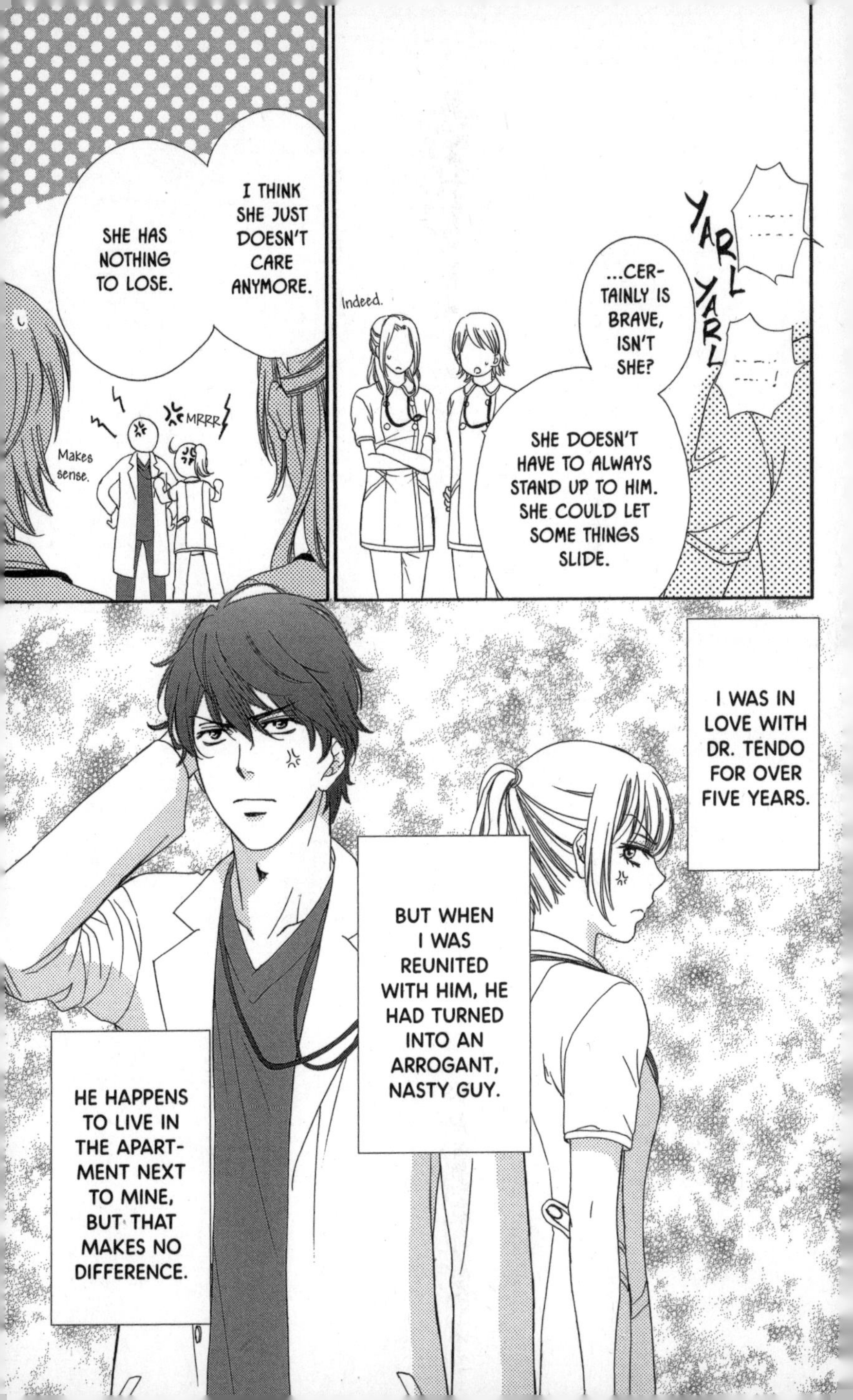
YARL YARL
...CER-TAINLY IS BRAVE, ISN'T SHE?
Indeed.
SHE DOESN'T HAVE TO ALWAYS STAND UP TO HIM. SHE COULD LET SOME THINGS SLIDE.
I THINK SHE JUST DOESN'T CARE ANYMORE.
SHE HAS NOTHING TO LOSE.
MRRR
Makes sense.
I WAS IN LOVE WITH DR. TENDO FOR OVER FIVE YEARS.
BUT WHEN I WAS REUNITED WITH HIM, HE HAD TURNED INTO AN ARROGANT, NASTY GUY.
HE HAPPENS TO LIVE IN THE APART-MENT NEXT TO MINE, BUT THAT MAKES NO DIFFERENCE.

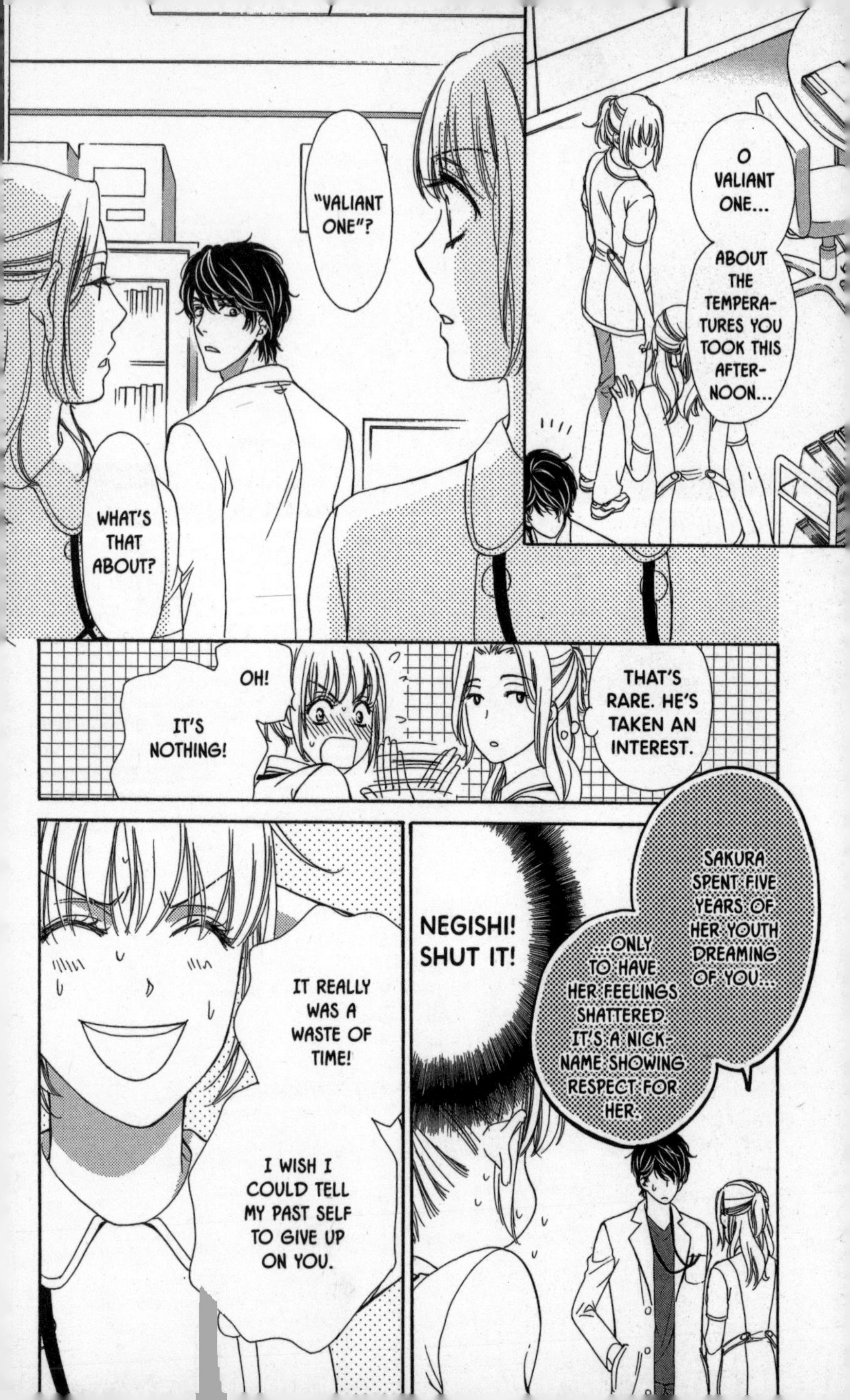
O VALIANT ONE...
ABOUT THE TEMPERATURES YOU TOOK THIS AFTERNOON...
"VALIANT ONE"?
WHAT'S THAT ABOUT?
THAT'S RARE. HE'S TAKEN AN INTEREST.
OH!
IT'S NOTHING!
SAKURA SPENT FIVE YEARS OF HER YOUTH DREAMING OF YOU...
...ONLY TO HAVE HER FEELINGS SHATTERED. IT'S A NICKNAME SHOWING RESPECT FOR HER.
NEGISHI! SHUT IT!
IT REALLY WAS A WASTE OF TIME!
I WISH I COULD TELL MY PAST SELF TO GIVE UP ON YOU.

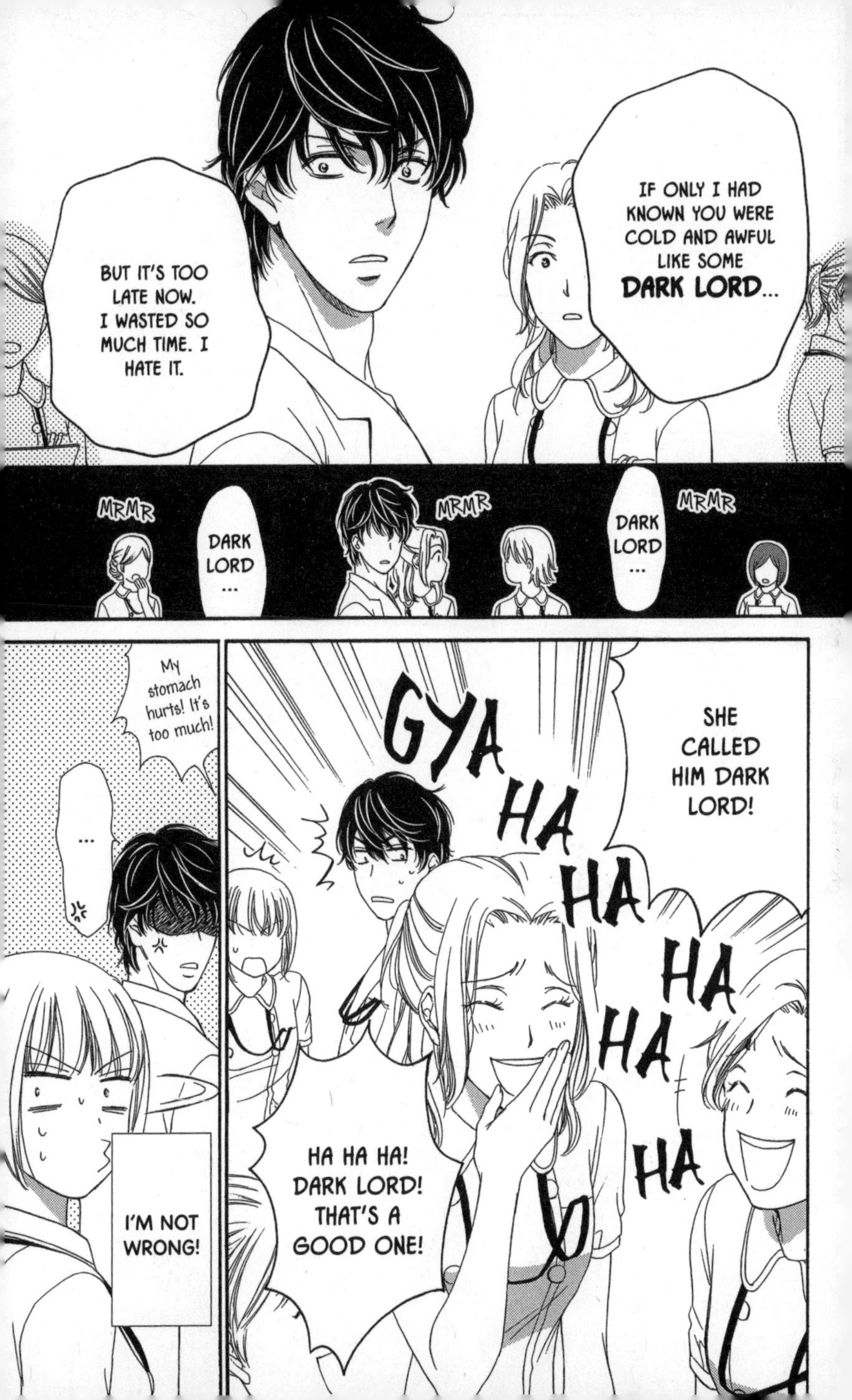
IF ONLY I HAD KNOWN YOU WERE COLD AND AWFUL LIKE SOME **DARK LORD**...
BUT IT'S TOO LATE NOW. I WASTED SO MUCH TIME. I HATE IT.
MRMR
DARK LORD ...
MRMR
DARK LORD ...
MRMR
SHE CALLED HIM DARK LORD!
GYA HA HA HA HA HA HA
HA HA HA! DARK LORD! THAT'S A GOOD ONE!
My stomach hurts! It's too much!
...
I'M NOT WRONG!

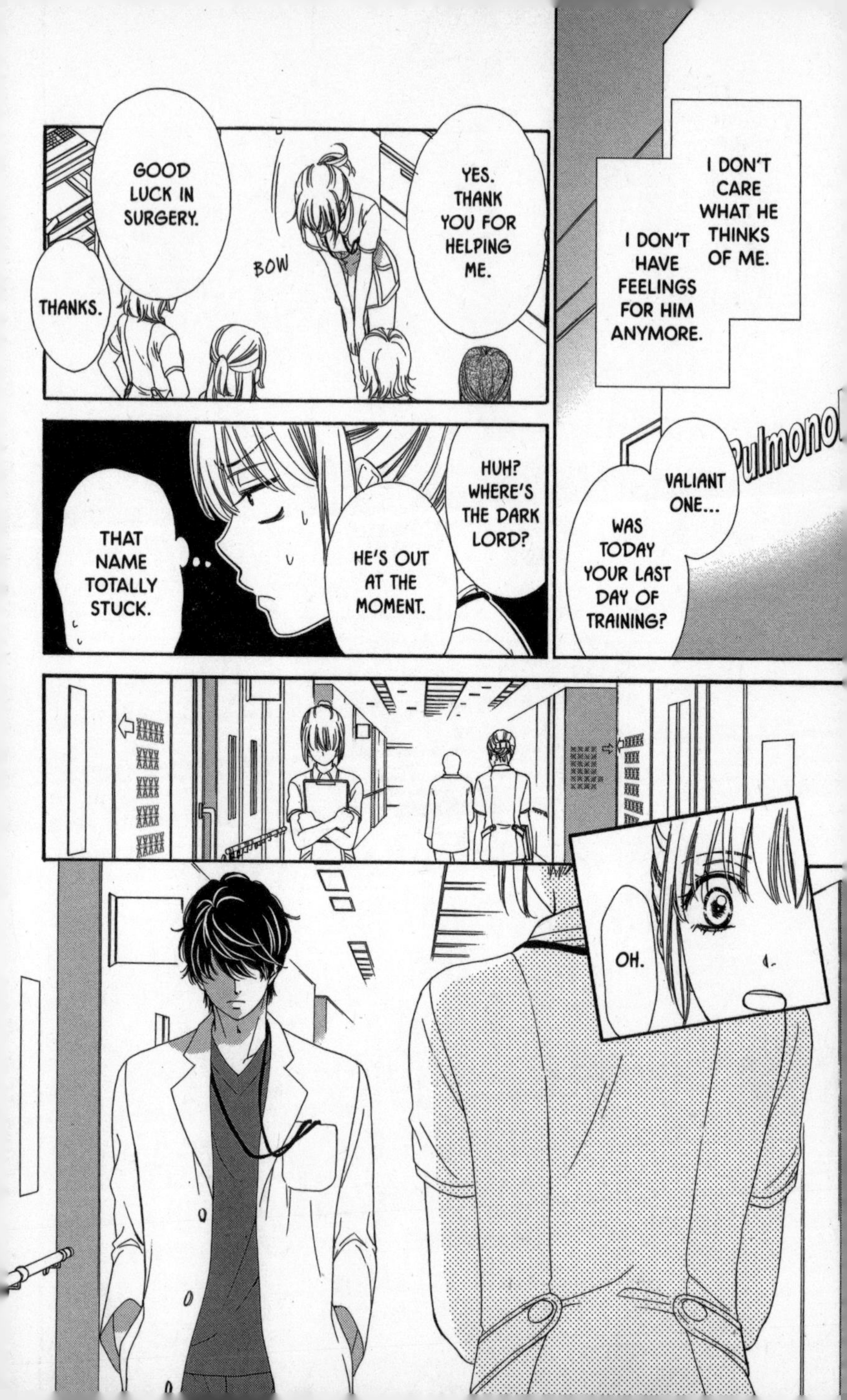
I DON'T CARE WHAT HE THINKS OF ME.
I DON'T HAVE FEELINGS FOR HIM ANYMORE.
Pulmonol
VALIANT ONE...
WAS TODAY YOUR LAST DAY OF TRAINING?
YES. THANK YOU FOR HELPING ME.
BOW
GOOD LUCK IN SURGERY.
THANKS.
HUH? WHERE'S THE DARK LORD?
HE'S OUT AT THE MOMENT.
THAT NAME TOTALLY STUCK.
OH.

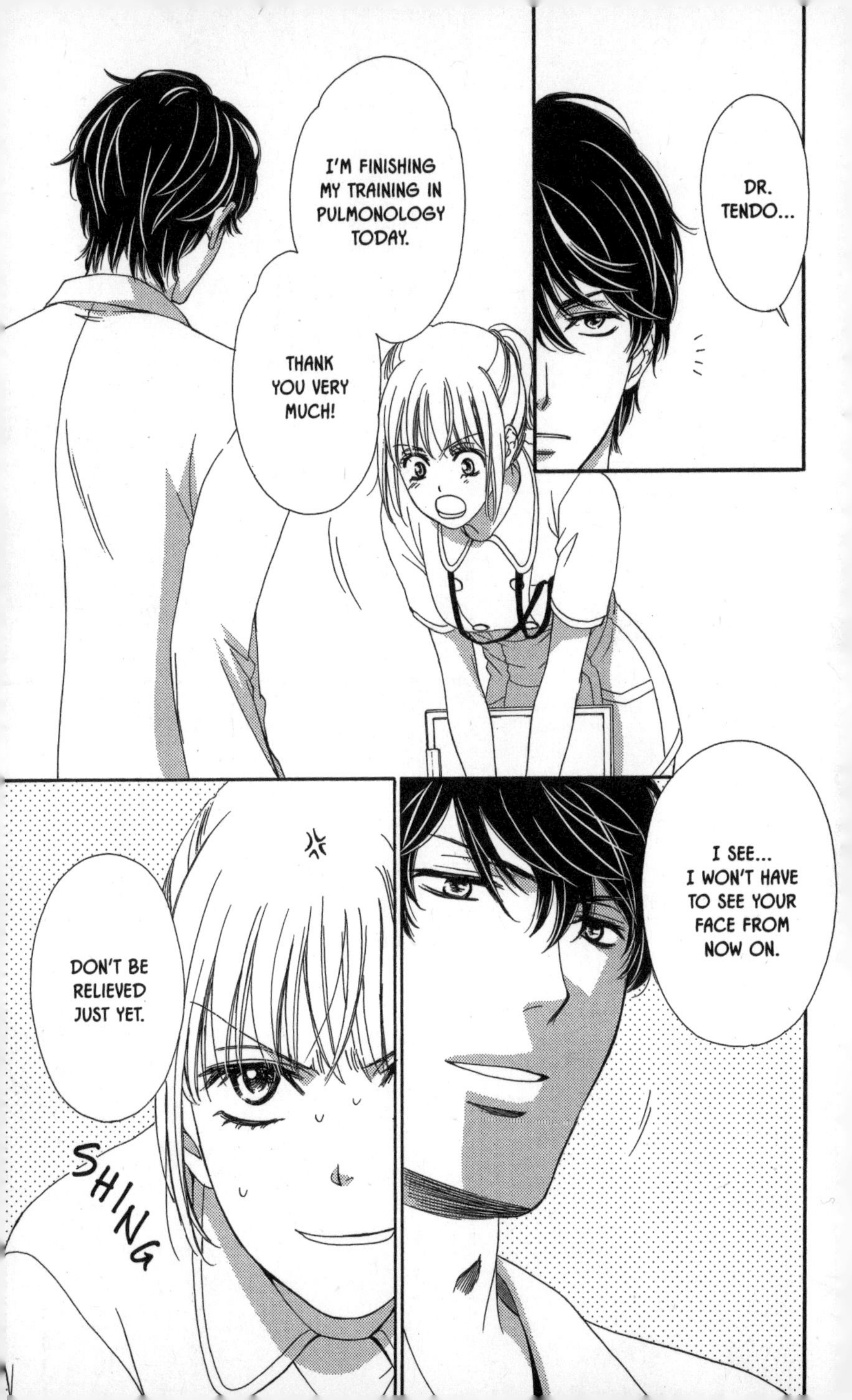
DR. TENDO...
I'M FINISHING MY TRAINING IN PULMONOLOGY TODAY.
THANK YOU VERY MUCH!
I SEE... I WON'T HAVE TO SEE YOUR FACE FROM NOW ON.
DON'T BE RELIEVED JUST YET.
SHING

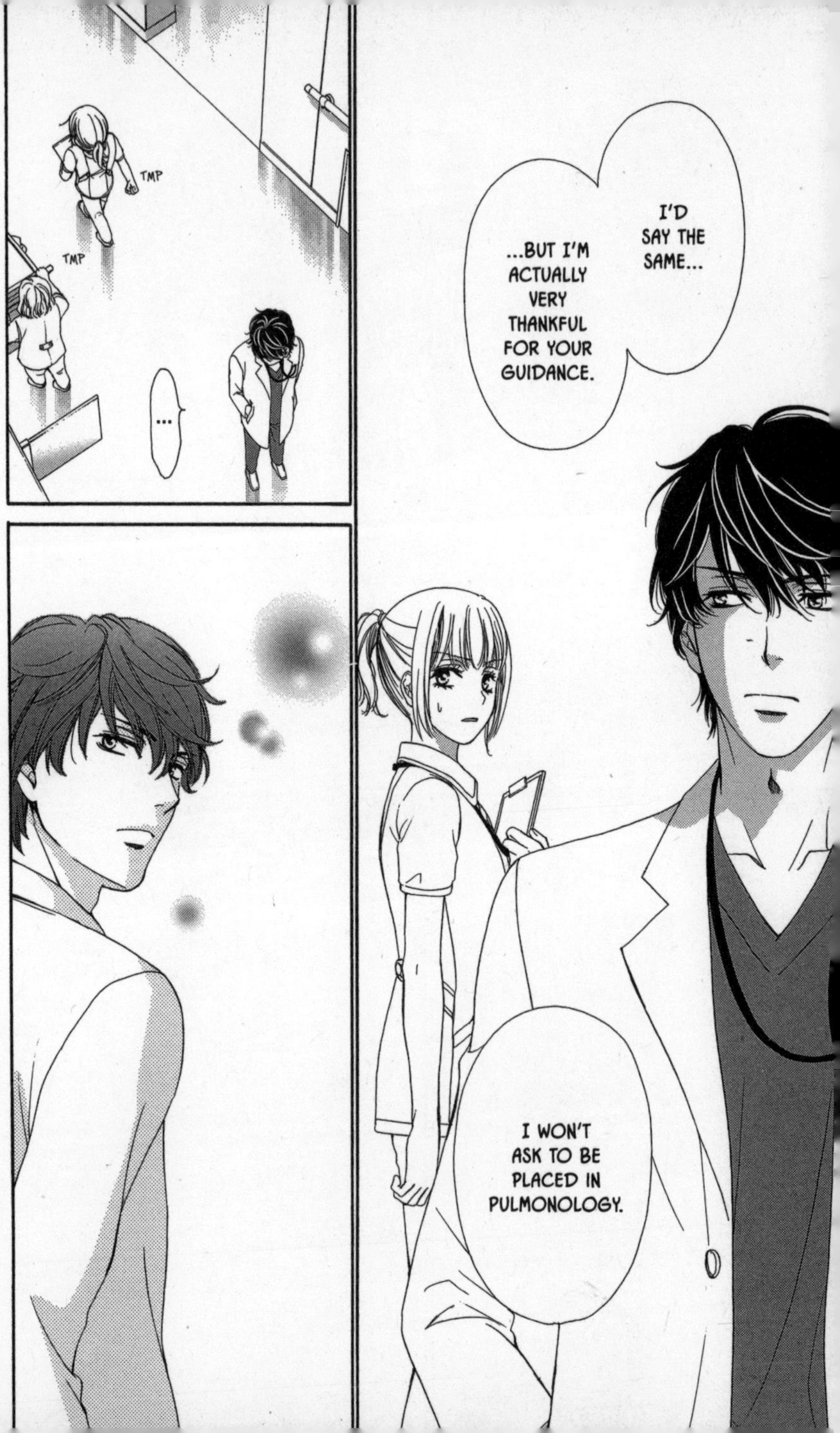
I'D SAY THE SAME...
...BUT I'M ACTUALLY VERY THANKFUL FOR YOUR GUIDANCE.
I WON'T ASK TO BE PLACED IN PULMONOLOGY.
TMP
TMP
...

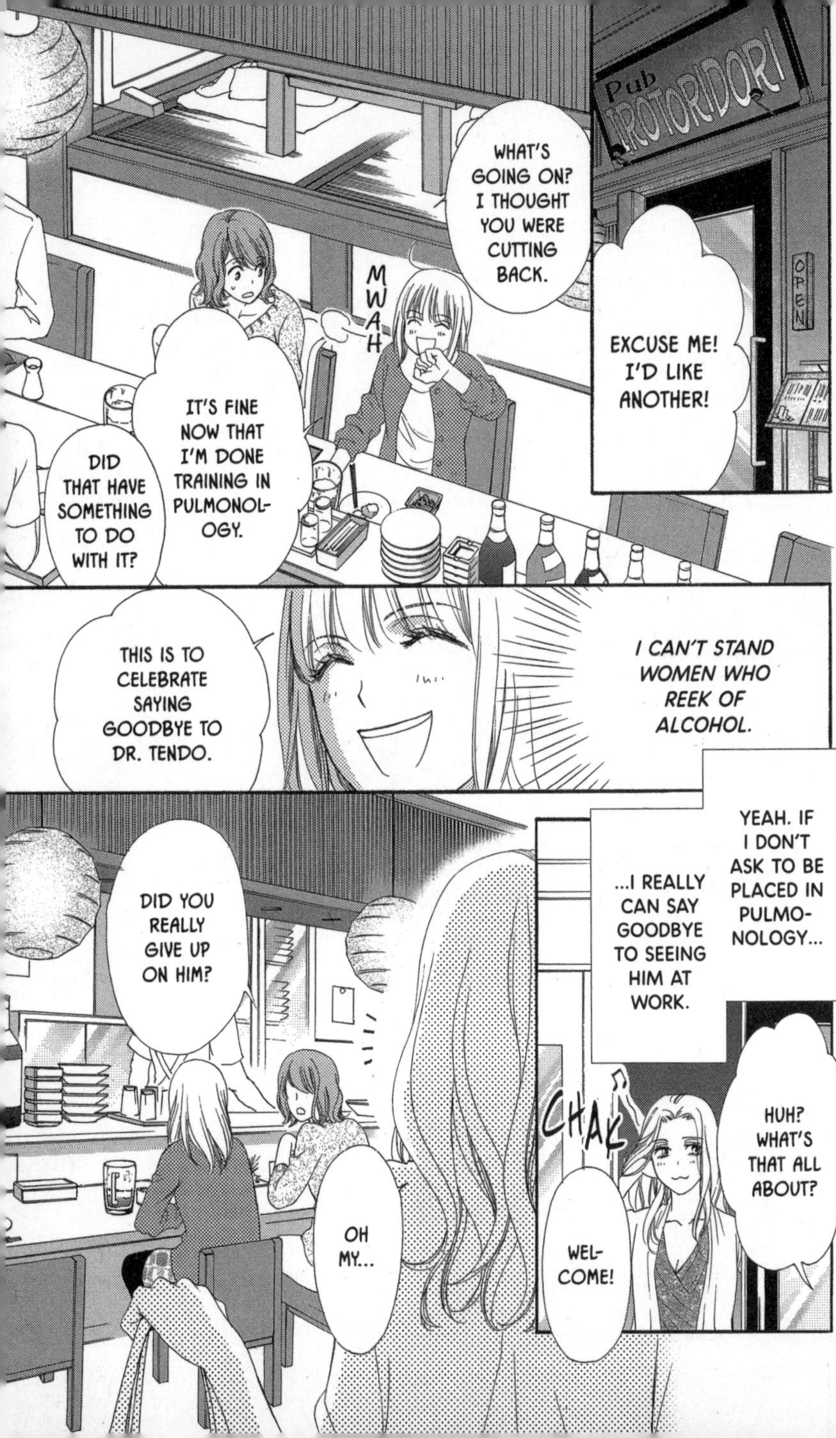
Pub
IROTORIDORI
OPEN
EXCUSE ME! I'D LIKE ANOTHER!
WHAT'S GOING ON? I THOUGHT YOU WERE CUTTING BACK.
MWAH
IT'S FINE NOW THAT I'M DONE TRAINING IN PULMONOLOGY.
DID THAT HAVE SOMETHING TO DO WITH IT?
I CAN'T STAND WOMEN WHO REEK OF ALCOHOL.
THIS IS TO CELEBRATE SAYING GOODBYE TO DR. TENDO.
DID YOU REALLY GIVE UP ON HIM?
YEAH. IF I DON'T ASK TO BE PLACED IN PULMONOLOGY...
...I REALLY CAN SAY GOODBYE TO SEEING HIM AT WORK.
HUH? WHAT'S THAT ALL ABOUT?
CHAK
WELCOME!
OH MY...

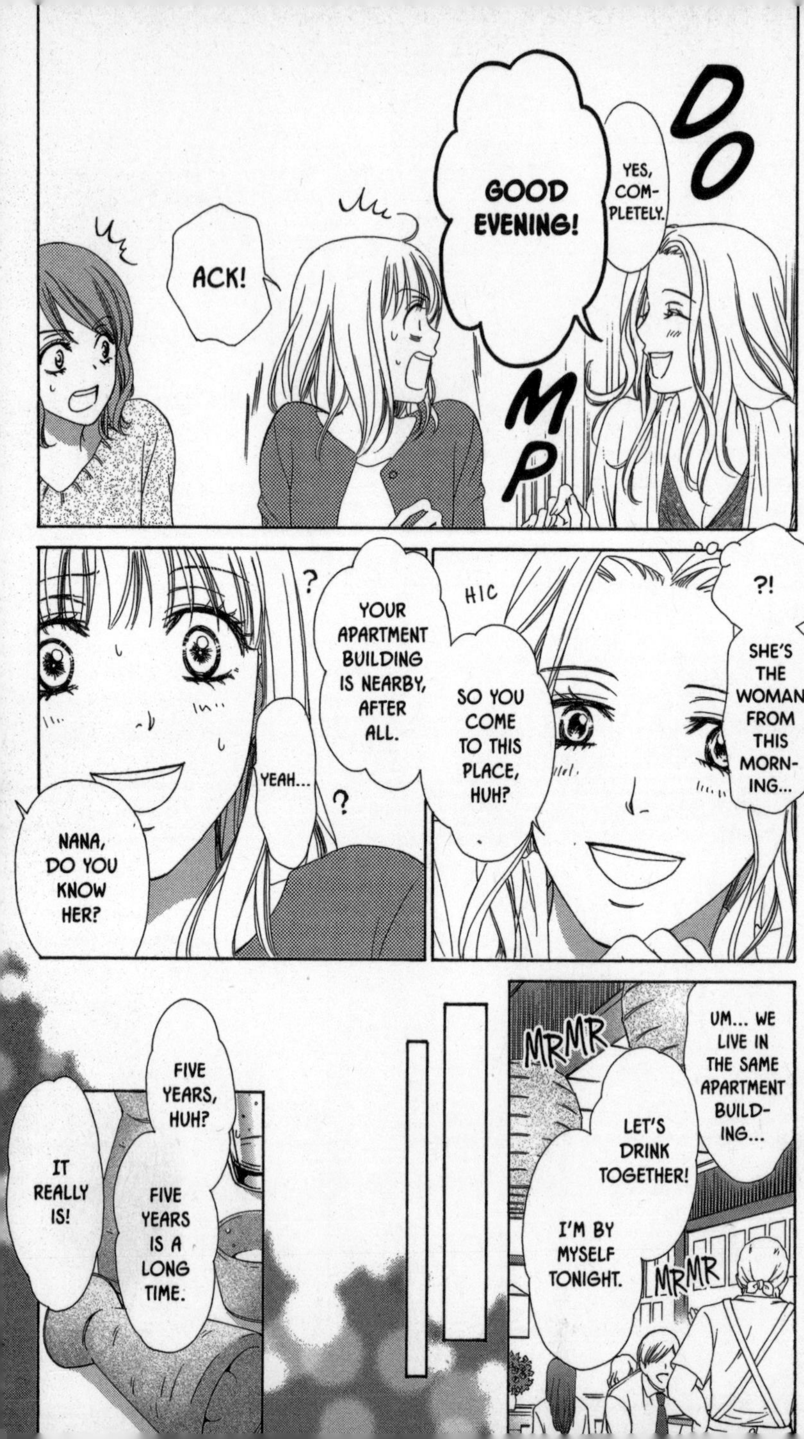
DOMP
YES, COMPLETELY.
GOOD EVENING!
ACK!
?!
SHE'S THE WOMAN FROM THIS MORNING...
HIC
SO YOU COME TO THIS PLACE, HUH?
YOUR APARTMENT BUILDING IS NEARBY, AFTER ALL.
?
YEAH...
?
NANA, DO YOU KNOW HER?
UM... WE LIVE IN THE SAME APARTMENT BUILDING...
MRMR
LET'S DRINK TOGETHER!
I'M BY MYSELF TONIGHT.
MRMR
FIVE YEARS, HUH?
IT REALLY IS!
FIVE YEARS IS A LONG TIME.

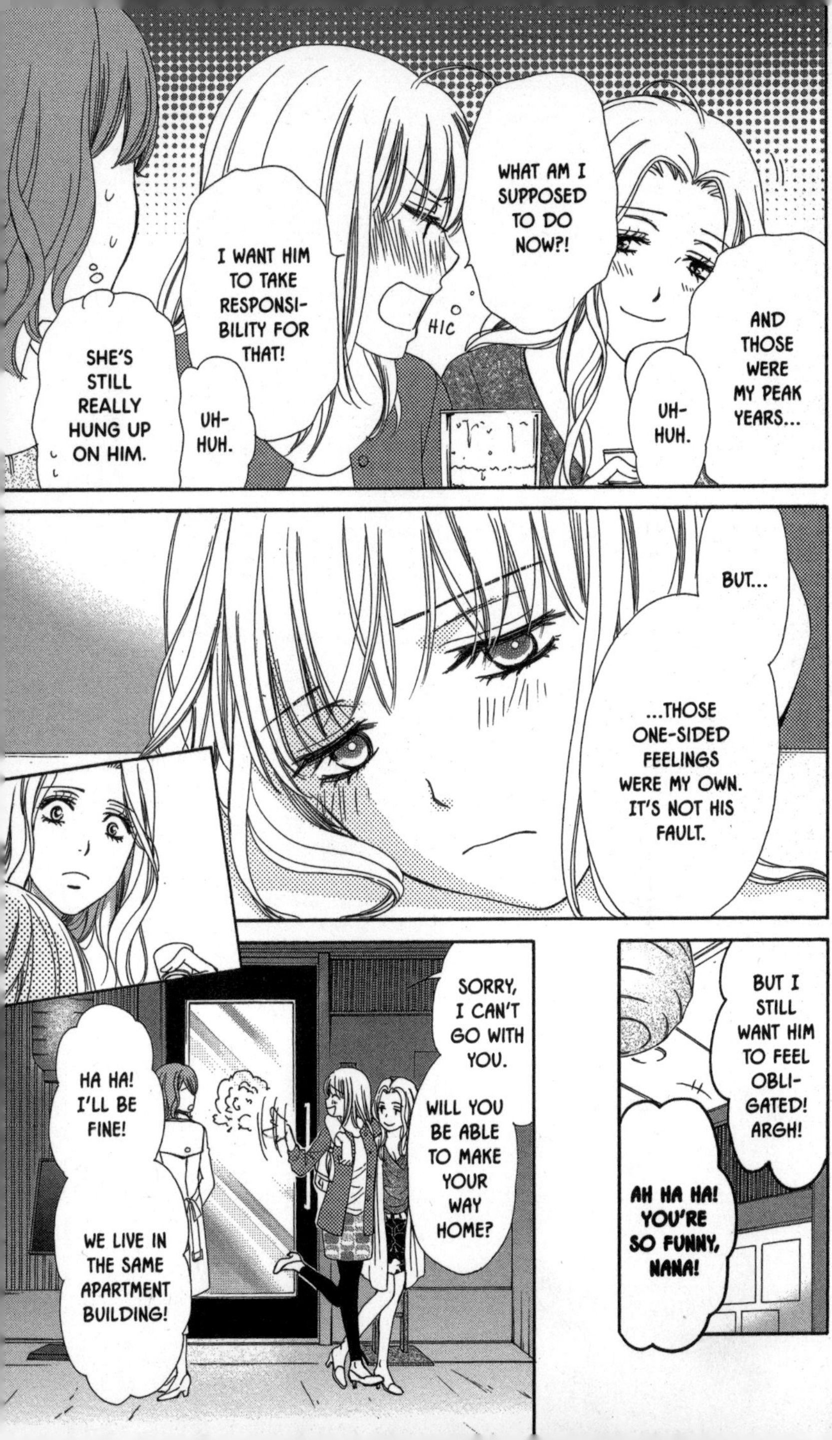
WHAT AM I SUPPOSED TO DO NOW?!
AND THOSE WERE MY PEAK YEARS...
UH-HUH.
I WANT HIM TO TAKE RESPONSIBILITY FOR THAT!
HIC
UH-HUH.
SHE'S STILL REALLY HUNG UP ON HIM.
BUT...
...THOSE ONE-SIDED FEELINGS WERE MY OWN. IT'S NOT HIS FAULT.
BUT I STILL WANT HIM TO FEEL OBLIGATED! ARGH!
AH HA HA! YOU'RE SO FUNNY, NANA!
SORRY, I CAN'T GO WITH YOU.
WILL YOU BE ABLE TO MAKE YOUR WAY HOME?
HA HA! I'LL BE FINE!
WE LIVE IN THE SAME APARTMENT BUILDING!

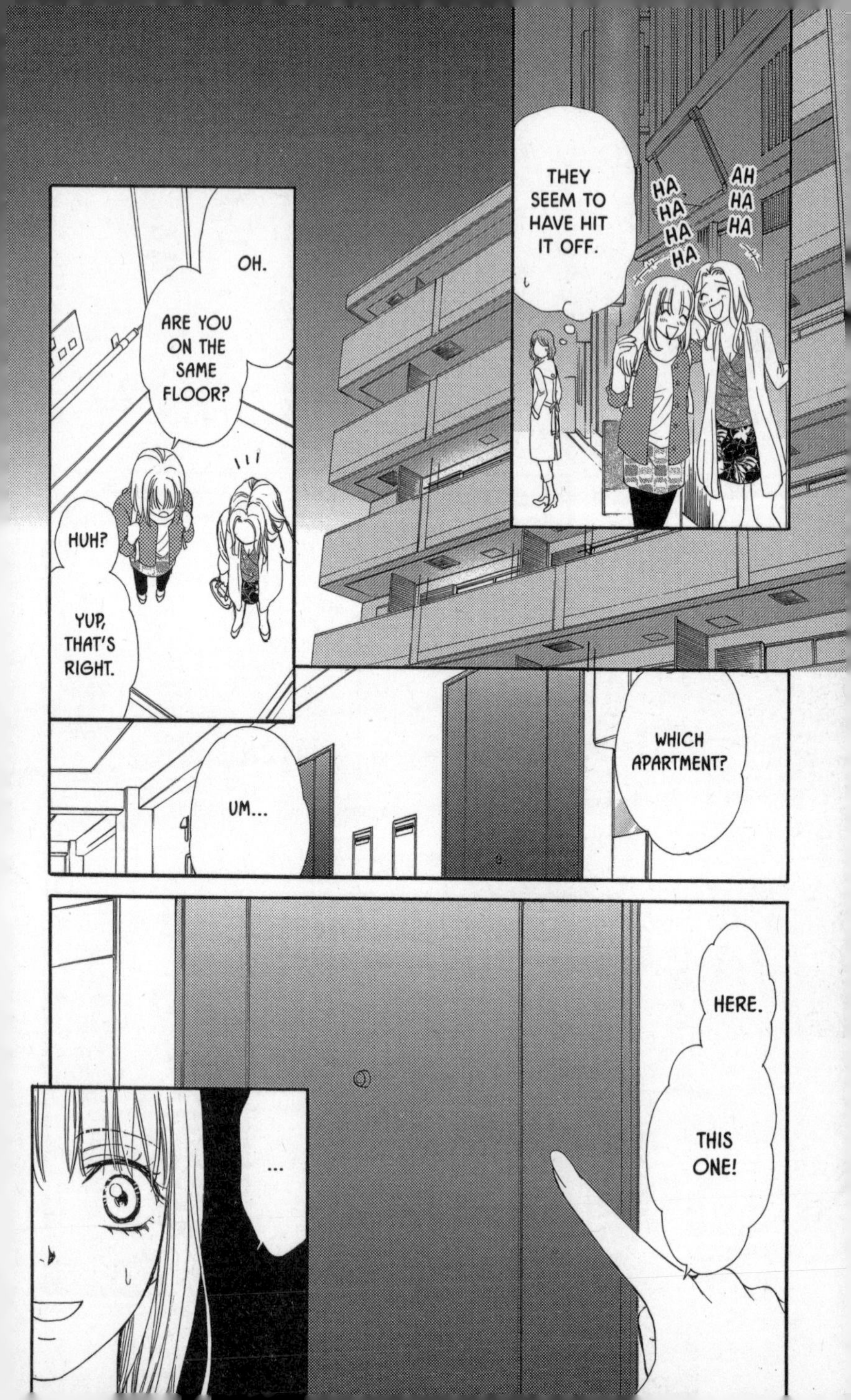
AH HA HA HA
HA HA HA HA
THEY SEEM TO HAVE HIT IT OFF.
OH.
ARE YOU ON THE SAME FLOOR?
HUH?
YUP, THAT'S RIGHT.
WHICH APARTMENT?
UM...
HERE.
THIS ONE!
...

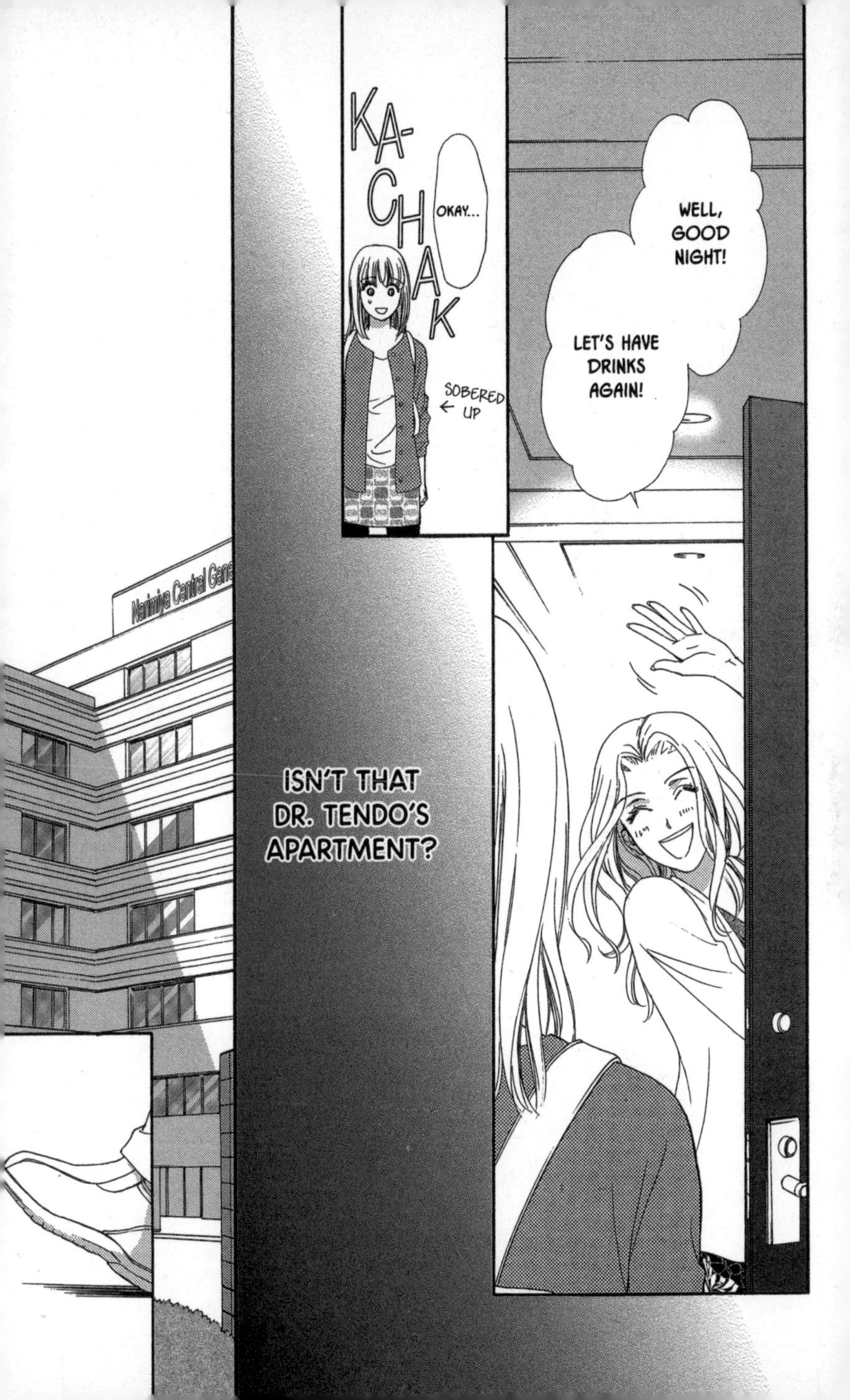
WELL, GOOD NIGHT!
LET'S HAVE DRINKS AGAIN!
KA-CHAK
OKAY...
SOBERED UP
ISN'T THAT DR. TENDO'S APARTMENT?
Narimiya Central Gene

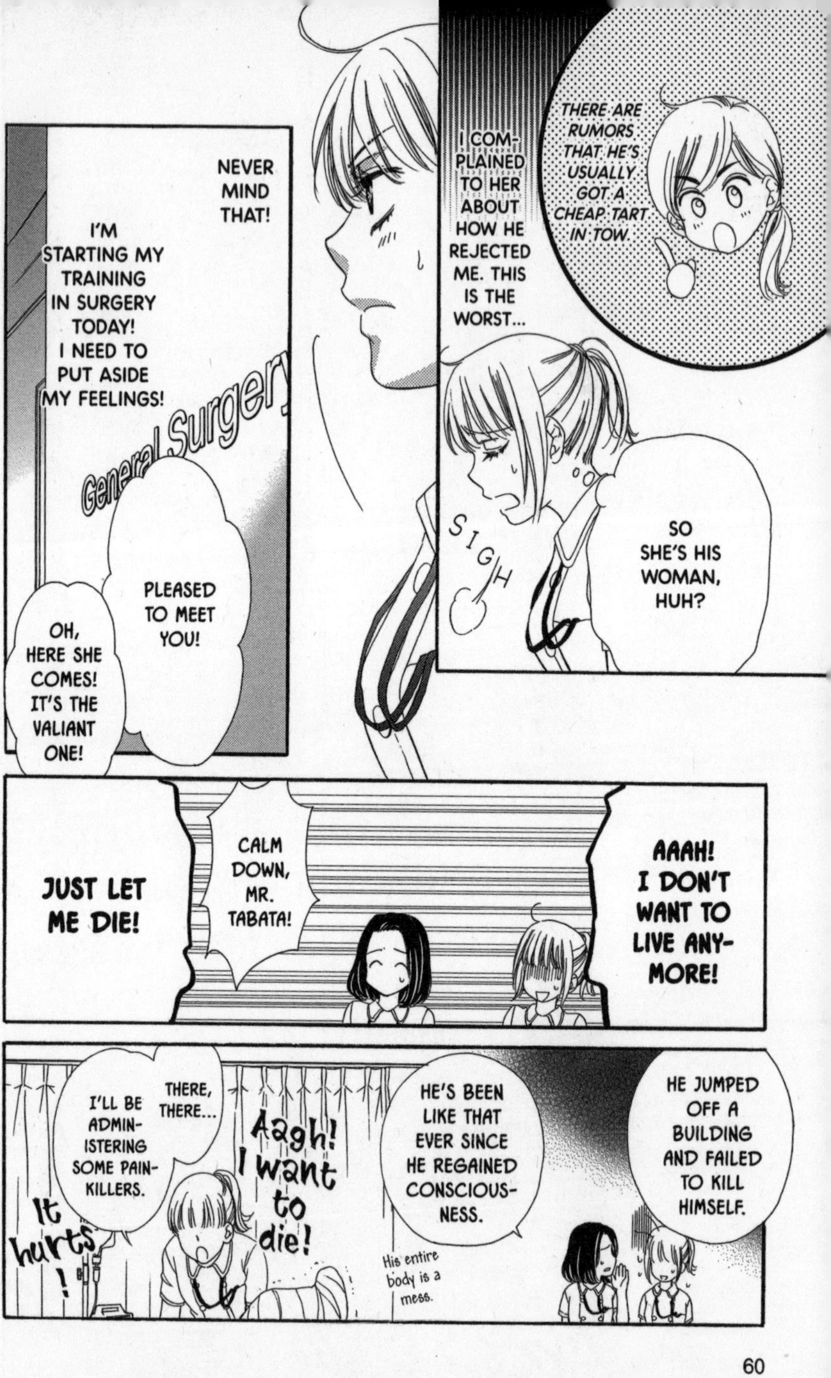
THERE ARE RUMORS THAT HE'S USUALLY GOT A CHEAP TART IN TOW.
I COMPLAINED TO HER ABOUT HOW HE REJECTED ME. THIS IS THE WORST...
SO SHE'S HIS WOMAN, HUH?
SIGH
NEVER MIND THAT!
I'M STARTING MY TRAINING IN SURGERY TODAY! I NEED TO PUT ASIDE MY FEELINGS!
General Surgery
PLEASED TO MEET YOU!
OH, HERE SHE COMES! IT'S THE VALIANT ONE!
AAAH! I DON'T WANT TO LIVE ANYMORE!
CALM DOWN, MR. TABATA!
JUST LET ME DIE!
HE JUMPED OFF A BUILDING AND FAILED TO KILL HIMSELF.
HE'S BEEN LIKE THAT EVER SINCE HE REGAINED CONSCIOUSNESS.
His entire body is a mess.
Aagh! I want to die!
THERE, THERE...
I'LL BE ADMINISTERING SOME PAINKILLERS.
It hurts!

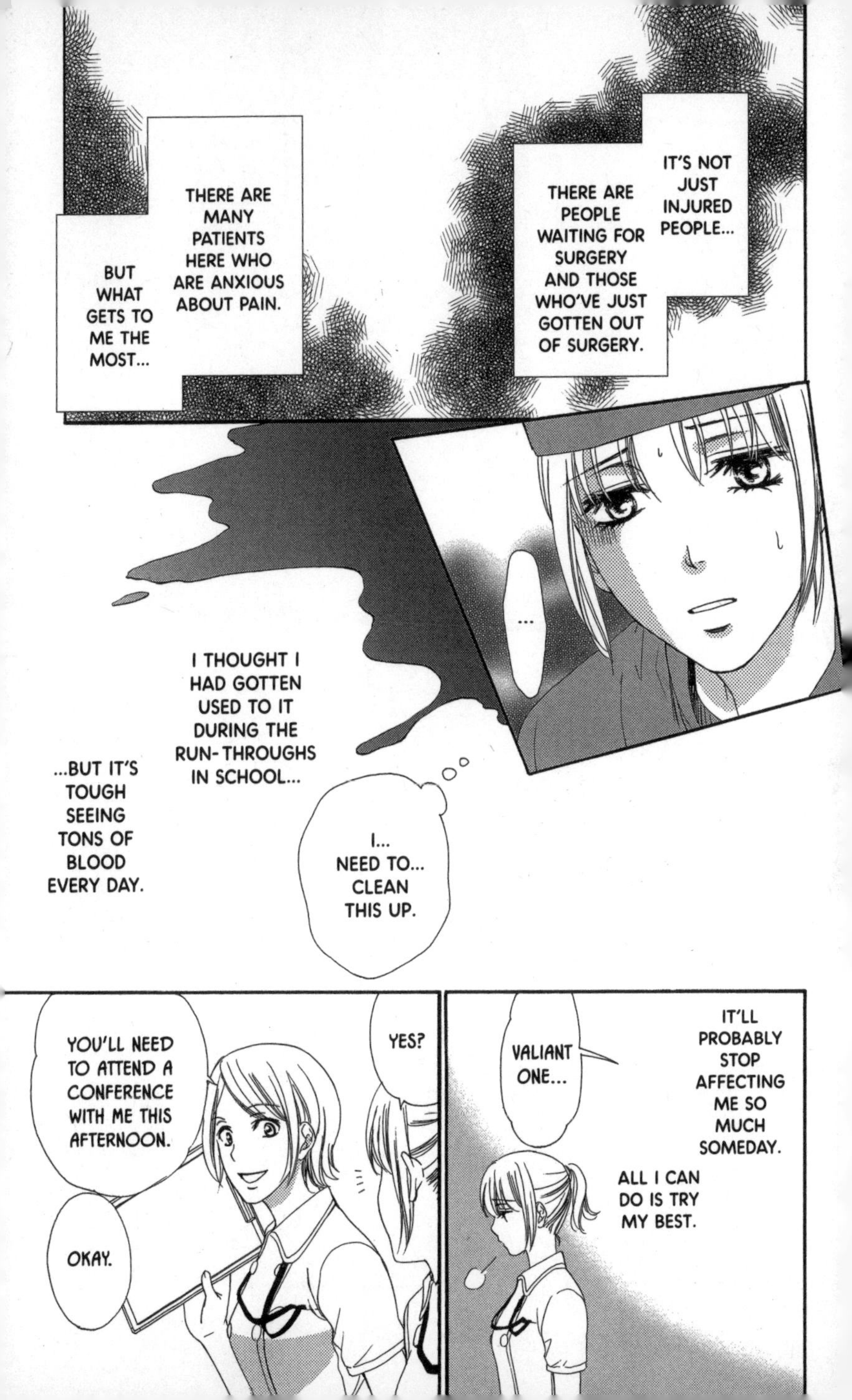
IT'S NOT JUST INJURED PEOPLE...
THERE ARE PEOPLE WAITING FOR SURGERY AND THOSE WHO'VE JUST GOTTEN OUT OF SURGERY.
THERE ARE MANY PATIENTS HERE WHO ARE ANXIOUS ABOUT PAIN.
BUT WHAT GETS TO ME THE MOST...
...
I THOUGHT I HAD GOTTEN USED TO IT DURING THE RUN-THROUGHS IN SCHOOL...
...BUT IT'S TOUGH SEEING TONS OF BLOOD EVERY DAY.
I... NEED TO... CLEAN THIS UP.
IT'LL PROBABLY STOP AFFECTING ME SO MUCH SOMEDAY.
VALIANT ONE...
ALL I CAN DO IS TRY MY BEST.
YES?
YOU'LL NEED TO ATTEND A CONFERENCE WITH ME THIS AFTERNOON.
OKAY.

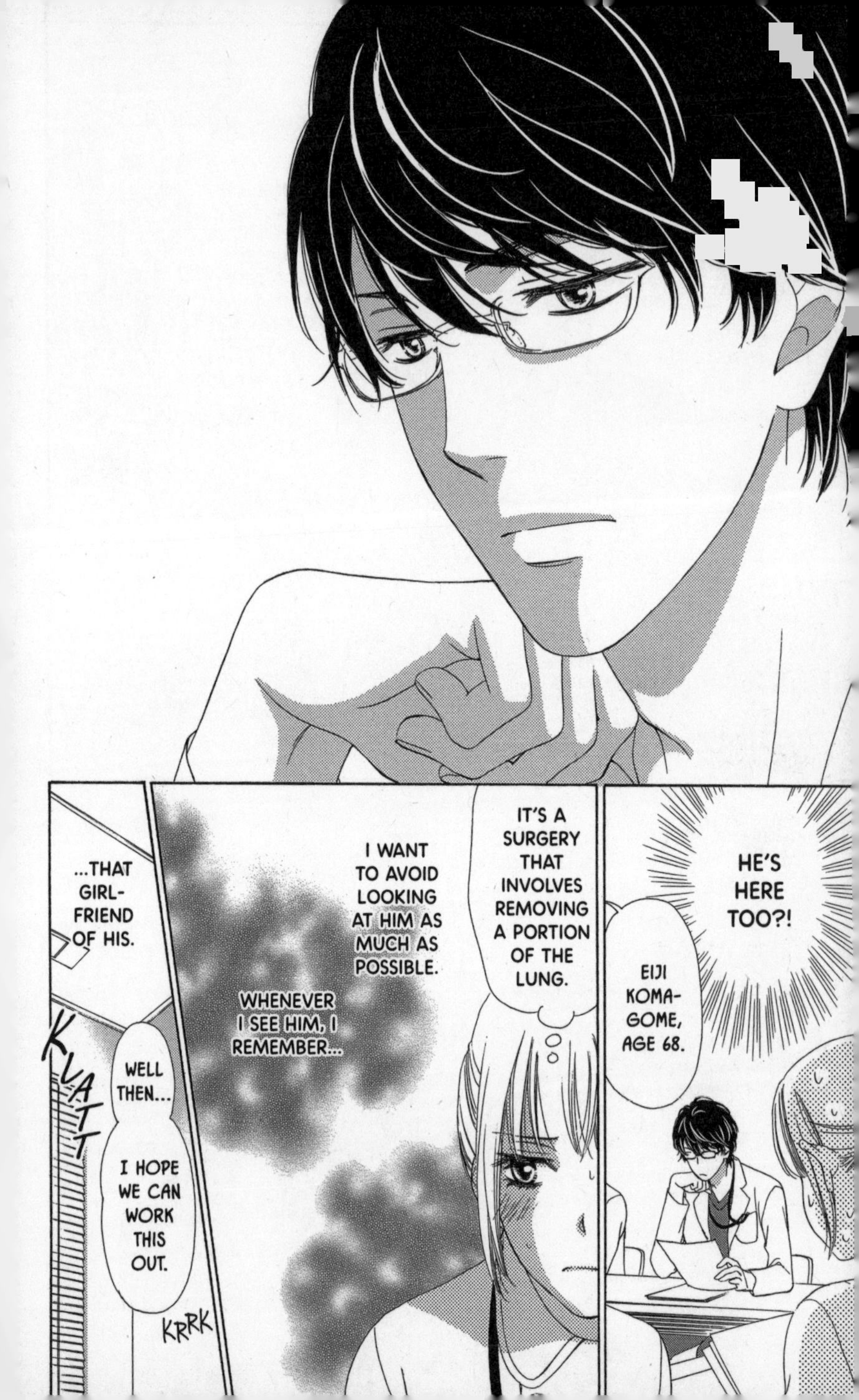
HE'S HERE TOO?!
EIJI KOMAGOME, AGE 68.
IT'S A SURGERY THAT INVOLVES REMOVING A PORTION OF THE LUNG.
I WANT TO AVOID LOOKING AT HIM AS MUCH AS POSSIBLE.
WHENEVER I SEE HIM, I REMEMBER...
...THAT GIRLFRIEND OF HIS.
KLATT
WELL THEN...
I HOPE WE CAN WORK THIS OUT.
KRRK

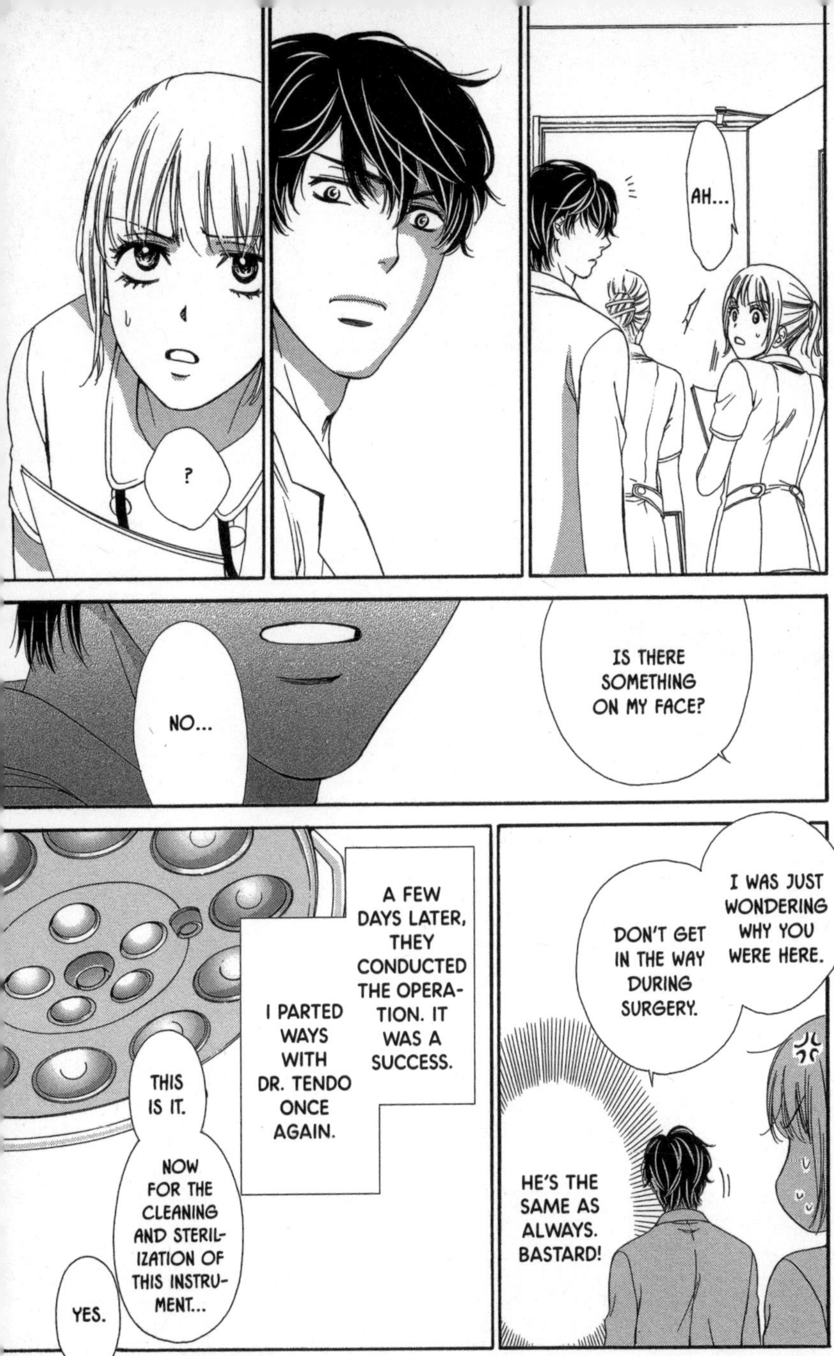
AH...
?
IS THERE SOMETHING ON MY FACE?
NO...
I WAS JUST WONDERING WHY YOU WERE HERE.
DON'T GET IN THE WAY DURING SURGERY.
HE'S THE SAME AS ALWAYS. BASTARD!
A FEW DAYS LATER, THEY CONDUCTED THE OPERA-TION. IT WAS A SUCCESS.
I PARTED WAYS WITH DR. TENDO ONCE AGAIN.
THIS IS IT.
NOW FOR THE CLEANING AND STERIL-IZATION OF THIS INSTRU-MENT...
YES.

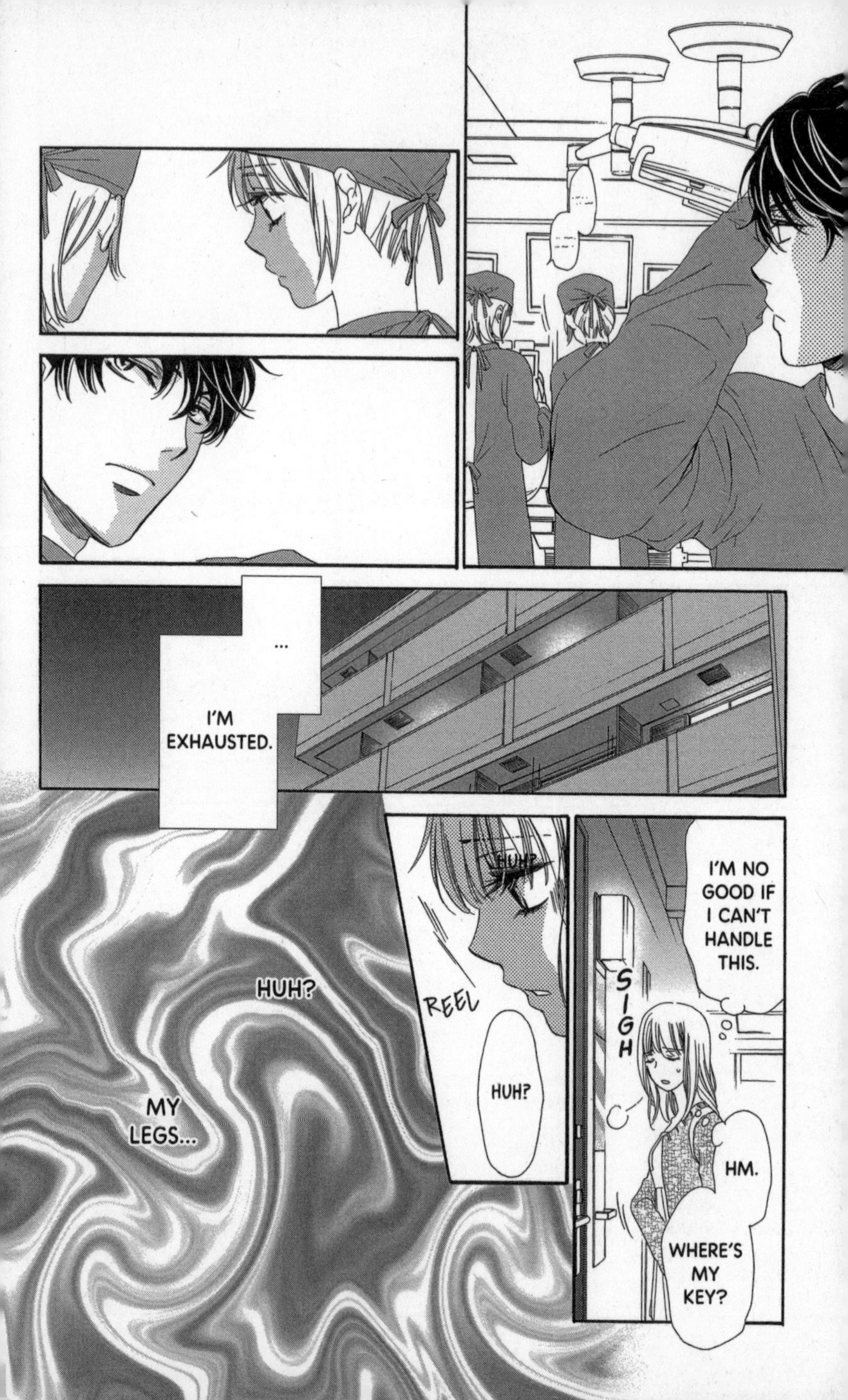
...
I'M EXHAUSTED.
I'M NO GOOD IF I CAN'T HANDLE THIS.
SIGH
HM.
WHERE'S MY KEY?
HUH?
REEL
HUH?
HUH?
MY LEGS...

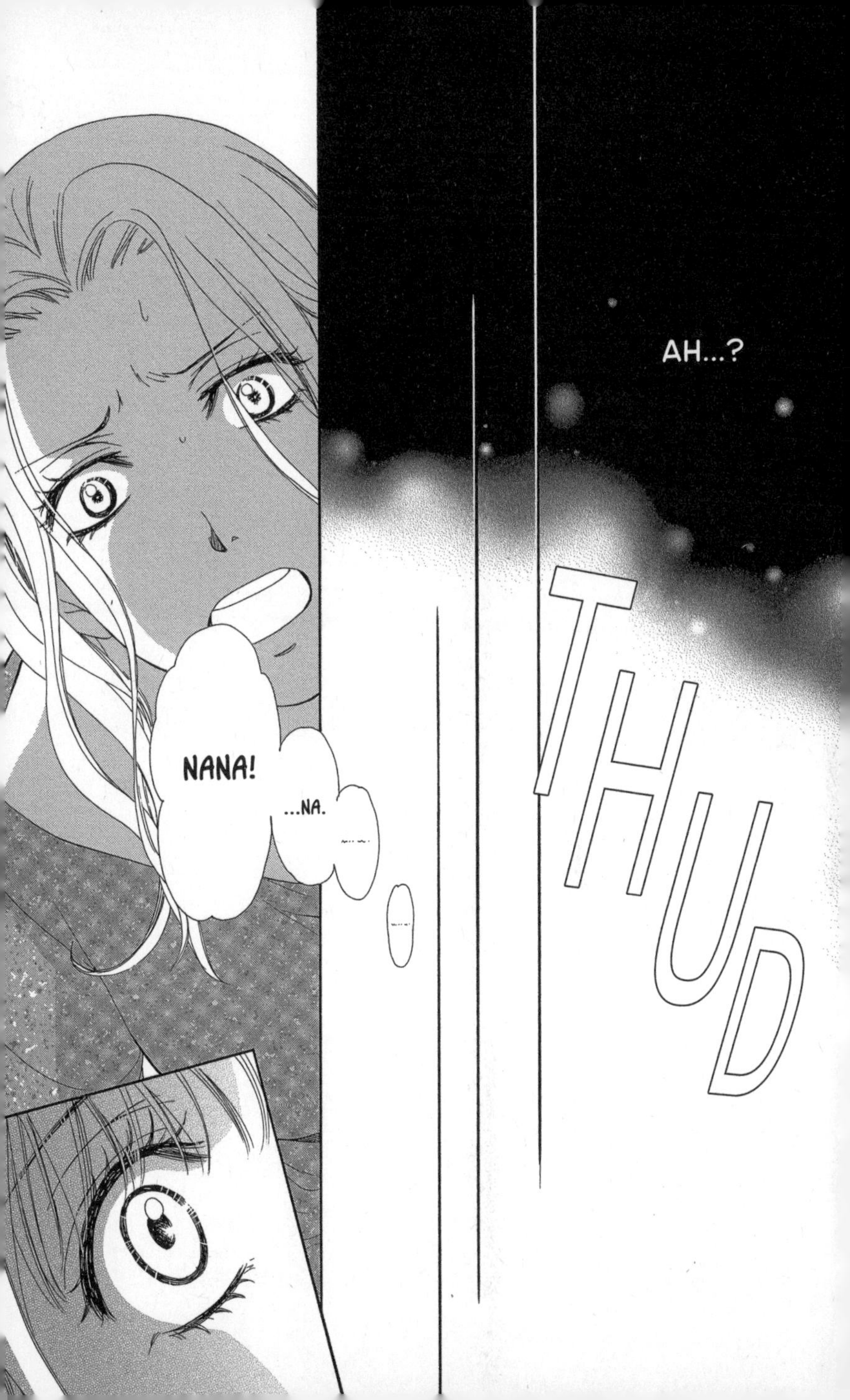
AH...?
THUD
NANA!
...NA.

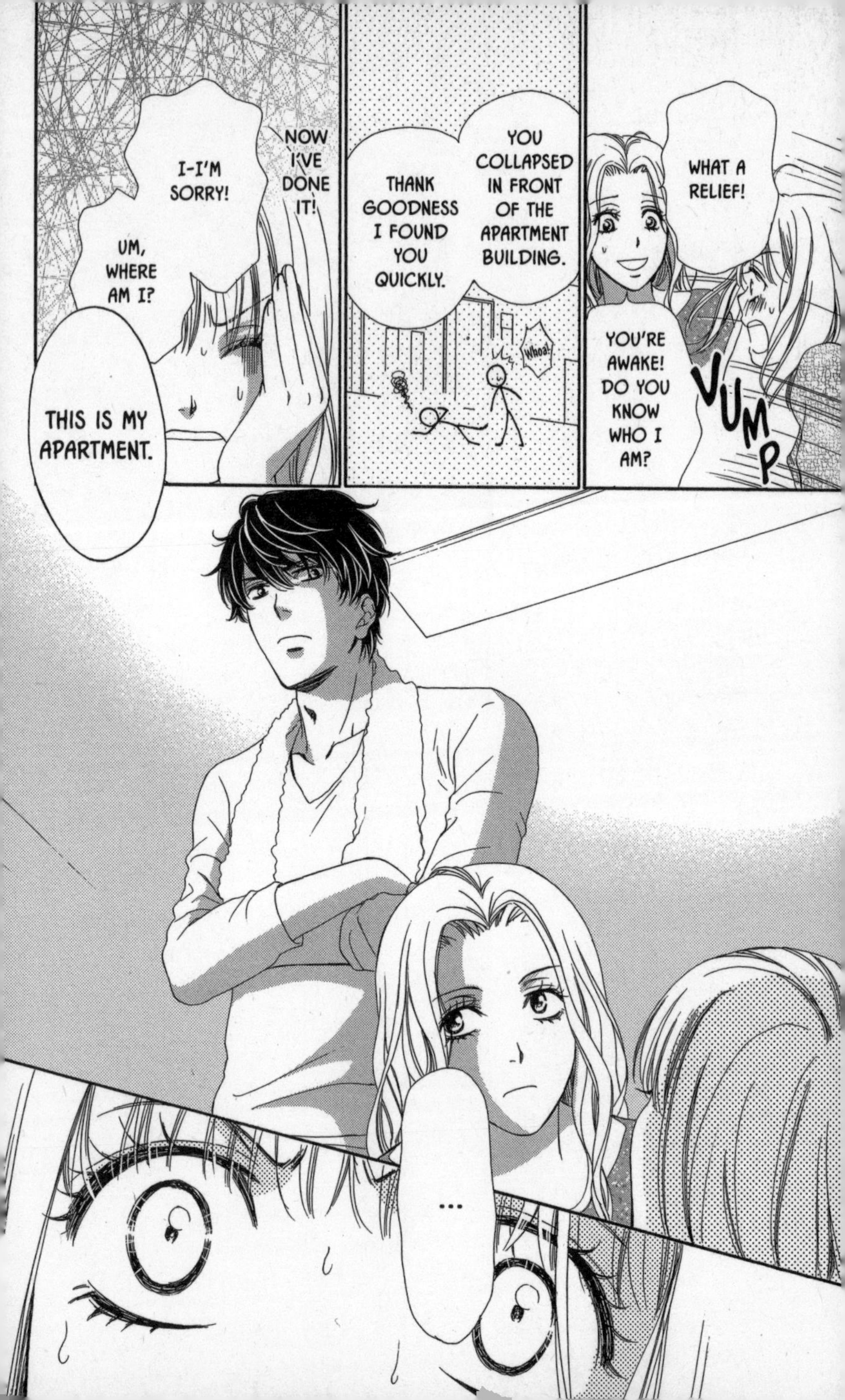
WHAT A RELIEF!
YOU'RE AWAKE! DO YOU KNOW WHO I AM?
VUMP
YOU COLLAPSED IN FRONT OF THE APARTMENT BUILDING.
THANK GOODNESS I FOUND YOU QUICKLY.
Whoa!
NOW I'VE DONE IT!
I-I'M SORRY!
UM, WHERE AM I?
THIS IS MY APARTMENT.
...

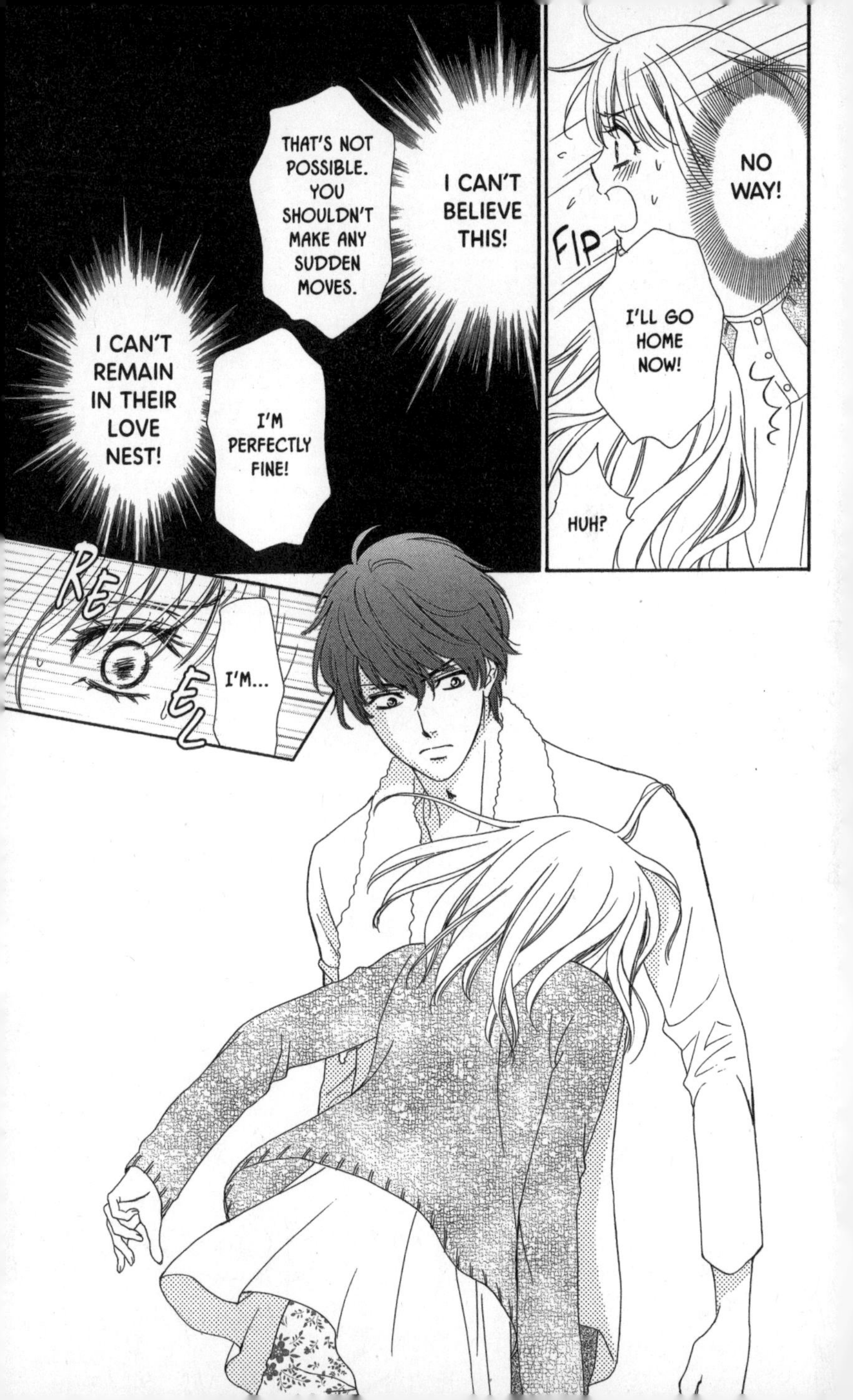
NO WAY!
FIP
I'LL GO HOME NOW!
HUH?
I CAN'T BELIEVE THIS!
THAT'S NOT POSSIBLE. YOU SHOULDN'T MAKE ANY SUDDEN MOVES.
I'M PERFECTLY FINE!
I CAN'T REMAIN IN THEIR LOVE NEST!
REEL
I'M...

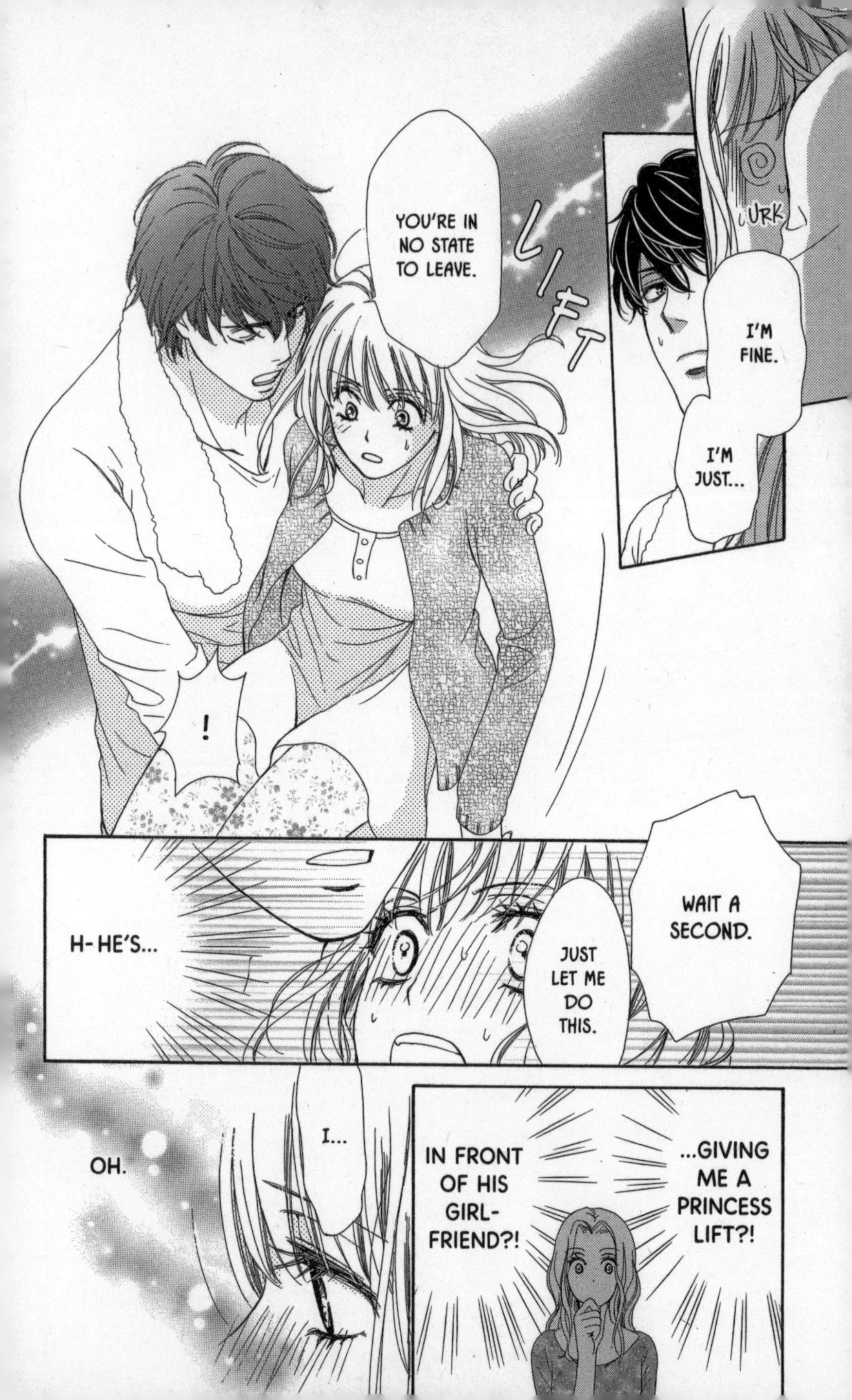
URK
I'M FINE.
I'M JUST...
YOU'RE IN NO STATE TO LEAVE.
LIFT
!
WAIT A SECOND.
JUST LET ME DO THIS.
H-HE'S...
...GIVING ME A PRINCESS LIFT?!
IN FRONT OF HIS GIRL-FRIEND?!
I...
OH.

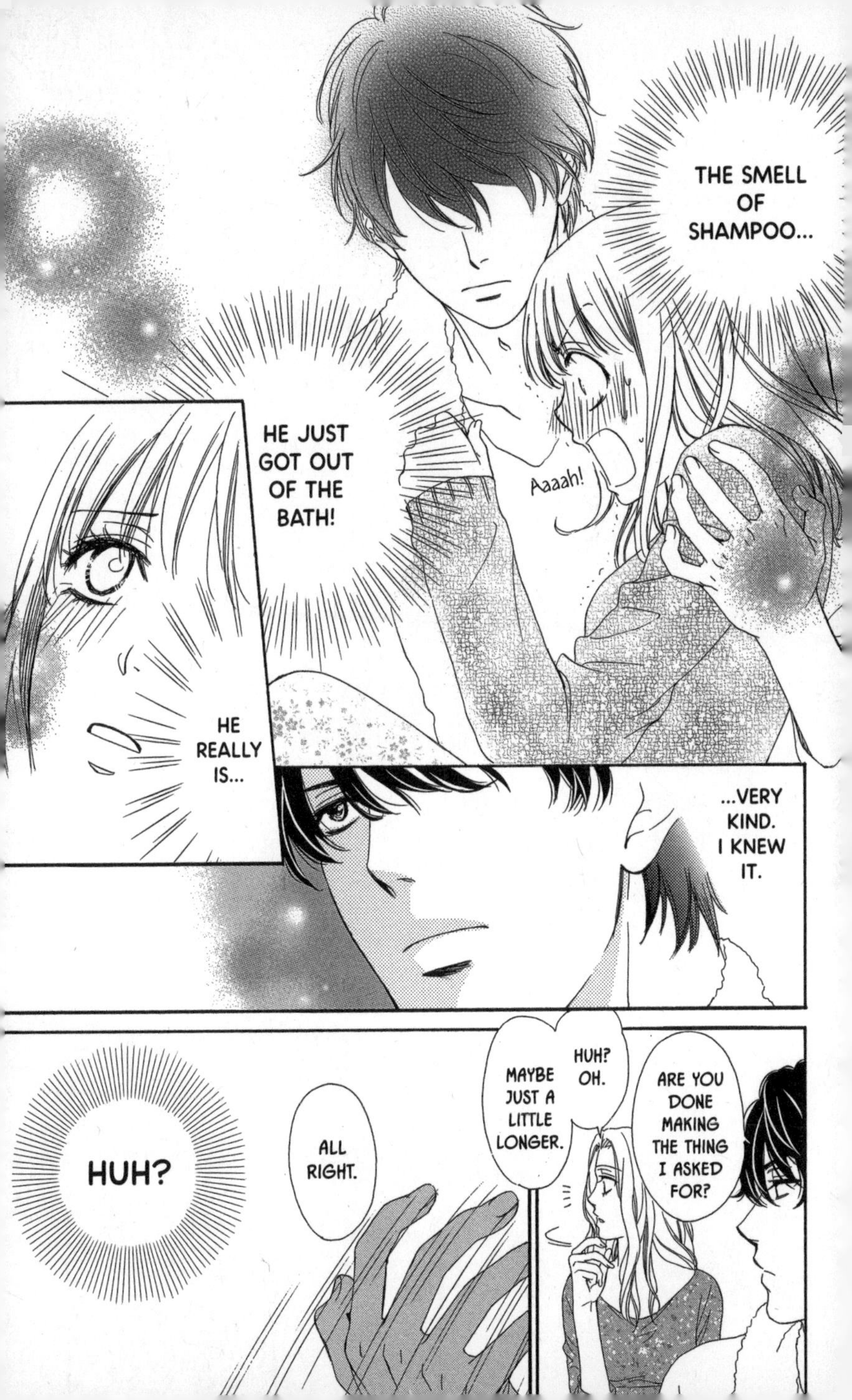
THE SMELL OF SHAMPOO...
Aaaah!
HE JUST GOT OUT OF THE BATH!
HE REALLY IS...
...VERY KIND. I KNEW IT.
ARE YOU DONE MAKING THE THING I ASKED FOR?
HUH? OH.
MAYBE JUST A LITTLE LONGER.
ALL RIGHT.
HUH?

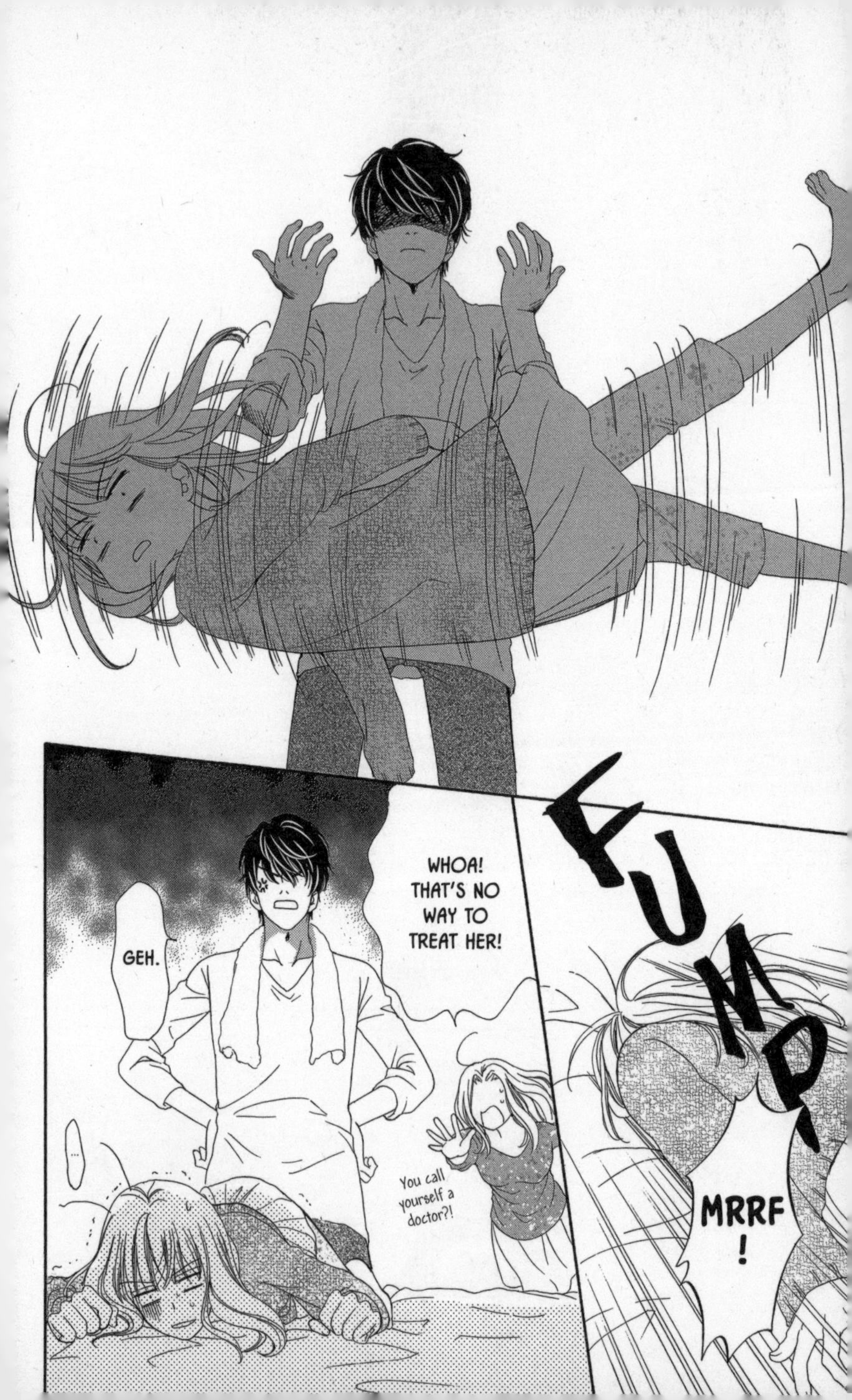
FUMP!
MRRF!
WHOA! THAT'S NO WAY TO TREAT HER!
You call yourself a doctor?!
GEH.
...

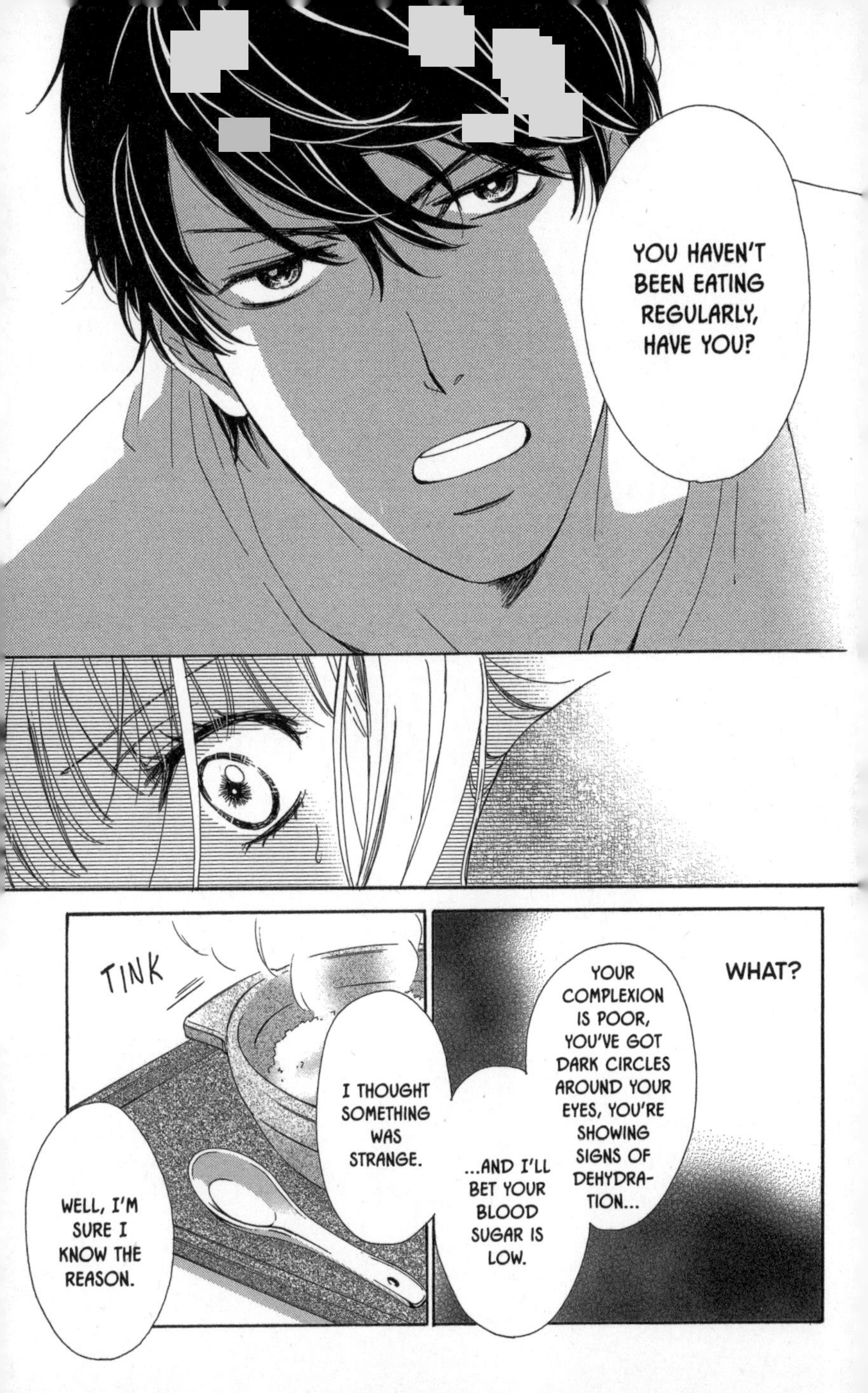
YOU HAVEN'T BEEN EATING REGULARLY, HAVE YOU?
WHAT?
YOUR COMPLEXION IS POOR, YOU'VE GOT DARK CIRCLES AROUND YOUR EYES, YOU'RE SHOWING SIGNS OF DEHYDRA-TION...
...AND I'LL BET YOUR BLOOD SUGAR IS LOW.
TINK
I THOUGHT SOMETHING WAS STRANGE.
WELL, I'M SURE I KNOW THE REASON.

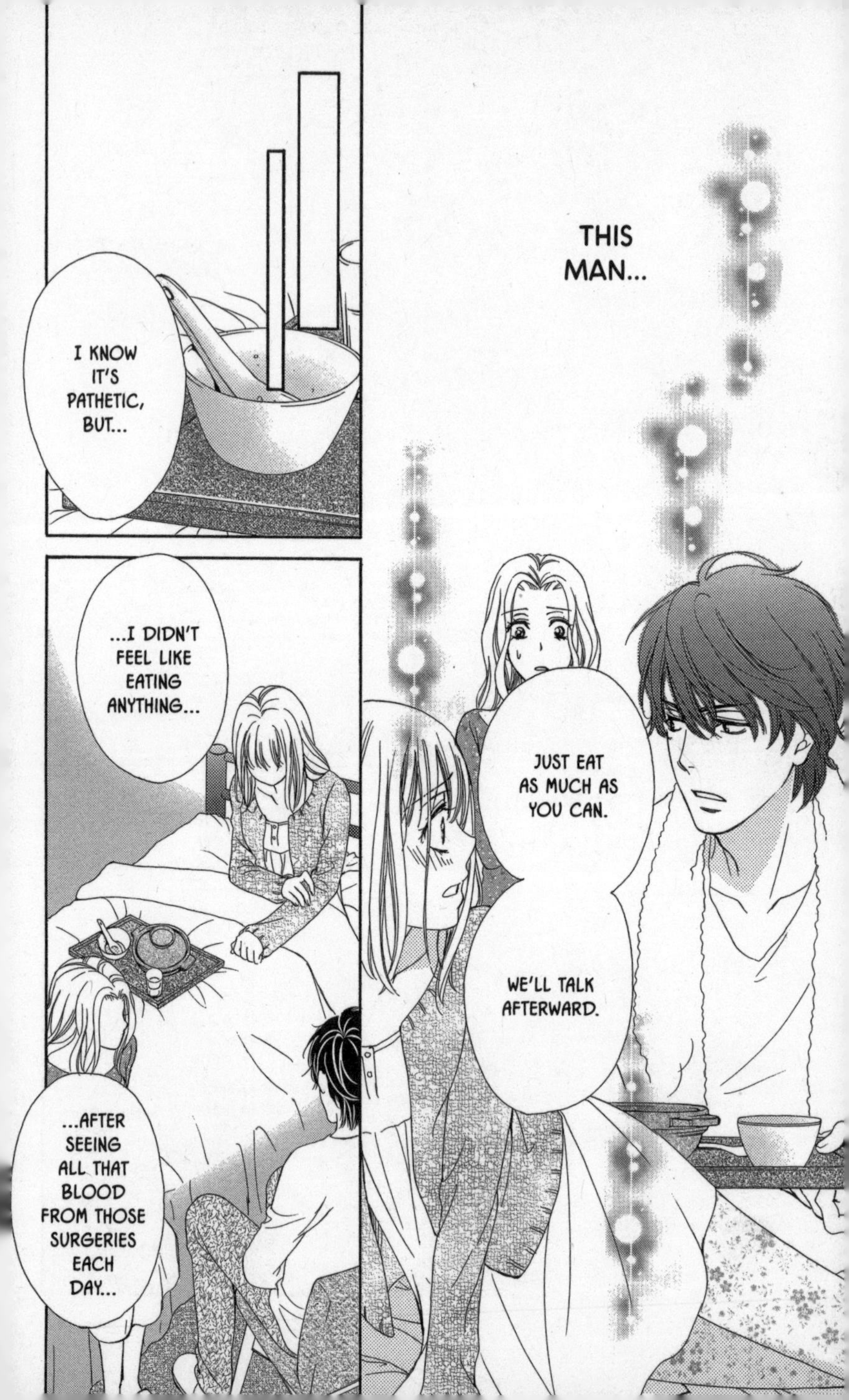
THIS MAN...
JUST EAT AS MUCH AS YOU CAN.
WE'LL TALK AFTERWARD.
I KNOW IT'S PATHETIC, BUT...
...I DIDN'T FEEL LIKE EATING ANYTHING...
...AFTER SEEING ALL THAT BLOOD FROM THOSE SURGERIES EACH DAY...

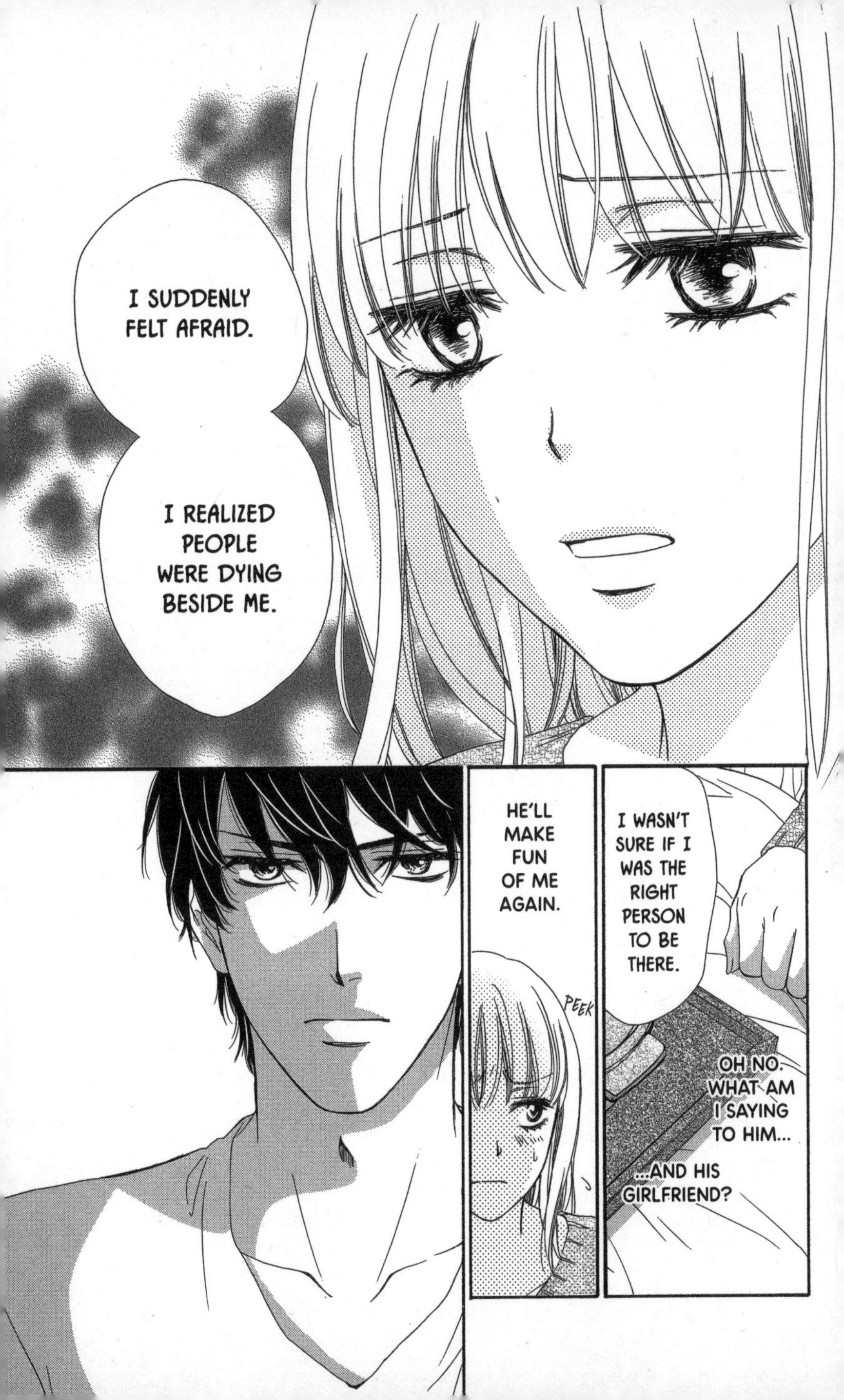
I SUDDENLY FELT AFRAID.
I REALIZED PEOPLE WERE DYING BESIDE ME.
I WASN'T SURE IF I WAS THE RIGHT PERSON TO BE THERE.
OH NO. WHAT AM I SAYING TO HIM...
...AND HIS GIRLFRIEND?
HE'LL MAKE FUN OF ME AGAIN.
PEEK

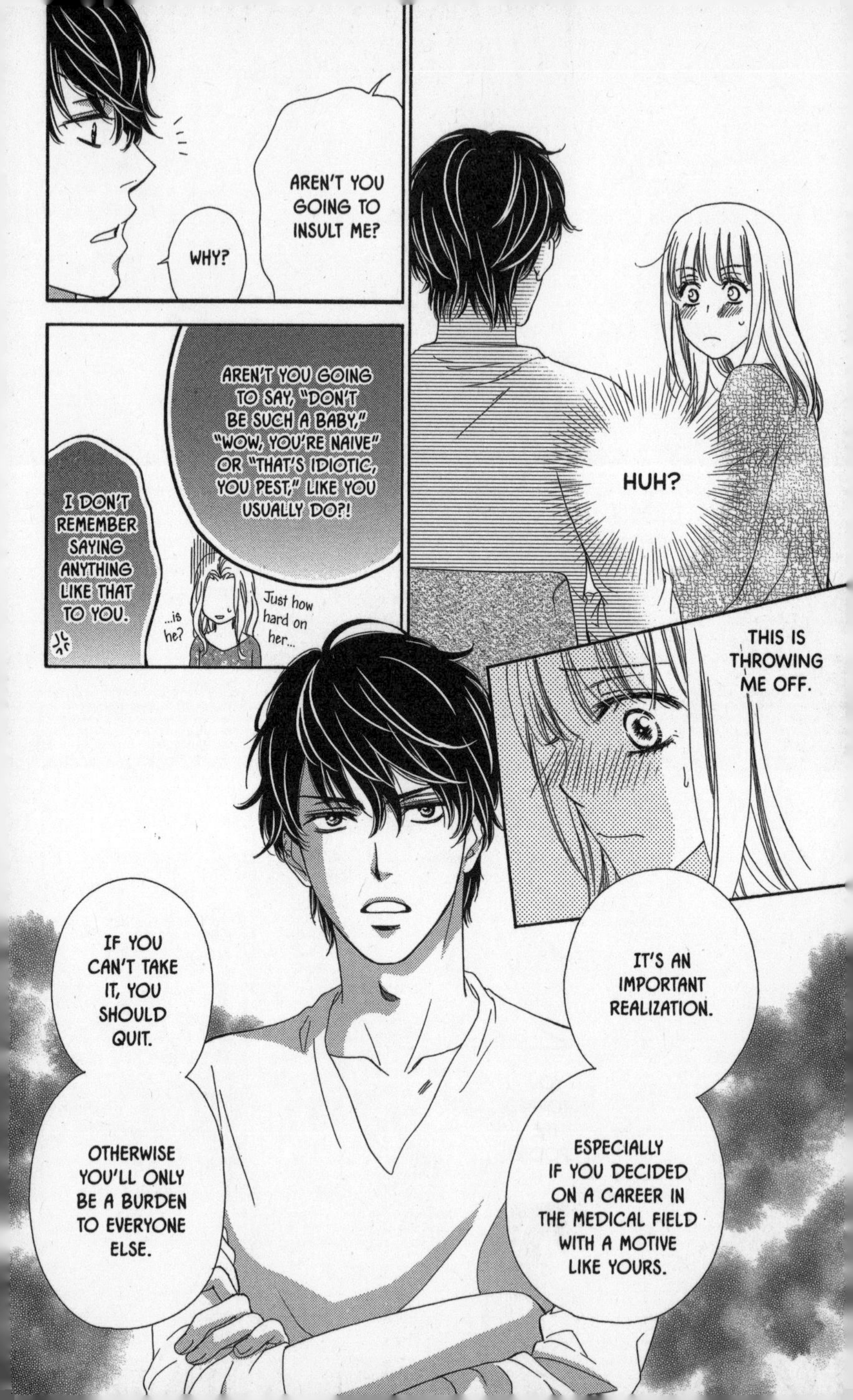
HUH?
AREN'T YOU GOING TO INSULT ME?
WHY?
AREN'T YOU GOING TO SAY, "DON'T BE SUCH A BABY," "WOW, YOU'RE NAIVE" OR "THAT'S IDIOTIC, YOU PEST," LIKE YOU USUALLY DO?!
I DON'T REMEMBER SAYING ANYTHING LIKE THAT TO YOU.
Just how hard on her...
...is he?
THIS IS THROWING ME OFF.
IT'S AN IMPORTANT REALIZATION.
ESPECIALLY IF YOU DECIDED ON A CAREER IN THE MEDICAL FIELD WITH A MOTIVE LIKE YOURS.
IF YOU CAN'T TAKE IT, YOU SHOULD QUIT.
OTHERWISE YOU'LL ONLY BE A BURDEN TO EVERYONE ELSE.

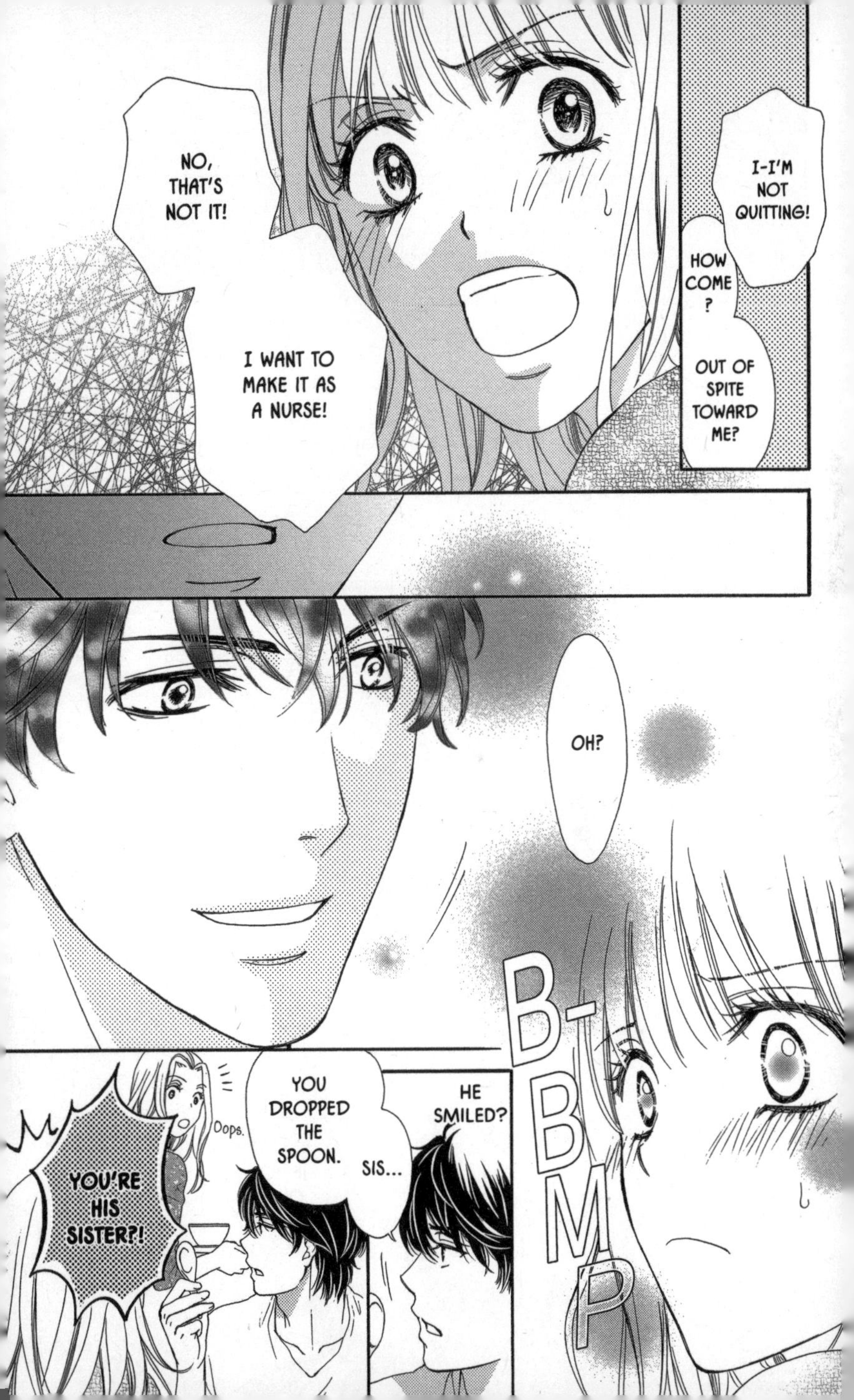

I-I'M NOT QUITTING!
HOW COME?
OUT OF SPITE TOWARD ME?
NO, THAT'S NOT IT!
I WANT TO MAKE IT AS A NURSE!
OH?
B-BMP
HE SMILED?
SIS...
YOU DROPPED THE SPOON.
Oops.
YOU'RE HIS SISTER?!

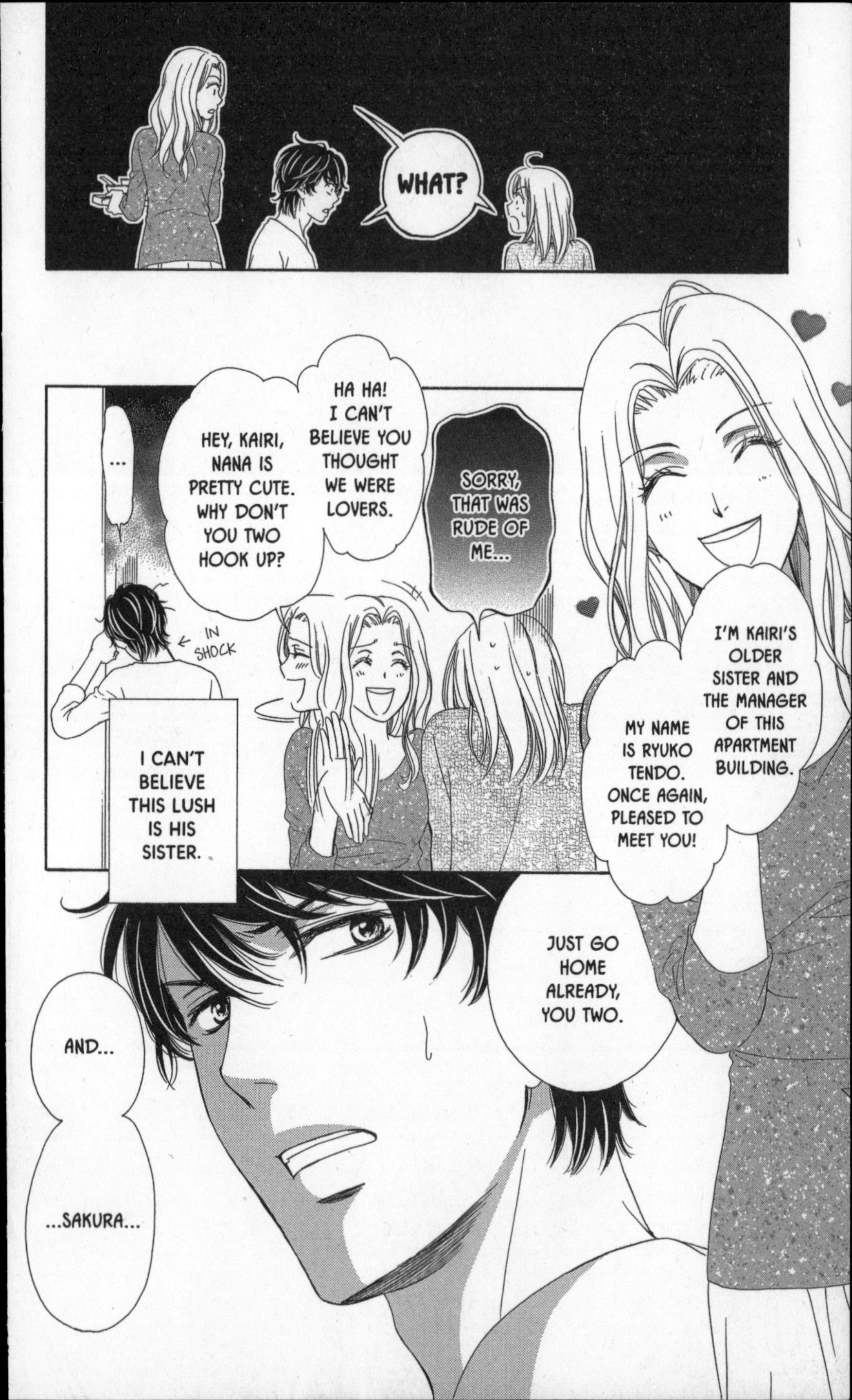
WHAT?
I'M KAIRI'S OLDER SISTER AND THE MANAGER OF THIS APARTMENT BUILDING.
MY NAME IS RYUKO TENDO. ONCE AGAIN, PLEASED TO MEET YOU!
SORRY, THAT WAS RUDE OF ME...
HA HA! I CAN'T BELIEVE YOU THOUGHT WE WERE LOVERS.
HEY, KAIRI, NANA IS PRETTY CUTE. WHY DON'T YOU TWO HOOK UP?
...
IN SHOCK
I CAN'T BELIEVE THIS LUSH IS HIS SISTER.
JUST GO HOME ALREADY, YOU TWO.
AND...
...SAKURA...

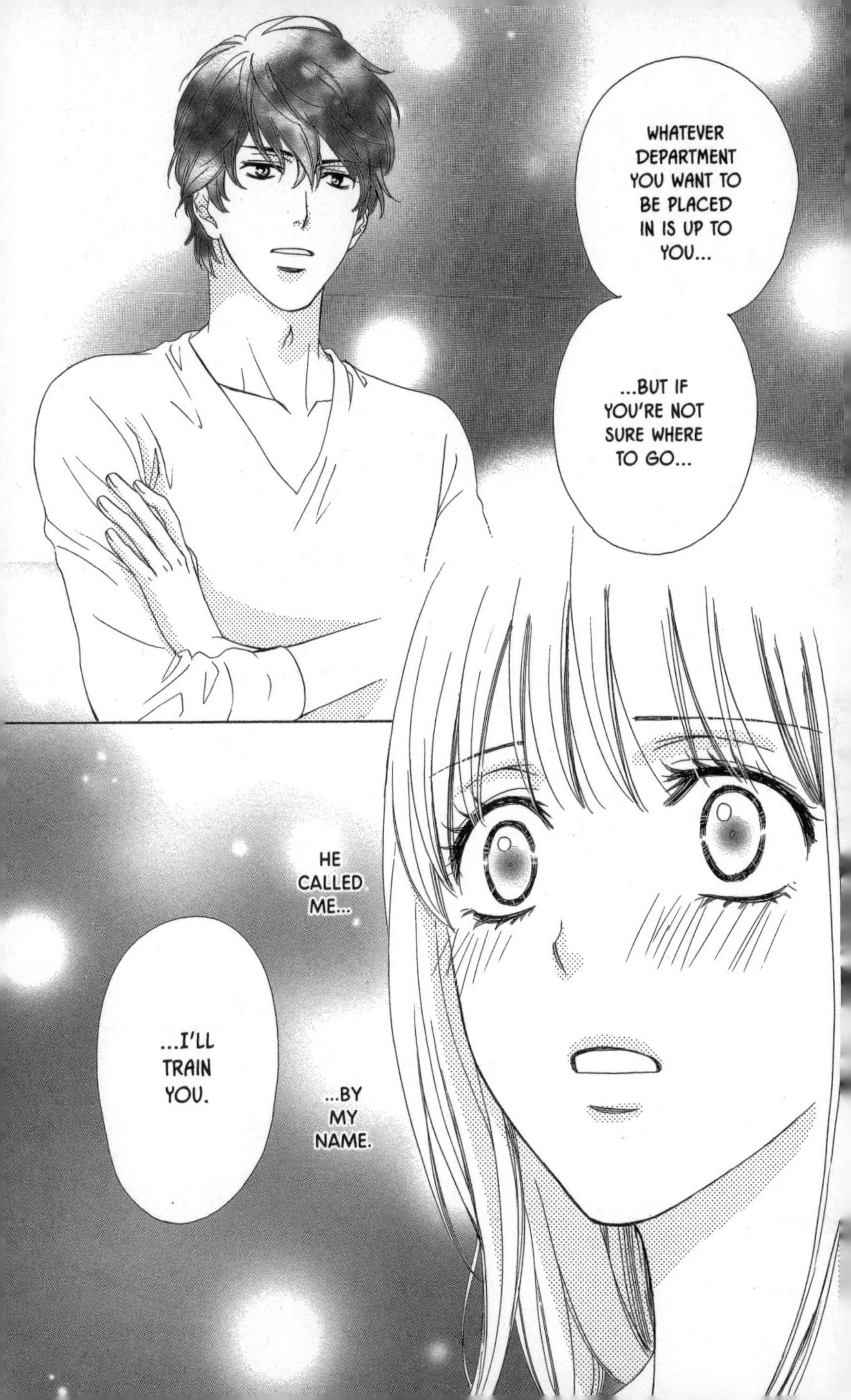
WHATEVER DEPARTMENT YOU WANT TO BE PLACED IN IS UP TO YOU...
...BUT IF YOU'RE NOT SURE WHERE TO GO...
HE CALLED ME...
...I'LL TRAIN YOU.
...BY MY NAME.

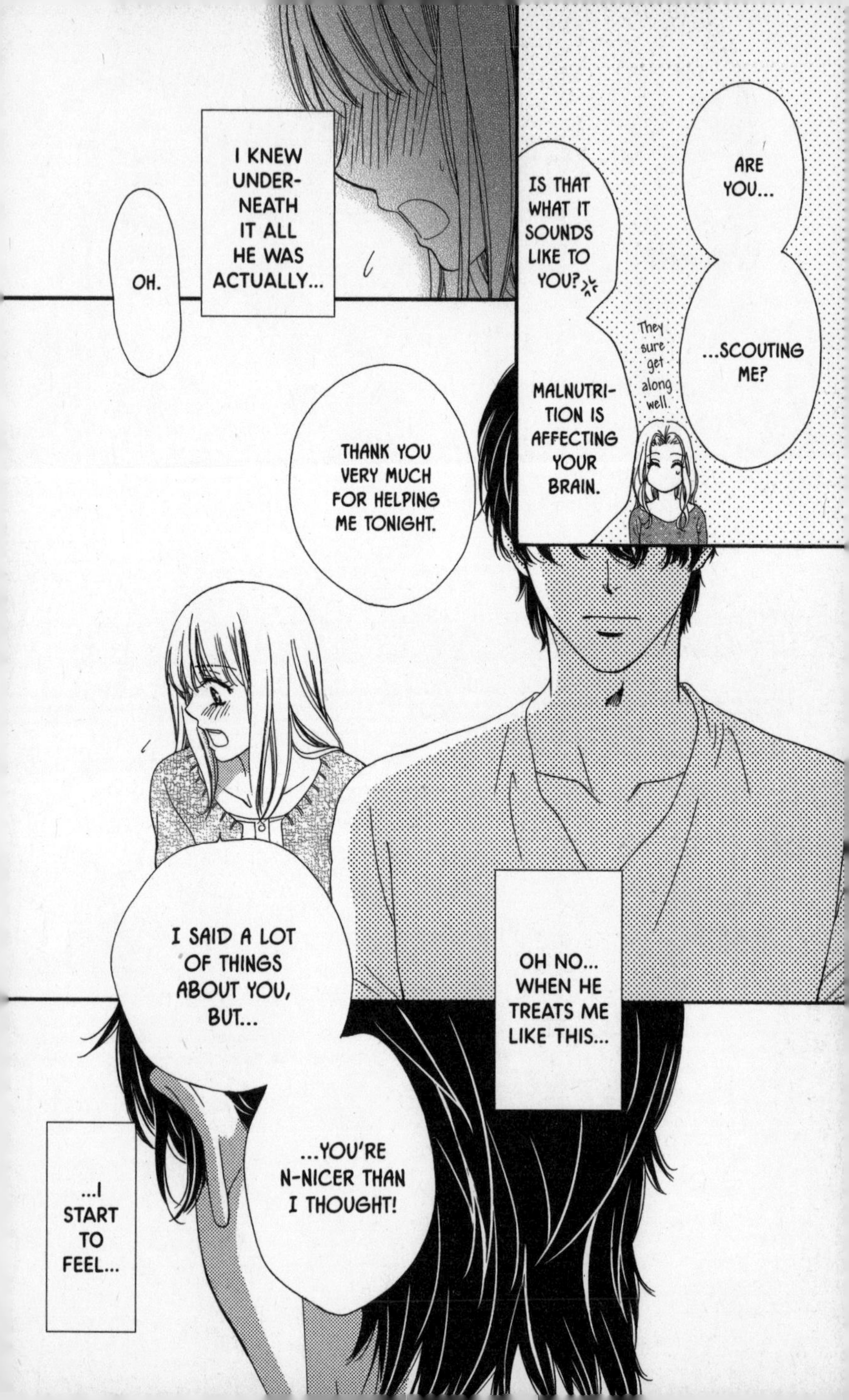
ARE YOU...
...SCOUTING ME?
IS THAT WHAT IT SOUNDS LIKE TO YOU?
MALNUTRITION IS AFFECTING YOUR BRAIN.
They sure get along well.
I KNEW UNDERNEATH IT ALL HE WAS ACTUALLY...
OH.
THANK YOU VERY MUCH FOR HELPING ME TONIGHT.
I SAID A LOT OF THINGS ABOUT YOU, BUT...
OH NO... WHEN HE TREATS ME LIKE THIS...
...YOU'RE N-NICER THAN I THOUGHT!
...I START TO FEEL...

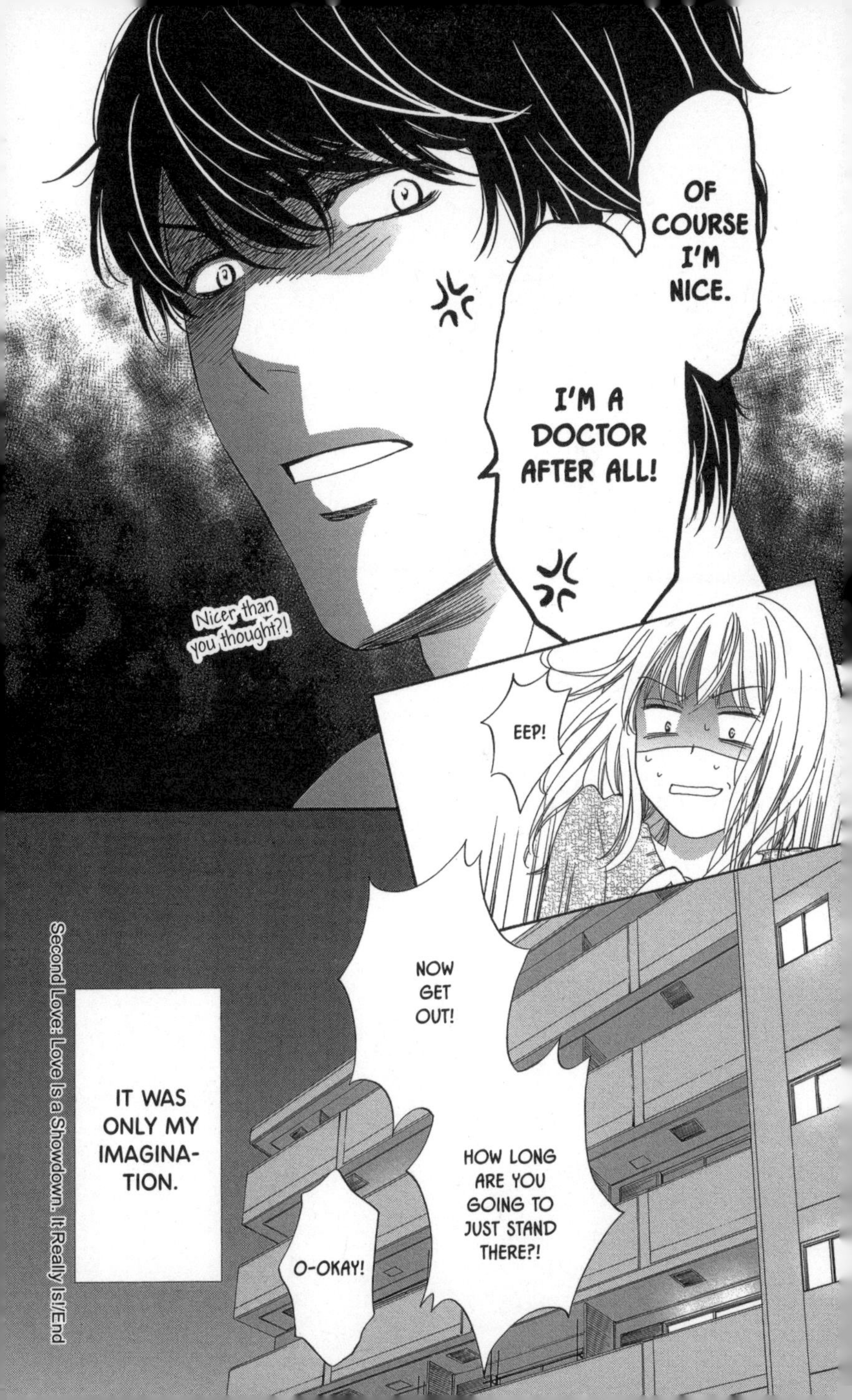
OF COURSE I'M NICE.
I'M A DOCTOR AFTER ALL!
Nicer than you thought?!
EEP!
NOW GET OUT!
HOW LONG ARE YOU GOING TO JUST STAND THERE?!
O-OKAY!
IT WAS ONLY MY IMAGINATION.

Second Love: Love Is a Showdown. It Really Is!/End

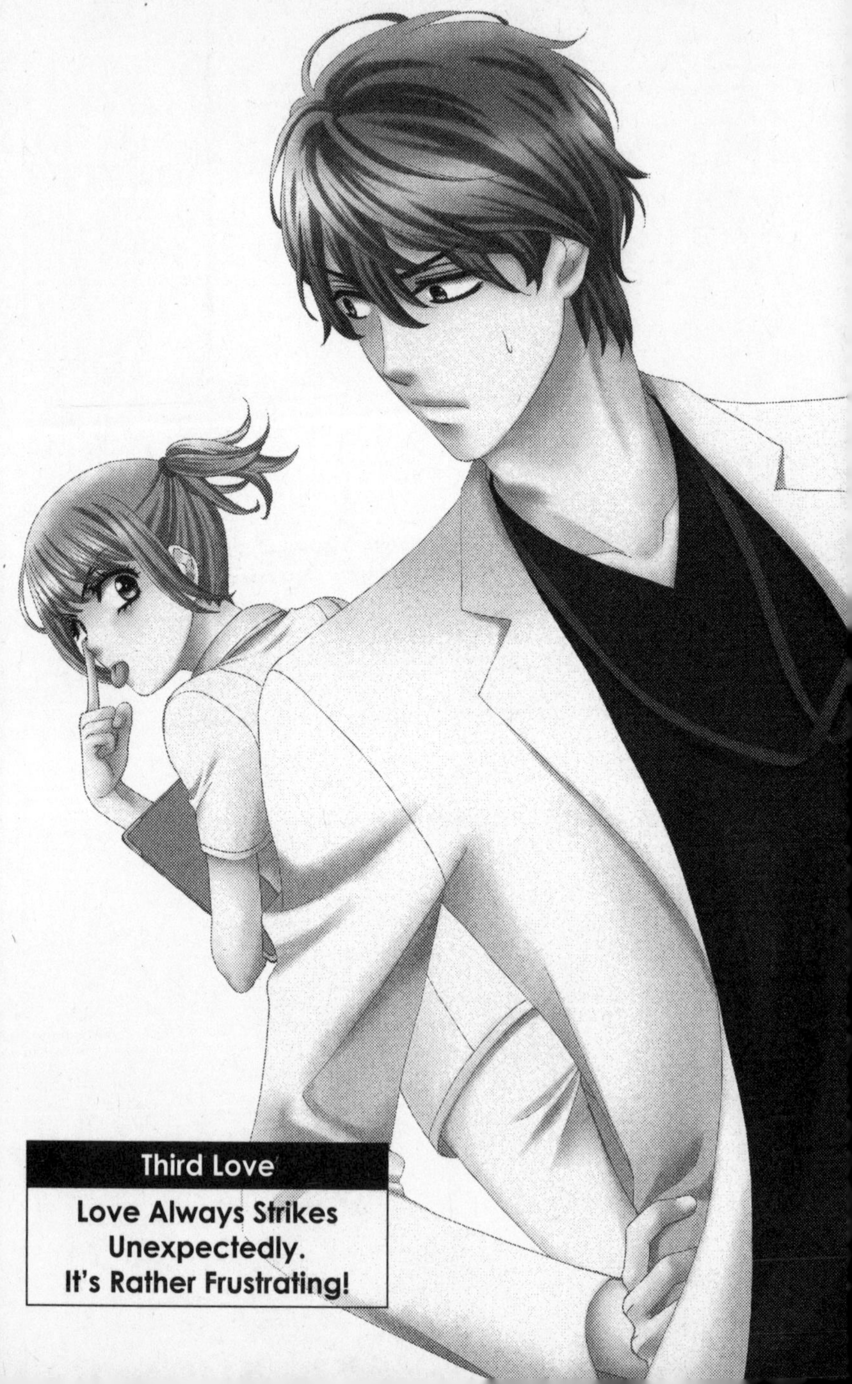

Third Love

Love Always Strikes Unexpectedly. It's Rather Frustrating!

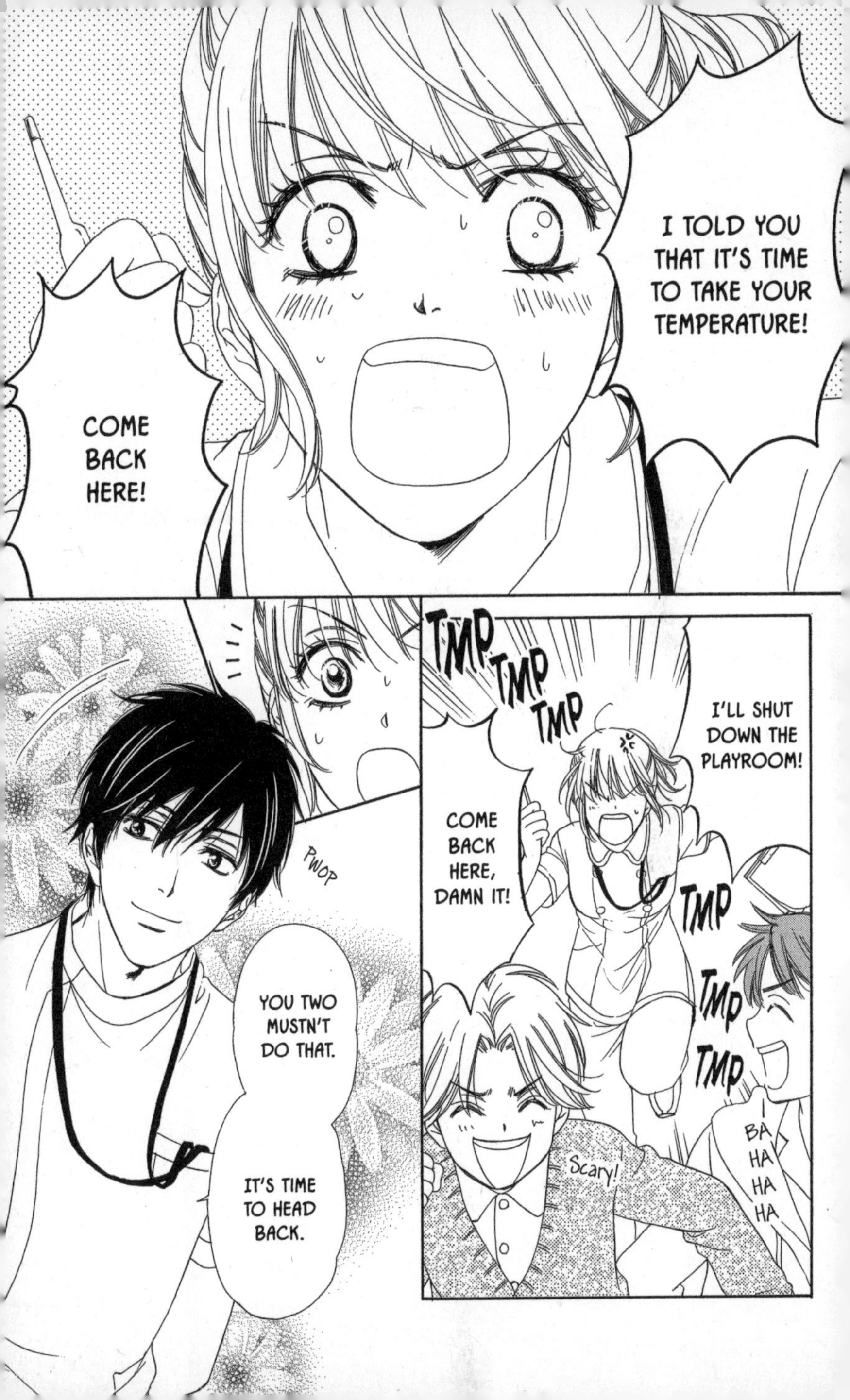
I TOLD YOU THAT IT'S TIME TO TAKE YOUR TEMPERATURE!
COME BACK HERE!
TMP TMP TMP
I'LL SHUT DOWN THE PLAYROOM!
COME BACK HERE, DAMN IT!
TMP TMP TMP
BA HA HA HA
Scary!
PWOP
YOU TWO MUSTN'T DO THAT.
IT'S TIME TO HEAD BACK.

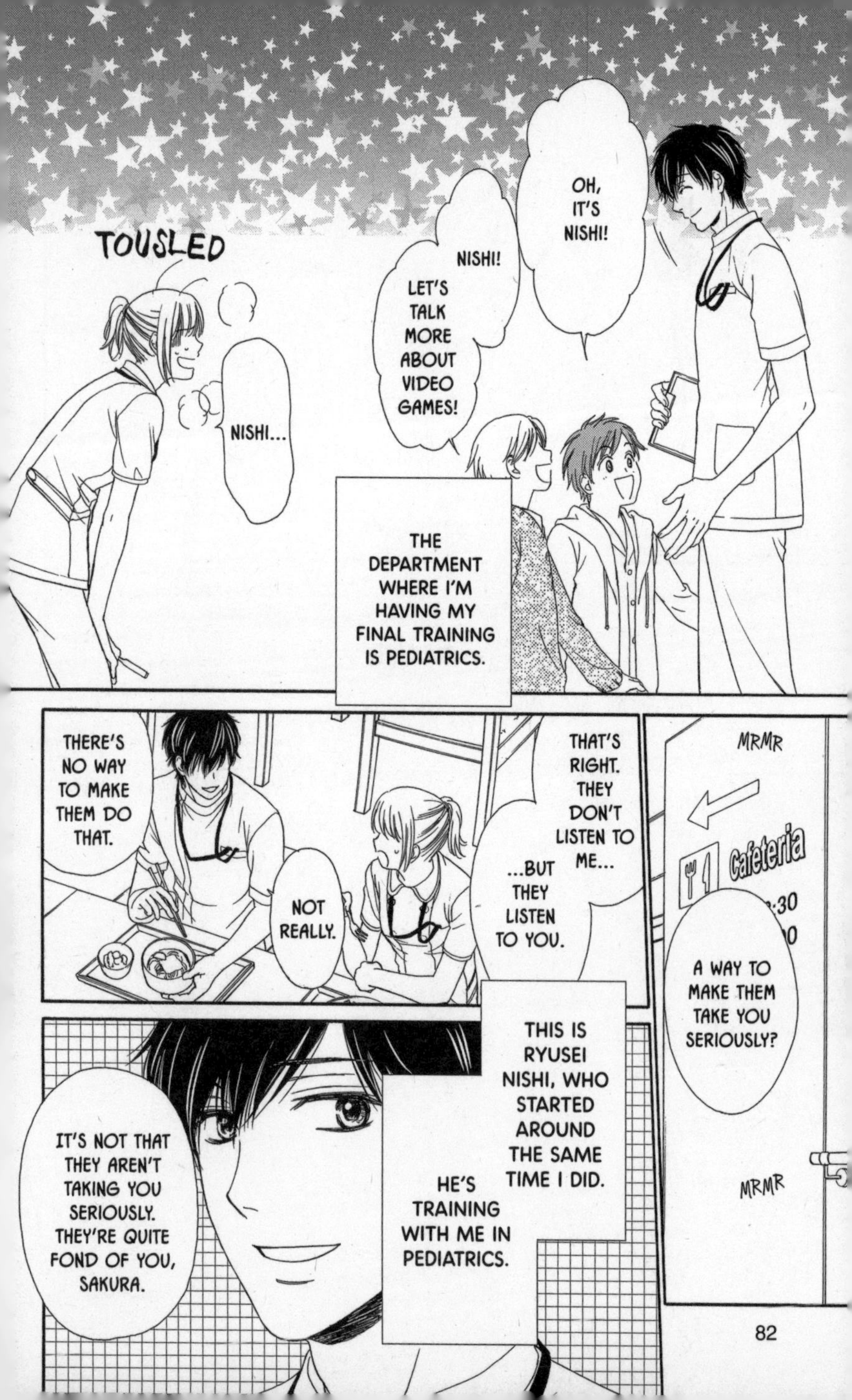
OH, IT'S NISHI!
NISHI! LET'S TALK MORE ABOUT VIDEO GAMES!
TOUSLED
NISHI...
THE DEPARTMENT WHERE I'M HAVING MY FINAL TRAINING IS PEDIATRICS.
MRMR
Cafeteria
A WAY TO MAKE THEM TAKE YOU SERIOUSLY?
MRMR
THAT'S RIGHT. THEY DON'T LISTEN TO ME...
...BUT THEY LISTEN TO YOU.
NOT REALLY.
THERE'S NO WAY TO MAKE THEM DO THAT.
THIS IS RYUSEI NISHI, WHO STARTED AROUND THE SAME TIME I DID.
HE'S TRAINING WITH ME IN PEDIATRICS.
IT'S NOT THAT THEY AREN'T TAKING YOU SERIOUSLY. THEY'RE QUITE FOND OF YOU, SAKURA.

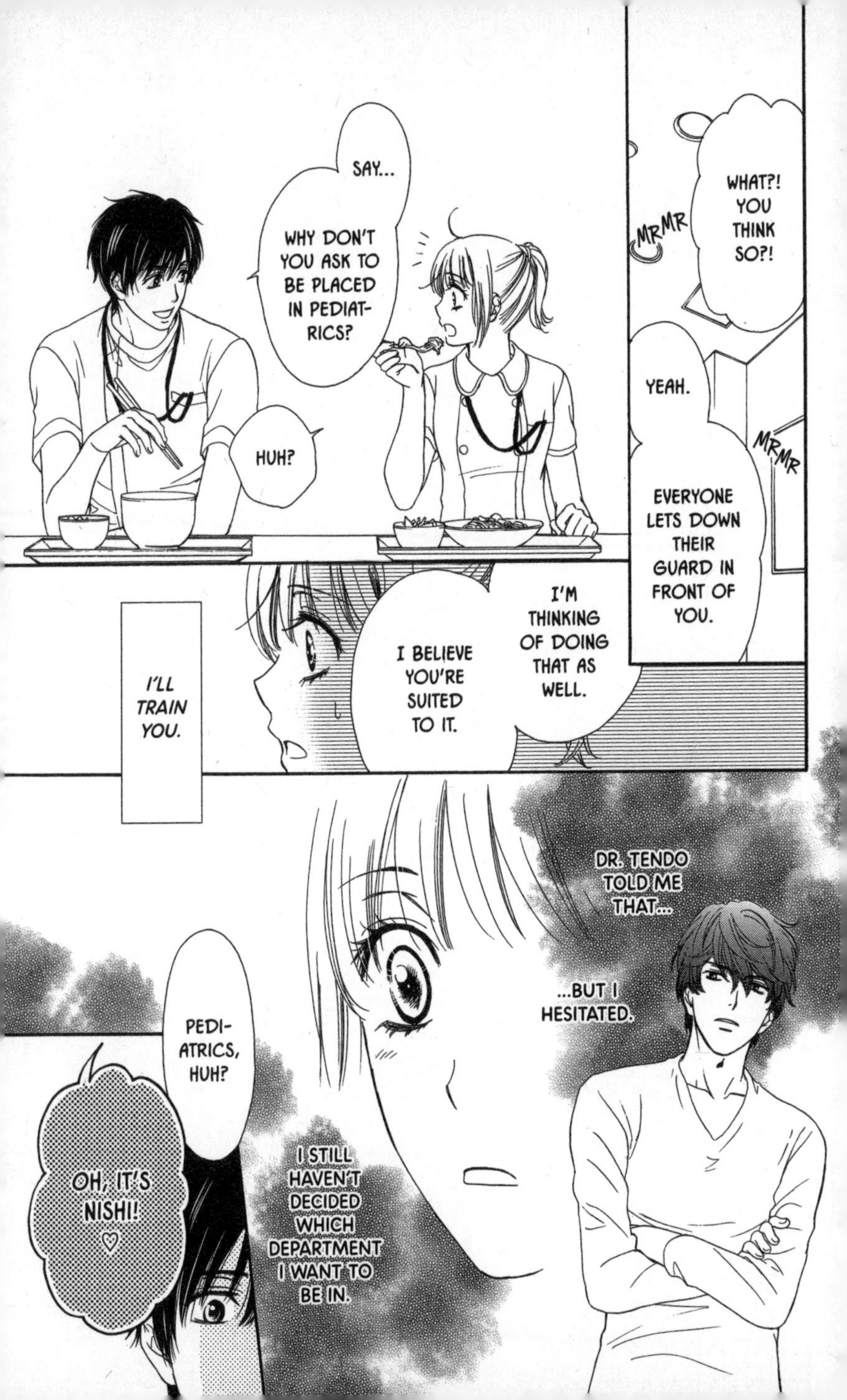
WHAT?! YOU THINK SO?!
MRMR
YEAH.
MRMR
EVERYONE LETS DOWN THEIR GUARD IN FRONT OF YOU.
SAY...
WHY DON'T YOU ASK TO BE PLACED IN PEDIAT-RICS?
HUH?
I'M THINKING OF DOING THAT AS WELL.
I BELIEVE YOU'RE SUITED TO IT.
I'LL TRAIN YOU.
DR. TENDO TOLD ME THAT...
...BUT I HESITATED.
PEDI-ATRICS, HUH?
I STILL HAVEN'T DECIDED WHICH DEPARTMENT I WANT TO BE IN.
OH, IT'S NISHI! ♡

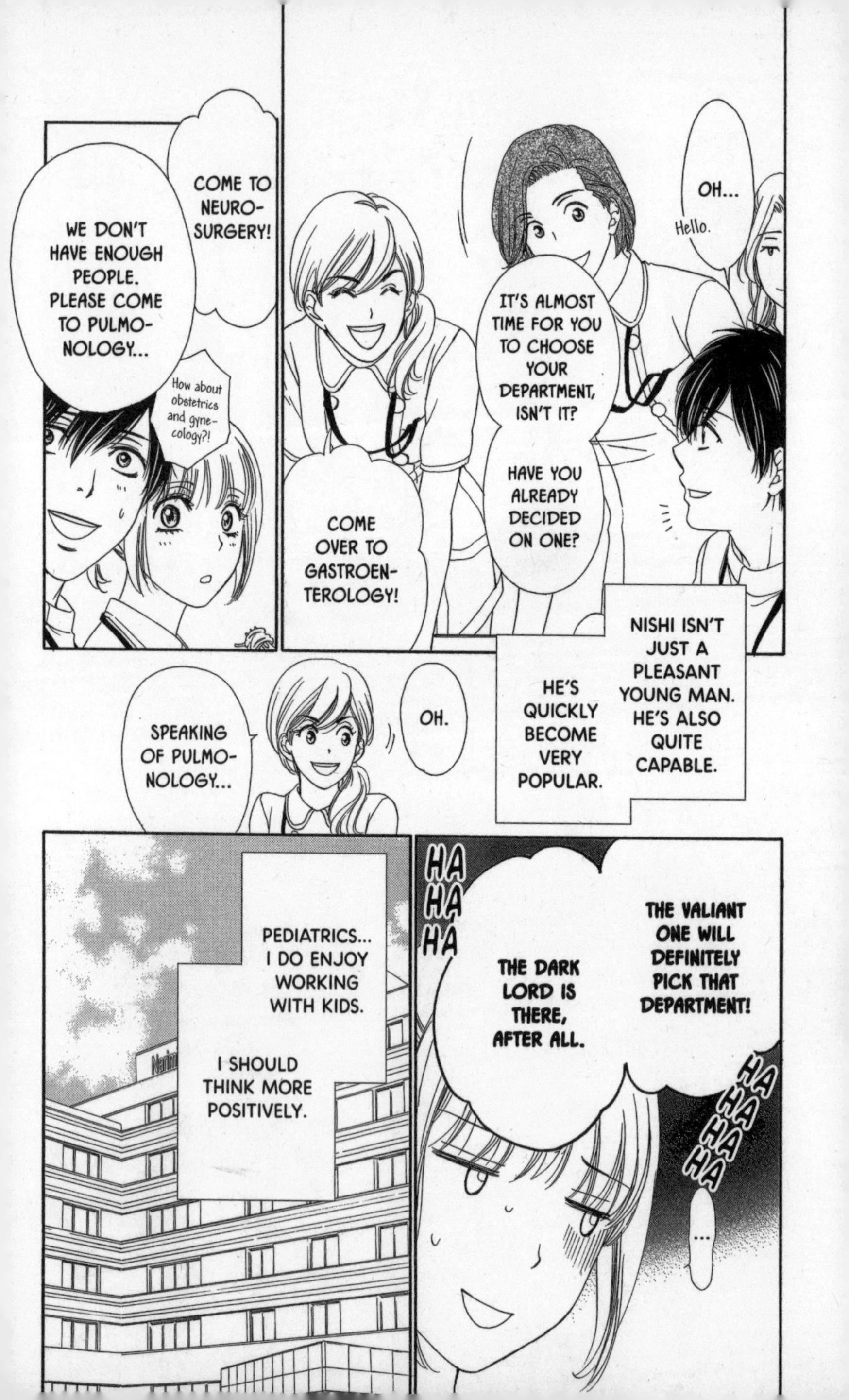
OH...
Hello.
IT'S ALMOST TIME FOR YOU TO CHOOSE YOUR DEPARTMENT, ISN'T IT?
HAVE YOU ALREADY DECIDED ON ONE?
COME OVER TO GASTROEN-TEROLOGY!
COME TO NEURO-SURGERY!
WE DON'T HAVE ENOUGH PEOPLE. PLEASE COME TO PULMO-NOLOGY...
How about obstetrics and gyne-cology?!
NISHI ISN'T JUST A PLEASANT YOUNG MAN. HE'S ALSO QUITE CAPABLE.
HE'S QUICKLY BECOME VERY POPULAR.
OH.
SPEAKING OF PULMO-NOLOGY...
HA HA HA
THE VALIANT ONE WILL DEFINITELY PICK THAT DEPARTMENT!
THE DARK LORD IS THERE, AFTER ALL.
HA HA HA HA
...
PEDIATRICS... I DO ENJOY WORKING WITH KIDS.
I SHOULD THINK MORE POSITIVELY.

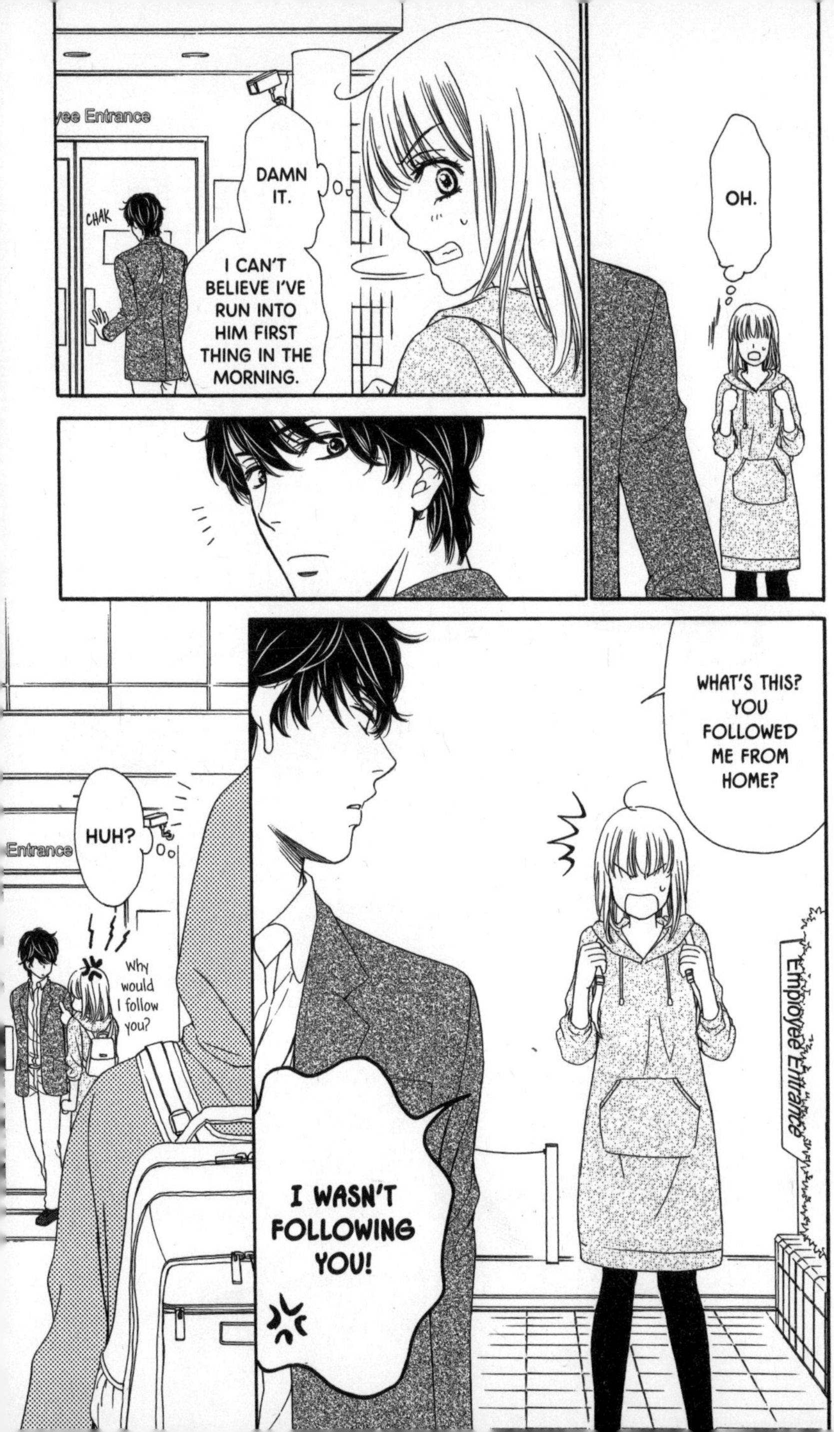
OH.
DAMN IT.
I CAN'T BELIEVE I'VE RUN INTO HIM FIRST THING IN THE MORNING.
yee Entrance
CHAK
WHAT'S THIS? YOU FOLLOWED ME FROM HOME?
Employee Entrance
I WASN'T FOLLOWING YOU!
HUH?
Entrance
Why would I follow you?

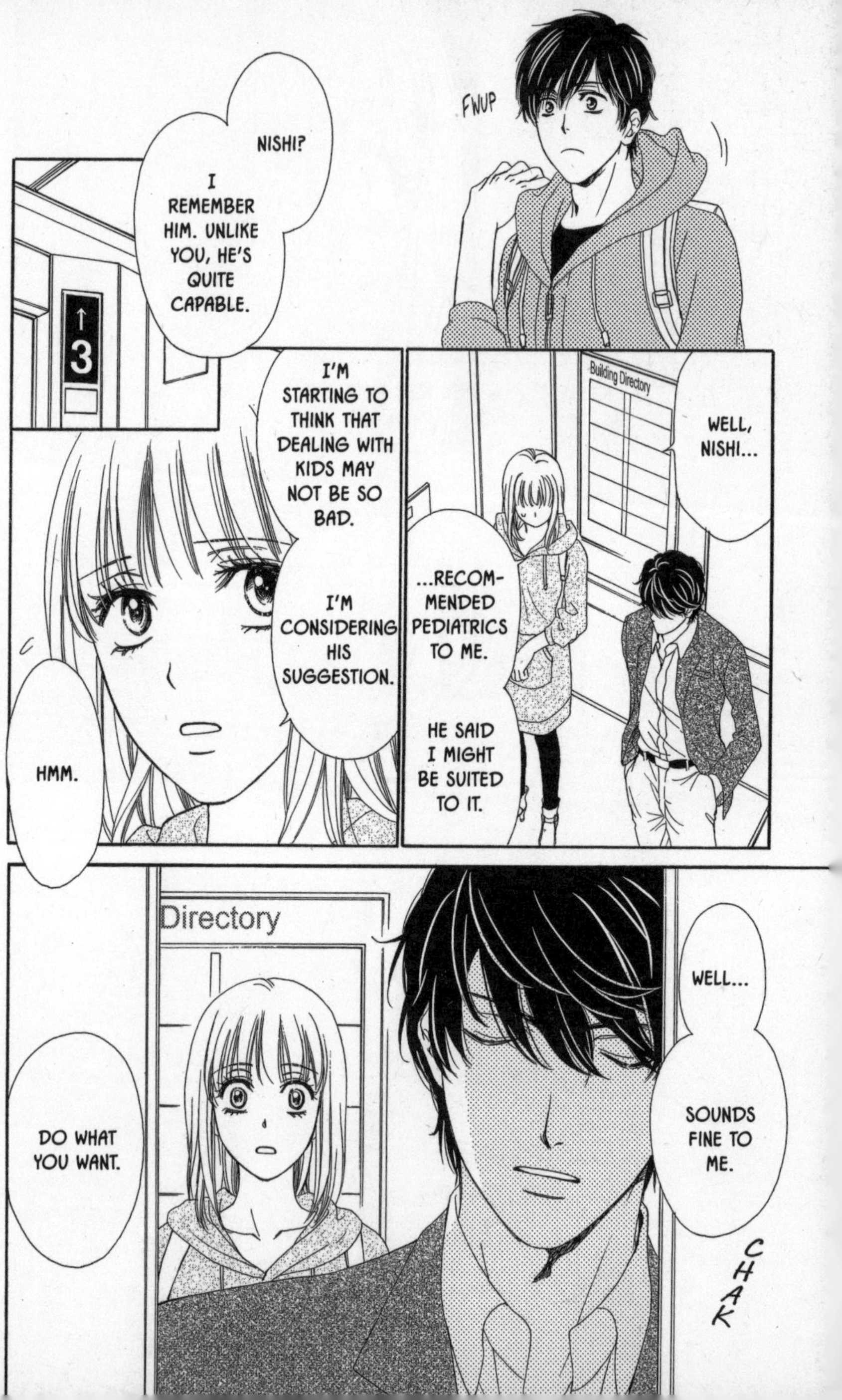
FWUP
NISHI?
I REMEMBER HIM. UNLIKE YOU, HE'S QUITE CAPABLE.
↑ 3
Building Directory
WELL, NISHI...
...RECOMMENDED PEDIATRICS TO ME.
HE SAID I MIGHT BE SUITED TO IT.
I'M STARTING TO THINK THAT DEALING WITH KIDS MAY NOT BE SO BAD.
I'M CONSIDERING HIS SUGGESTION.
HMM.
Directory
WELL...
SOUNDS FINE TO ME.
CHAK
DO WHAT YOU WANT.

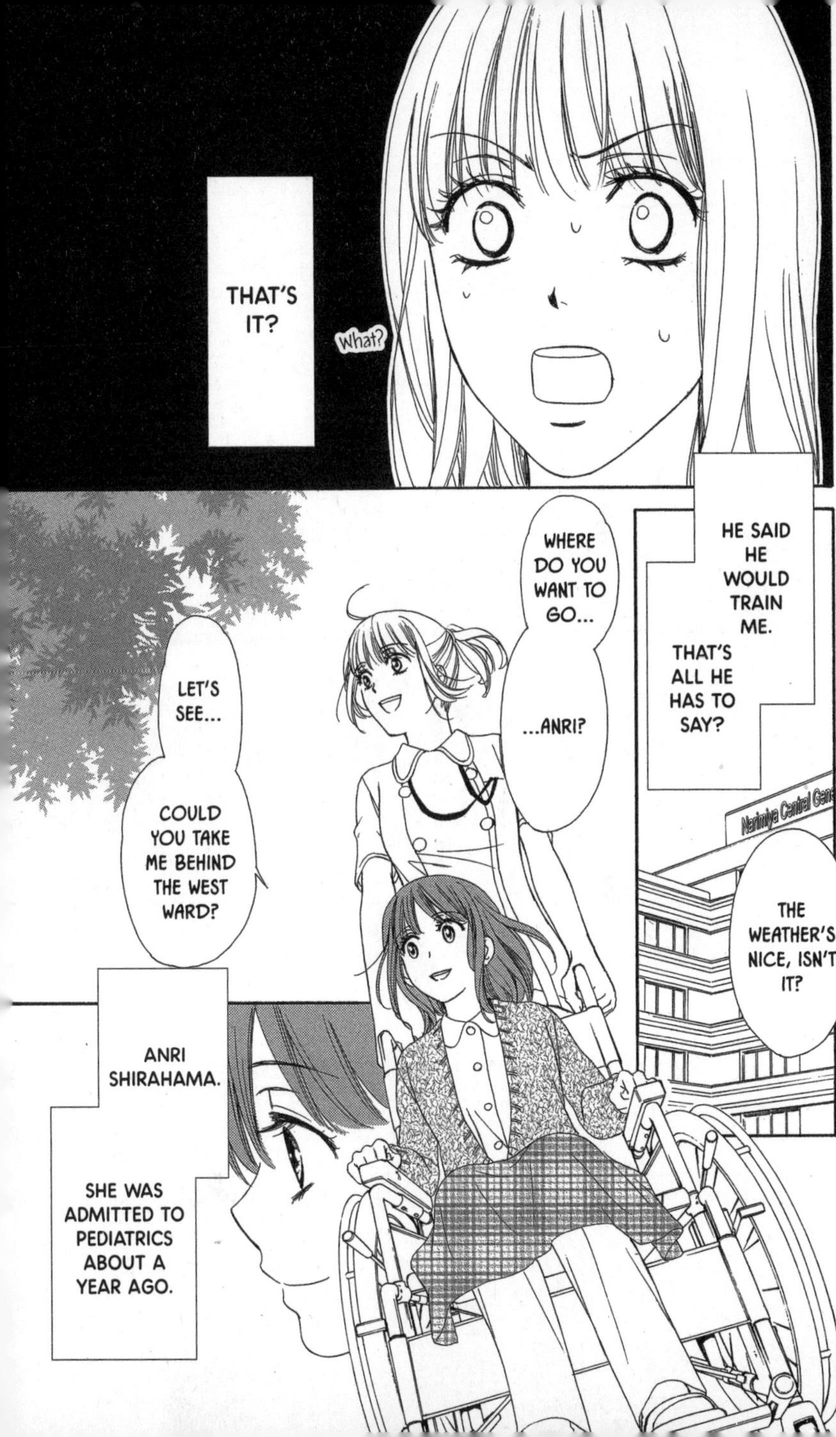

What?
THAT'S IT?
HE SAID HE WOULD TRAIN ME.
THAT'S ALL HE HAS TO SAY?
WHERE DO YOU WANT TO GO...
...ANRI?
Narimiya Central Gene
THE WEATHER'S NICE, ISN'T IT?
LET'S SEE...
COULD YOU TAKE ME BEHIND THE WEST WARD?
ANRI SHIRAHAMA.
SHE WAS ADMITTED TO PEDIATRICS ABOUT A YEAR AGO.

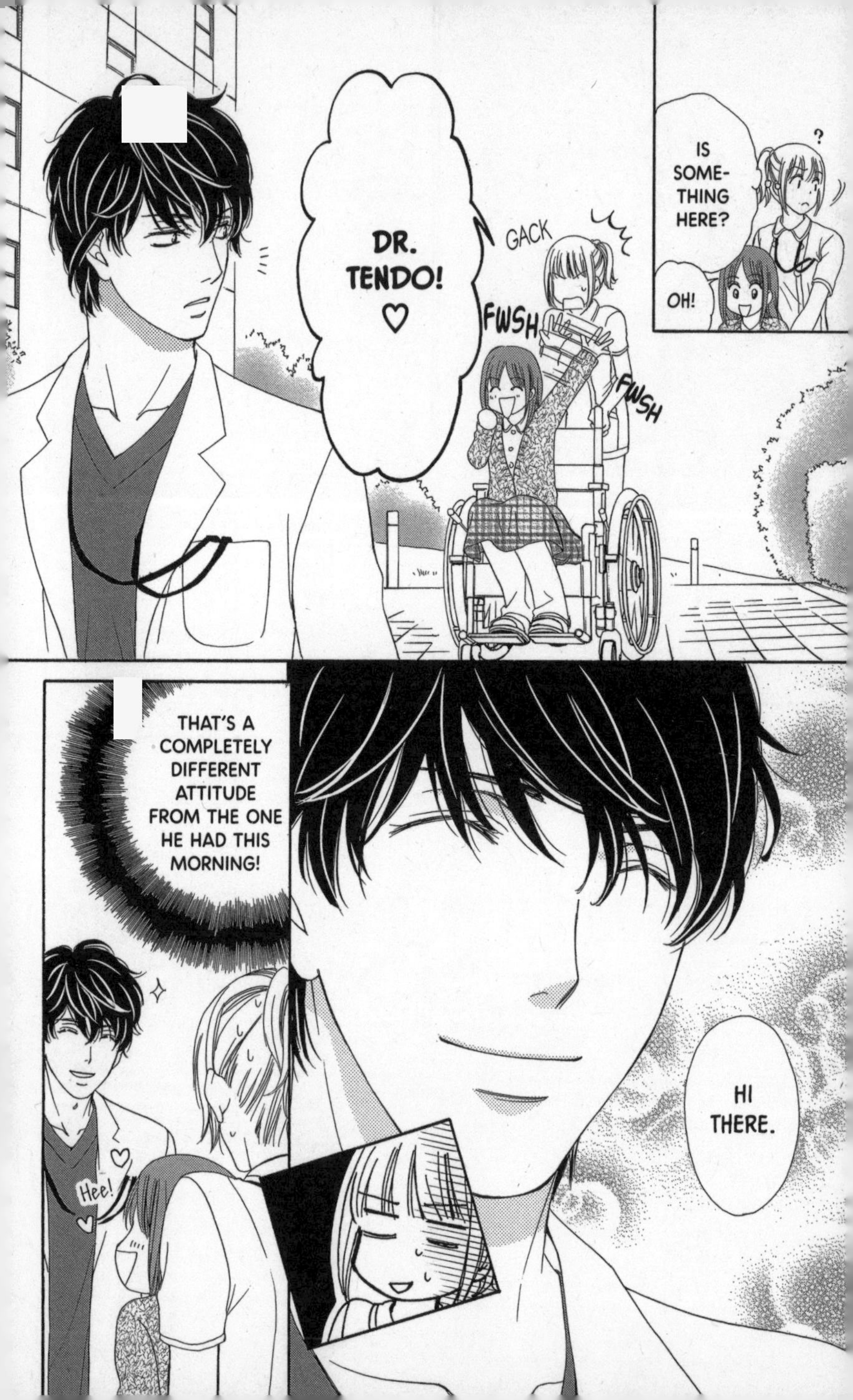
IS SOMETHING HERE?
?
OH!
GACK
DR. TENDO! ♡
FWSH
FWSH
HI THERE.
THAT'S A COMPLETELY DIFFERENT ATTITUDE FROM THE ONE HE HAD THIS MORNING!
Hee!

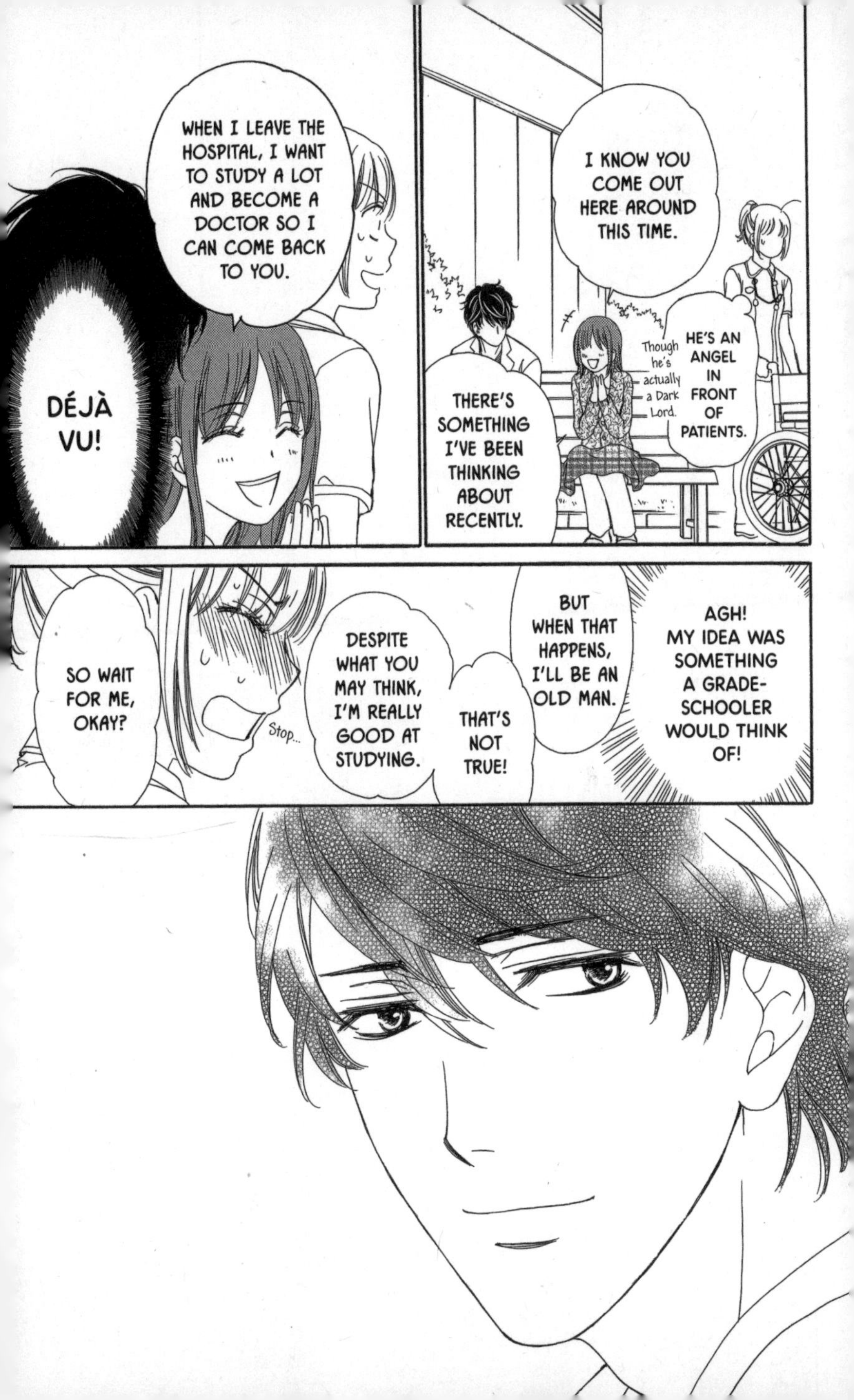
I KNOW YOU COME OUT HERE AROUND THIS TIME.
HE'S AN ANGEL IN FRONT OF PATIENTS.
Though he's actually a Dark Lord.
THERE'S SOMETHING I'VE BEEN THINKING ABOUT RECENTLY.
WHEN I LEAVE THE HOSPITAL, I WANT TO STUDY A LOT AND BECOME A DOCTOR SO I CAN COME BACK TO YOU.
DÉJÀ VU!
AGH! MY IDEA WAS SOMETHING A GRADE-SCHOOLER WOULD THINK OF!
BUT WHEN THAT HAPPENS, I'LL BE AN OLD MAN.
THAT'S NOT TRUE!
DESPITE WHAT YOU MAY THINK, I'M REALLY GOOD AT STUDYING.
Stop...
SO WAIT FOR ME, OKAY?

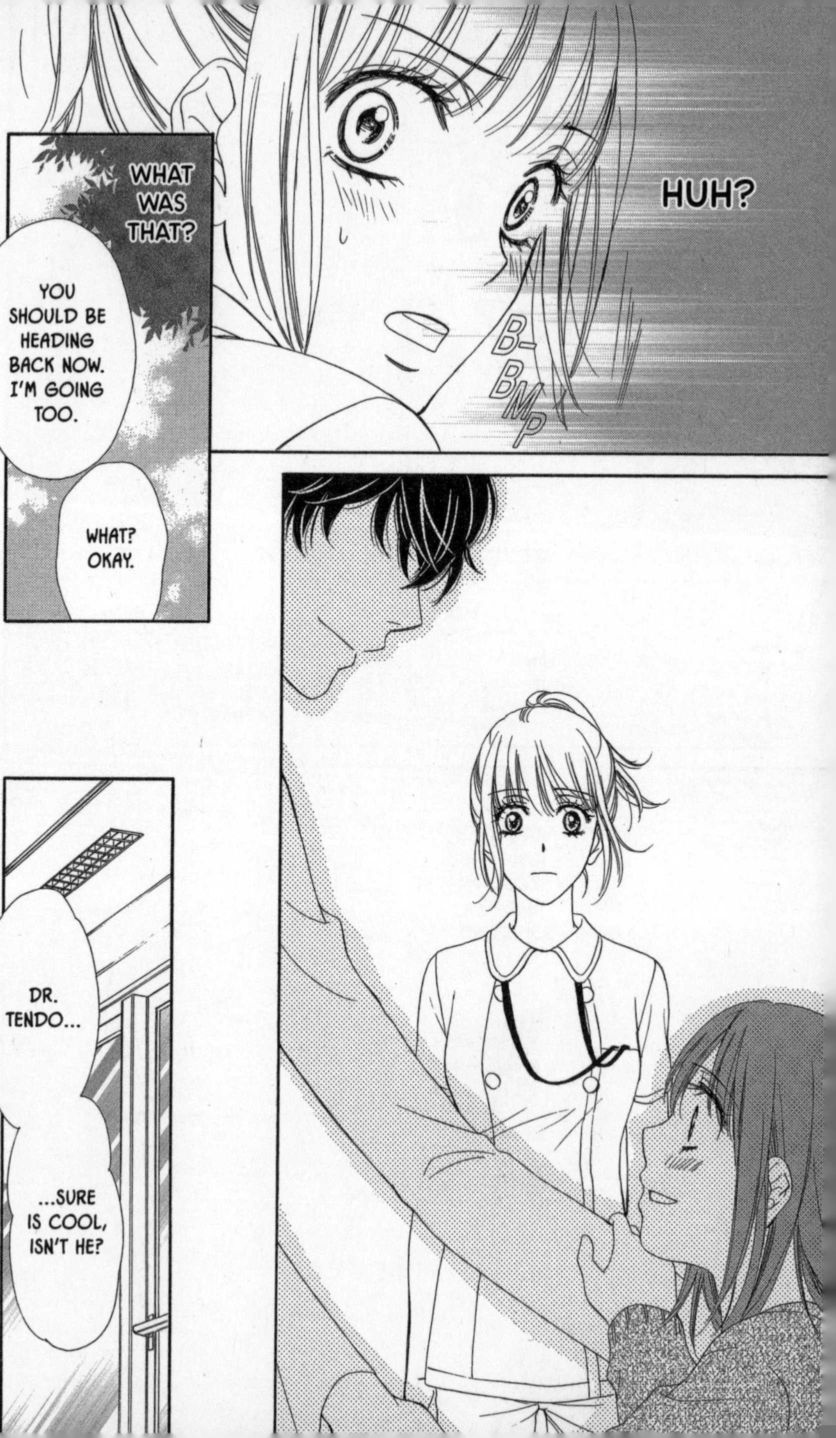
HUH?
B-BMP
WHAT WAS THAT?
YOU SHOULD BE HEADING BACK NOW. I'M GOING TOO.
WHAT? OKAY.
DR. TENDO...
...SURE IS COOL, ISN'T HE?

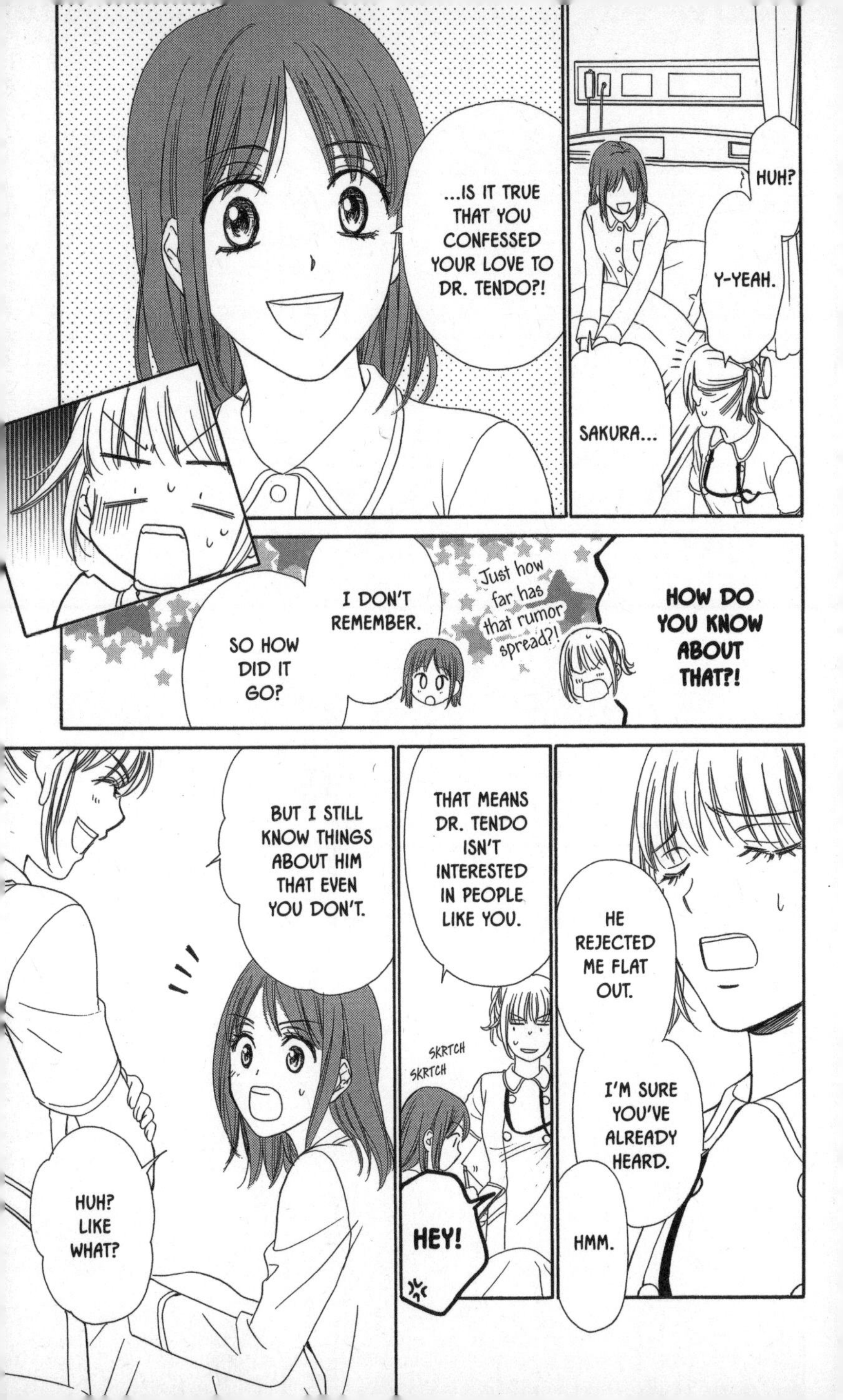
HUH?
Y-YEAH.
SAKURA...
...IS IT TRUE THAT YOU CONFESSED YOUR LOVE TO DR. TENDO?!
HOW DO YOU KNOW ABOUT THAT?!
Just how far has that rumor spread?!
I DON'T REMEMBER.
SO HOW DID IT GO?
HE REJECTED ME FLAT OUT.
I'M SURE YOU'VE ALREADY HEARD.
HMM.
THAT MEANS DR. TENDO ISN'T INTERESTED IN PEOPLE LIKE YOU.
SKRTCH
SKRTCH
HEY!
BUT I STILL KNOW THINGS ABOUT HIM THAT EVEN YOU DON'T.
HUH? LIKE WHAT?

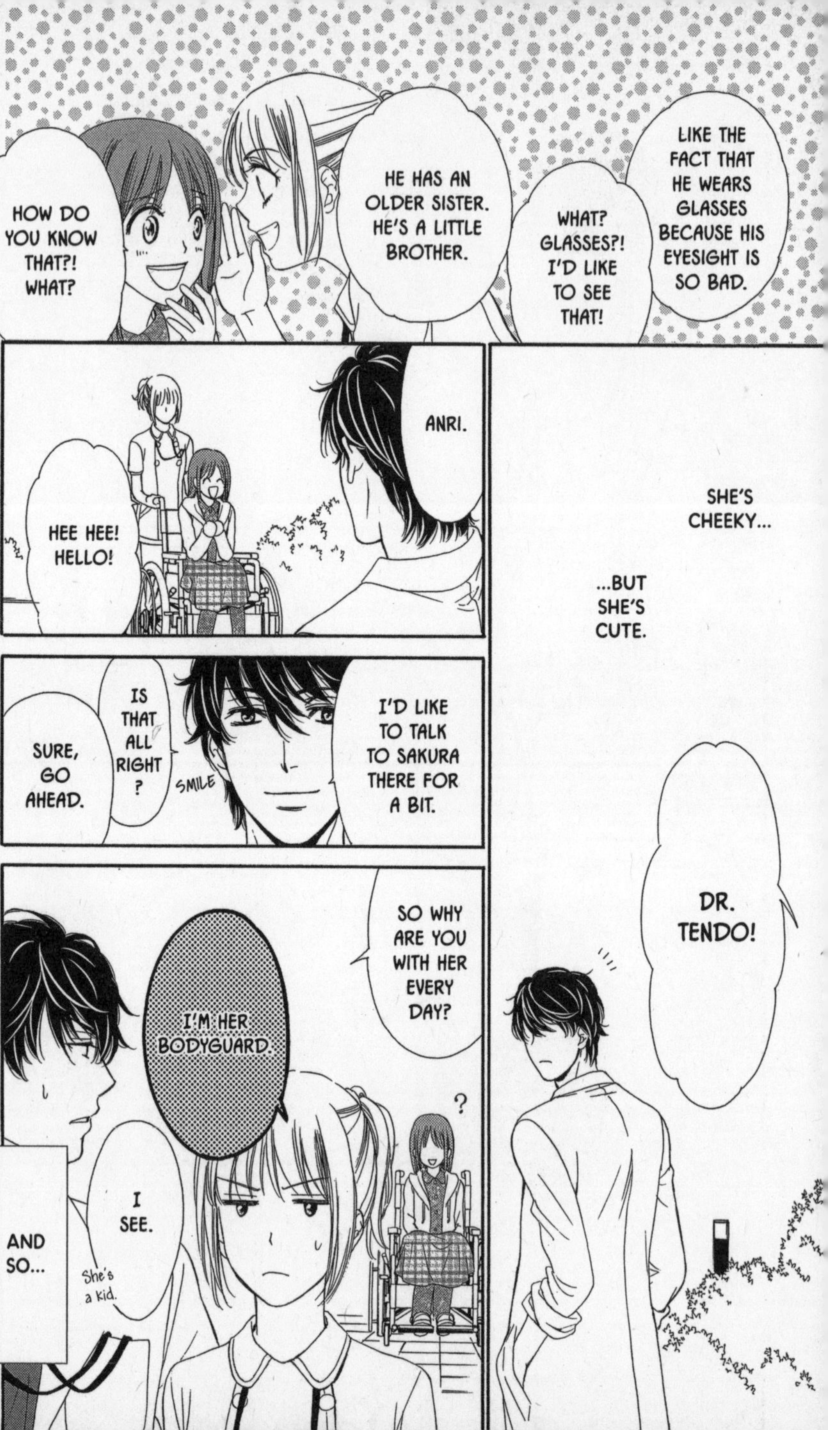
LIKE THE FACT THAT HE WEARS GLASSES BECAUSE HIS EYESIGHT IS SO BAD.
WHAT? GLASSES?! I'D LIKE TO SEE THAT!
HE HAS AN OLDER SISTER. HE'S A LITTLE BROTHER.
HOW DO YOU KNOW THAT?! WHAT?
SHE'S CHEEKY...
...BUT SHE'S CUTE.
DR. TENDO!
ANRI.
HEE HEE! HELLO!
I'D LIKE TO TALK TO SAKURA THERE FOR A BIT.
IS THAT ALL RIGHT?
SMILE
SURE, GO AHEAD.
SO WHY ARE YOU WITH HER EVERY DAY?
I'M HER BODYGUARD.
?
I SEE.
She's a kid.
AND SO...

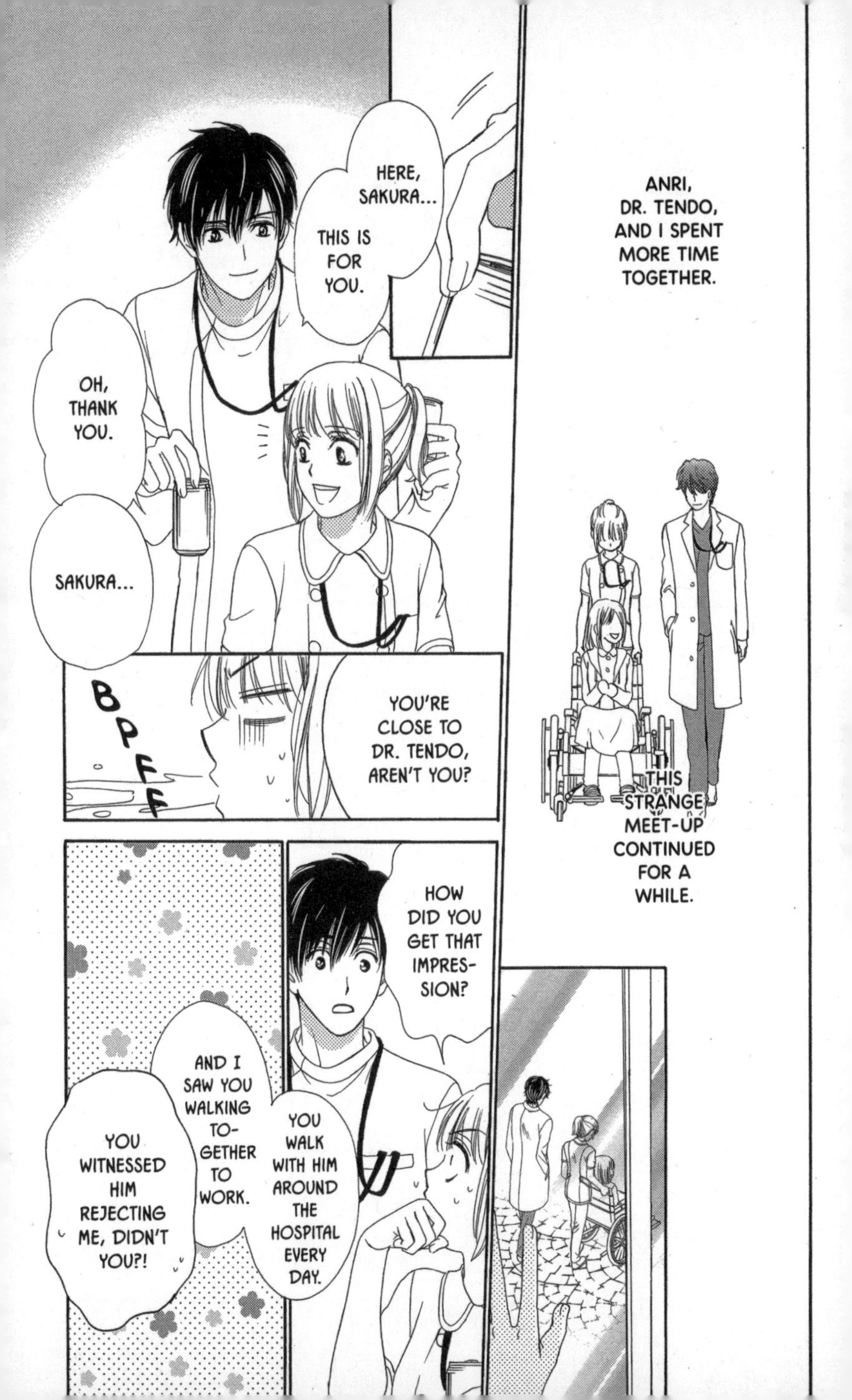

ANRI, DR. TENDO, AND I SPENT MORE TIME TOGETHER.
THIS STRANGE MEET-UP CONTINUED FOR A WHILE.
HERE, SAKURA...
THIS IS FOR YOU.
OH, THANK YOU.
SAKURA...
BPFF
YOU'RE CLOSE TO DR. TENDO, AREN'T YOU?
HOW DID YOU GET THAT IMPRES-SION?
YOU WALK WITH HIM AROUND THE HOSPITAL EVERY DAY.
AND I SAW YOU WALKING TO-GETHER TO WORK.
YOU WITNESSED HIM REJECTING ME, DIDN'T YOU?!

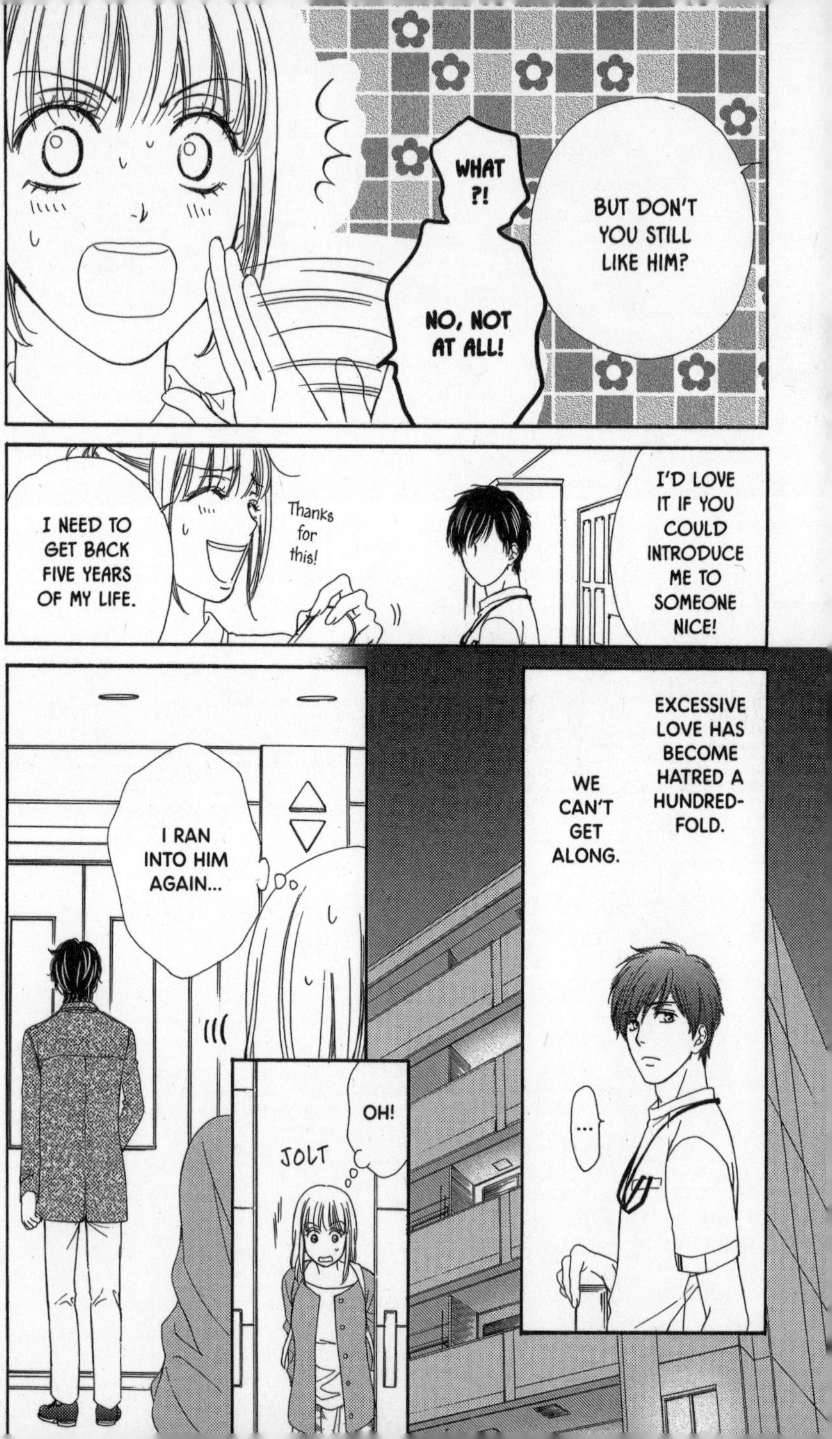
BUT DON'T YOU STILL LIKE HIM?
WHAT?!
NO, NOT AT ALL!
I'D LOVE IT IF YOU COULD INTRODUCE ME TO SOMEONE NICE!
Thanks for this!
I NEED TO GET BACK FIVE YEARS OF MY LIFE.
EXCESSIVE LOVE HAS BECOME HATRED A HUNDRED-FOLD.
WE CAN'T GET ALONG.
...
I RAN INTO HIM AGAIN...
OH!
JOLT

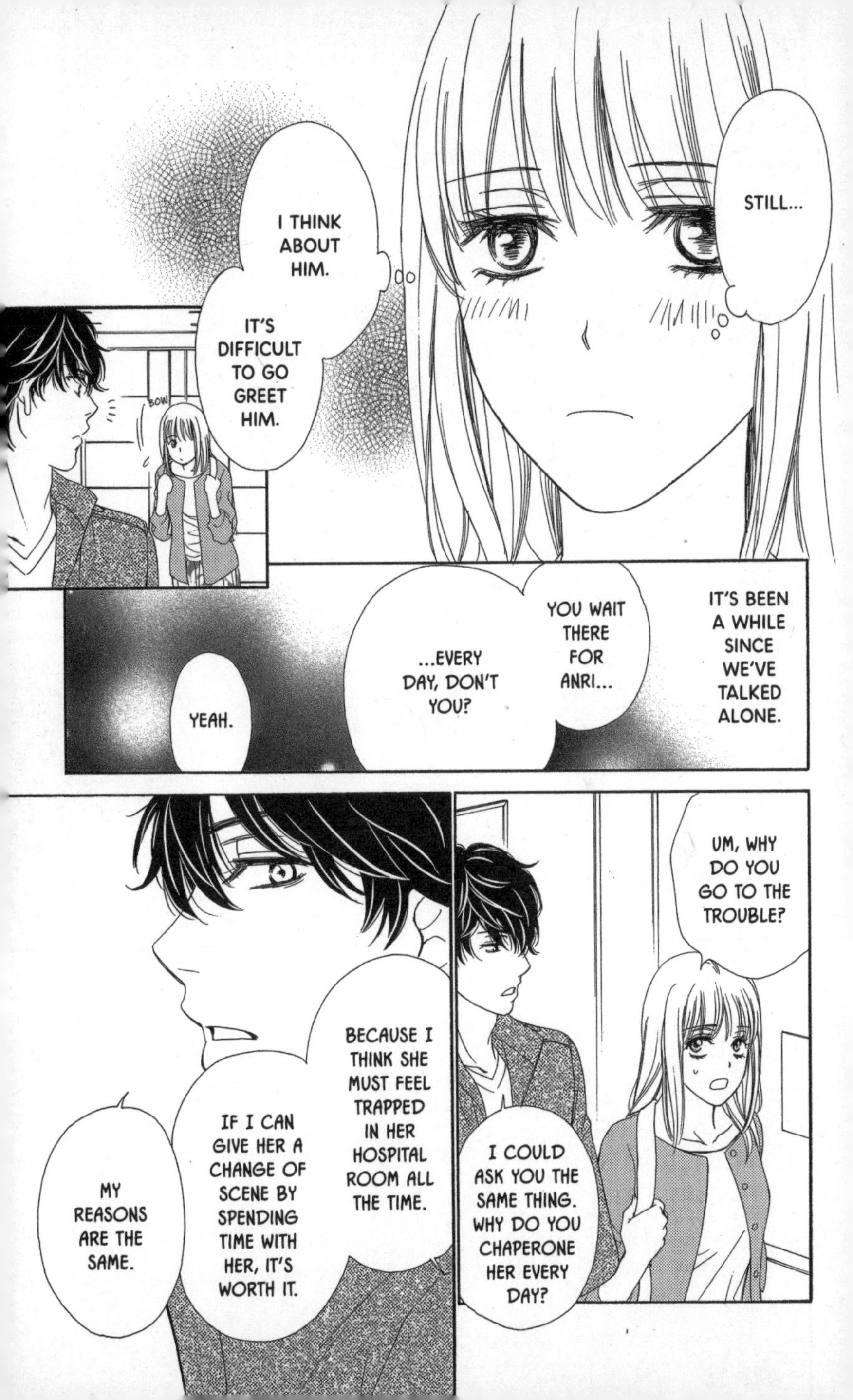
STILL...
I THINK ABOUT HIM.
IT'S DIFFICULT TO GO GREET HIM.
BOW
IT'S BEEN A WHILE SINCE WE'VE TALKED ALONE.
YOU WAIT THERE FOR ANRI...
...EVERY DAY, DON'T YOU?
YEAH.
UM, WHY DO YOU GO TO THE TROUBLE?
I COULD ASK YOU THE SAME THING. WHY DO YOU CHAPERONE HER EVERY DAY?
BECAUSE I THINK SHE MUST FEEL TRAPPED IN HER HOSPITAL ROOM ALL THE TIME.
IF I CAN GIVE HER A CHANGE OF SCENE BY SPENDING TIME WITH HER, IT'S WORTH IT.
MY REASONS ARE THE SAME.

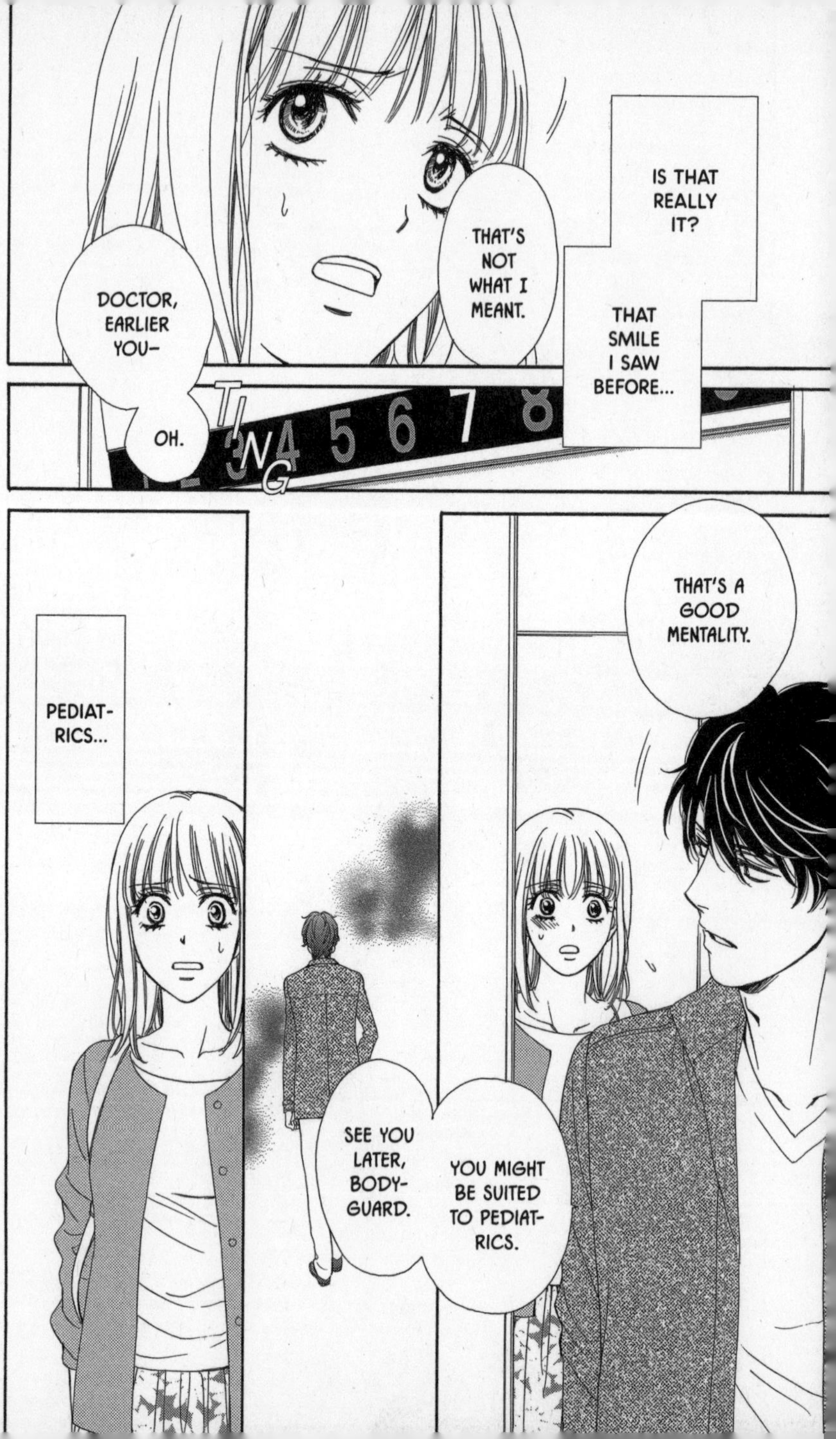
IS THAT REALLY IT?
THAT SMILE I SAW BEFORE...
THAT'S NOT WHAT I MEANT.
DOCTOR, EARLIER YOU–
OH.
TING
THAT'S A GOOD MENTALITY.
YOU MIGHT BE SUITED TO PEDIATRICS.
SEE YOU LATER, BODYGUARD.
PEDIATRICS...

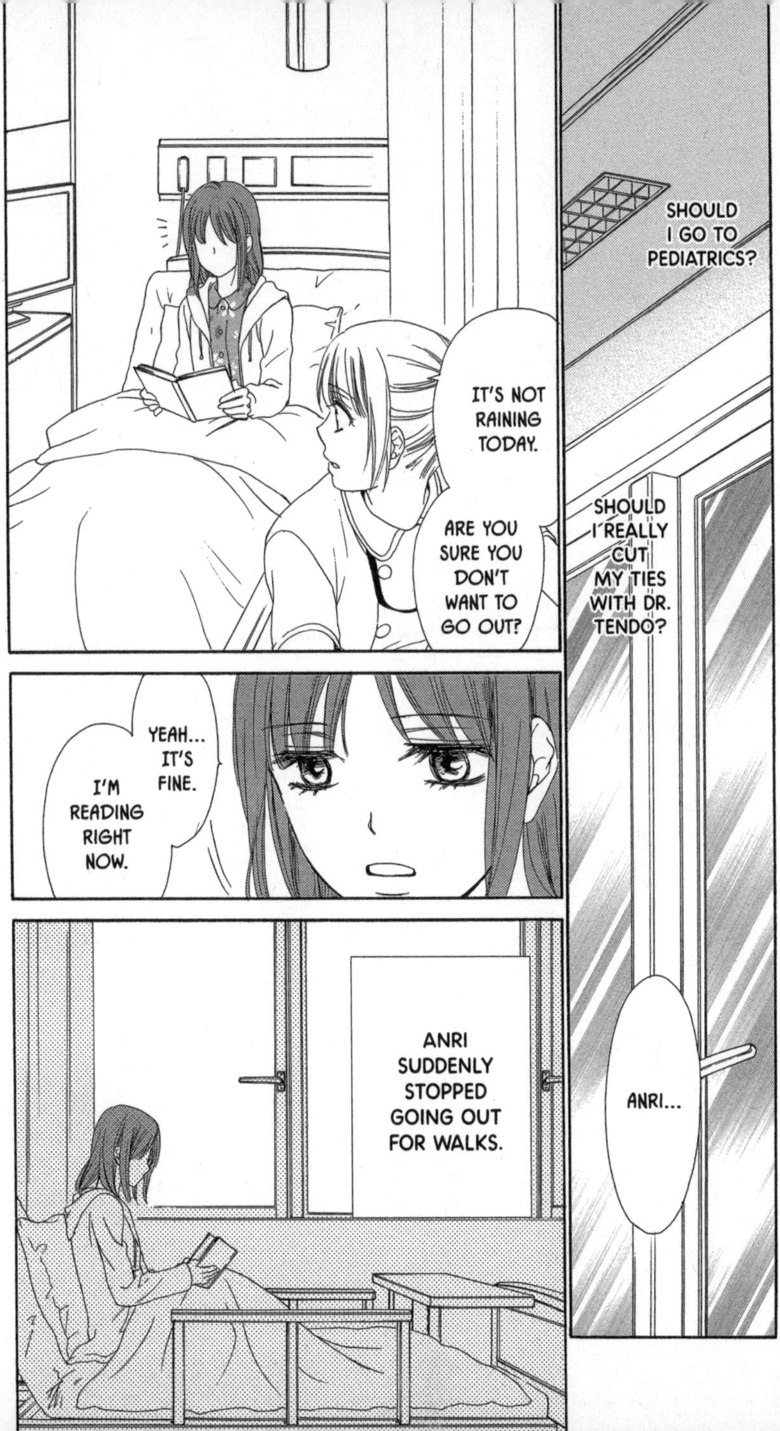
SHOULD I GO TO PEDIATRICS?
SHOULD I REALLY CUT MY TIES WITH DR. TENDO?
ANRI...
IT'S NOT RAINING TODAY.
ARE YOU SURE YOU DON'T WANT TO GO OUT?
YEAH... IT'S FINE.
I'M READING RIGHT NOW.
ANRI SUDDENLY STOPPED GOING OUT FOR WALKS.

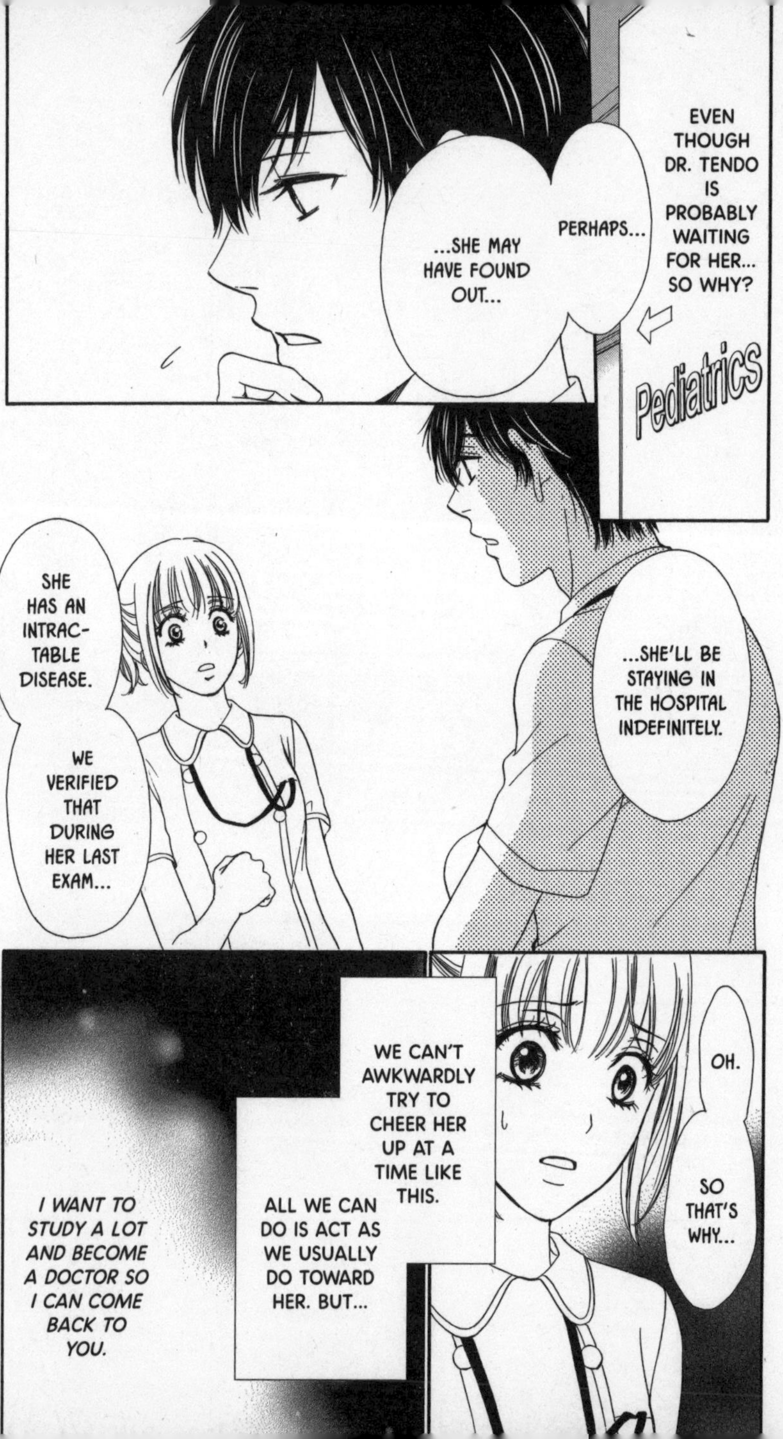
EVEN THOUGH DR. TENDO IS PROBABLY WAITING FOR HER... SO WHY?
PERHAPS...
...SHE MAY HAVE FOUND OUT...
Pediatrics
SHE HAS AN INTRAC-TABLE DISEASE.
WE VERIFIED THAT DURING HER LAST EXAM...
...SHE'LL BE STAYING IN THE HOSPITAL INDEFINITELY.
OH.
SO THAT'S WHY...
WE CAN'T AWKWARDLY TRY TO CHEER HER UP AT A TIME LIKE THIS.
ALL WE CAN DO IS ACT AS WE USUALLY DO TOWARD HER. BUT...
I WANT TO STUDY A LOT AND BECOME A DOCTOR SO I CAN COME BACK TO YOU.

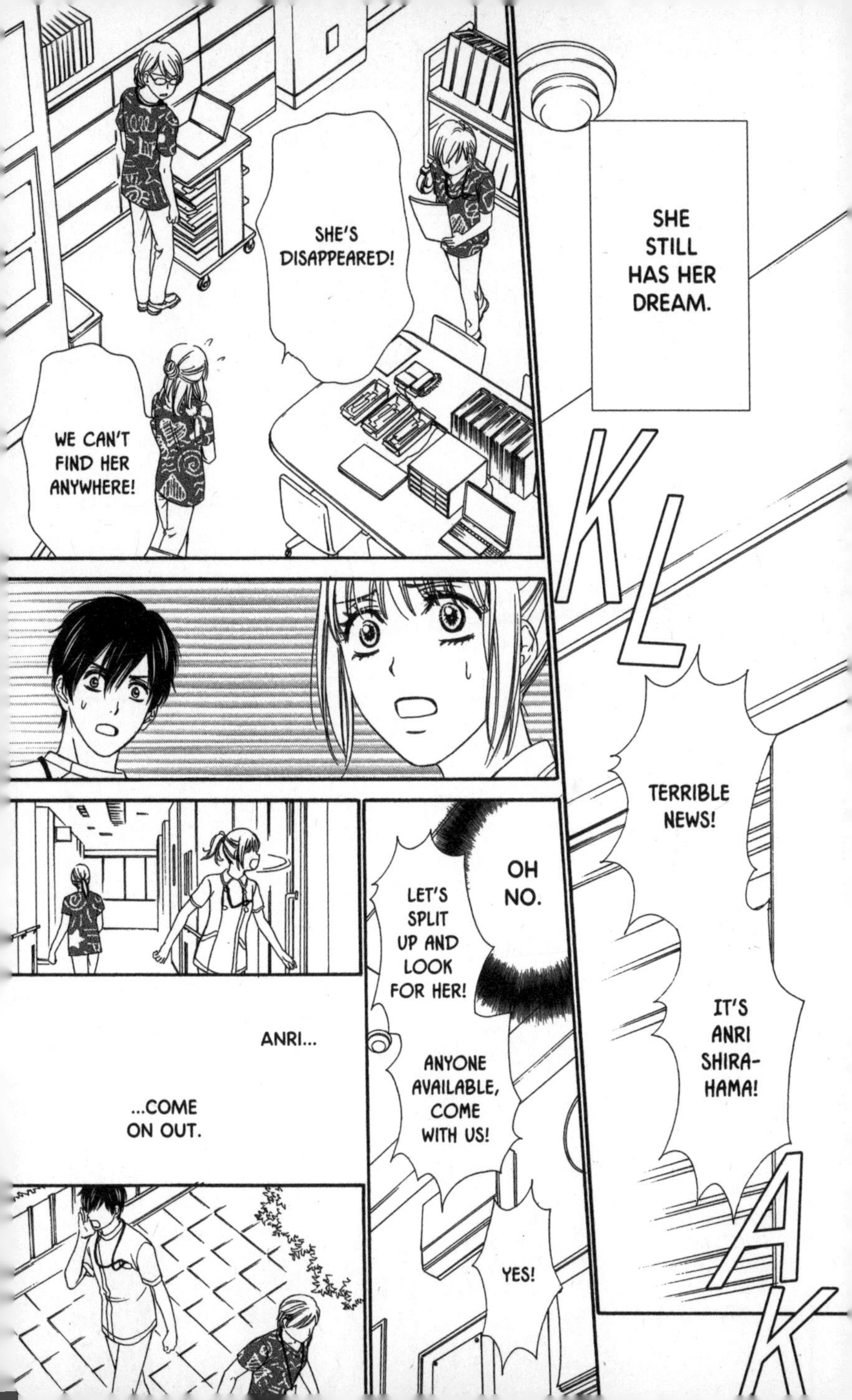
SHE STILL HAS HER DREAM.
KL
TERRIBLE NEWS!
IT'S ANRI SHIRAHAMA!
AK
SHE'S DISAPPEARED!
WE CAN'T FIND HER ANYWHERE!
OH NO.
LET'S SPLIT UP AND LOOK FOR HER!
ANYONE AVAILABLE, COME WITH US!
YES!
ANRI...
...COME ON OUT.

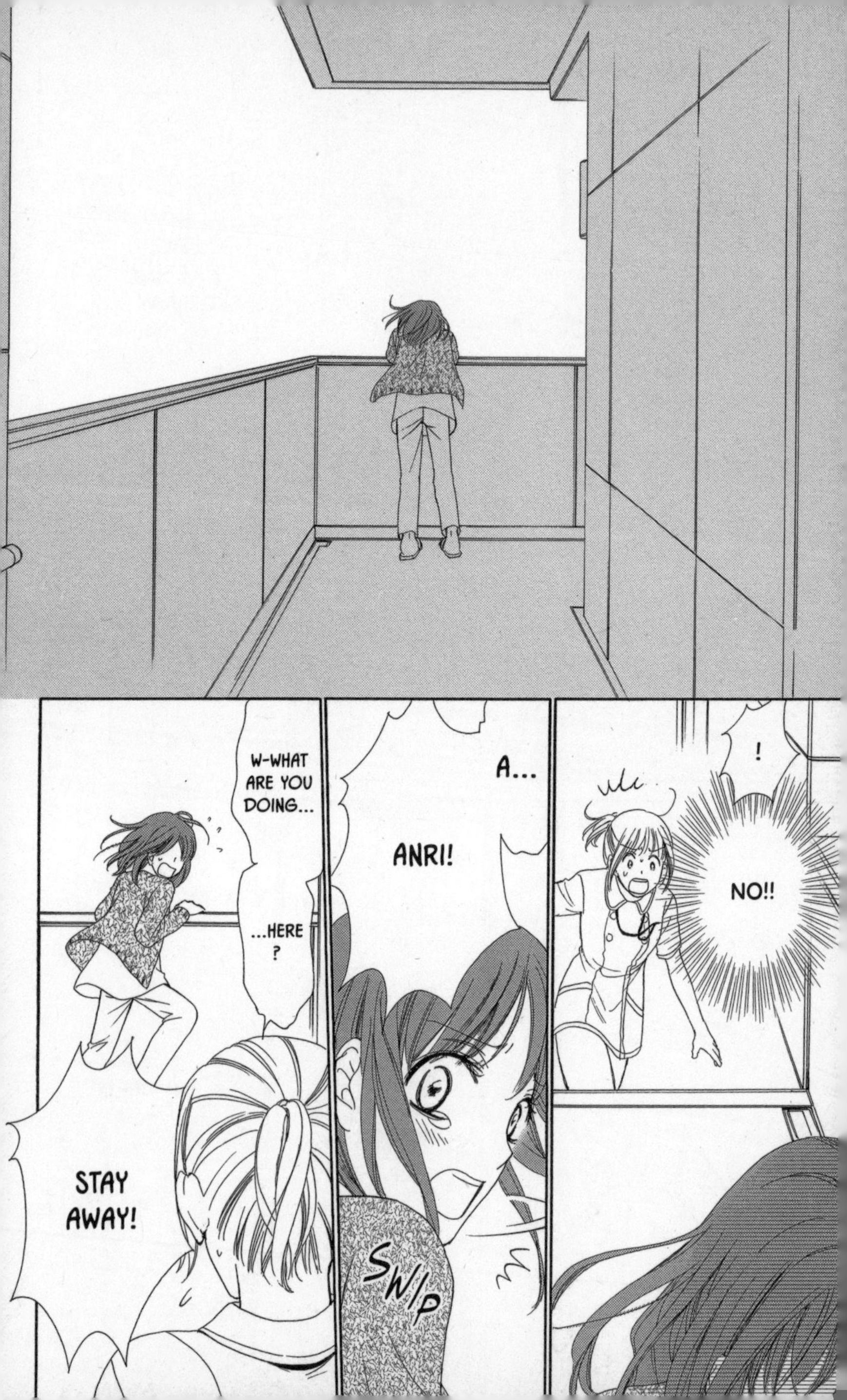
!
NO!!
A...
ANRI!
SWIP
W-WHAT ARE YOU DOING... ...HERE?
STAY AWAY!

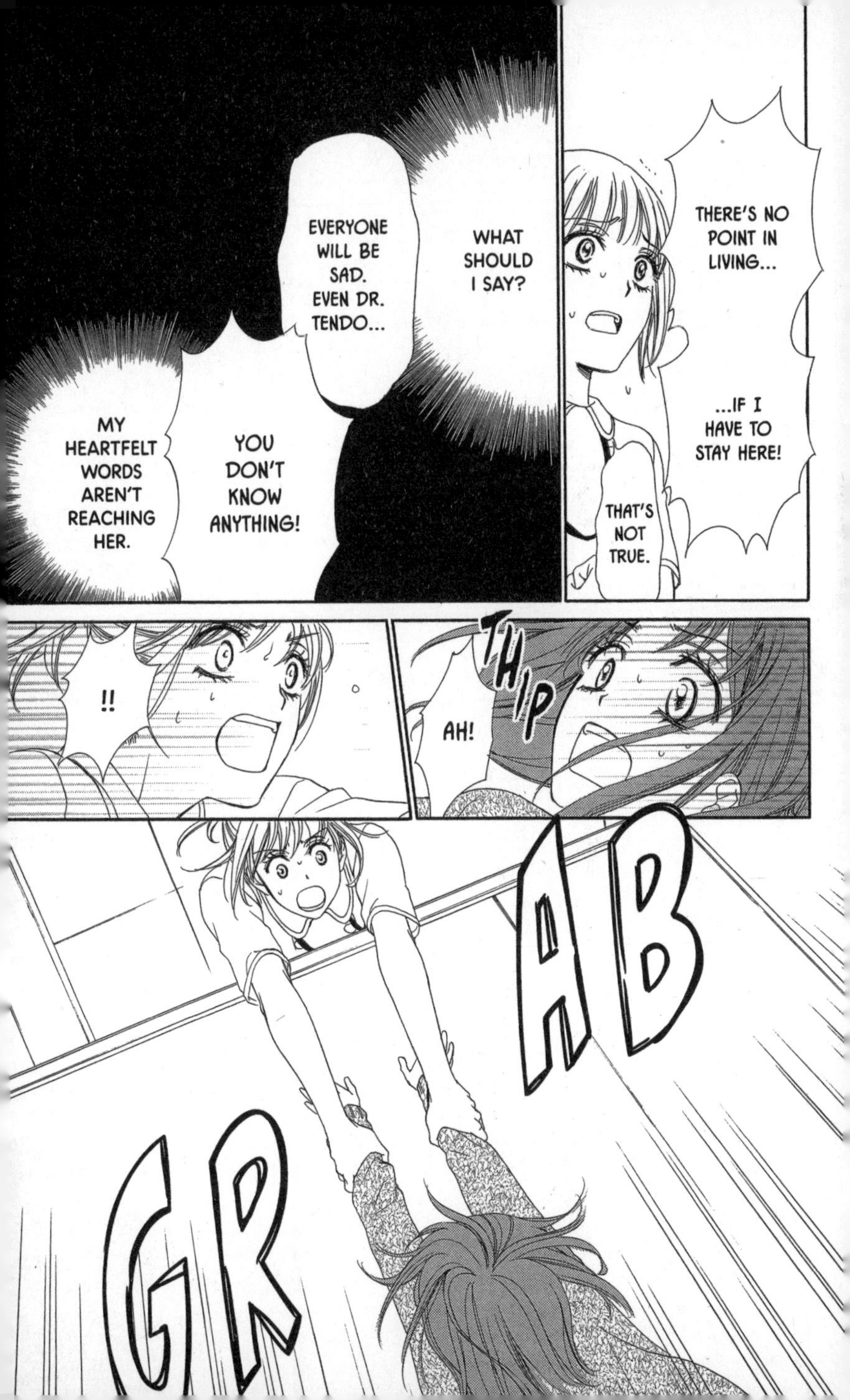
THERE'S NO POINT IN LIVING...
...IF I HAVE TO STAY HERE!
THAT'S NOT TRUE.
WHAT SHOULD I SAY?
EVERYONE WILL BE SAD. EVEN DR. TENDO...
YOU DON'T KNOW ANYTHING!
MY HEARTFELT WORDS AREN'T REACHING HER.
THIP
AH!
!!
GRAB

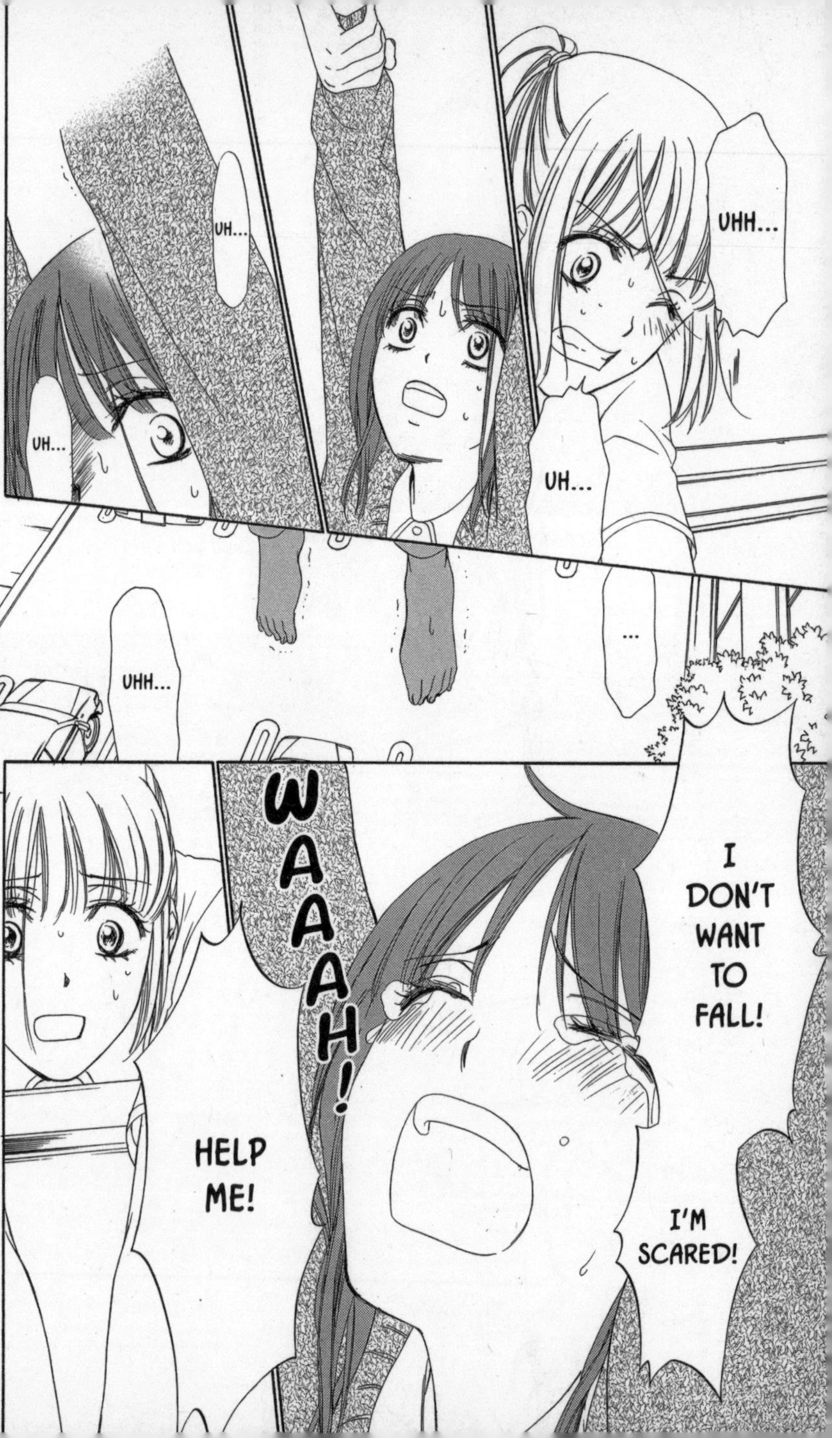
UHH...
UH...
UH...
UH...
...
UHH...
I DON'T WANT TO FALL!
I'M SCARED!
WAAAAH!
HELP ME!

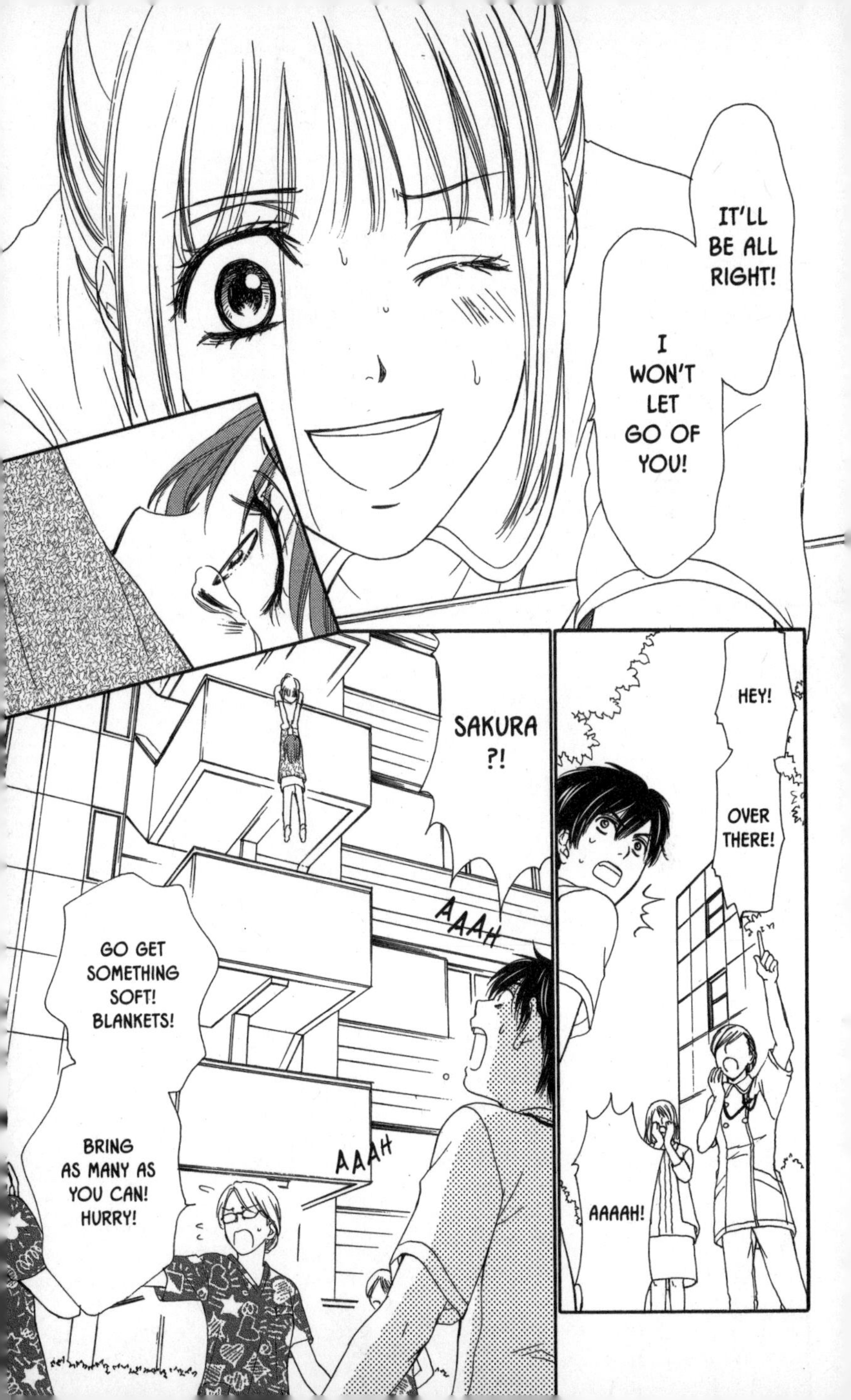
IT'LL BE ALL RIGHT!
I WON'T LET GO OF YOU!
HEY!
OVER THERE!
AAAAH!
SAKURA?!
AAAH
GO GET SOMETHING SOFT! BLANKETS!
BRING AS MANY AS YOU CAN! HURRY!
AAAH

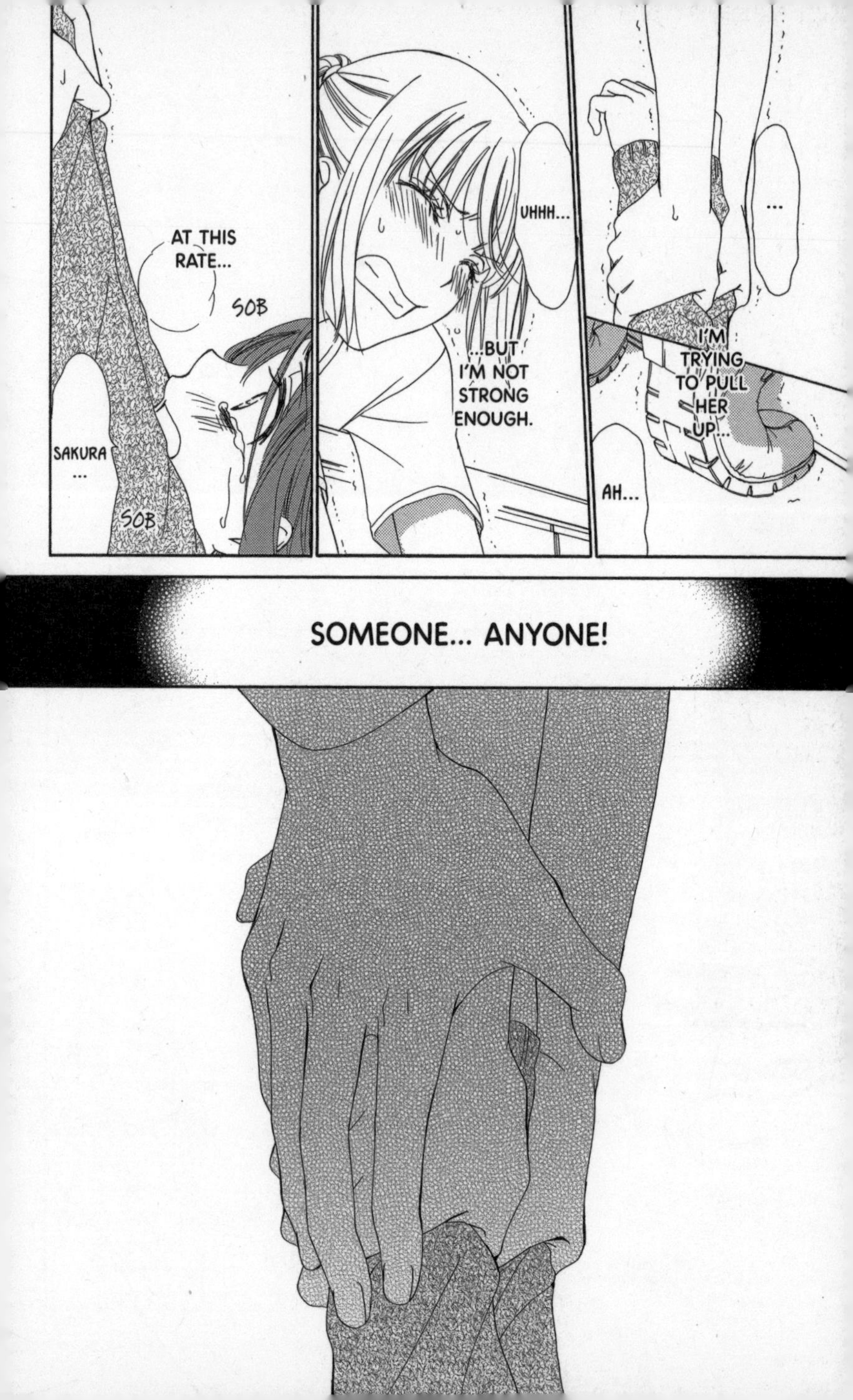
...
I'M TRYING TO PULL HER UP...
AH...
UHHH...
...BUT I'M NOT STRONG ENOUGH.
AT THIS RATE...
SOB
SAKURA ...
SOB
SOMEONE... ANYONE!

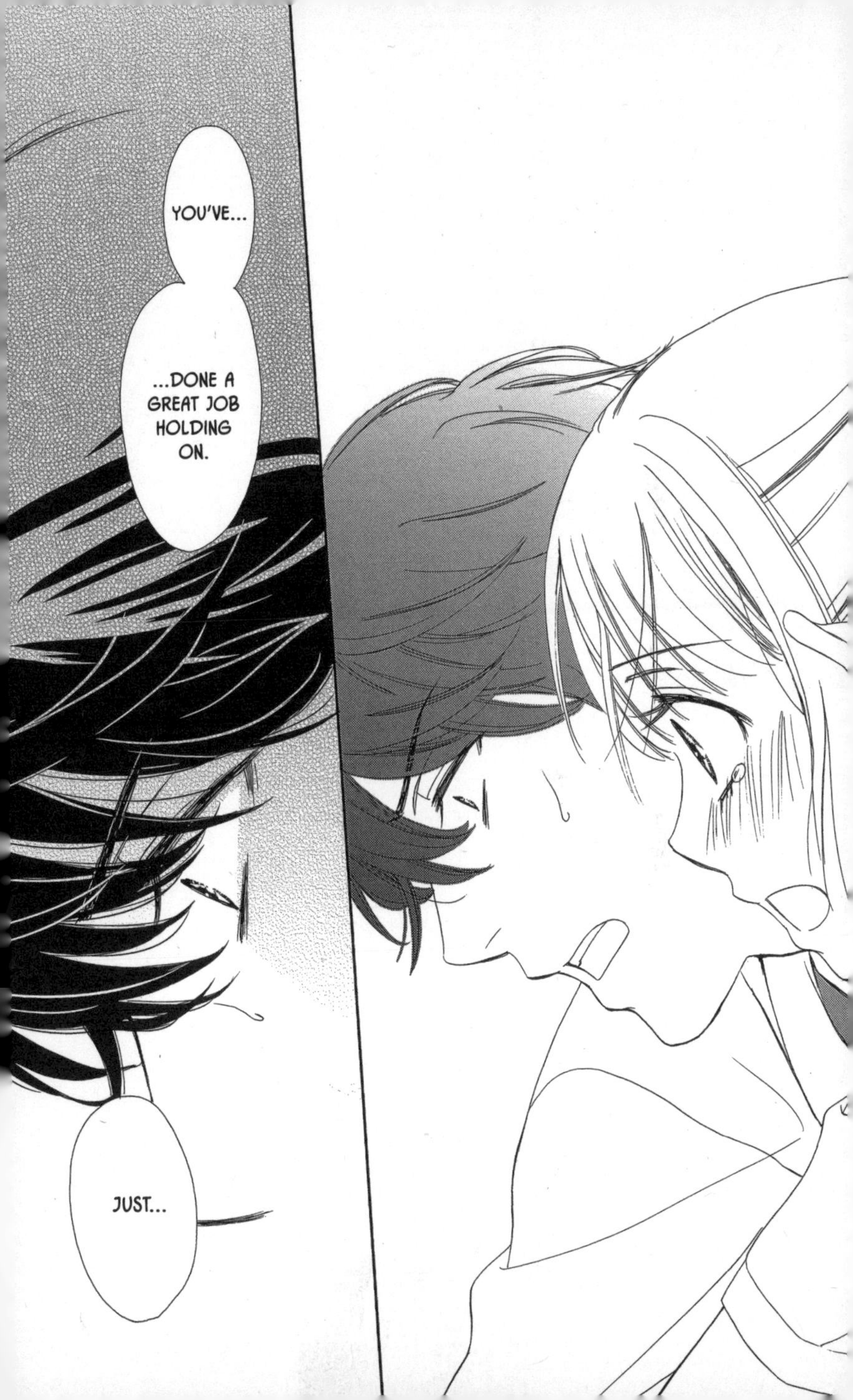
YOU'VE...
...DONE A GREAT JOB HOLDING ON.
JUST...

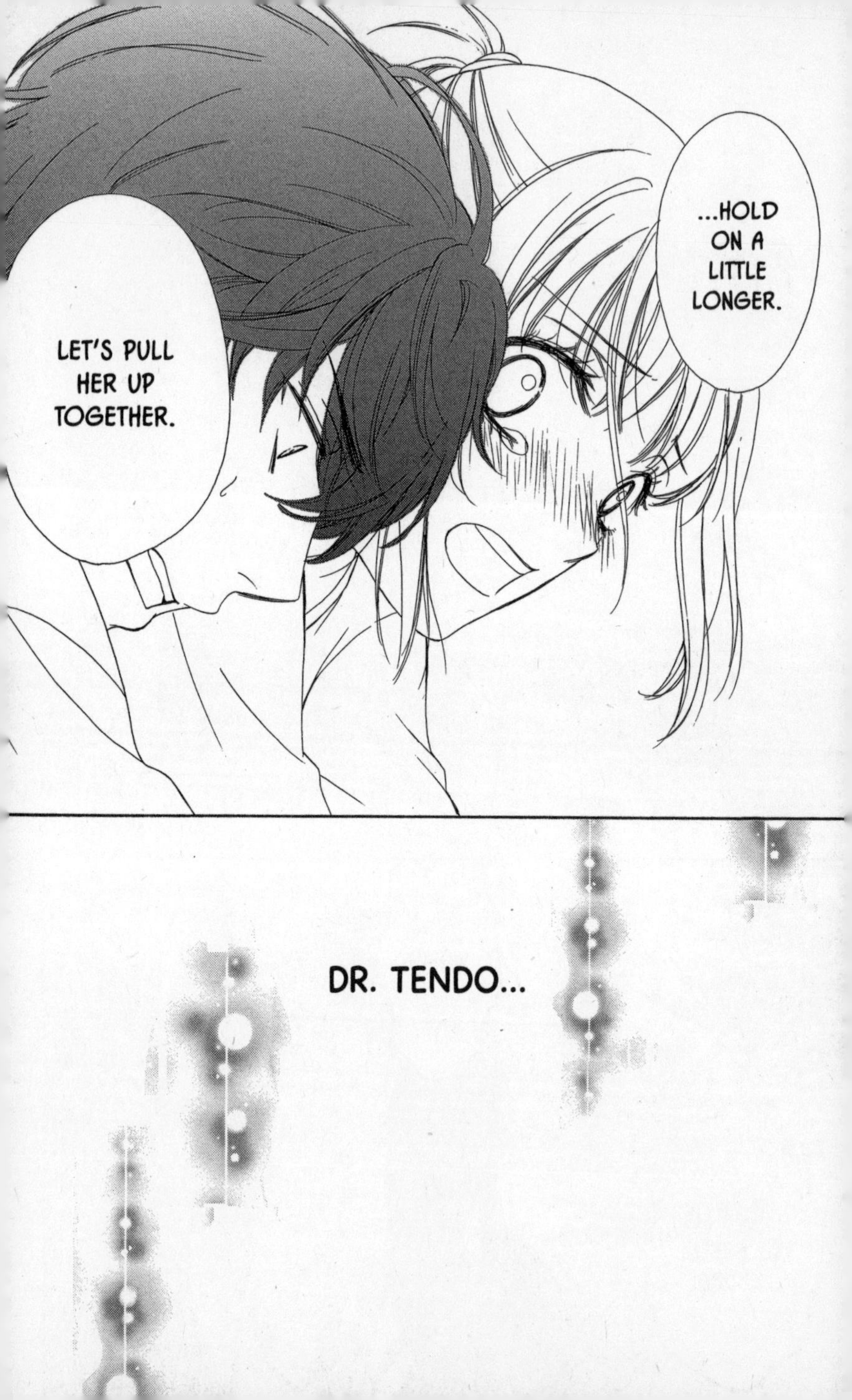
...HOLD ON A LITTLE LONGER.
LET'S PULL HER UP TOGETHER.
DR. TENDO...

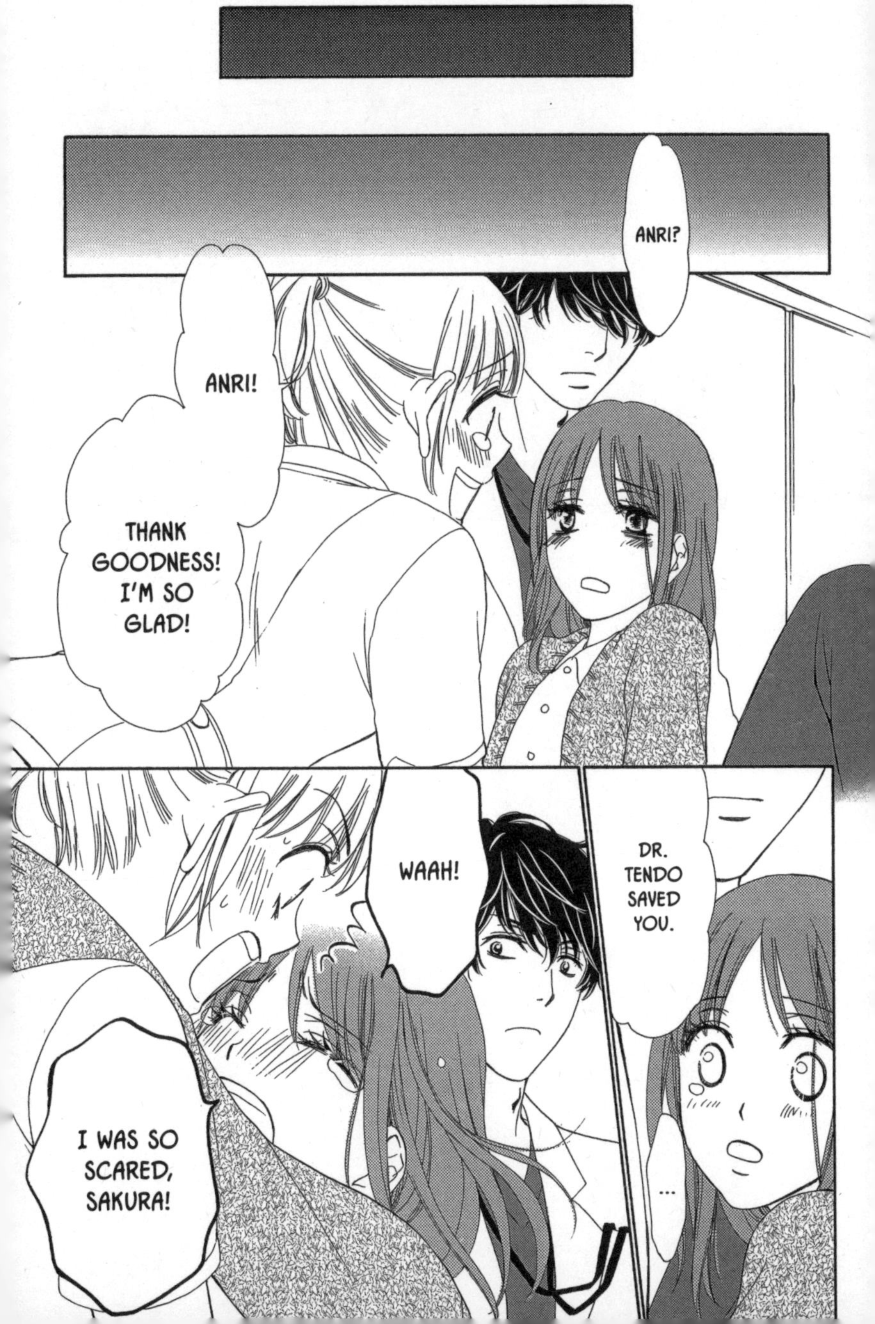
ANRI?
ANRI!
THANK GOODNESS! I'M SO GLAD!
DR. TENDO SAVED YOU.
...
WAAH!
I WAS SO SCARED, SAKURA!

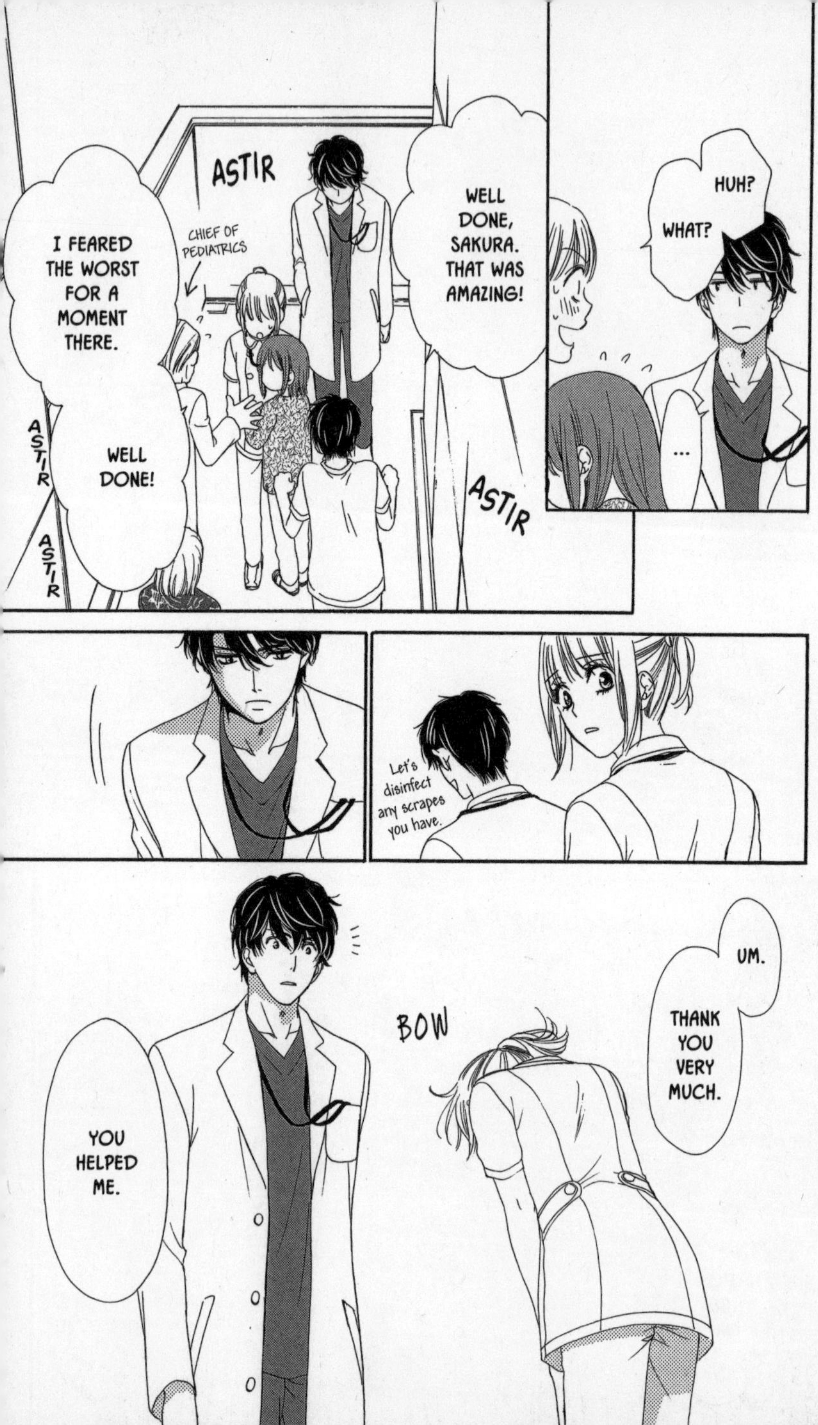
HUH?
WHAT?
...
WELL DONE, SAKURA. THAT WAS AMAZING!
ASTIR
ASTIR
CHIEF OF PEDIATRICS
I FEARED THE WORST FOR A MOMENT THERE.
WELL DONE!
ASTIR
ASTIR
Let's disinfect any scrapes you have.
UM.
THANK YOU VERY MUCH.
BOW
YOU HELPED ME.

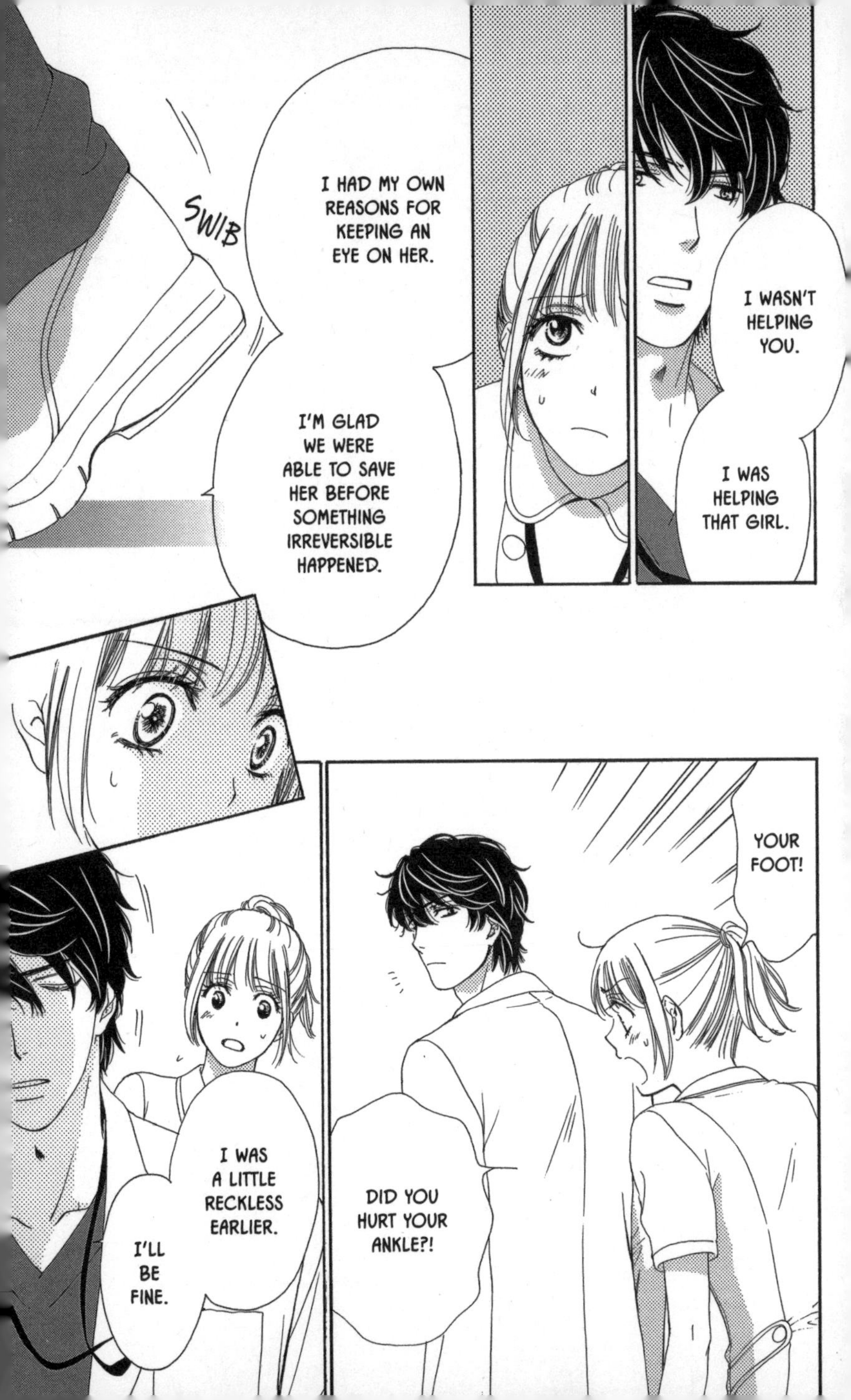
I WASN'T HELPING YOU.
I WAS HELPING THAT GIRL.
SWIB
I HAD MY OWN REASONS FOR KEEPING AN EYE ON HER.
I'M GLAD WE WERE ABLE TO SAVE HER BEFORE SOMETHING IRREVERSIBLE HAPPENED.
YOUR FOOT!
DID YOU HURT YOUR ANKLE?!
I WAS A LITTLE RECKLESS EARLIER.
I'LL BE FINE.

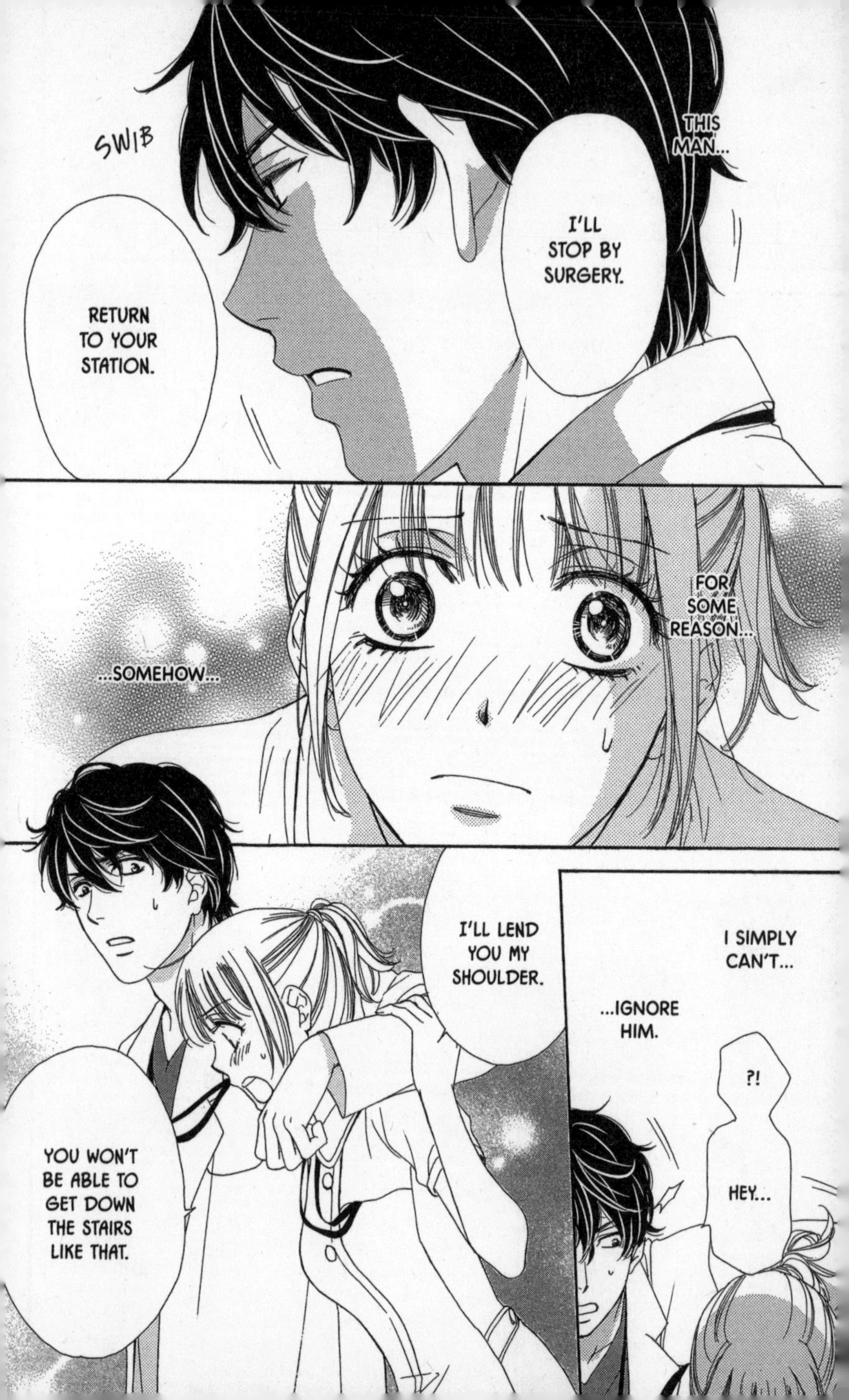
THIS MAN...
I'LL STOP BY SURGERY.
SWIB
RETURN TO YOUR STATION.
FOR SOME REASON...
...SOMEHOW...
I SIMPLY CAN'T...
...IGNORE HIM.
?!
HEY...
I'LL LEND YOU MY SHOULDER.
YOU WON'T BE ABLE TO GET DOWN THE STAIRS LIKE THAT.

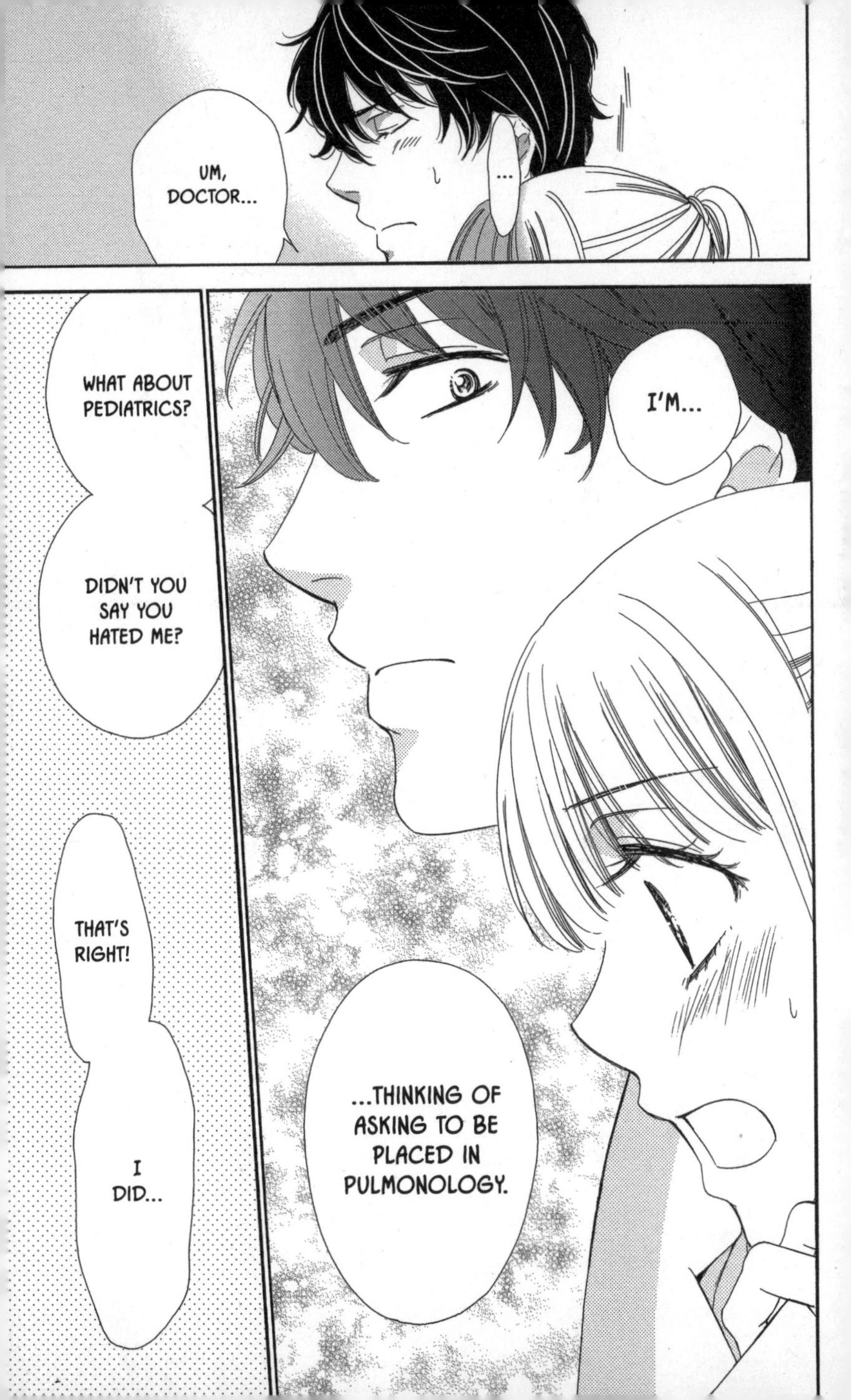
...
UM, DOCTOR...
I'M...
...THINKING OF ASKING TO BE PLACED IN PULMONOLOGY.
WHAT ABOUT PEDIATRICS?
DIDN'T YOU SAY YOU HATED ME?
THAT'S RIGHT!
I DID...

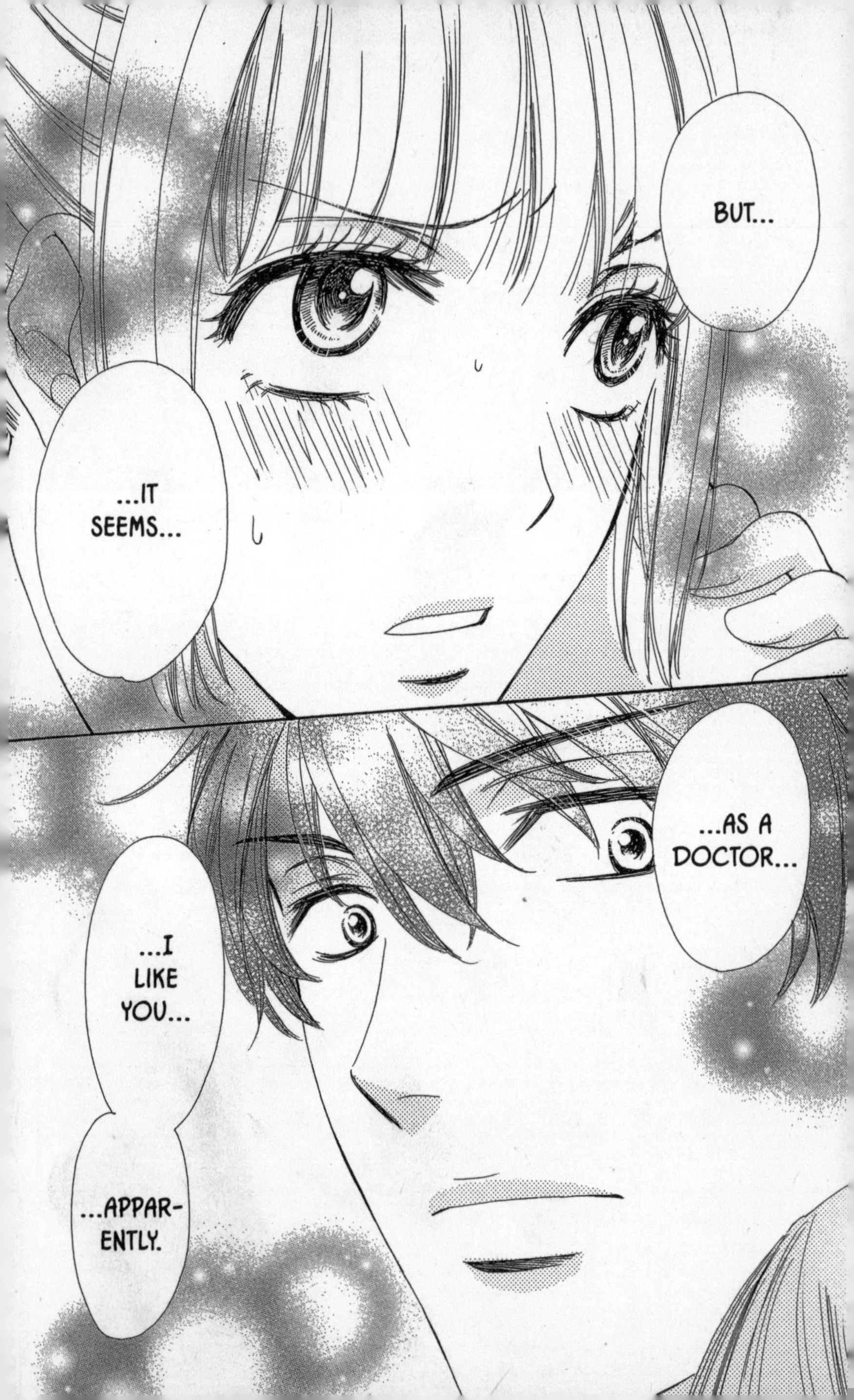
BUT...
...IT SEEMS...
...AS A DOCTOR...
...I LIKE YOU...
...APPARENTLY.

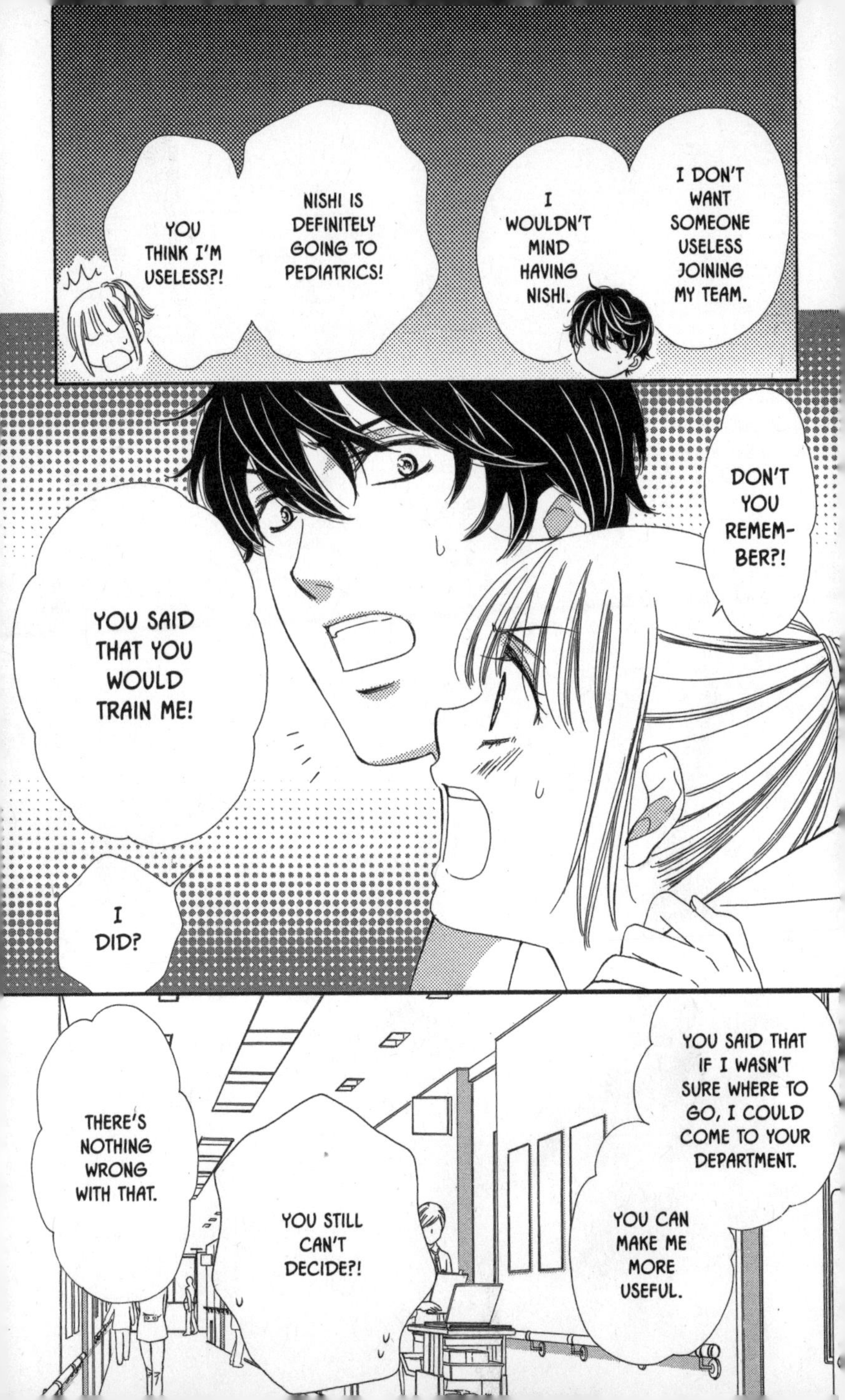
I DON'T WANT SOMEONE USELESS JOINING MY TEAM.
I WOULDN'T MIND HAVING NISHI.
NISHI IS DEFINITELY GOING TO PEDIATRICS!
YOU THINK I'M USELESS?!
DON'T YOU REMEM-BER?!
YOU SAID THAT YOU WOULD TRAIN ME!
I DID?
YOU SAID THAT IF I WASN'T SURE WHERE TO GO, I COULD COME TO YOUR DEPARTMENT.
YOU CAN MAKE ME MORE USEFUL.
YOU STILL CAN'T DECIDE?!
THERE'S NOTHING WRONG WITH THAT.

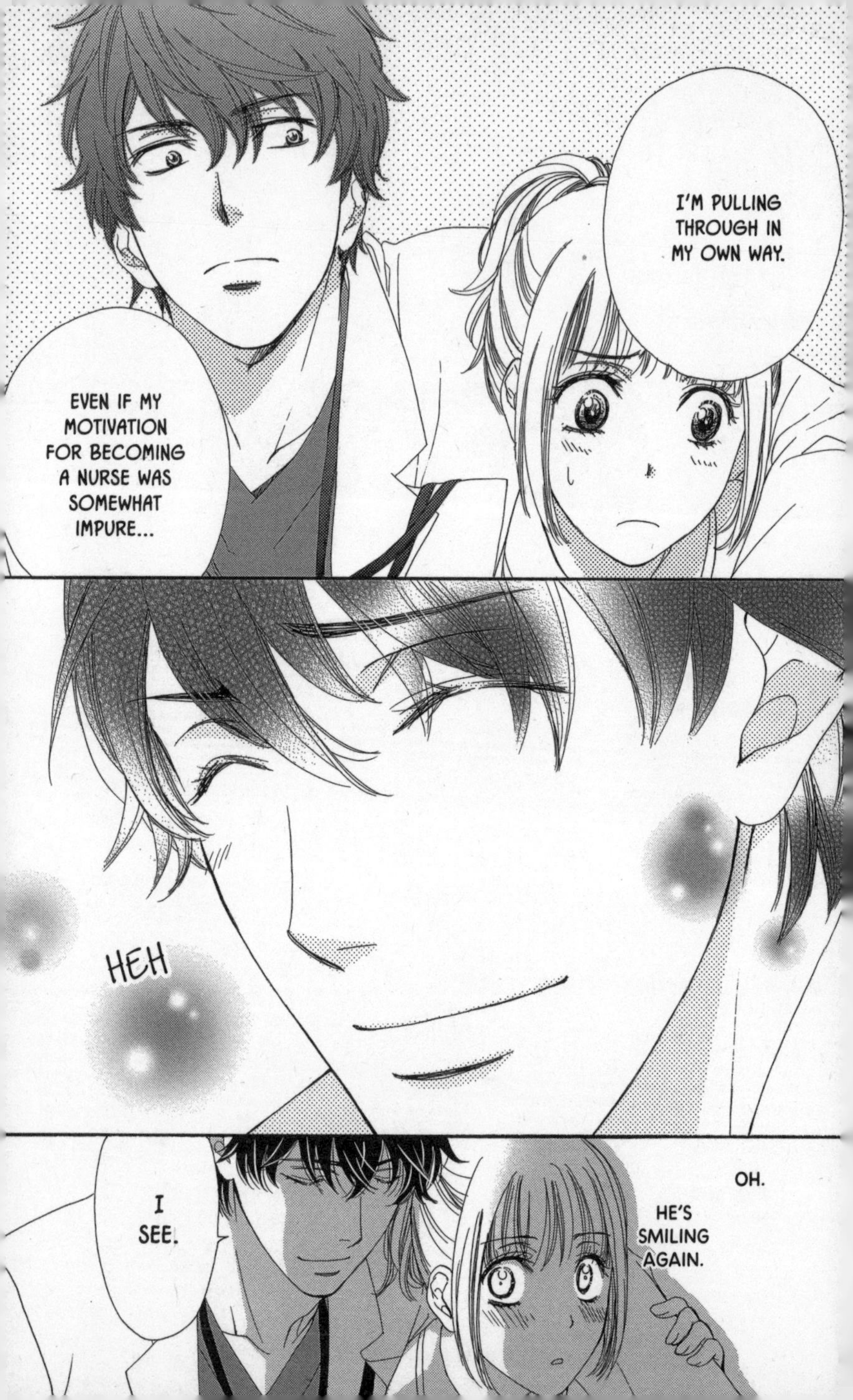
I'M PULLING THROUGH IN MY OWN WAY.
EVEN IF MY MOTIVATION FOR BECOMING A NURSE WAS SOMEWHAT IMPURE...
HEH
OH.
HE'S SMILING AGAIN.
I SEE.

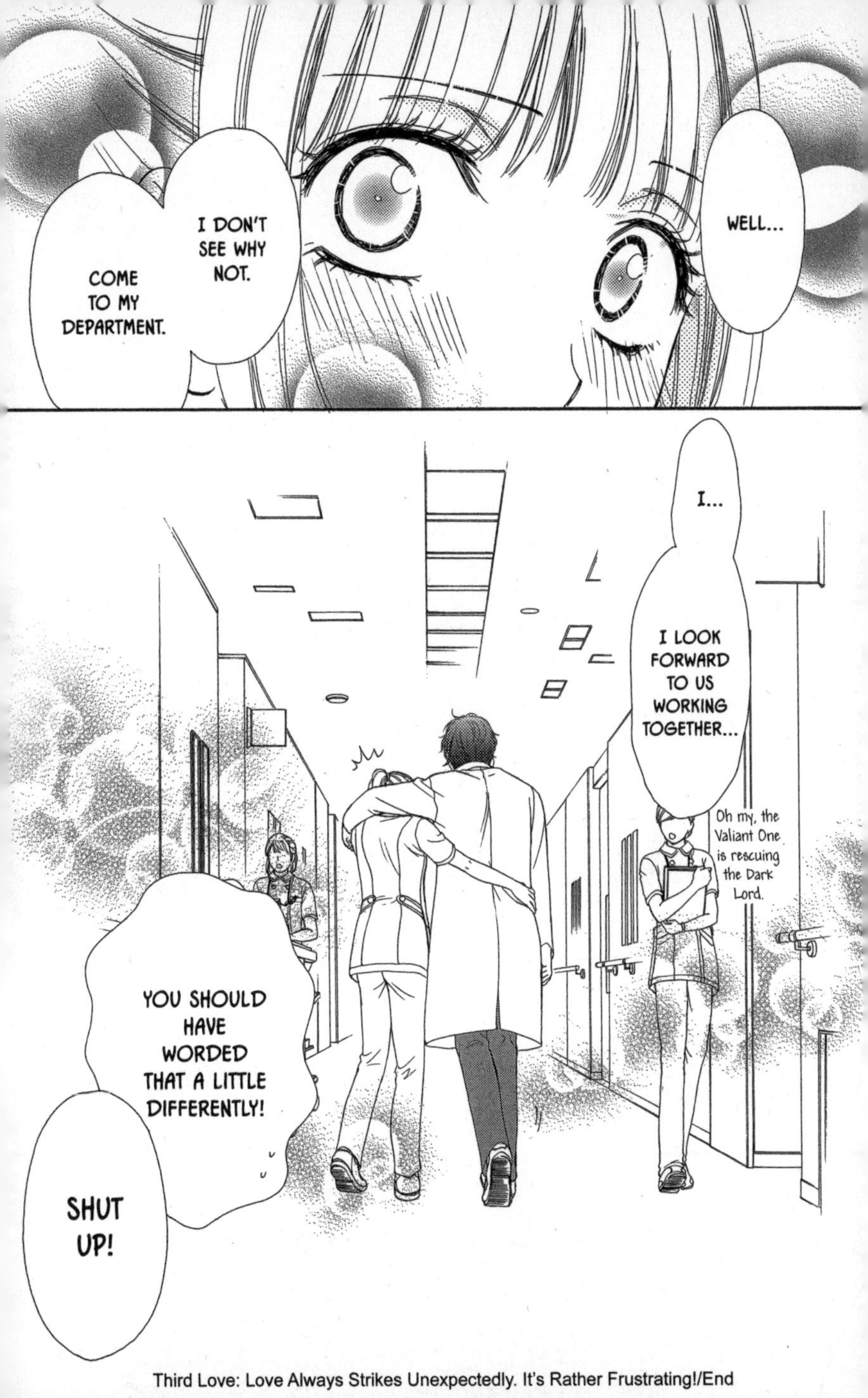
WELL...
I DON'T SEE WHY NOT.
COME TO MY DEPARTMENT.
I...
I LOOK FORWARD TO US WORKING TOGETHER...
Oh my, the Valiant One is rescuing the Dark Lord.
YOU SHOULD HAVE WORDED THAT A LITTLE DIFFERENTLY!
SHUT UP!

Third Love: Love Always Strikes Unexpectedly. It's Rather Frustrating!/End

@ A pair of doctors
Standing next to Tendo is Katagiri from *Happy Marriage?!*
I'm not sure if he'll appear in the story. (*laugh*)

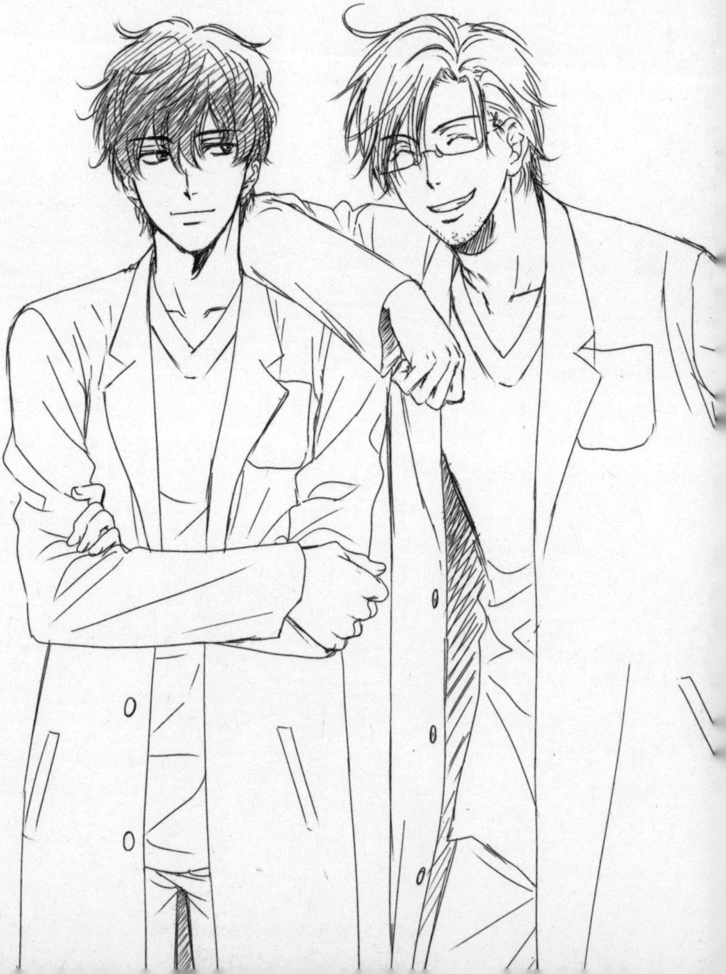

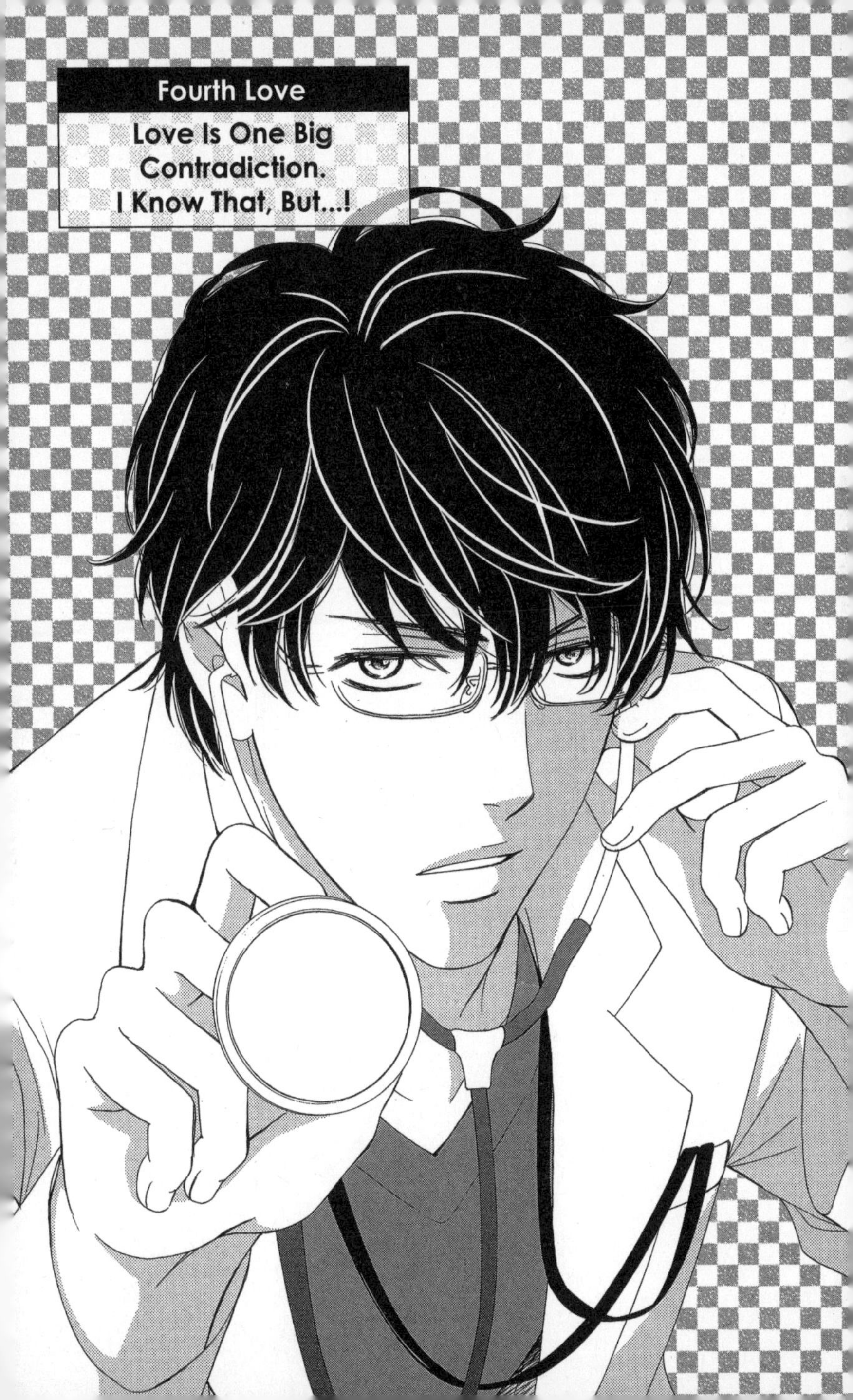
Fourth Love
Love Is One Big Contradiction. I Know That, But...!

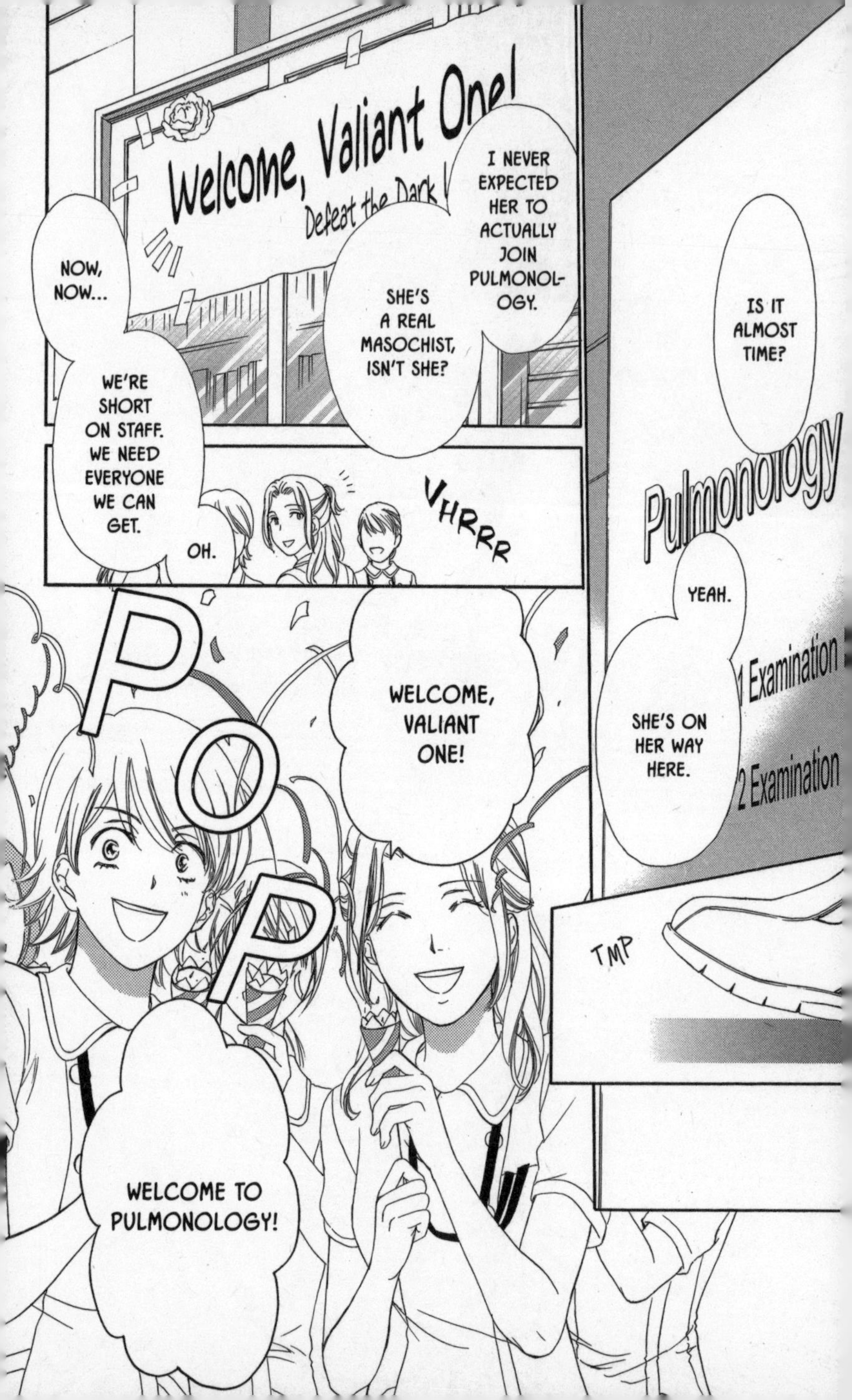
Pulmonology
IS IT ALMOST TIME?
YEAH.
1 Examination
2 Examination
SHE'S ON HER WAY HERE.
Welcome, Valiant One!
Defeat the Dark
I NEVER EXPECTED HER TO ACTUALLY JOIN PULMONOLOGY.
SHE'S A REAL MASOCHIST, ISN'T SHE?
NOW, NOW...
WE'RE SHORT ON STAFF. WE NEED EVERYONE WE CAN GET.
VHRRR
OH.
TMP
POP
WELCOME, VALIANT ONE!
POP
WELCOME TO PULMONOLOGY!

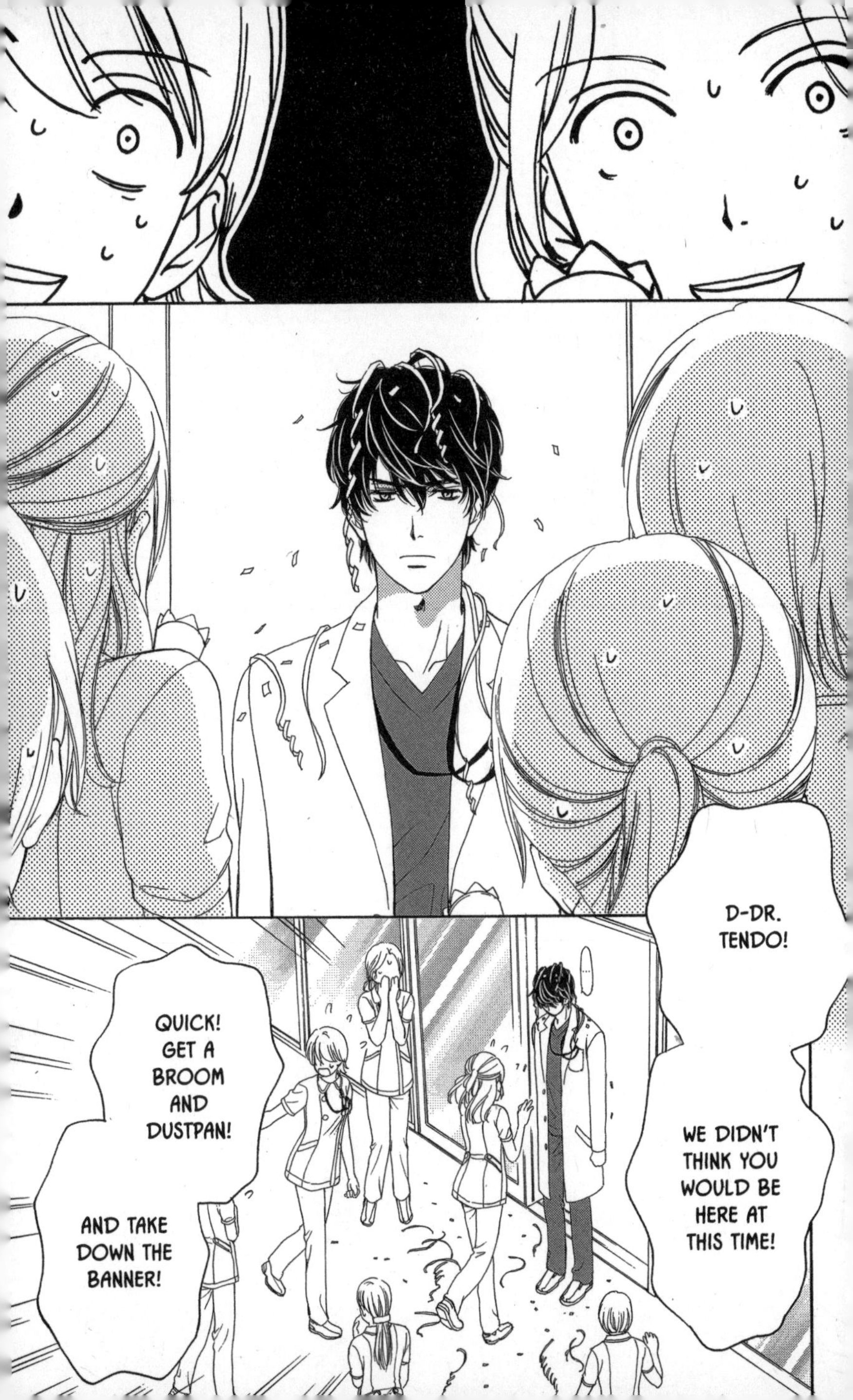
D-DR. TENDO!
WE DIDN'T THINK YOU WOULD BE HERE AT THIS TIME!
...
QUICK! GET A BROOM AND DUSTPAN!
AND TAKE DOWN THE BANNER!

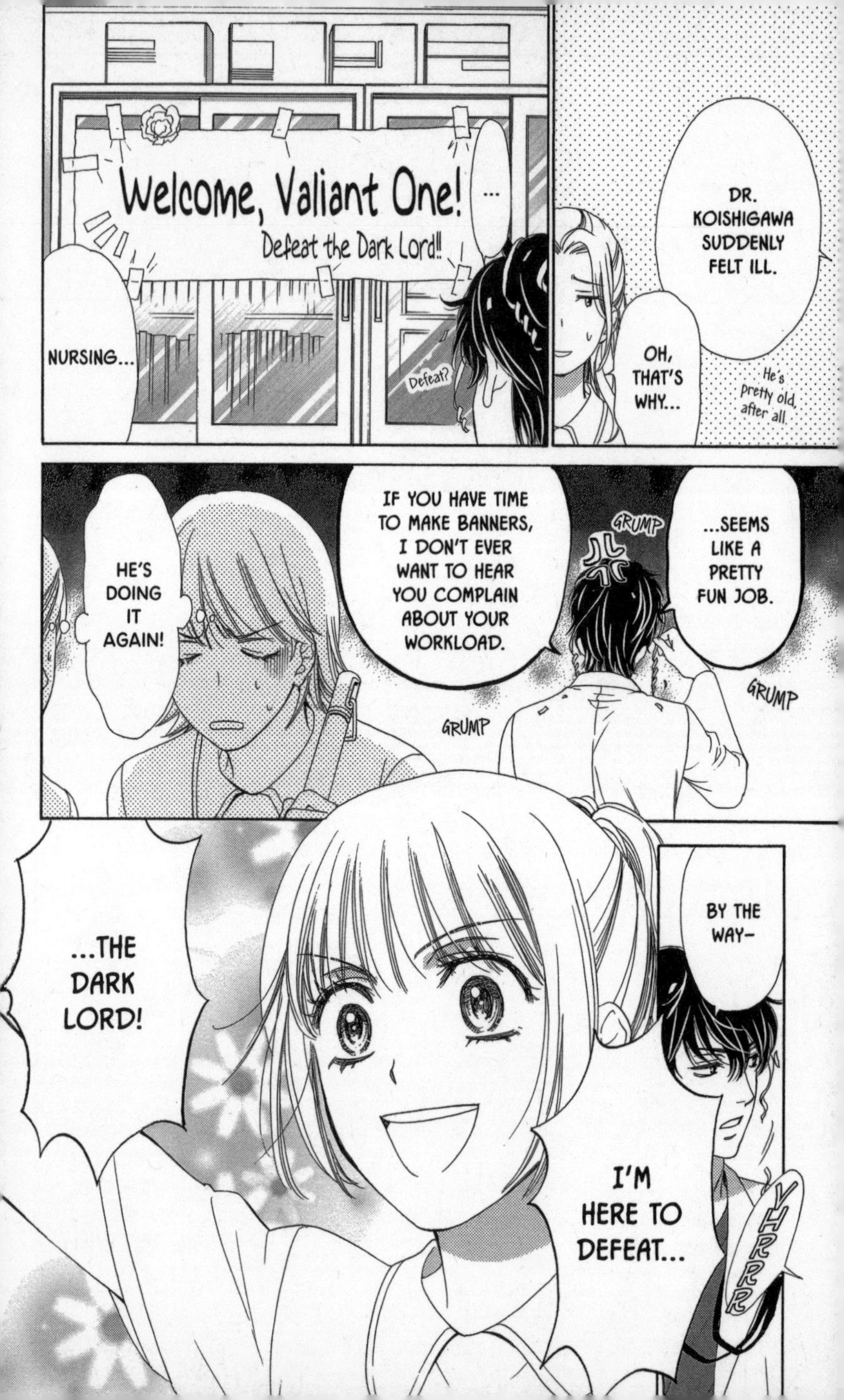
DR. KOISHIGAWA SUDDENLY FELT ILL.
OH, THAT'S WHY...
He's pretty old, after all.
...
Welcome, Valiant One!
Defeat the Dark Lord!!
Defeat?
NURSING...
...SEEMS LIKE A PRETTY FUN JOB.
GRUMP
GRUMP
GRUMP
IF YOU HAVE TIME TO MAKE BANNERS, I DON'T EVER WANT TO HEAR YOU COMPLAIN ABOUT YOUR WORKLOAD.
HE'S DOING IT AGAIN!
BY THE WAY–
VHRRR
I'M HERE TO DEFEAT...
...THE DARK LORD!

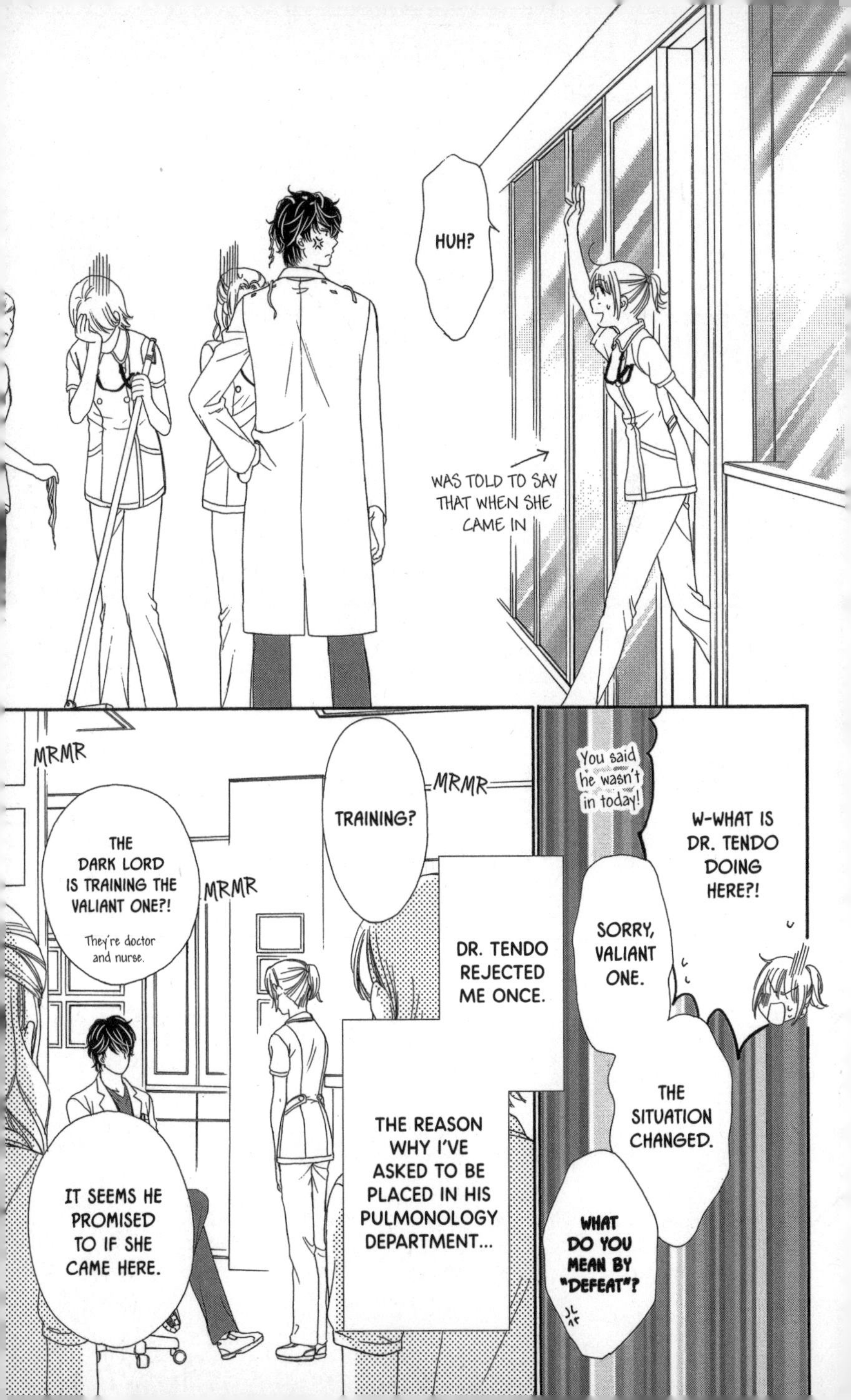
HUH?
WAS TOLD TO SAY THAT WHEN SHE CAME IN
W-WHAT IS DR. TENDO DOING HERE?!
You said he wasn't in today!
SORRY, VALIANT ONE.
THE SITUATION CHANGED.
WHAT DO YOU MEAN BY "DEFEAT"?
MRMR
TRAINING?
DR. TENDO REJECTED ME ONCE.
THE REASON WHY I'VE ASKED TO BE PLACED IN HIS PULMONOLOGY DEPARTMENT...
MRMR
THE DARK LORD IS TRAINING THE VALIANT ONE?!
They're doctor and nurse.
MRMR
IT SEEMS HE PROMISED TO IF SHE CAME HERE.

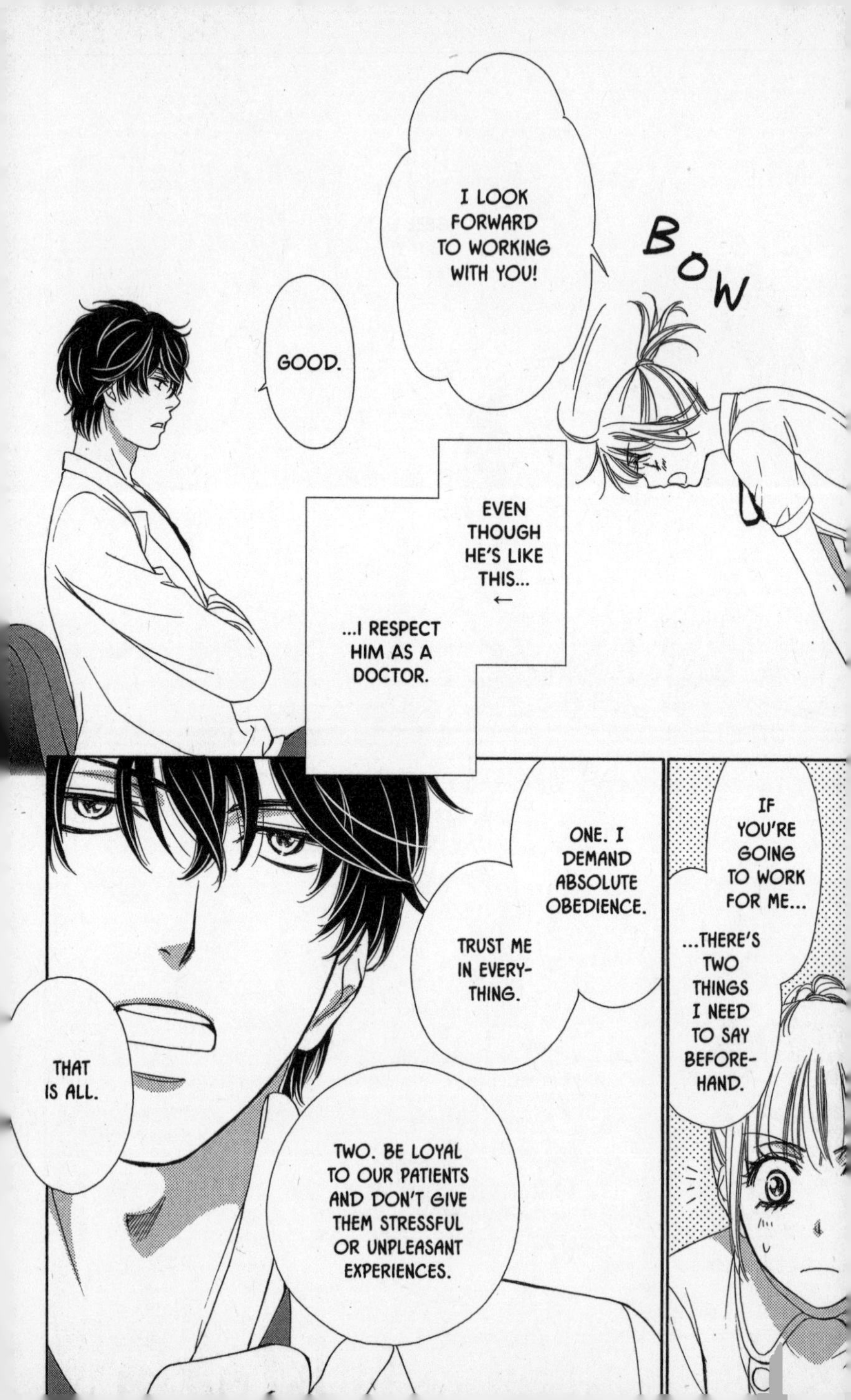
BOW
I LOOK FORWARD TO WORKING WITH YOU!
GOOD.
EVEN THOUGH HE'S LIKE THIS... ←
...I RESPECT HIM AS A DOCTOR.
IF YOU'RE GOING TO WORK FOR ME...
...THERE'S TWO THINGS I NEED TO SAY BEFOREHAND.
ONE. I DEMAND ABSOLUTE OBEDIENCE.
TRUST ME IN EVERYTHING.
TWO. BE LOYAL TO OUR PATIENTS AND DON'T GIVE THEM STRESSFUL OR UNPLEASANT EXPERIENCES.
THAT IS ALL.

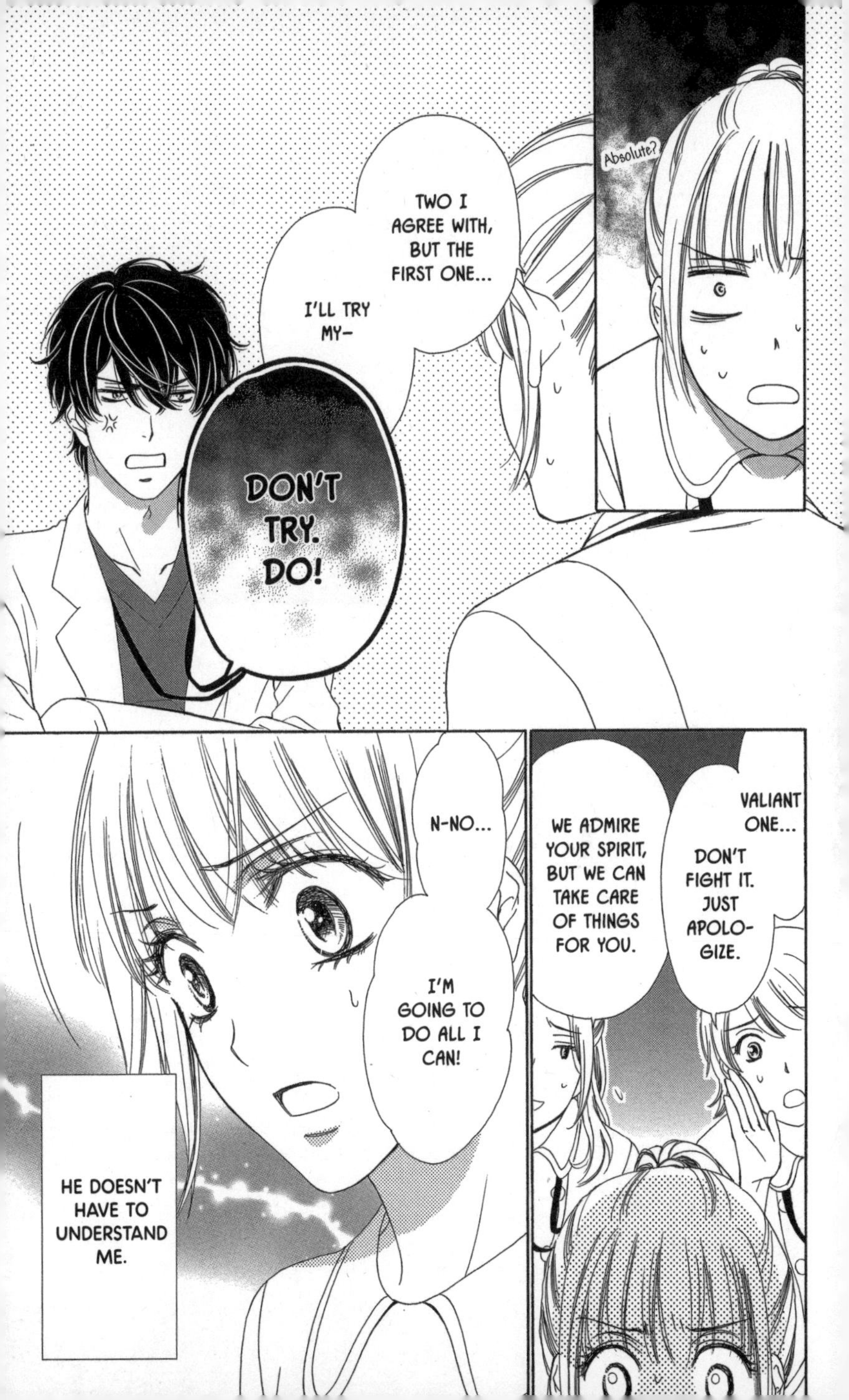
Absolute?
TWO I AGREE WITH, BUT THE FIRST ONE...
I'LL TRY MY—
DON'T TRY. DO!
VALIANT ONE... DON'T FIGHT IT. JUST APOLO-GIZE.
WE ADMIRE YOUR SPIRIT, BUT WE CAN TAKE CARE OF THINGS FOR YOU.
N-NO...
I'M GOING TO DO ALL I CAN!
HE DOESN'T HAVE TO UNDERSTAND ME.

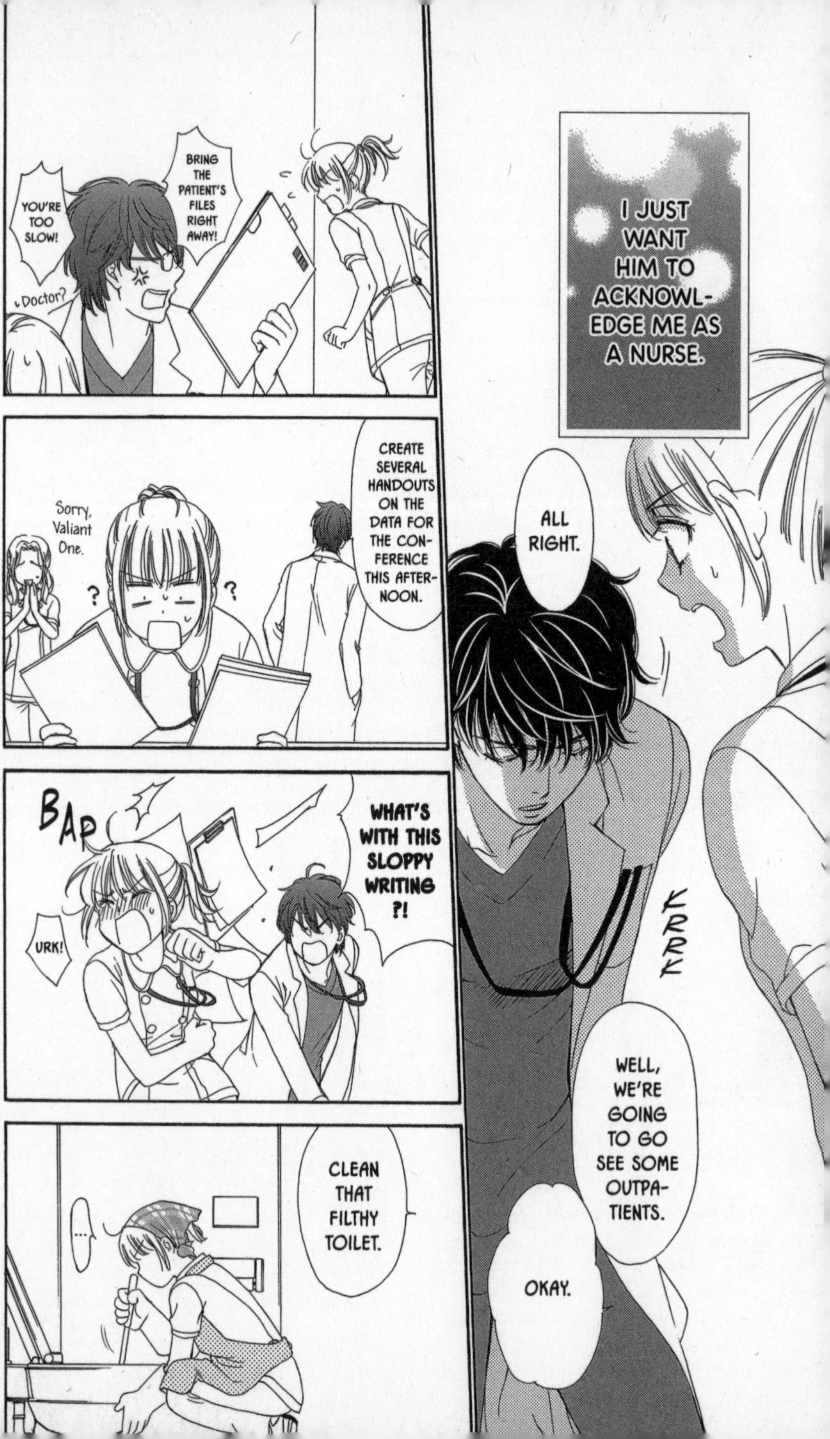
I JUST WANT HIM TO ACKNOWLEDGE ME AS A NURSE.
ALL RIGHT.
KRRK
WELL, WE'RE GOING TO GO SEE SOME OUTPATIENTS.
OKAY.
BRING THE PATIENT'S FILES RIGHT AWAY!
YOU'RE TOO SLOW!
Doctor?
CREATE SEVERAL HANDOUTS ON THE DATA FOR THE CONFERENCE THIS AFTERNOON.
?
?
Sorry, Valiant One.
WHAT'S WITH THIS SLOPPY WRITING?!
BAP
URK!
CLEAN THAT FILTHY TOILET.
...

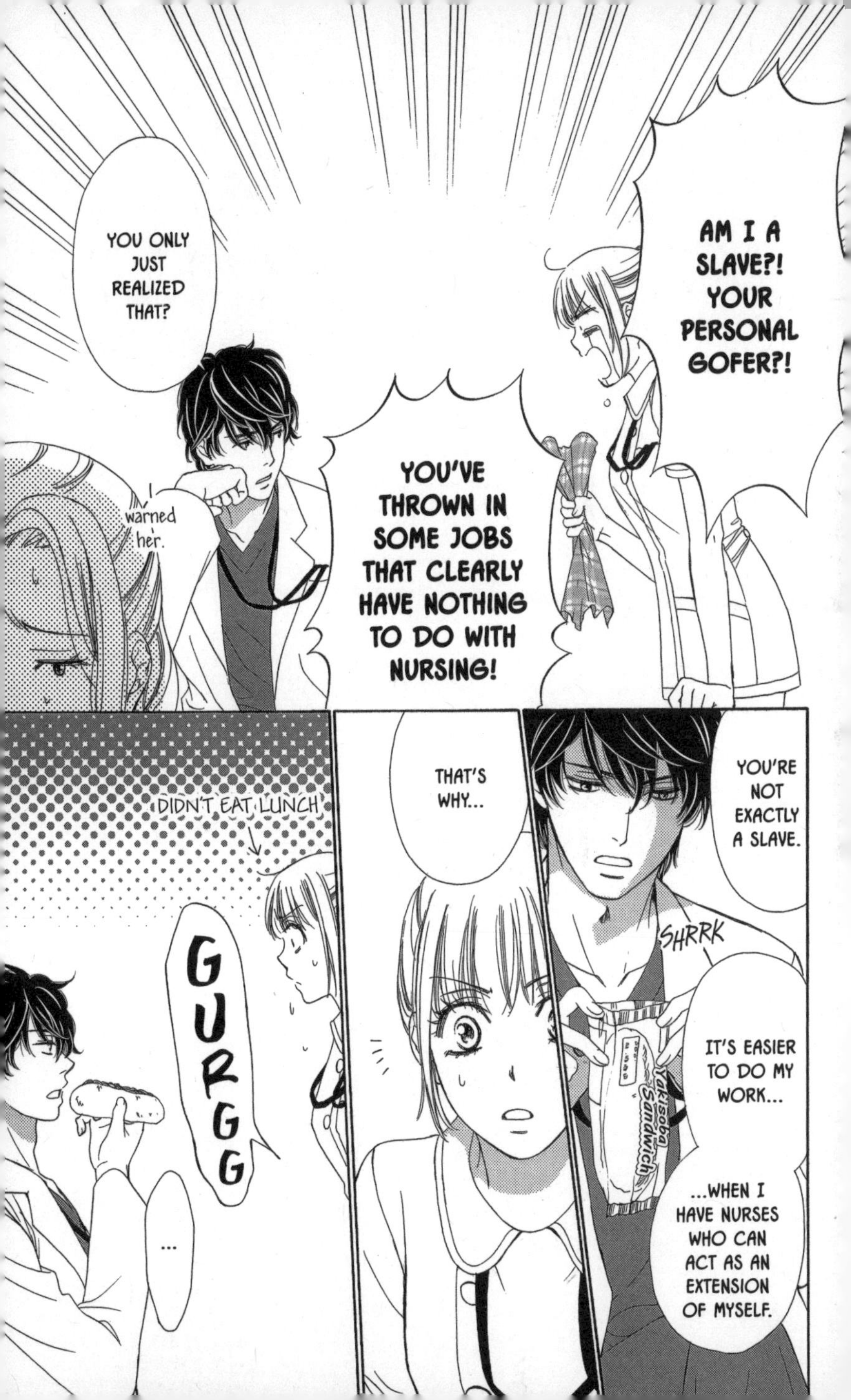
AM I A SLAVE?! YOUR PERSONAL GOFER?!
YOU'VE THROWN IN SOME JOBS THAT CLEARLY HAVE NOTHING TO DO WITH NURSING!
YOU ONLY JUST REALIZED THAT?
I warned her.
YOU'RE NOT EXACTLY A SLAVE.
SHRRK
IT'S EASIER TO DO MY WORK...
...WHEN I HAVE NURSES WHO CAN ACT AS AN EXTENSION OF MYSELF.
Yakisoba Sandwich
THAT'S WHY...
DIDN'T EAT LUNCH
GURGG
...

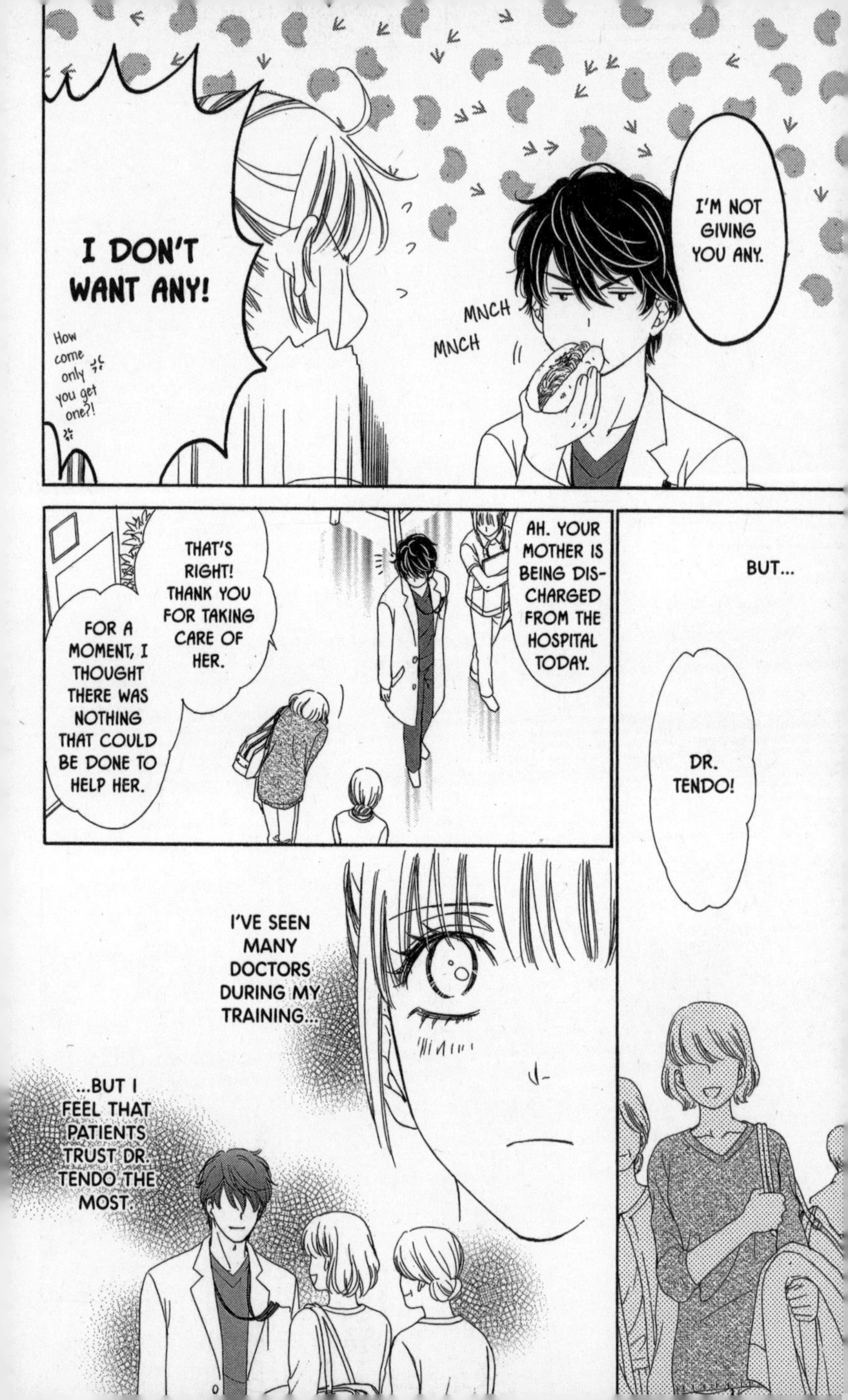
I'M NOT GIVING YOU ANY.
MNCH
MNCH
I DON'T WANT ANY!
How come only you get one?!
BUT...
DR. TENDO!
AH. YOUR MOTHER IS BEING DISCHARGED FROM THE HOSPITAL TODAY.
THAT'S RIGHT! THANK YOU FOR TAKING CARE OF HER.
FOR A MOMENT, I THOUGHT THERE WAS NOTHING THAT COULD BE DONE TO HELP HER.
I'VE SEEN MANY DOCTORS DURING MY TRAINING...
...BUT I FEEL THAT PATIENTS TRUST DR. TENDO THE MOST.

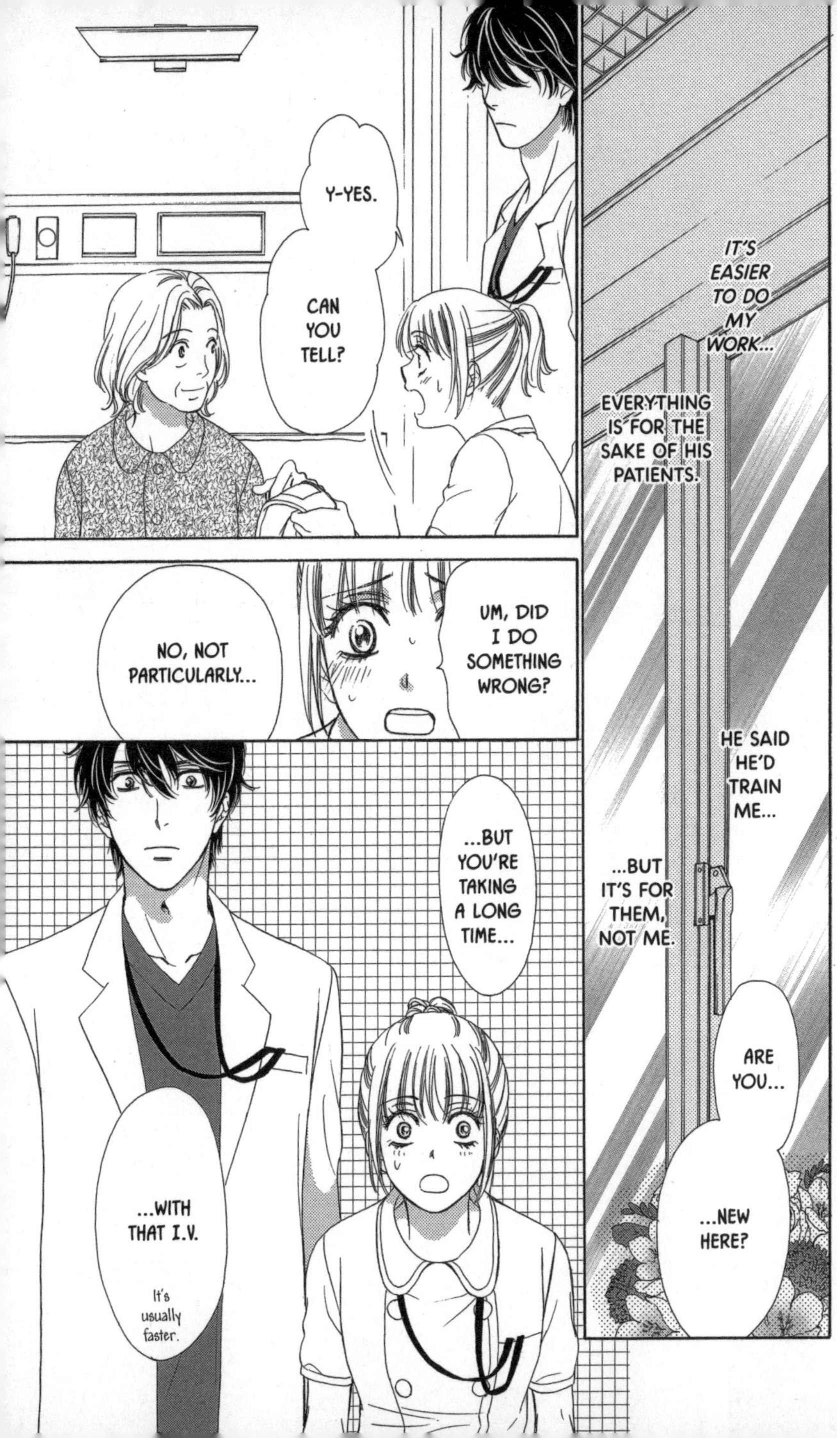
IT'S EASIER TO DO MY WORK...
EVERYTHING IS FOR THE SAKE OF HIS PATIENTS.
HE SAID HE'D TRAIN ME...
...BUT IT'S FOR THEM, NOT ME.
ARE YOU...
...NEW HERE?
Y-YES.
CAN YOU TELL?
UM, DID I DO SOMETHING WRONG?
NO, NOT PARTICULARLY...
...BUT YOU'RE TAKING A LONG TIME...
...WITH THAT I.V.
It's usually faster.

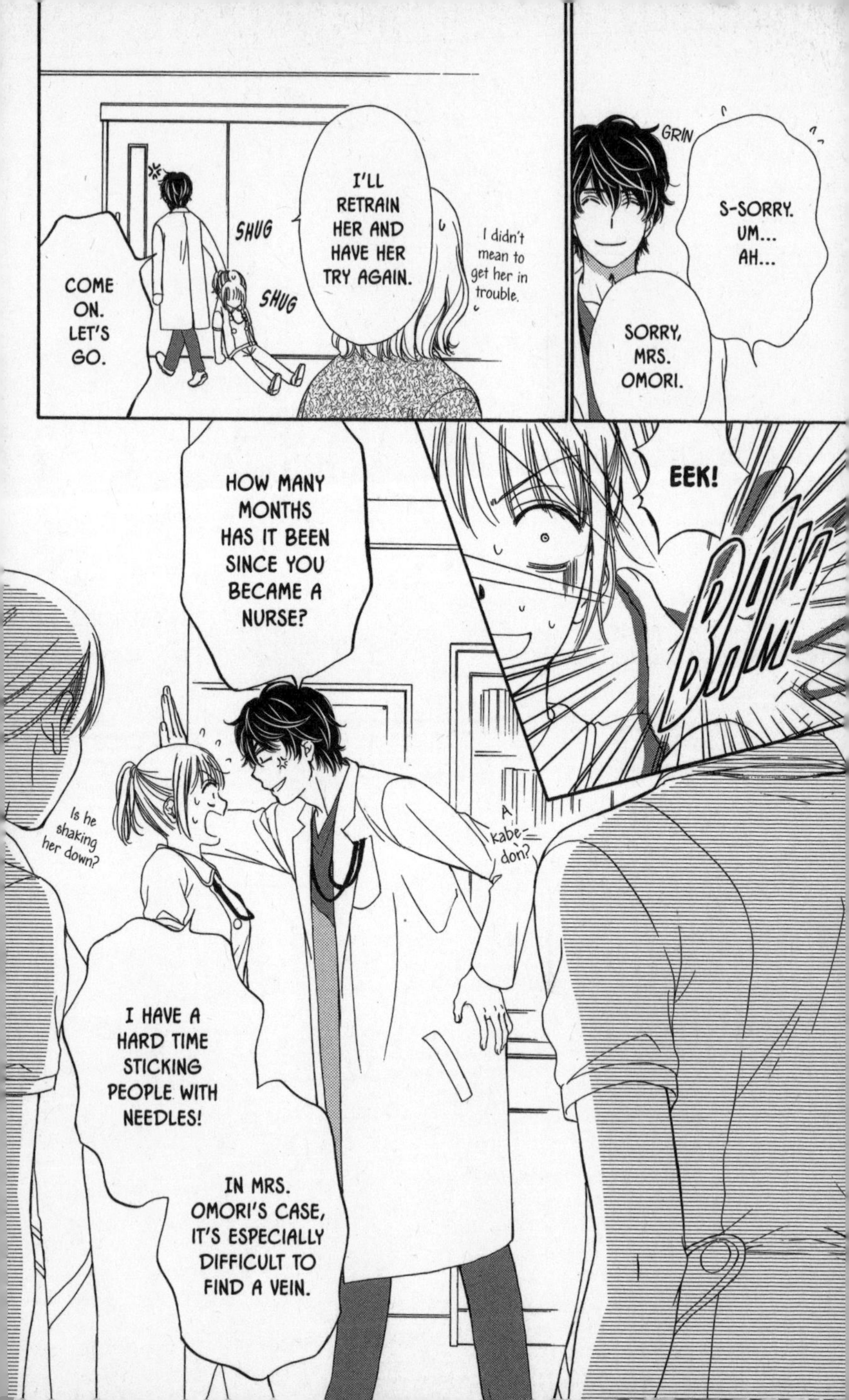

S-SORRY. UM... AH...
GRIN
SORRY, MRS. OMORI.
I'LL RETRAIN HER AND HAVE HER TRY AGAIN.
I didn't mean to get her in trouble.
SHUG
SHUG
COME ON. LET'S GO.
EEK!
BAM
HOW MANY MONTHS HAS IT BEEN SINCE YOU BECAME A NURSE?
A kabe-don?
Is he shaking her down?
I HAVE A HARD TIME STICKING PEOPLE WITH NEEDLES!
IN MRS. OMORI'S CASE, IT'S ESPECIALLY DIFFICULT TO FIND A VEIN.

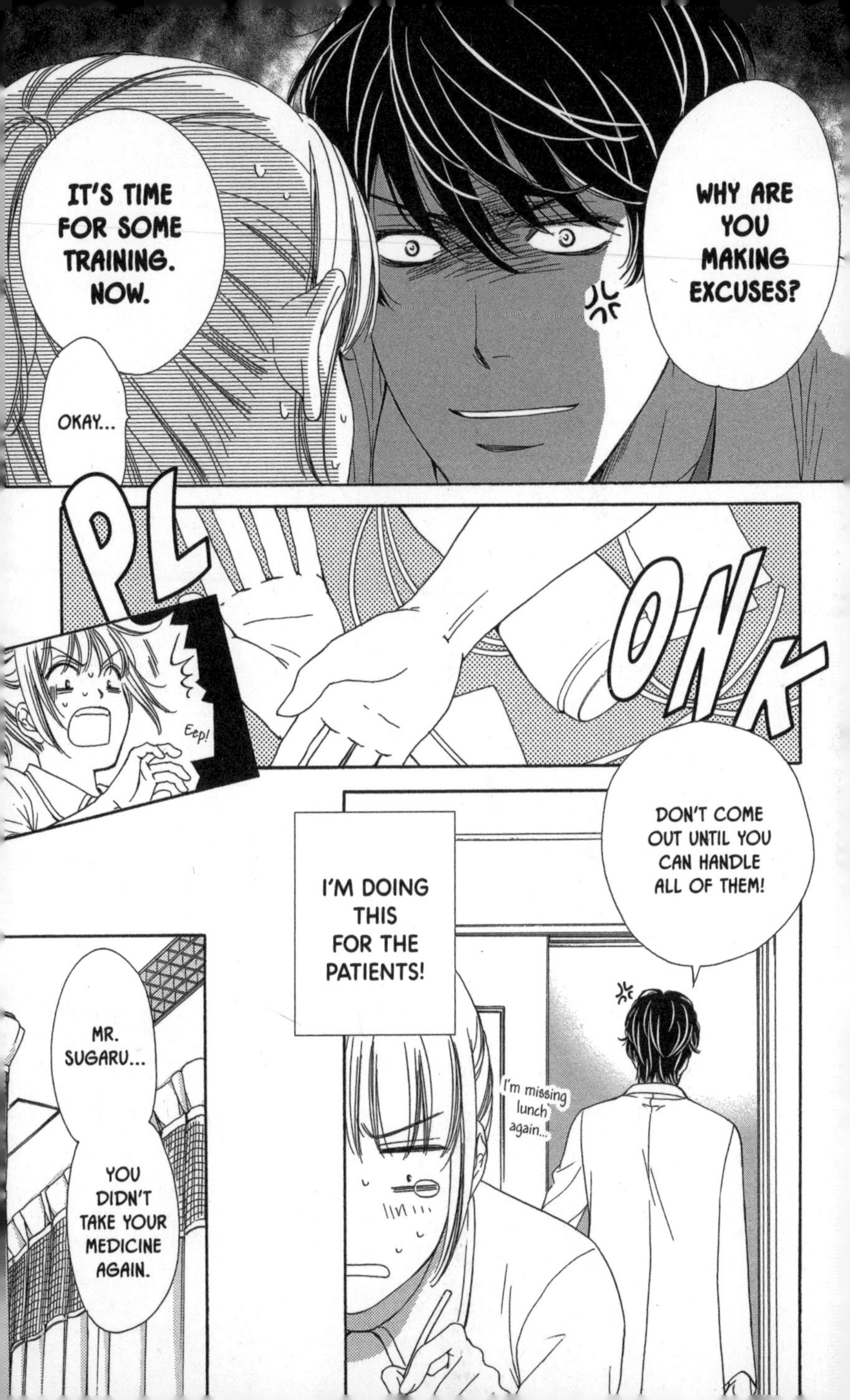
WHY ARE YOU MAKING EXCUSES?
IT'S TIME FOR SOME TRAINING. NOW.
OKAY...
PLONK
Eep!
DON'T COME OUT UNTIL YOU CAN HANDLE ALL OF THEM!
I'M DOING THIS FOR THE PATIENTS!
I'm missing lunch again...
MR. SUGARU...
YOU DIDN'T TAKE YOUR MEDICINE AGAIN.

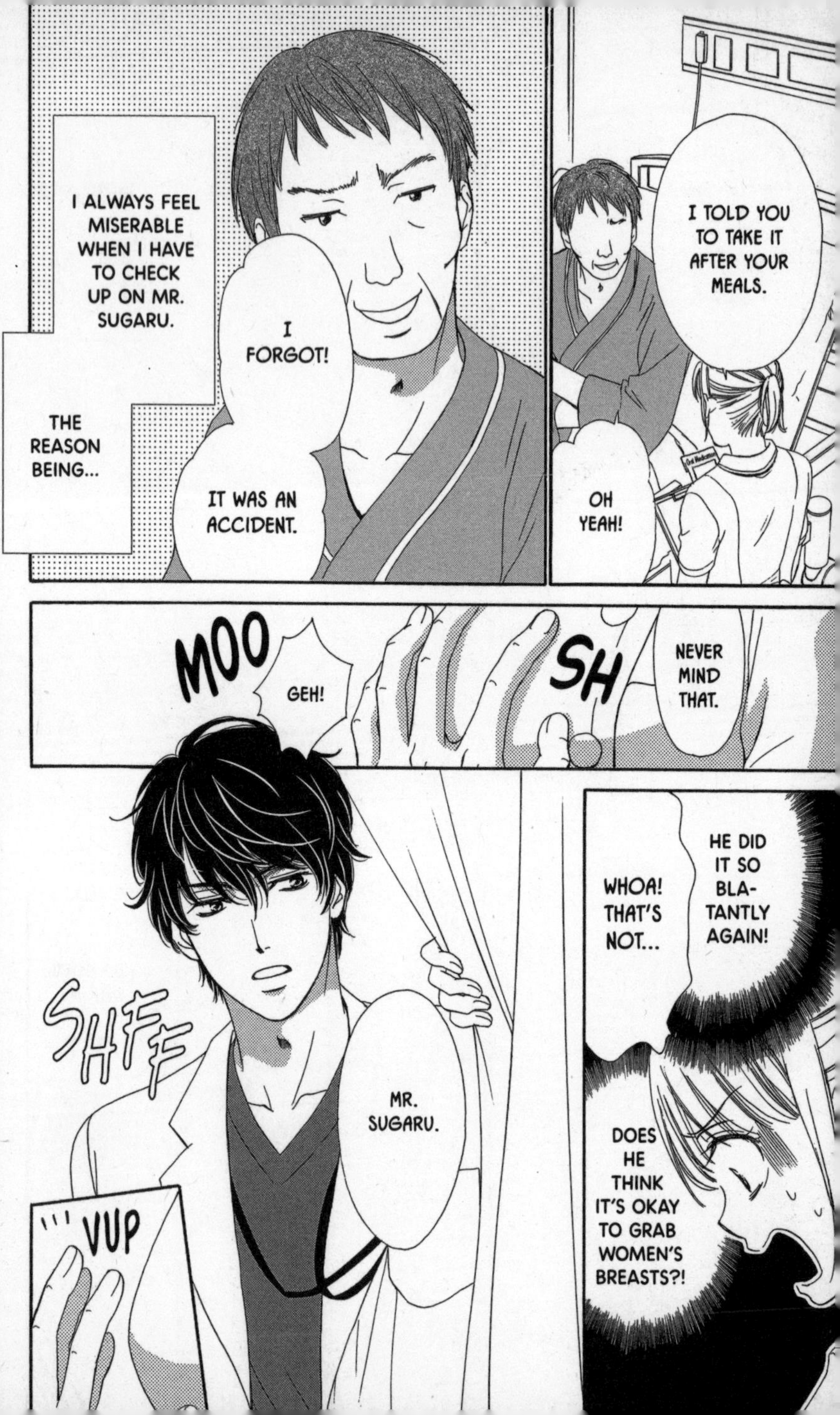
I TOLD YOU TO TAKE IT AFTER YOUR MEALS.
OH YEAH!
I ALWAYS FEEL MISERABLE WHEN I HAVE TO CHECK UP ON MR. SUGARU.
THE REASON BEING...
I FORGOT!
IT WAS AN ACCIDENT.
NEVER MIND THAT.
MOO
SH
GEH!
HE DID IT SO BLA-TANTLY AGAIN!
WHOA! THAT'S NOT...
DOES HE THINK IT'S OKAY TO GRAB WOMEN'S BREASTS?!
MR. SUGARU.
SHFF
VUP

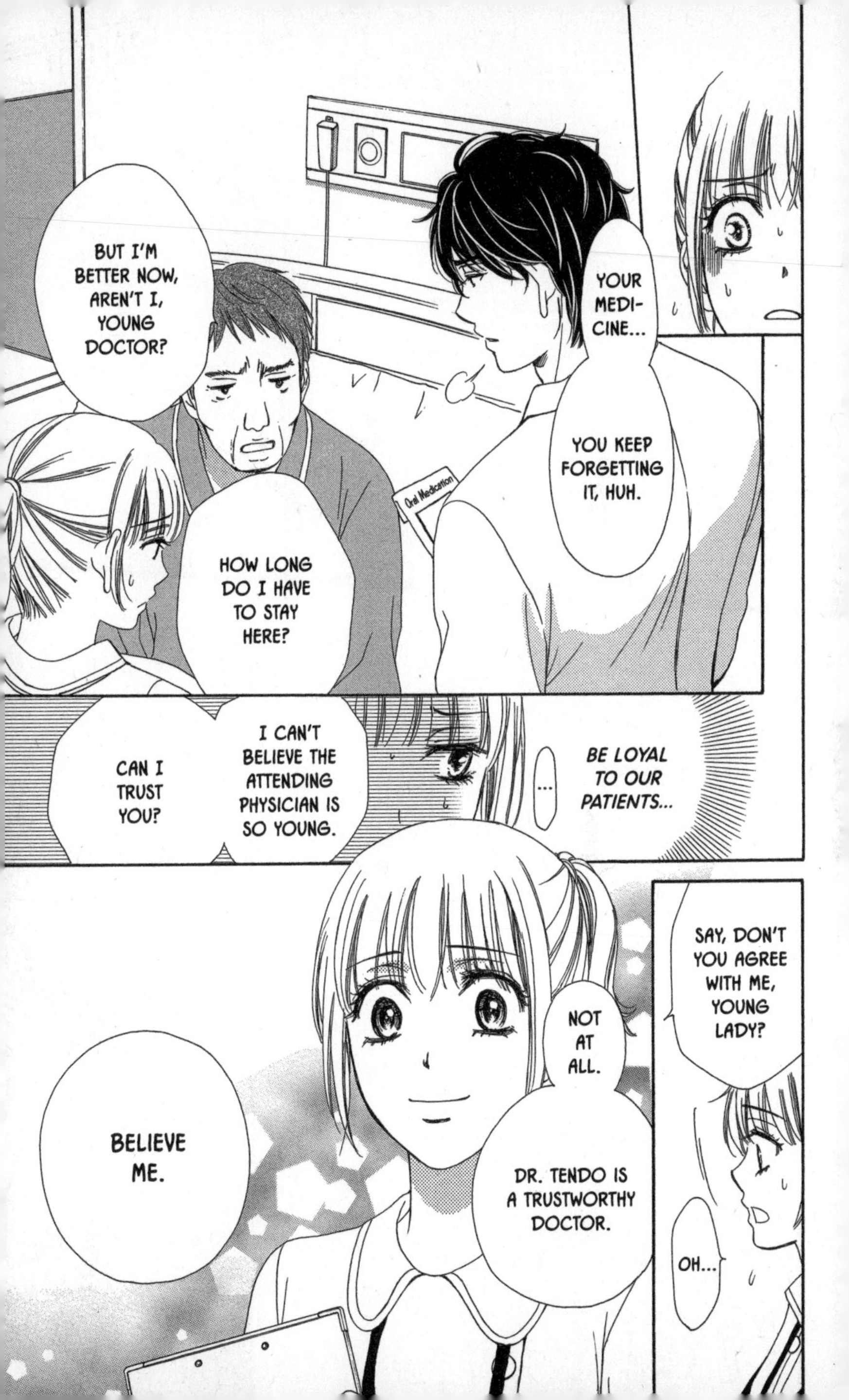
YOUR MEDICINE...
YOU KEEP FORGETTING IT, HUH.
BUT I'M BETTER NOW, AREN'T I, YOUNG DOCTOR?
HOW LONG DO I HAVE TO STAY HERE?
BE LOYAL TO OUR PATIENTS...
...
I CAN'T BELIEVE THE ATTENDING PHYSICIAN IS SO YOUNG.
CAN I TRUST YOU?
SAY, DON'T YOU AGREE WITH ME, YOUNG LADY?
OH...
NOT AT ALL.
DR. TENDO IS A TRUSTWORTHY DOCTOR.
BELIEVE ME.

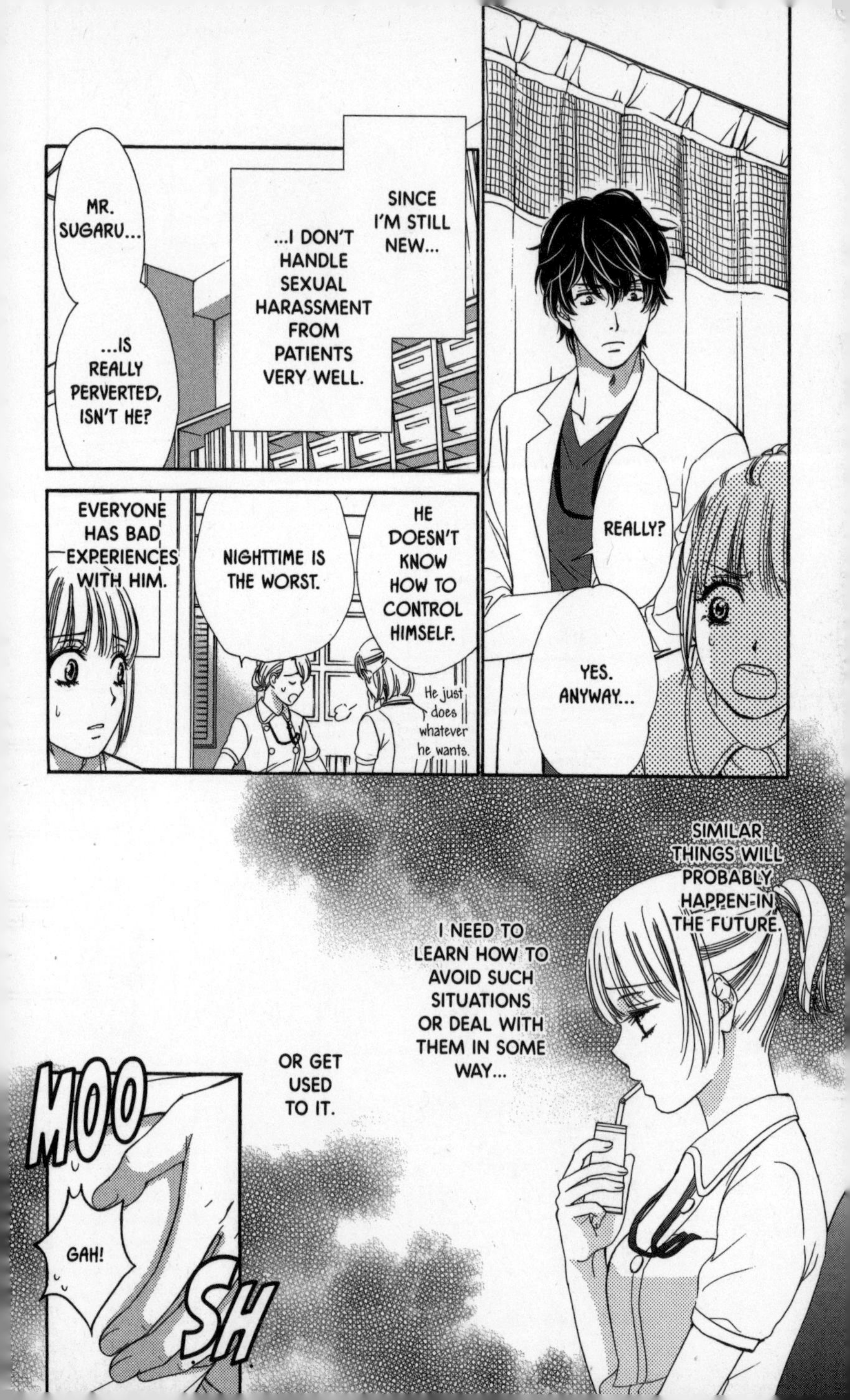
REALLY?
YES. ANYWAY...
SINCE I'M STILL NEW...
...I DON'T HANDLE SEXUAL HARASSMENT FROM PATIENTS VERY WELL.
MR. SUGARU...
...IS REALLY PERVERTED, ISN'T HE?
HE DOESN'T KNOW HOW TO CONTROL HIMSELF.
He just does whatever he wants.
NIGHTTIME IS THE WORST.
EVERYONE HAS BAD EXPERIENCES WITH HIM.
SIMILAR THINGS WILL PROBABLY HAPPEN IN THE FUTURE.
I NEED TO LEARN HOW TO AVOID SUCH SITUATIONS OR DEAL WITH THEM IN SOME WAY...
OR GET USED TO IT.
MOO
SH
GAH!

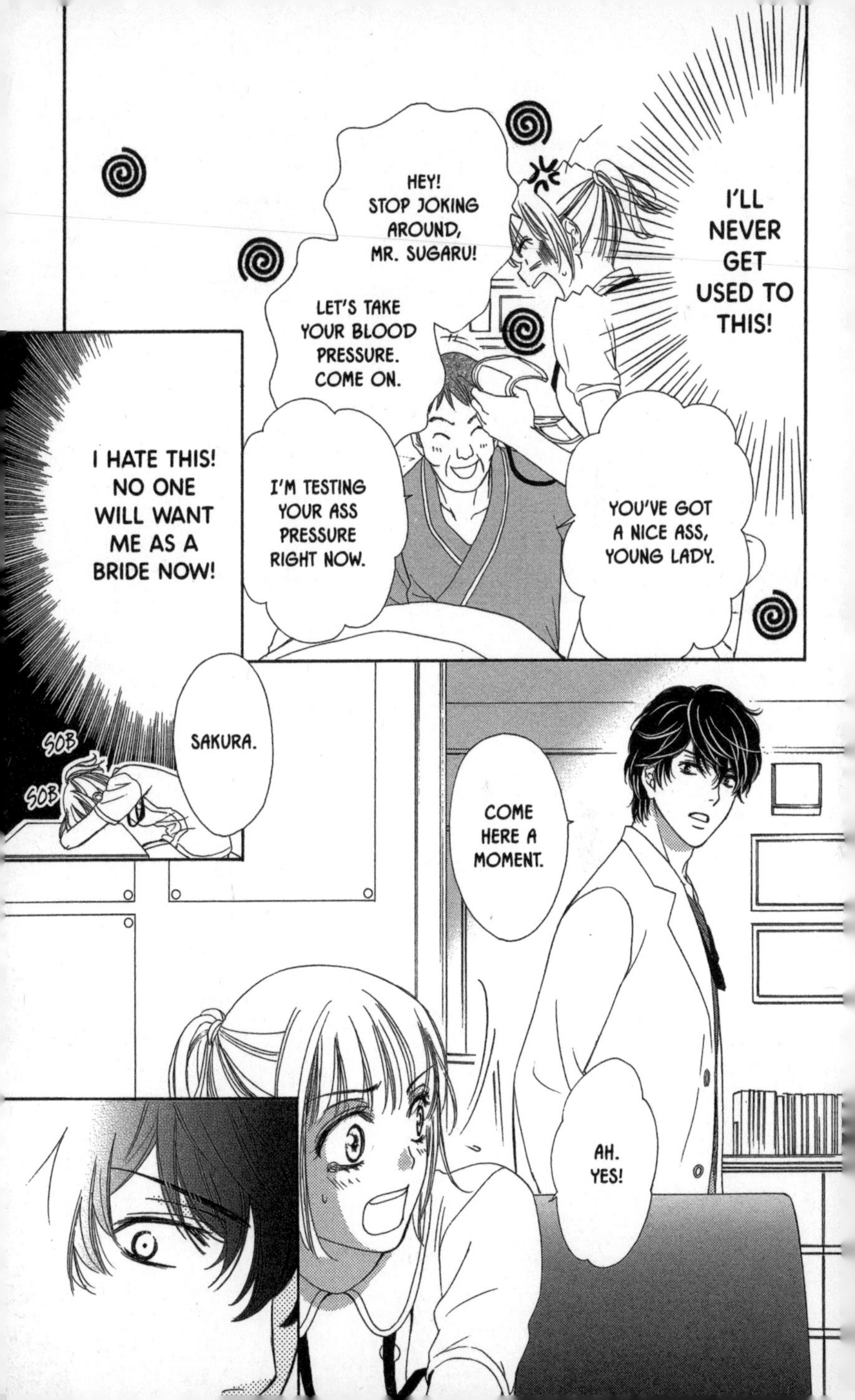
I'LL NEVER GET USED TO THIS!
HEY! STOP JOKING AROUND, MR. SUGARU!
LET'S TAKE YOUR BLOOD PRESSURE. COME ON.
YOU'VE GOT A NICE ASS, YOUNG LADY.
I'M TESTING YOUR ASS PRESSURE RIGHT NOW.
I HATE THIS! NO ONE WILL WANT ME AS A BRIDE NOW!
SOB
SOB
SAKURA.
COME HERE A MOMENT.
AH. YES!

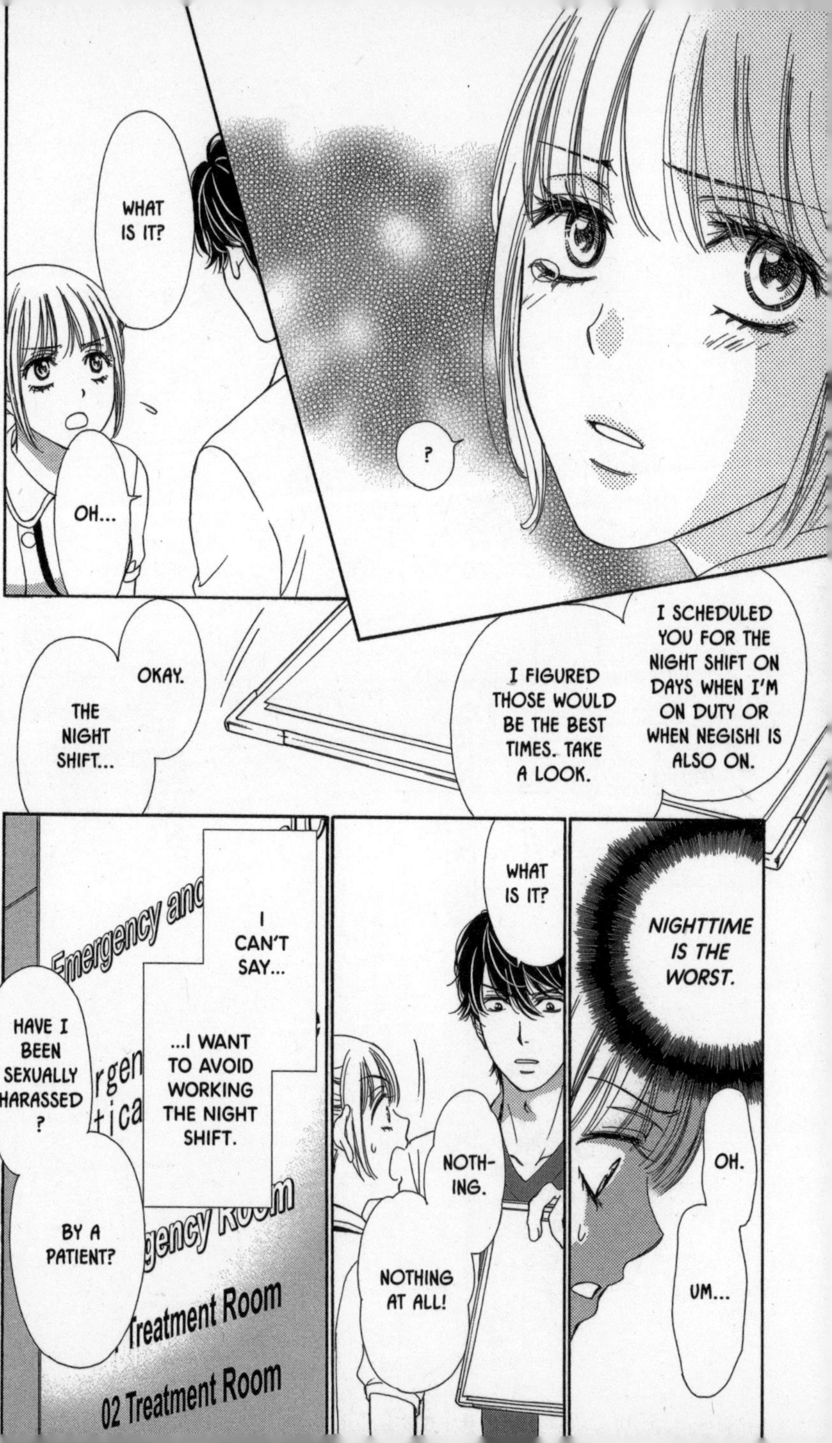
?
WHAT IS IT?
OH...
I SCHEDULED YOU FOR THE NIGHT SHIFT ON DAYS WHEN I'M ON DUTY OR WHEN NEGISHI IS ALSO ON.
I FIGURED THOSE WOULD BE THE BEST TIMES. TAKE A LOOK.
OKAY.
THE NIGHT SHIFT...
NIGHTTIME IS THE WORST.
OH.
UM...
WHAT IS IT?
NOTHING.
NOTHING AT ALL!
I CAN'T SAY...
...I WANT TO AVOID WORKING THE NIGHT SHIFT.
HAVE I BEEN SEXUALLY HARASSED?
BY A PATIENT?
Emergency and
Treatment Room
02 Treatment Room

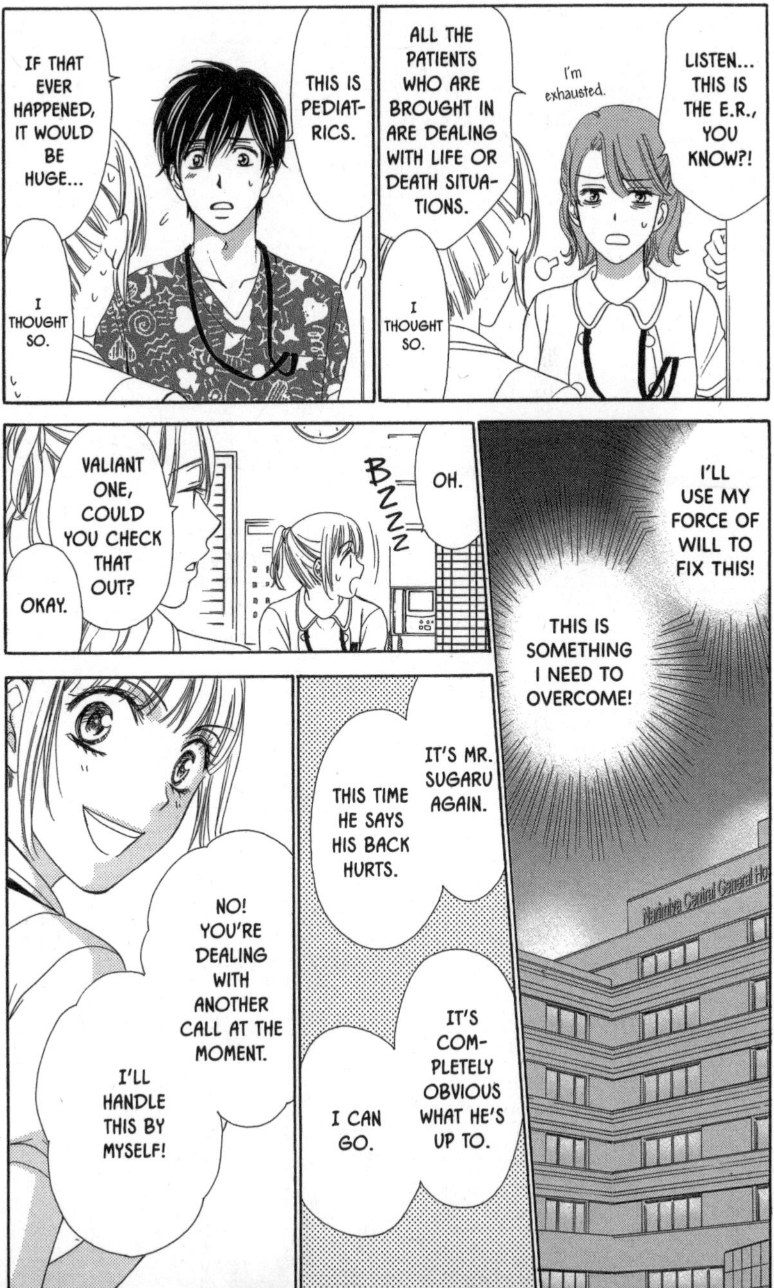
LISTEN... THIS IS THE E.R., YOU KNOW?!
I'm exhausted.
ALL THE PATIENTS WHO ARE BROUGHT IN ARE DEALING WITH LIFE OR DEATH SITUATIONS.
I THOUGHT SO.
THIS IS PEDIATRICS.
IF THAT EVER HAPPENED, IT WOULD BE HUGE...
I THOUGHT SO.
I'LL USE MY FORCE OF WILL TO FIX THIS!
THIS IS SOMETHING I NEED TO OVERCOME!
OH.
BZZZ
VALIANT ONE, COULD YOU CHECK THAT OUT?
OKAY.
IT'S MR. SUGARU AGAIN.
THIS TIME HE SAYS HIS BACK HURTS.
IT'S COMPLETELY OBVIOUS WHAT HE'S UP TO.
I CAN GO.
NO! YOU'RE DEALING WITH ANOTHER CALL AT THE MOMENT.
I'LL HANDLE THIS BY MYSELF!

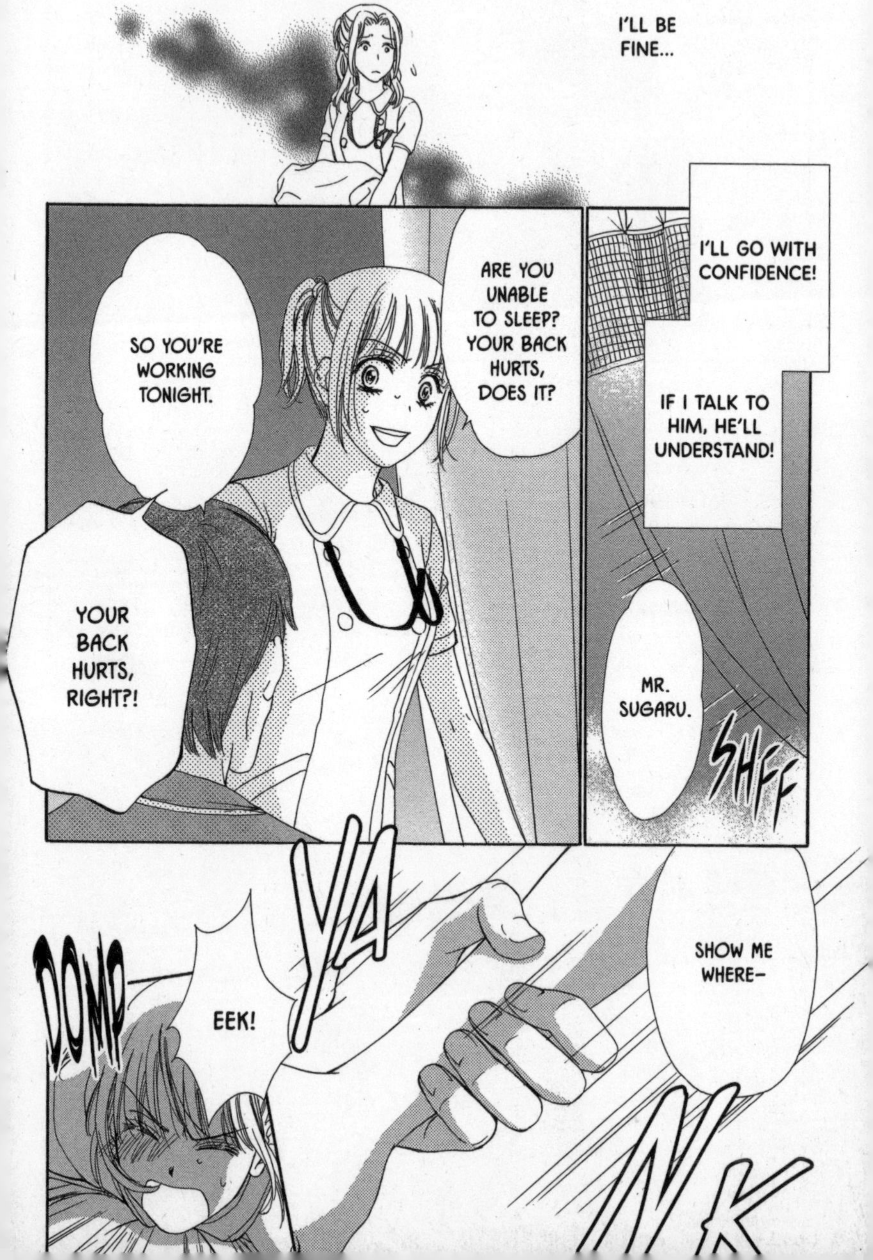
I'LL BE FINE...
I'LL GO WITH CONFIDENCE!
IF I TALK TO HIM, HE'LL UNDERSTAND!
MR. SUGARU.
SHFF
ARE YOU UNABLE TO SLEEP? YOUR BACK HURTS, DOES IT?
SO YOU'RE WORKING TONIGHT.
YOUR BACK HURTS, RIGHT?!
SHOW ME WHERE—
YANK
EEK!
DOMP

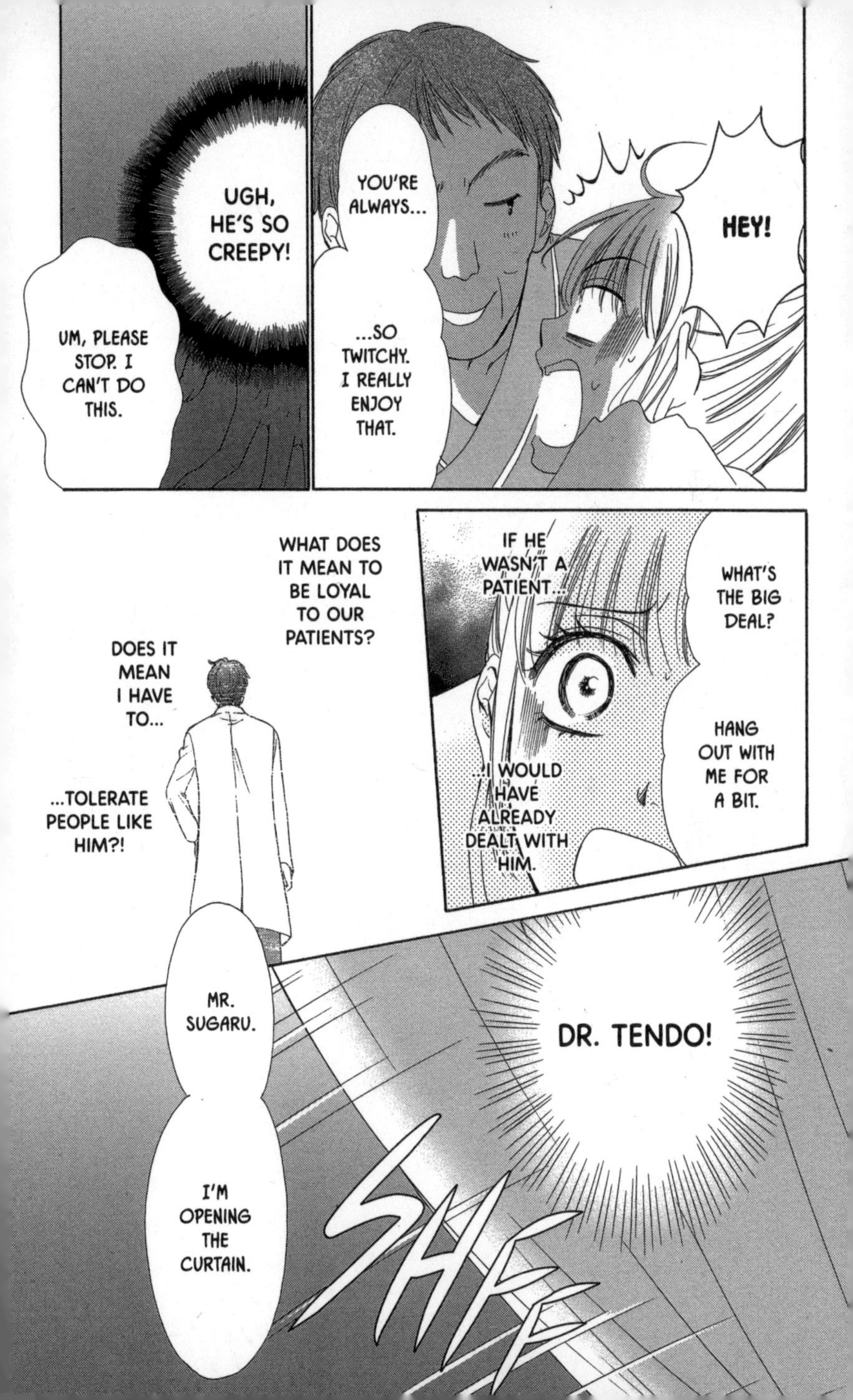
HEY!
YOU'RE ALWAYS...
...SO TWITCHY. I REALLY ENJOY THAT.
UGH, HE'S SO CREEPY!
UM, PLEASE STOP. I CAN'T DO THIS.
WHAT'S THE BIG DEAL?
HANG OUT WITH ME FOR A BIT.
IF HE WASN'T A PATIENT...
...I WOULD HAVE ALREADY DEALT WITH HIM.
WHAT DOES IT MEAN TO BE LOYAL TO OUR PATIENTS?
DOES IT MEAN I HAVE TO...
...TOLERATE PEOPLE LIKE HIM?!
DR. TENDO!
MR. SUGARU.
I'M OPENING THE CURTAIN.
SHFF

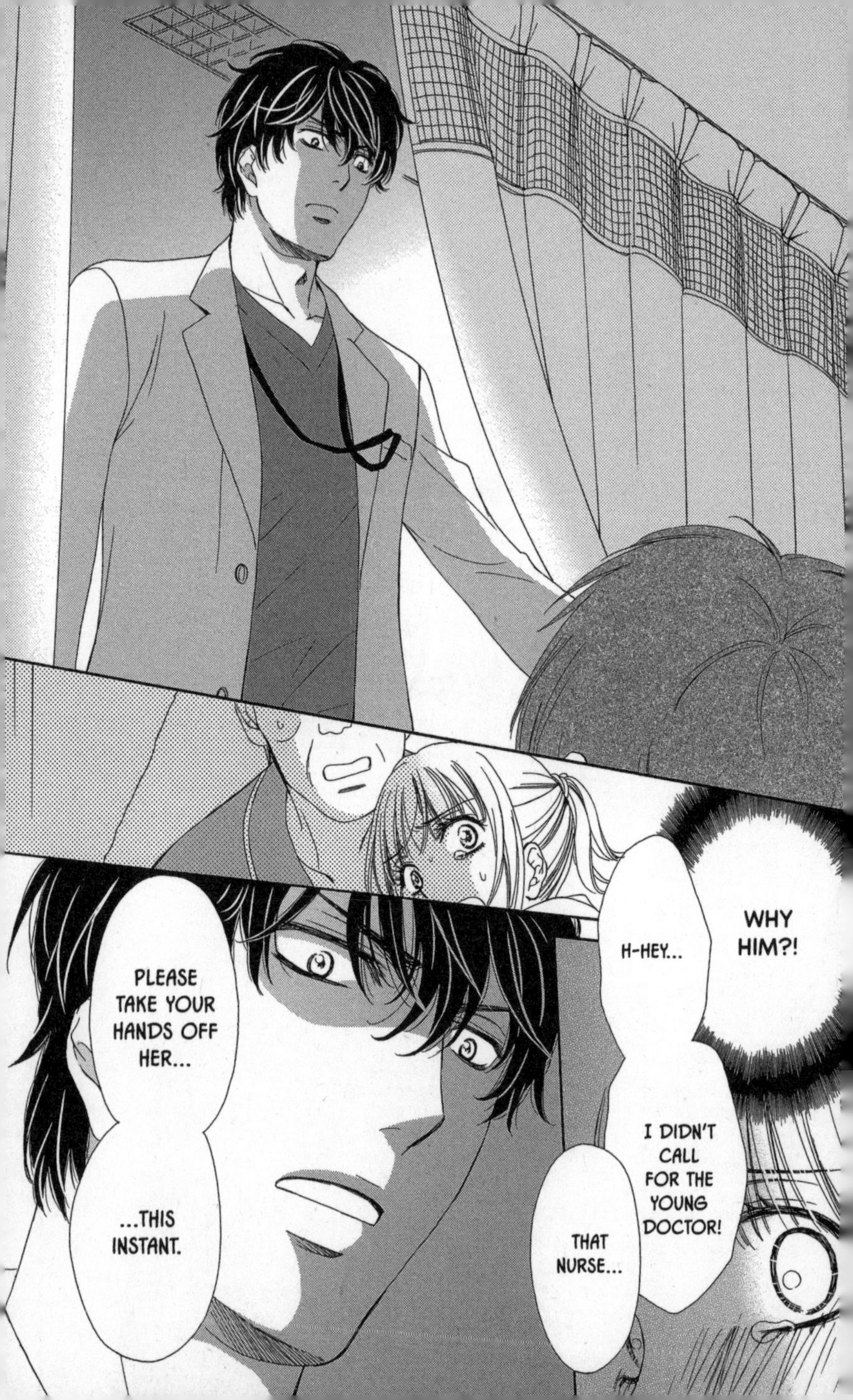
WHY HIM?!
H-HEY...
I DIDN'T CALL FOR THE YOUNG DOCTOR!
THAT NURSE...
PLEASE TAKE YOUR HANDS OFF HER...
...THIS INSTANT.

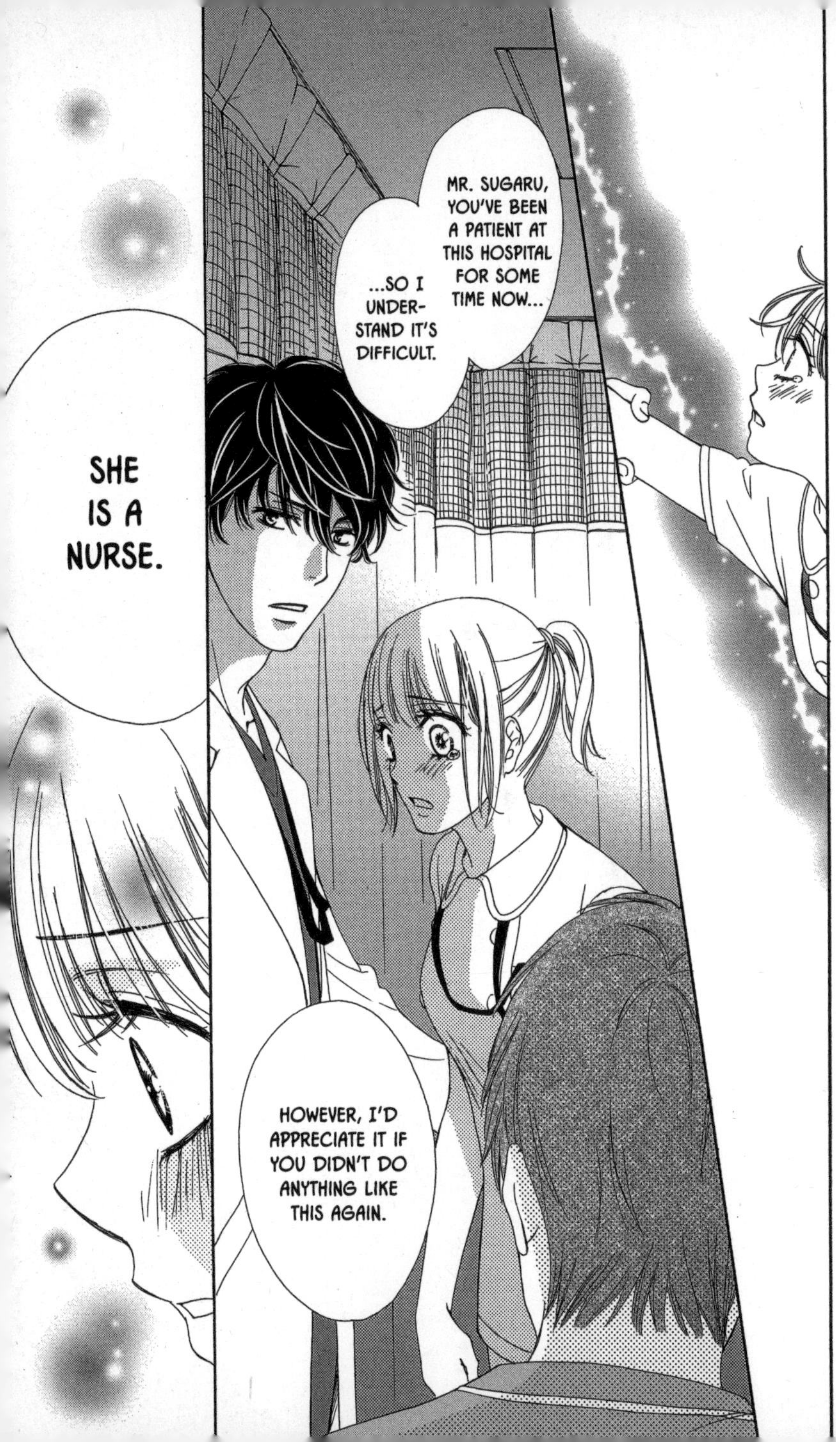
MR. SUGARU, YOU'VE BEEN A PATIENT AT THIS HOSPITAL FOR SOME TIME NOW...
...SO I UNDER-STAND IT'S DIFFICULT.
HOWEVER, I'D APPRECIATE IT IF YOU DIDN'T DO ANYTHING LIKE THIS AGAIN.
SHE IS A NURSE.

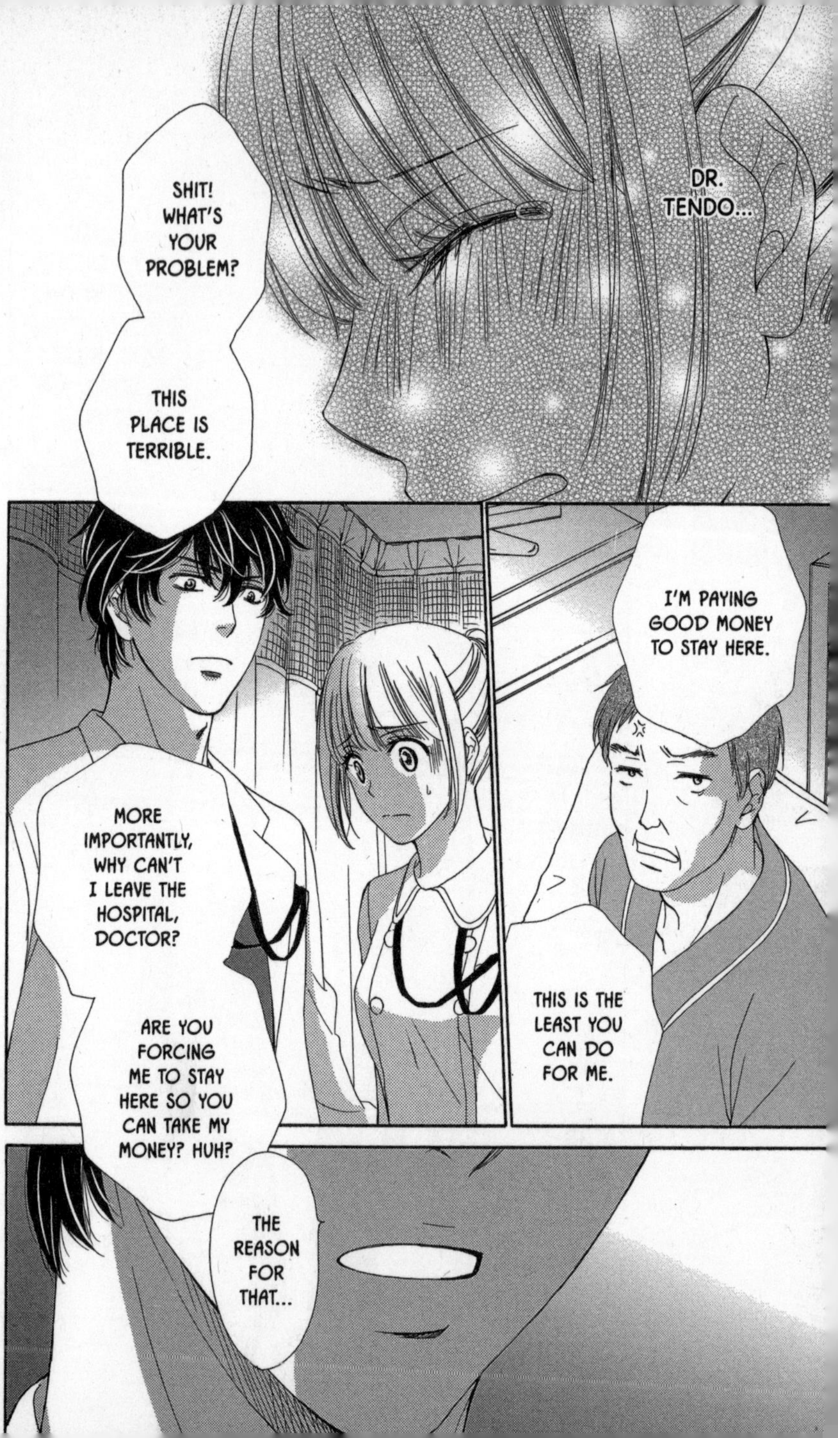
DR. TENDO...
SHIT! WHAT'S YOUR PROBLEM?
THIS PLACE IS TERRIBLE.
I'M PAYING GOOD MONEY TO STAY HERE.
THIS IS THE LEAST YOU CAN DO FOR ME.
MORE IMPORTANTLY, WHY CAN'T I LEAVE THE HOSPITAL, DOCTOR?
ARE YOU FORCING ME TO STAY HERE SO YOU CAN TAKE MY MONEY? HUH?
THE REASON FOR THAT...

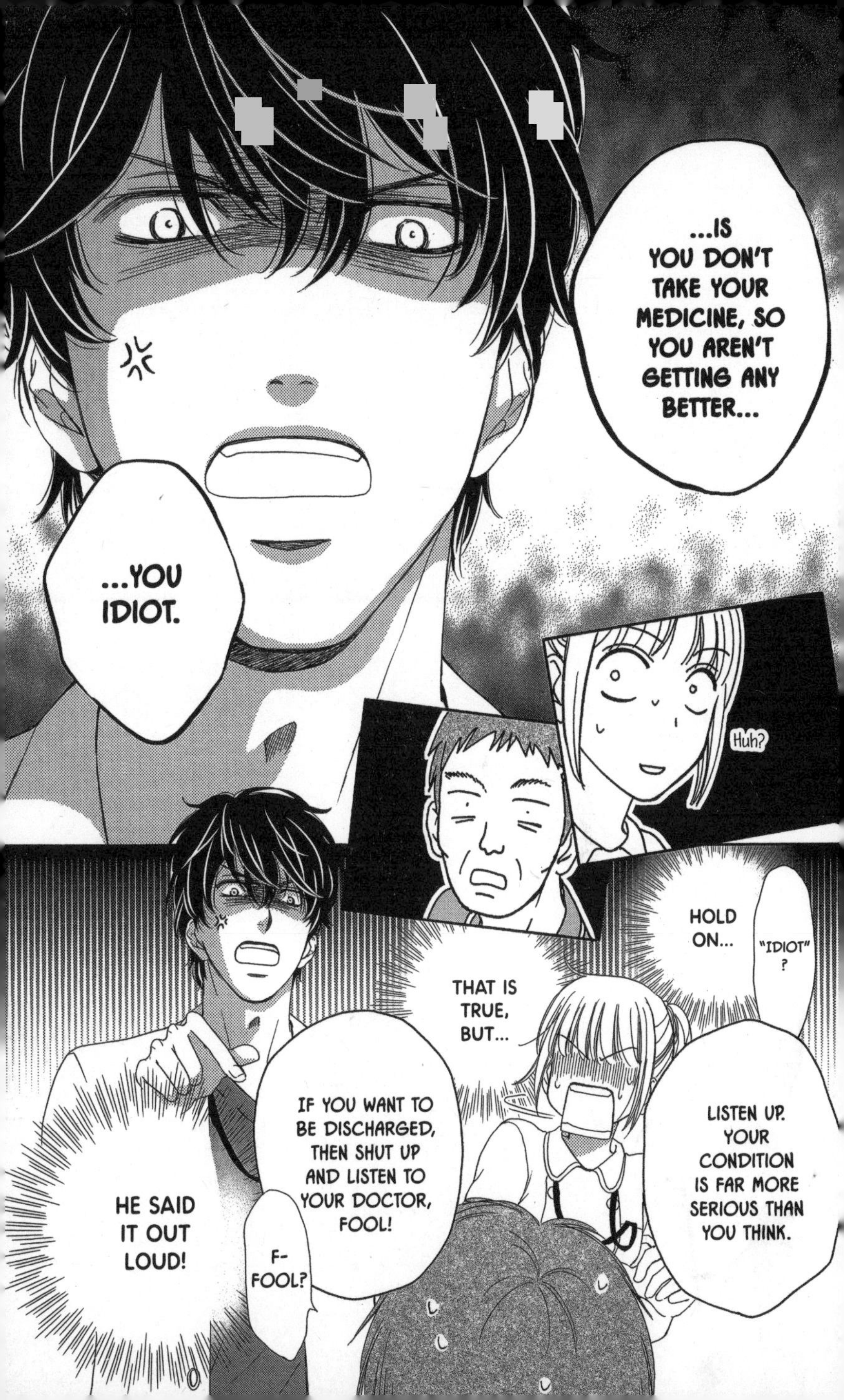
...IS YOU DON'T TAKE YOUR MEDICINE, SO YOU AREN'T GETTING ANY BETTER...
...YOU IDIOT.
Huh?
"IDIOT"?
HOLD ON...
THAT IS TRUE, BUT...
LISTEN UP. YOUR CONDITION IS FAR MORE SERIOUS THAN YOU THINK.
IF YOU WANT TO BE DISCHARGED, THEN SHUT UP AND LISTEN TO YOUR DOCTOR, FOOL!
F-FOOL?
HE SAID IT OUT LOUD!

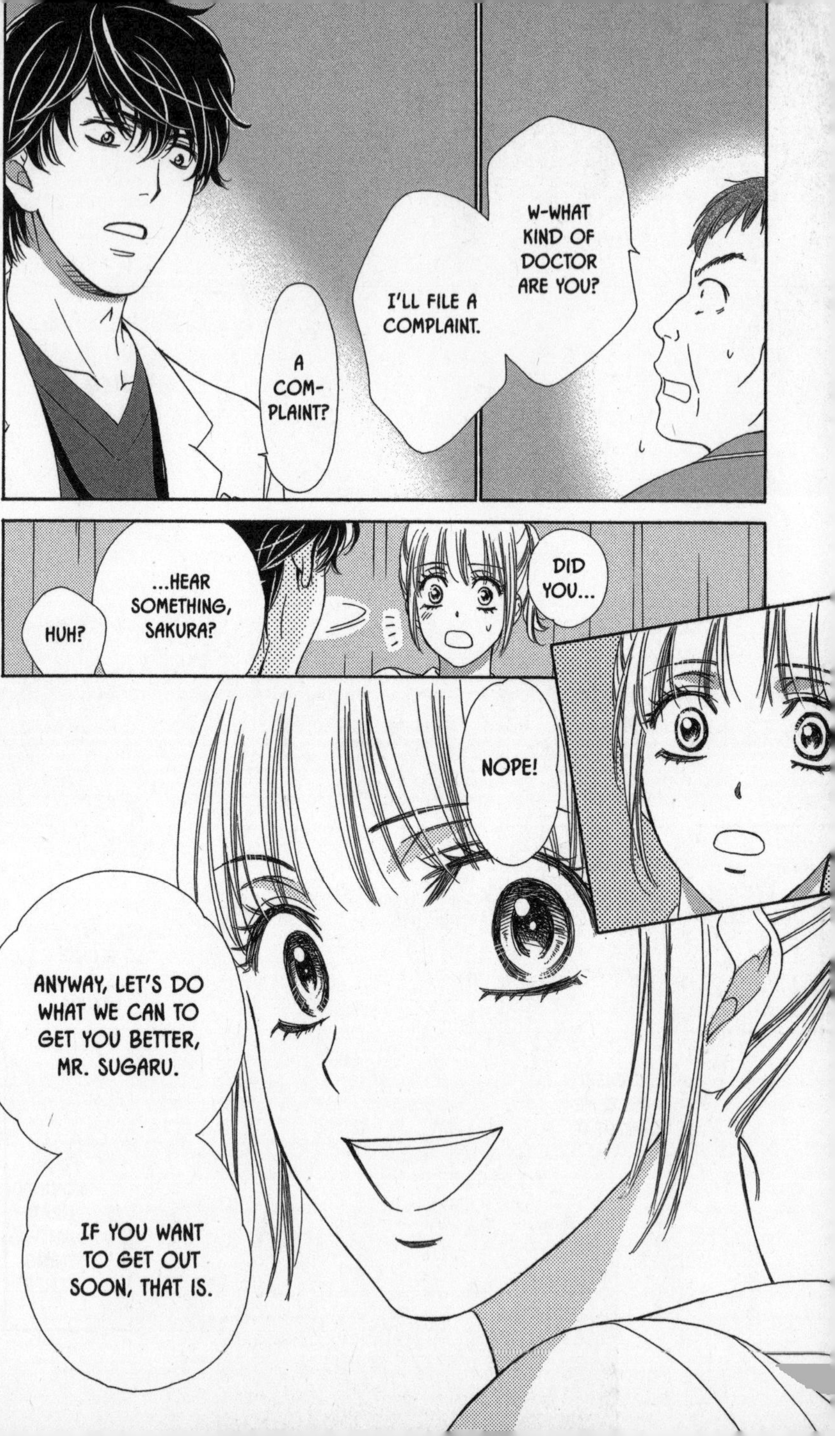
W-WHAT KIND OF DOCTOR ARE YOU?
I'LL FILE A COMPLAINT.
A COM-PLAINT?
DID YOU...
...HEAR SOMETHING, SAKURA?
HUH?
NOPE!
ANYWAY, LET'S DO WHAT WE CAN TO GET YOU BETTER, MR. SUGARU.
IF YOU WANT TO GET OUT SOON, THAT IS.

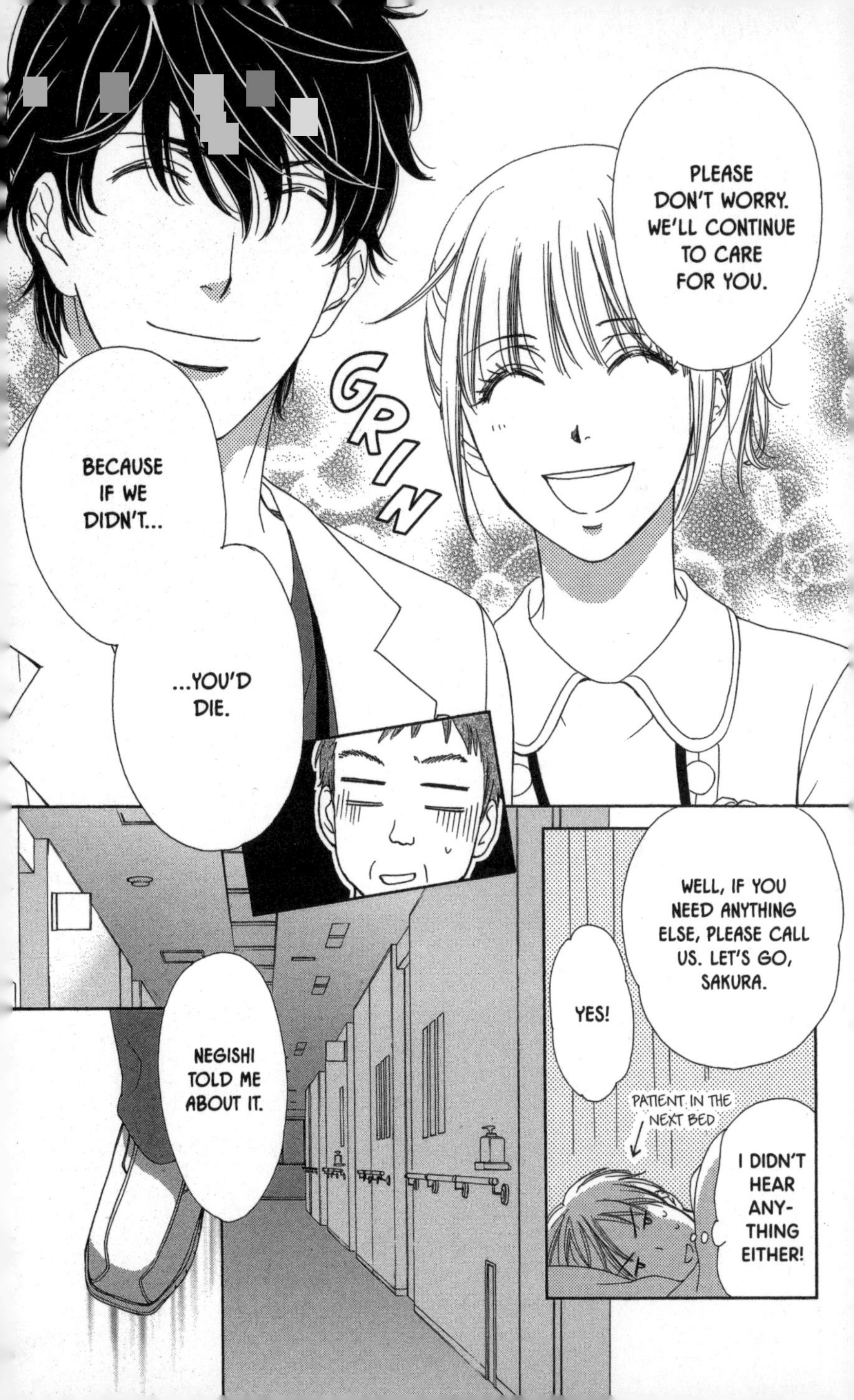
PLEASE DON'T WORRY. WE'LL CONTINUE TO CARE FOR YOU.
GRIN
BECAUSE IF WE DIDN'T...
...YOU'D DIE.
WELL, IF YOU NEED ANYTHING ELSE, PLEASE CALL US. LET'S GO, SAKURA.
YES!
PATIENT IN THE NEXT BED
I DIDN'T HEAR ANY-THING EITHER!
NEGISHI TOLD ME ABOUT IT.

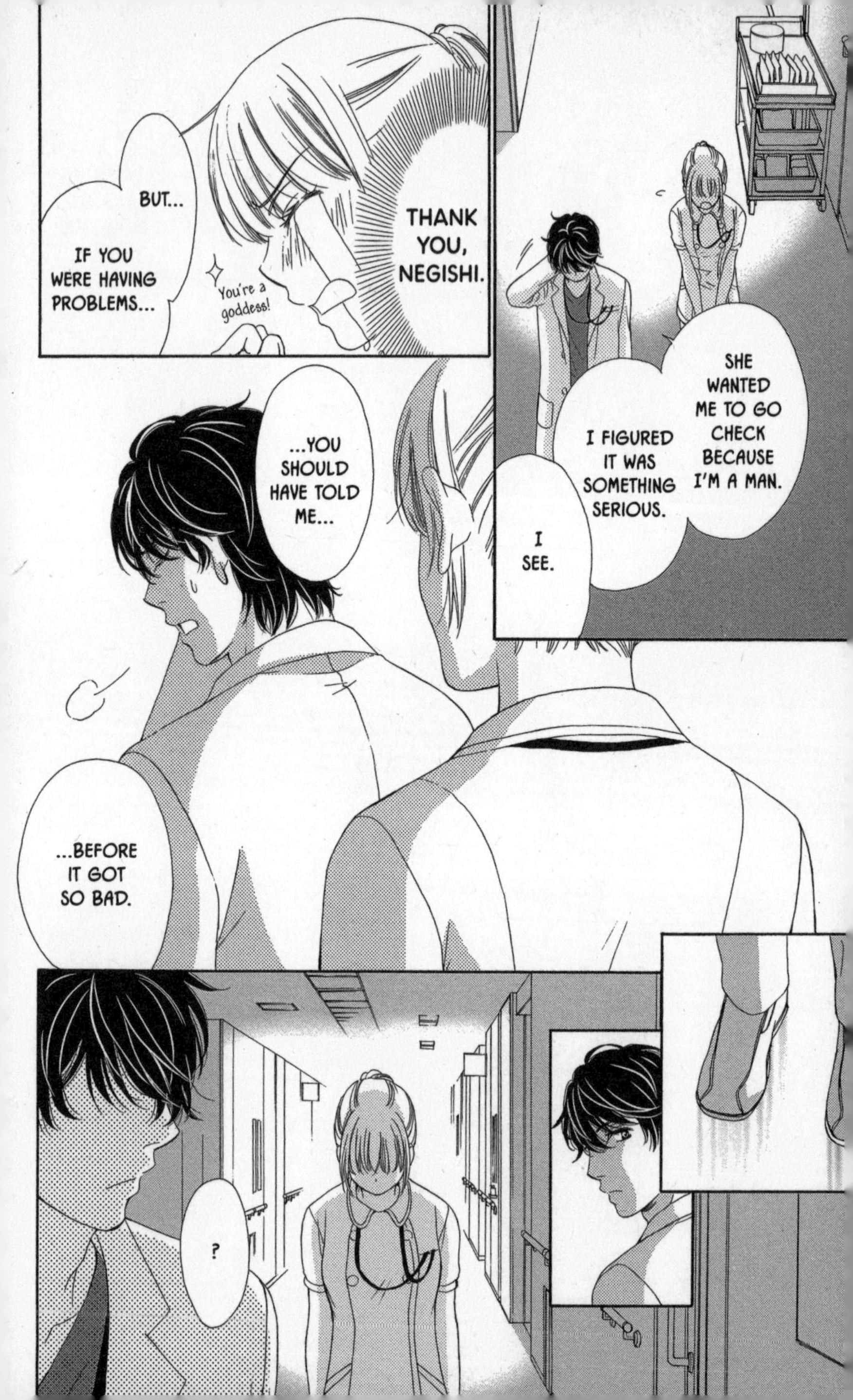
SHE WANTED ME TO GO CHECK BECAUSE I'M A MAN.
I FIGURED IT WAS SOMETHING SERIOUS.
I SEE.
THANK YOU, NEGISHI.
You're a goddess!
BUT...
IF YOU WERE HAVING PROBLEMS...
...YOU SHOULD HAVE TOLD ME...
...BEFORE IT GOT SO BAD.
?

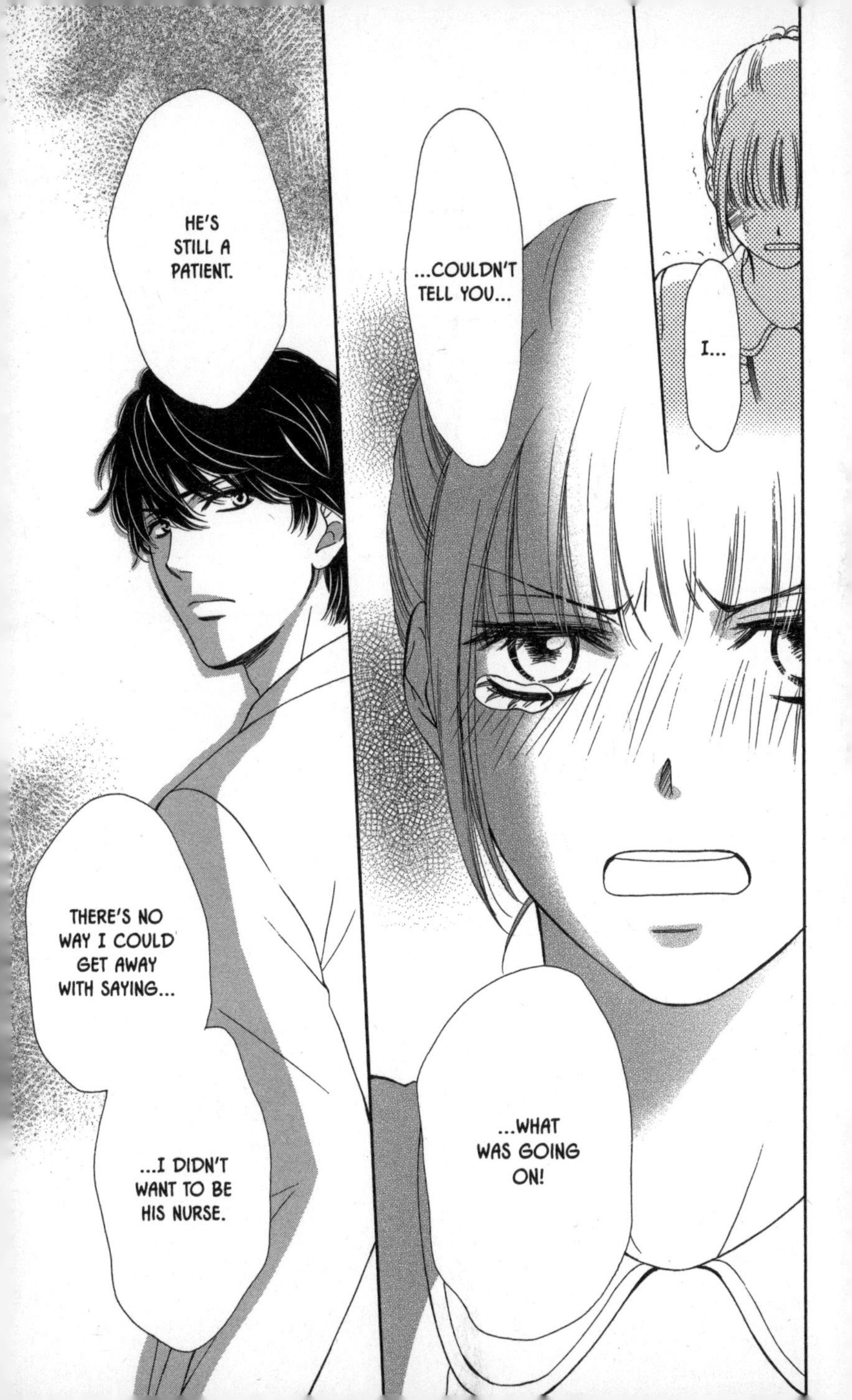
I...
...COULDN'T TELL YOU...
...WHAT WAS GOING ON!
HE'S STILL A PATIENT.
THERE'S NO WAY I COULD GET AWAY WITH SAYING...
...I DIDN'T WANT TO BE HIS NURSE.

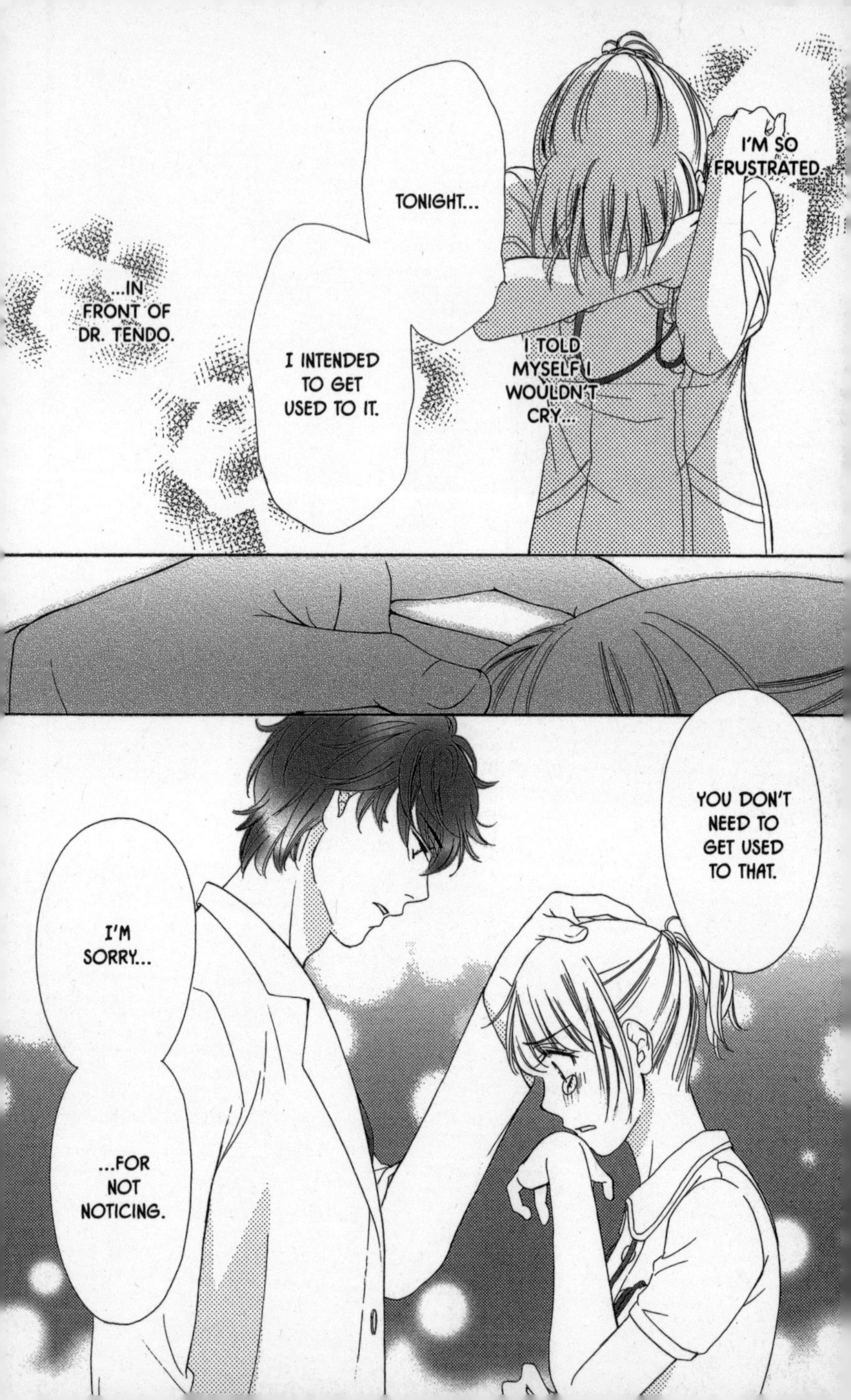
I'M SO FRUSTRATED.
I TOLD MYSELF I WOULDN'T CRY...
TONIGHT...
I INTENDED TO GET USED TO IT.
...IN FRONT OF DR. TENDO.
YOU DON'T NEED TO GET USED TO THAT.
I'M SORRY...
...FOR NOT NOTICING.

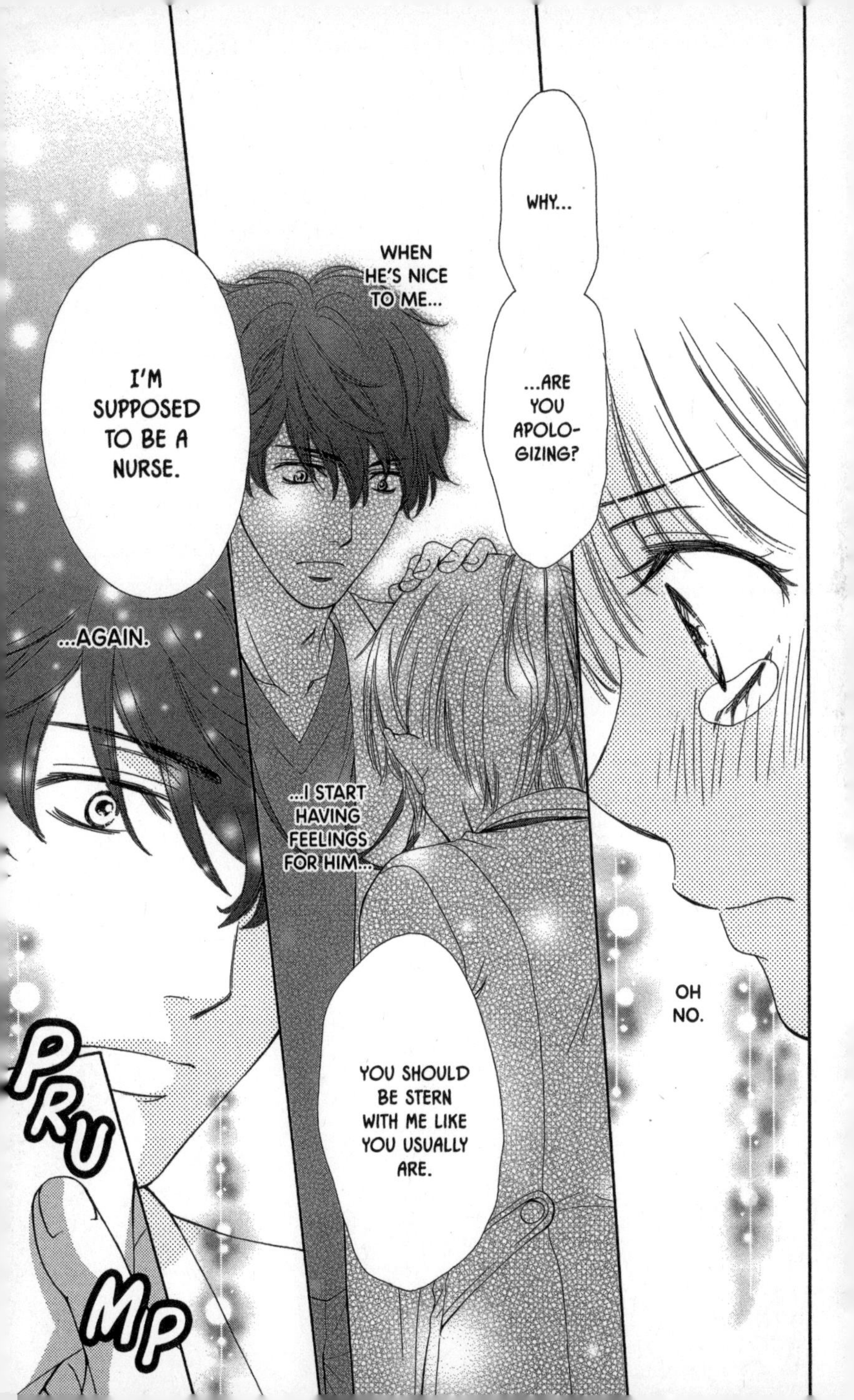
WHY...
...ARE YOU APOLOGIZING?
OH NO.
WHEN HE'S NICE TO ME...
...I START HAVING FEELINGS FOR HIM...
YOU SHOULD BE STERN WITH ME LIKE YOU USUALLY ARE.
I'M SUPPOSED TO BE A NURSE.
...AGAIN.
PRUMP

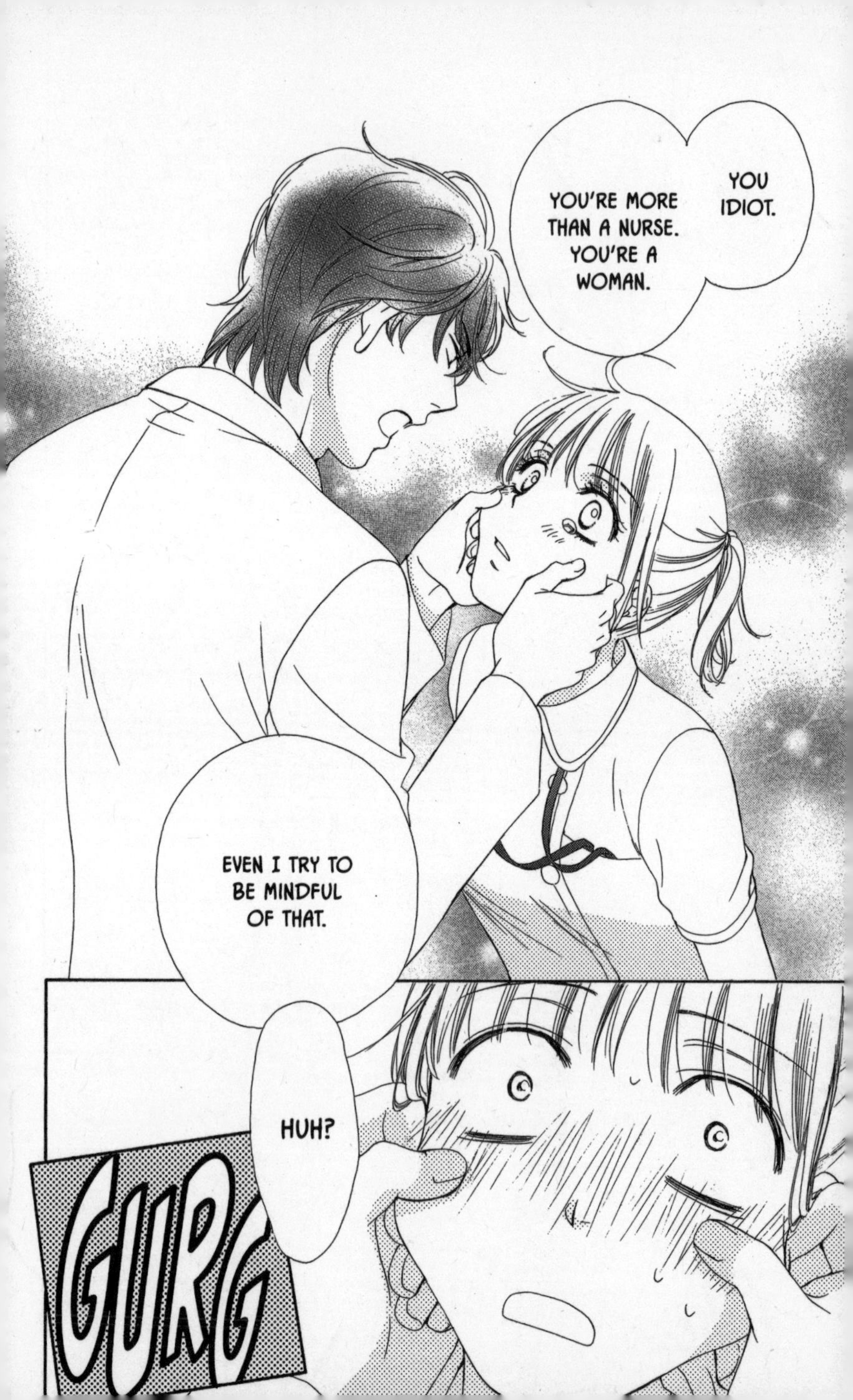
YOU IDIOT.
YOU'RE MORE THAN A NURSE. YOU'RE A WOMAN.
EVEN I TRY TO BE MINDFUL OF THAT.
HUH?
GURG

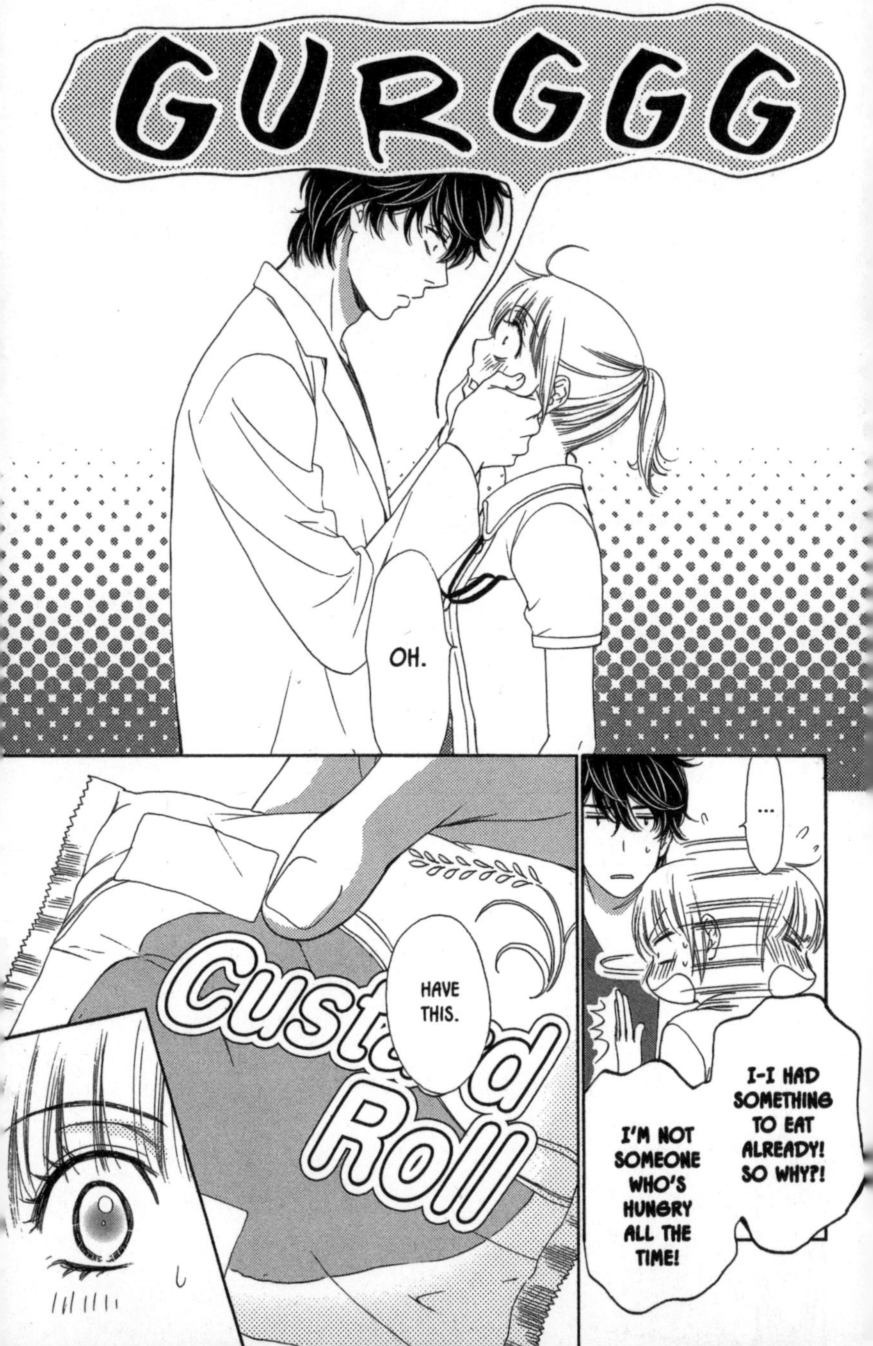
GURGGG
OH.
...
I-I HAD SOMETHING TO EAT ALREADY! SO WHY?!
I'M NOT SOMEONE WHO'S HUNGRY ALL THE TIME!
HAVE THIS.
Custa d
Roll

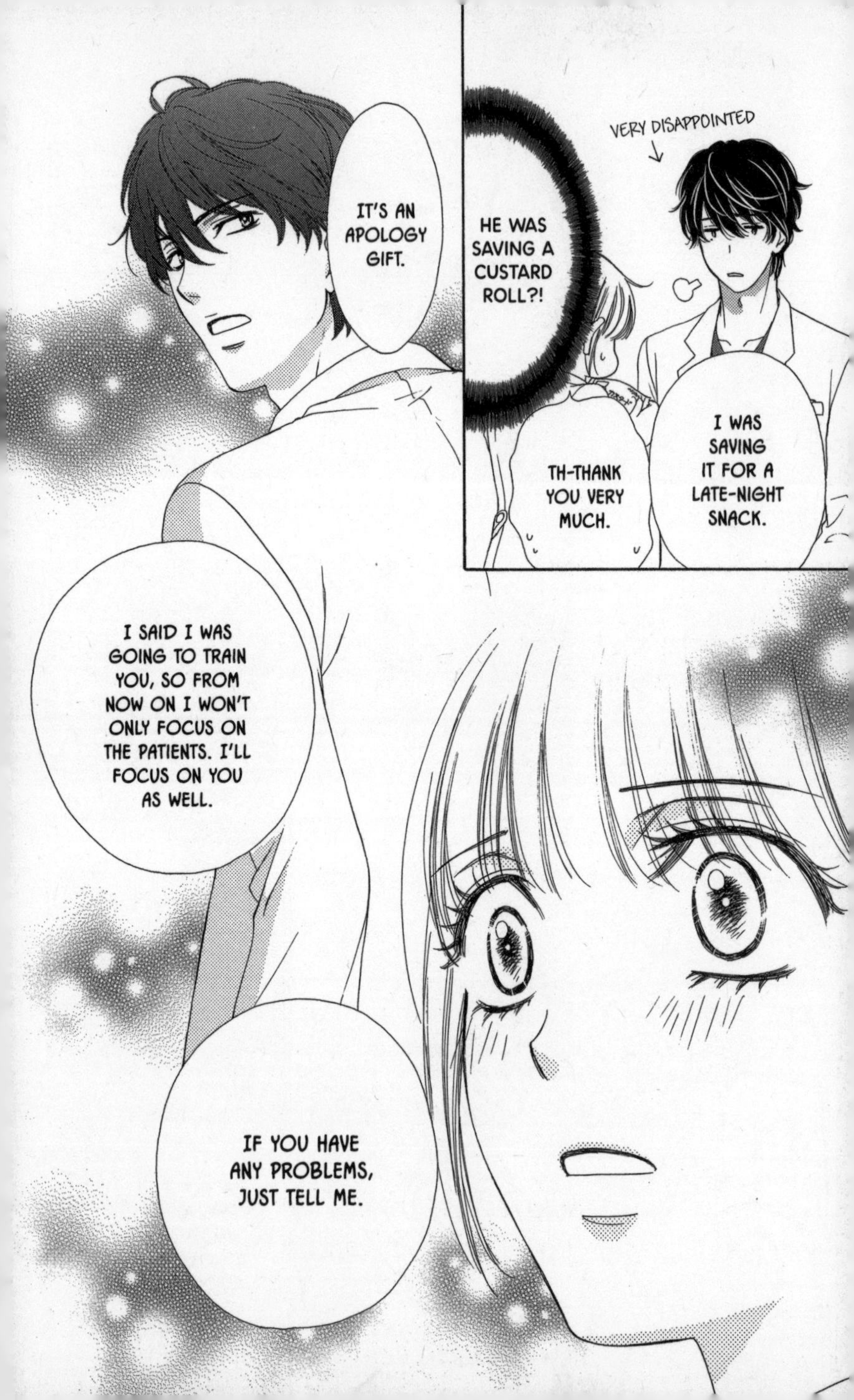
VERY DISAPPOINTED
I WAS SAVING IT FOR A LATE-NIGHT SNACK.
TH-THANK YOU VERY MUCH.
HE WAS SAVING A CUSTARD ROLL?!
IT'S AN APOLOGY GIFT.
I SAID I WAS GOING TO TRAIN YOU, SO FROM NOW ON I WON'T ONLY FOCUS ON THE PATIENTS. I'LL FOCUS ON YOU AS WELL.
IF YOU HAVE ANY PROBLEMS, JUST TELL ME.

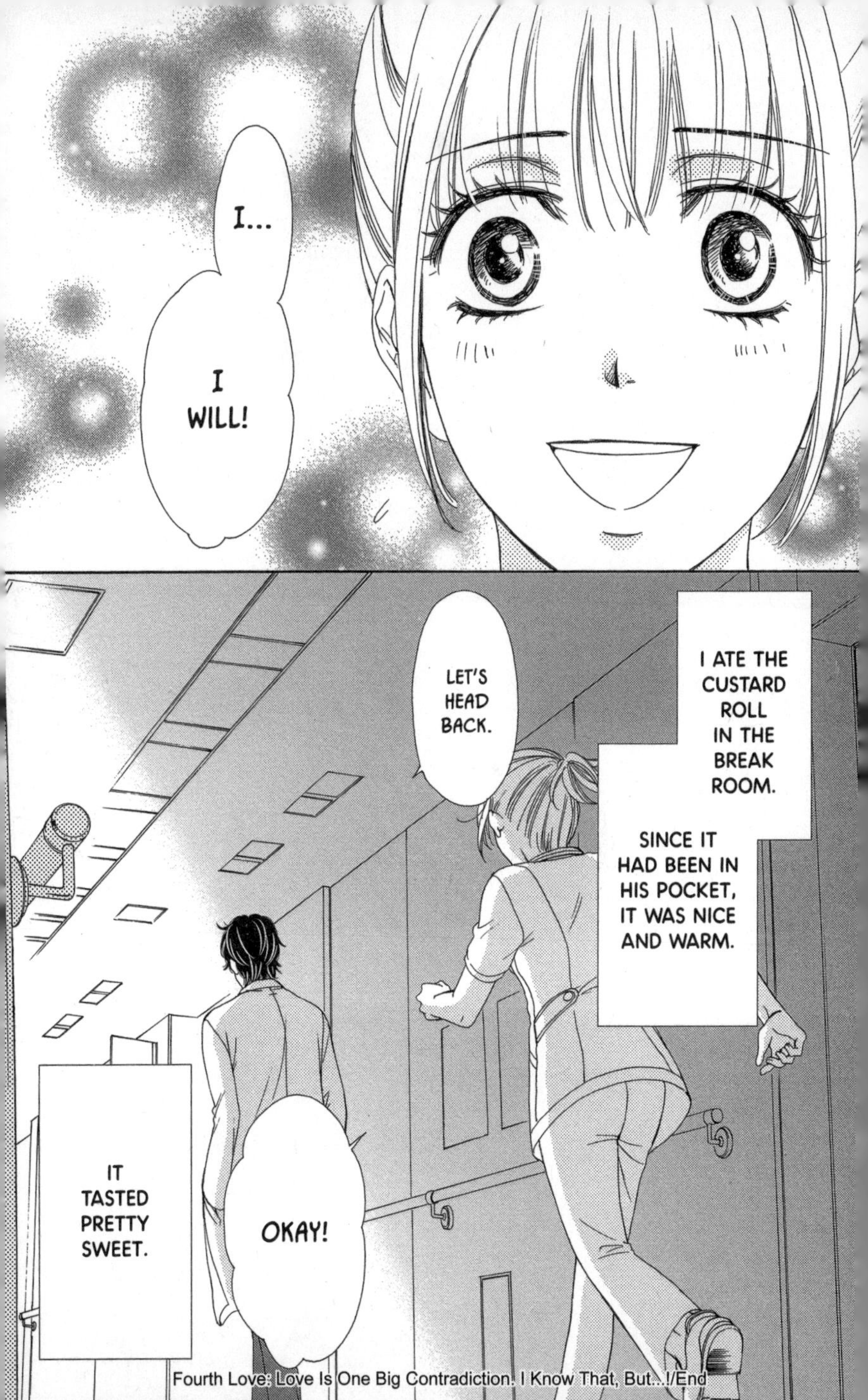
I...
I WILL!
I ATE THE CUSTARD ROLL IN THE BREAK ROOM.
LET'S HEAD BACK.
SINCE IT HAD BEEN IN HIS POCKET, IT WAS NICE AND WARM.
OKAY!
IT TASTED PRETTY SWEET.

Fourth Love: Love Is One Big Contradiction. I Know That, But...!/End

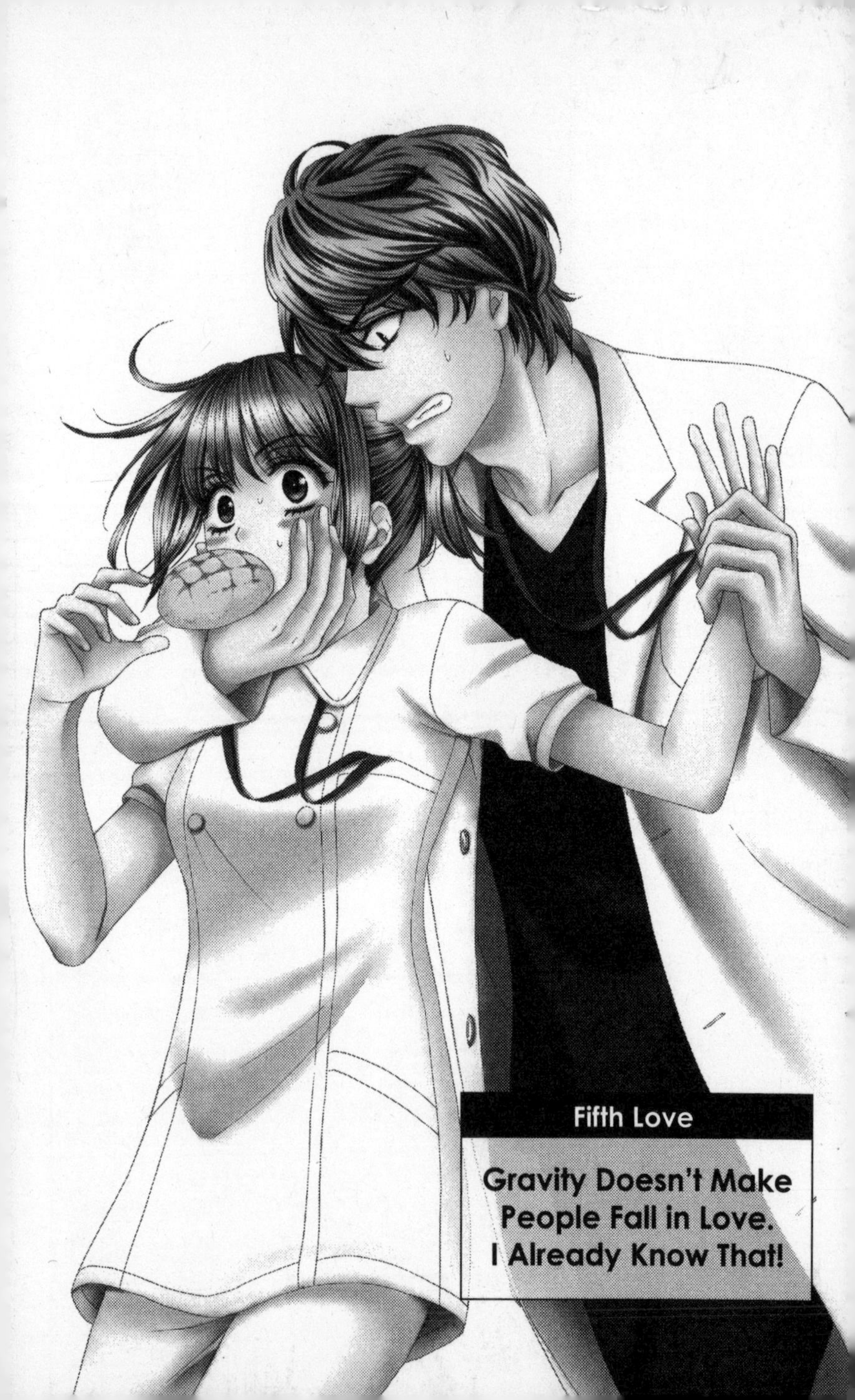
Fifth Love
Gravity Doesn't Make People Fall in Love. I Already Know That!

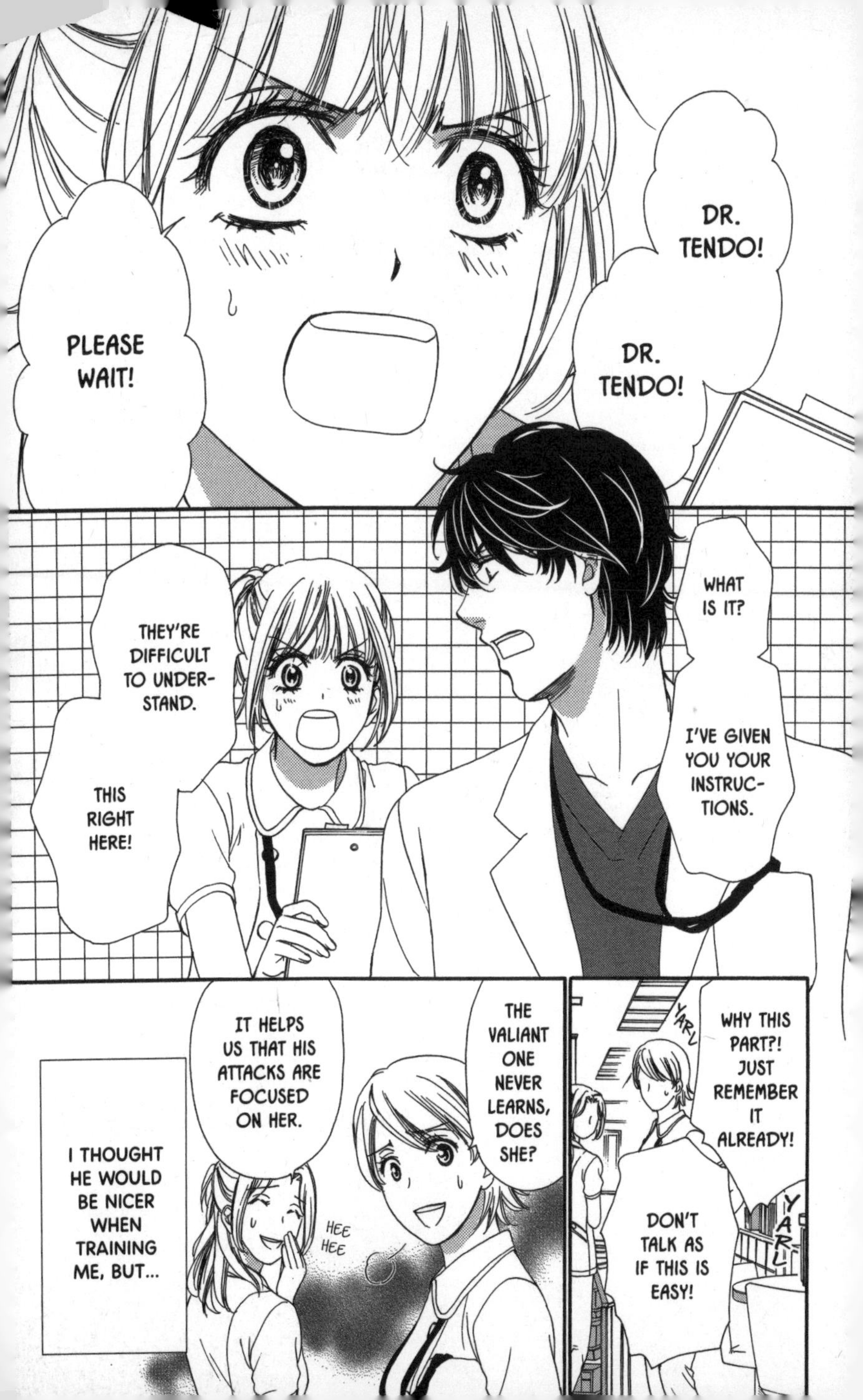
DR. TENDO!
DR. TENDO!
PLEASE WAIT!
WHAT IS IT?
I'VE GIVEN YOU YOUR INSTRUCTIONS.
THEY'RE DIFFICULT TO UNDERSTAND.
THIS RIGHT HERE!
YARL
WHY THIS PART?! JUST REMEMBER IT ALREADY!
YARL
DON'T TALK AS IF THIS IS EASY!
THE VALIANT ONE NEVER LEARNS, DOES SHE?
IT HELPS US THAT HIS ATTACKS ARE FOCUSED ON HER.
HEE HEE
I THOUGHT HE WOULD BE NICER WHEN TRAINING ME, BUT...

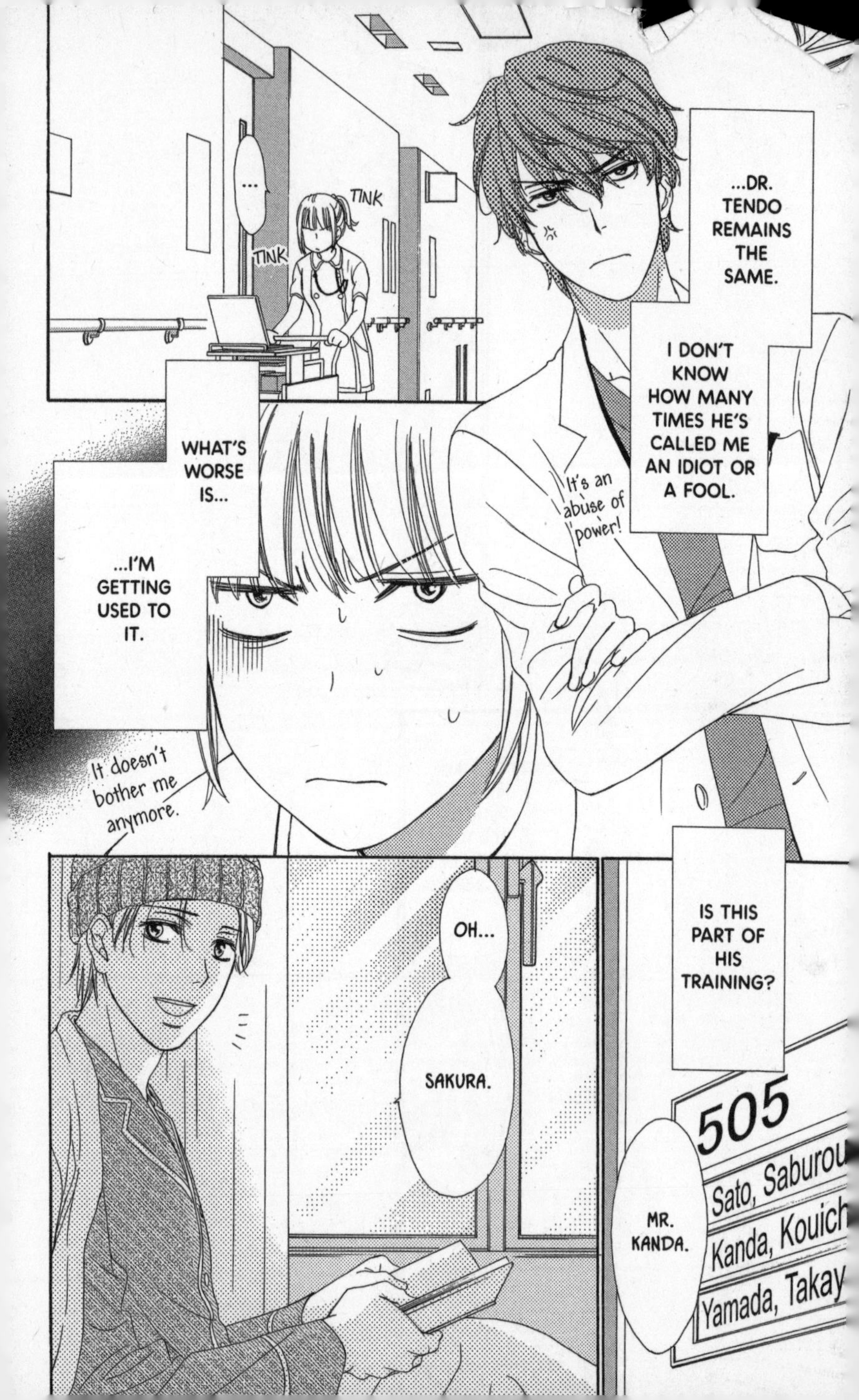
...DR. TENDO REMAINS THE SAME.
I DON'T KNOW HOW MANY TIMES HE'S CALLED ME AN IDIOT OR A FOOL.
It's an abuse of power!
...
TINK
TINK
WHAT'S WORSE IS...
...I'M GETTING USED TO IT.
It doesn't bother me anymore.
IS THIS PART OF HIS TRAINING?
505
Sato, Saburou
Kanda, Kouich
Yamada, Takay
MR. KANDA.
OH...
SAKURA.

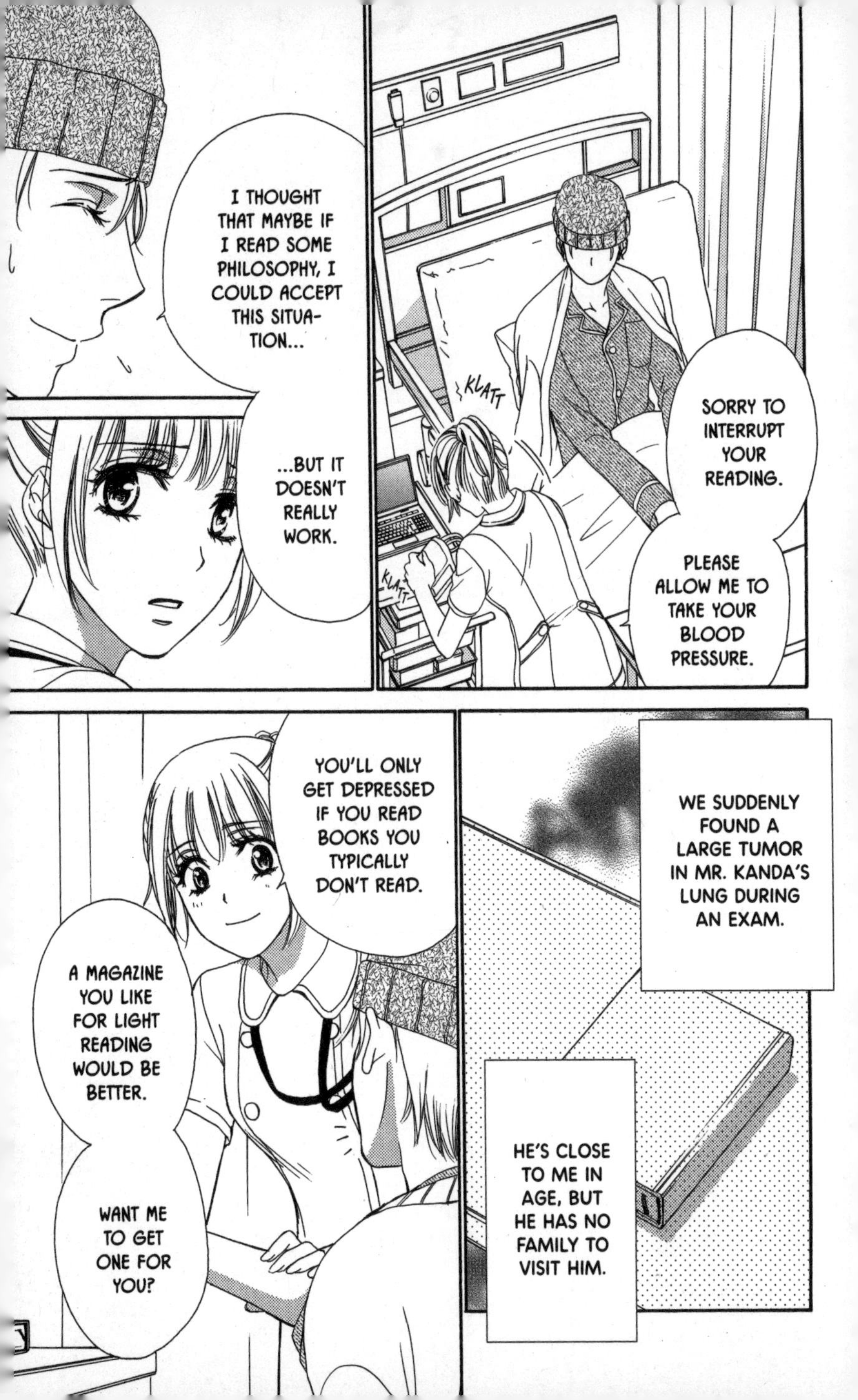
KLATT
SORRY TO INTERRUPT YOUR READING.
KLATT
PLEASE ALLOW ME TO TAKE YOUR BLOOD PRESSURE.
I THOUGHT THAT MAYBE IF I READ SOME PHILOSOPHY, I COULD ACCEPT THIS SITUA-TION...
...BUT IT DOESN'T REALLY WORK.
WE SUDDENLY FOUND A LARGE TUMOR IN MR. KANDA'S LUNG DURING AN EXAM.
HE'S CLOSE TO ME IN AGE, BUT HE HAS NO FAMILY TO VISIT HIM.
YOU'LL ONLY GET DEPRESSED IF YOU READ BOOKS YOU TYPICALLY DON'T READ.
A MAGAZINE YOU LIKE FOR LIGHT READING WOULD BE BETTER.
WANT ME TO GET ONE FOR YOU?

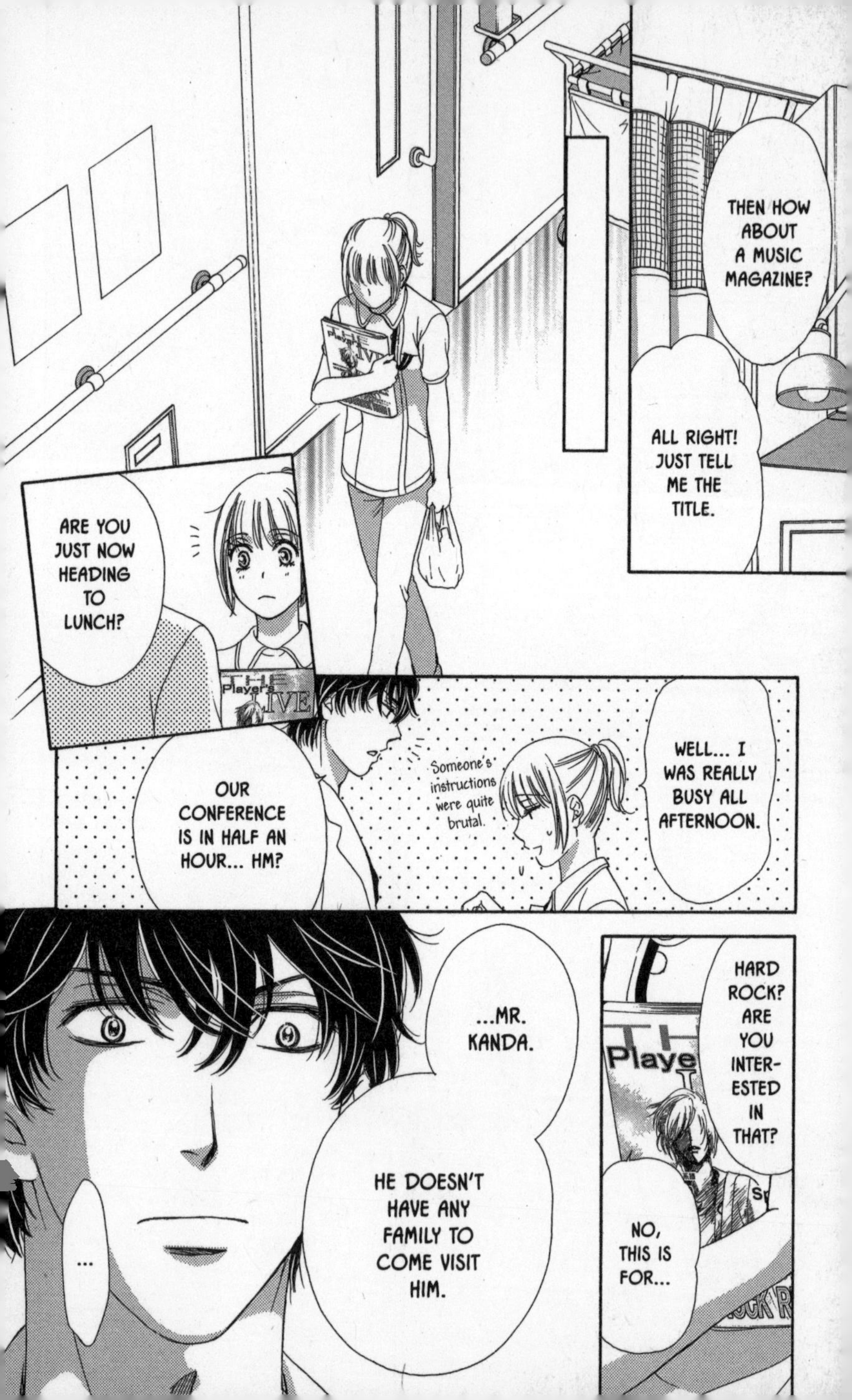
THEN HOW ABOUT A MUSIC MAGAZINE?
ALL RIGHT! JUST TELL ME THE TITLE.
ARE YOU JUST NOW HEADING TO LUNCH?
THE Player's LIVE
WELL... I WAS REALLY BUSY ALL AFTERNOON.
Someone's instructions were quite brutal.
OUR CONFERENCE IS IN HALF AN HOUR... HM?
HARD ROCK? ARE YOU INTERESTED IN THAT?
NO, THIS IS FOR...
...MR. KANDA.
HE DOESN'T HAVE ANY FAMILY TO COME VISIT HIM.
...

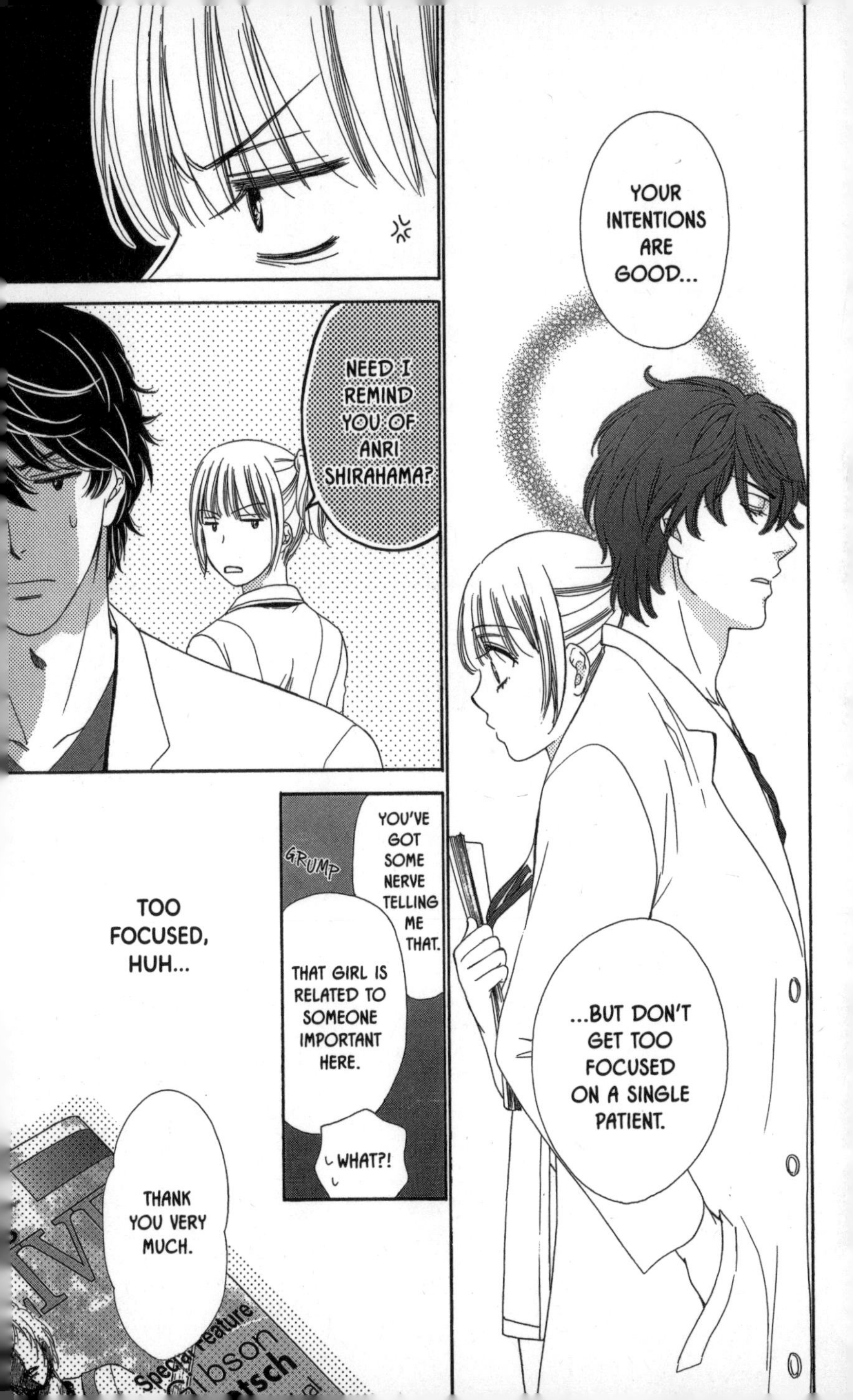
YOUR INTENTIONS ARE GOOD...
...BUT DON'T GET TOO FOCUSED ON A SINGLE PATIENT.
NEED I REMIND YOU OF ANRI SHIRAHAMA?
YOU'VE GOT SOME NERVE TELLING ME THAT.
GRUMP
THAT GIRL IS RELATED TO SOMEONE IMPORTANT HERE.
WHAT?!
TOO FOCUSED, HUH...
THANK YOU VERY MUCH.
Special feature

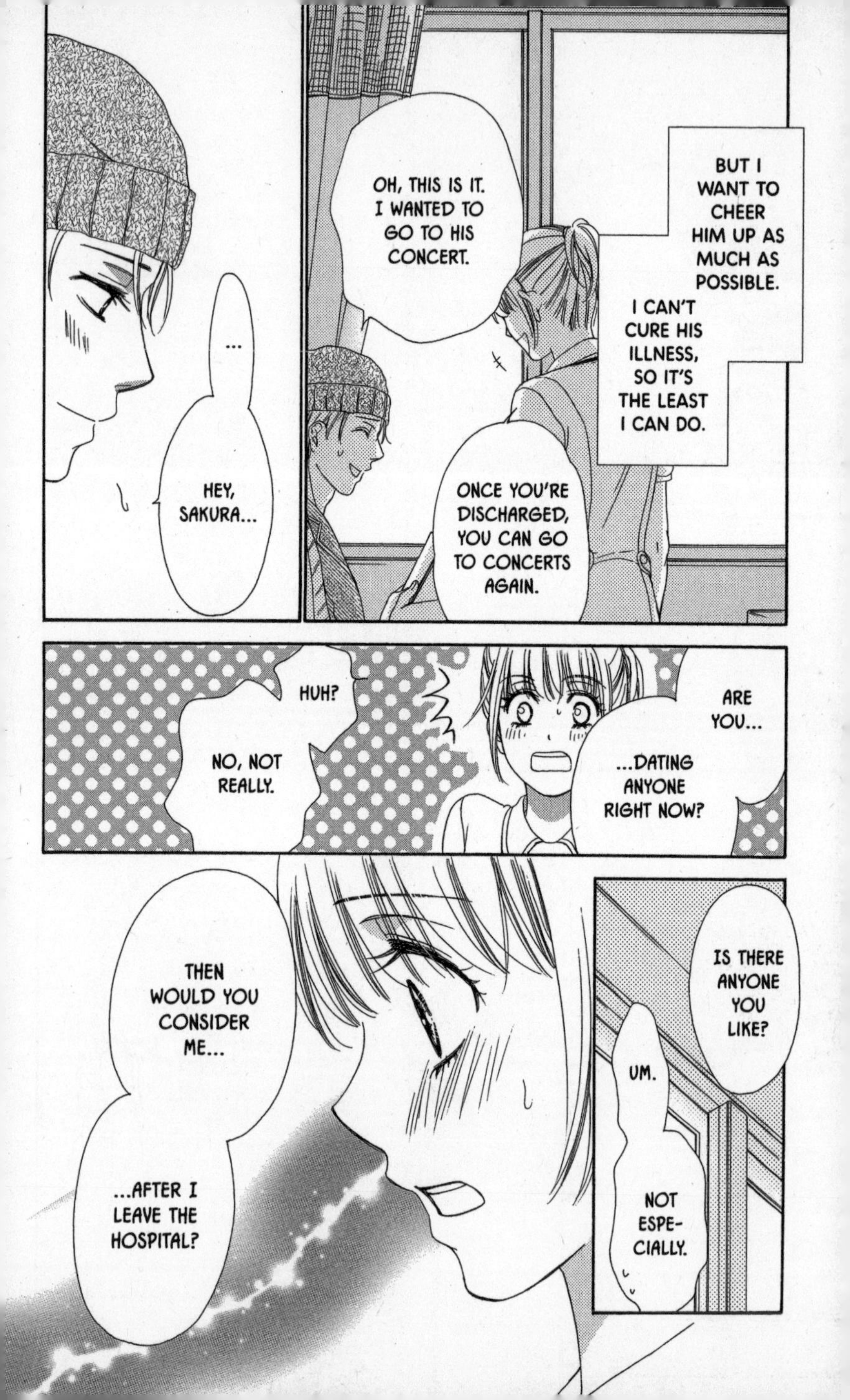
BUT I WANT TO CHEER HIM UP AS MUCH AS POSSIBLE.
I CAN'T CURE HIS ILLNESS, SO IT'S THE LEAST I CAN DO.
OH, THIS IS IT. I WANTED TO GO TO HIS CONCERT.
ONCE YOU'RE DISCHARGED, YOU CAN GO TO CONCERTS AGAIN.
...
HEY, SAKURA...
ARE YOU...
...DATING ANYONE RIGHT NOW?
HUH?
NO, NOT REALLY.
IS THERE ANYONE YOU LIKE?
UM.
NOT ESPECIALLY.
THEN WOULD YOU CONSIDER ME...
...AFTER I LEAVE THE HOSPITAL?

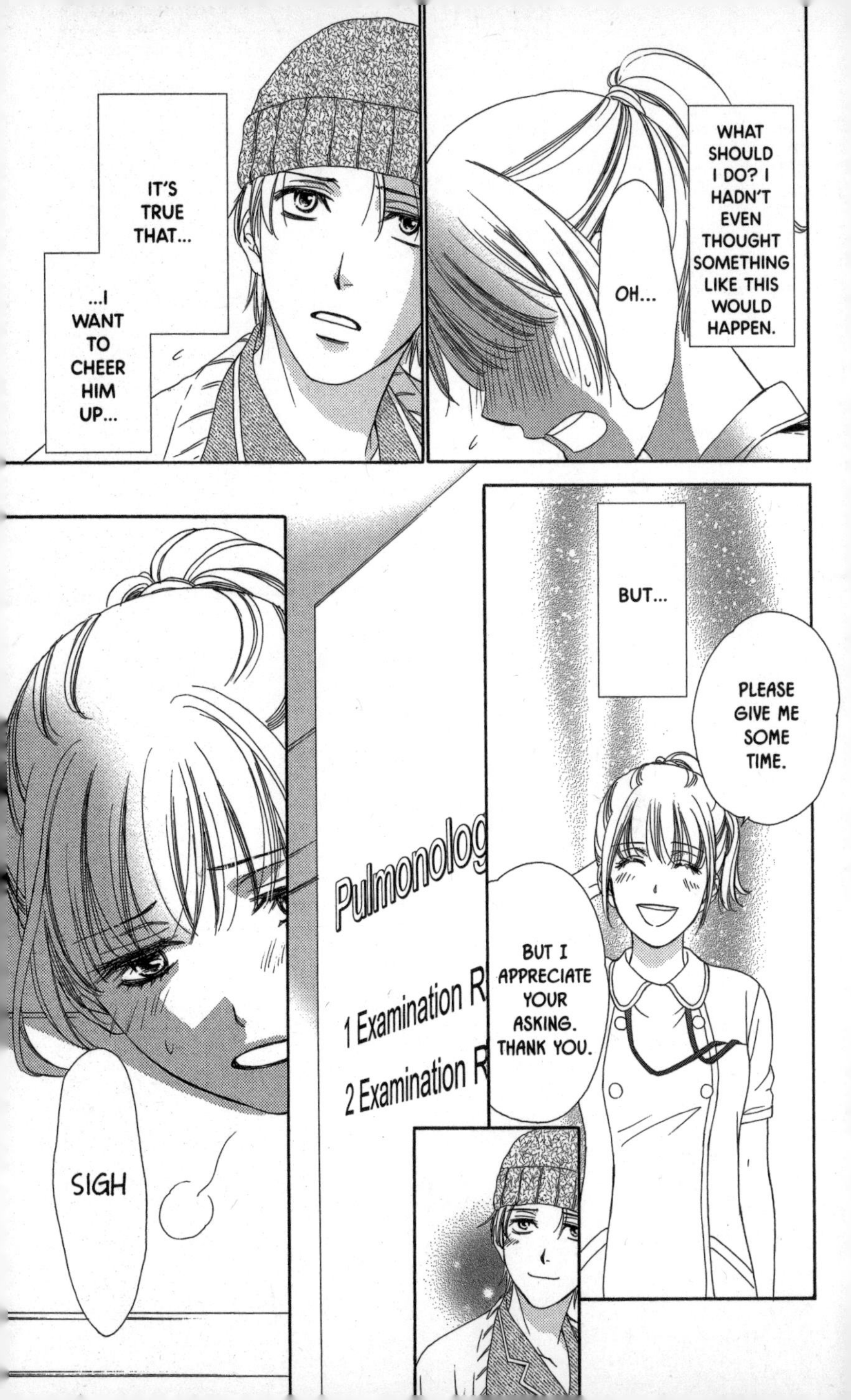
WHAT SHOULD I DO? I HADN'T EVEN THOUGHT SOMETHING LIKE THIS WOULD HAPPEN.
OH...
IT'S TRUE THAT...
...I WANT TO CHEER HIM UP...
BUT...
PLEASE GIVE ME SOME TIME.
BUT I APPRECIATE YOUR ASKING. THANK YOU.
Pulmonolog
1 Examination R
2 Examination R
SIGH

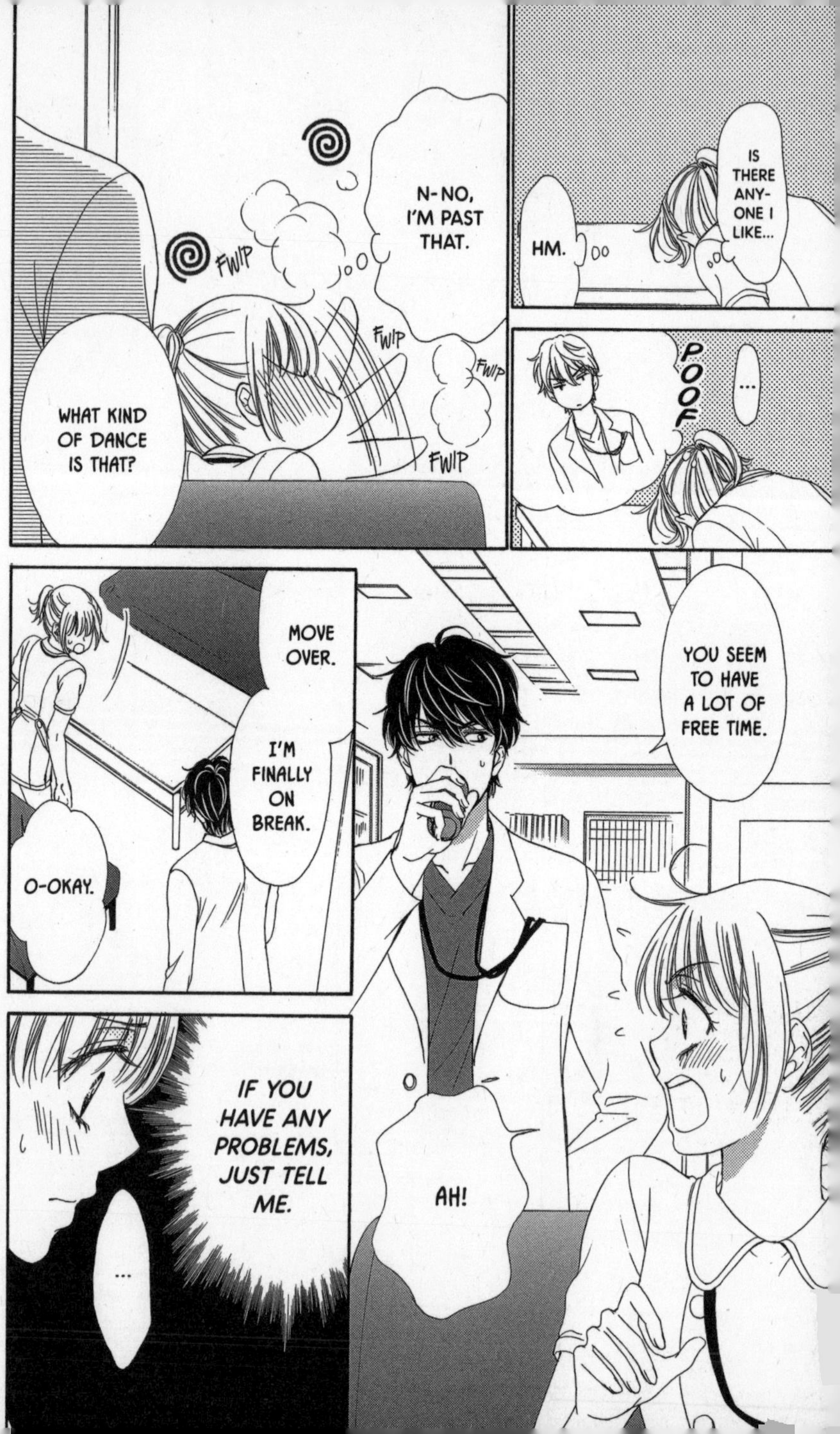
IS THERE ANY-ONE I LIKE...
HM.
...
POOF
N-NO, I'M PAST THAT.
FWIP
FWIP
FWIP
FWIP
WHAT KIND OF DANCE IS THAT?
YOU SEEM TO HAVE A LOT OF FREE TIME.
AH!
MOVE OVER.
I'M FINALLY ON BREAK.
O-OKAY.
IF YOU HAVE ANY PROBLEMS, JUST TELL ME.
...

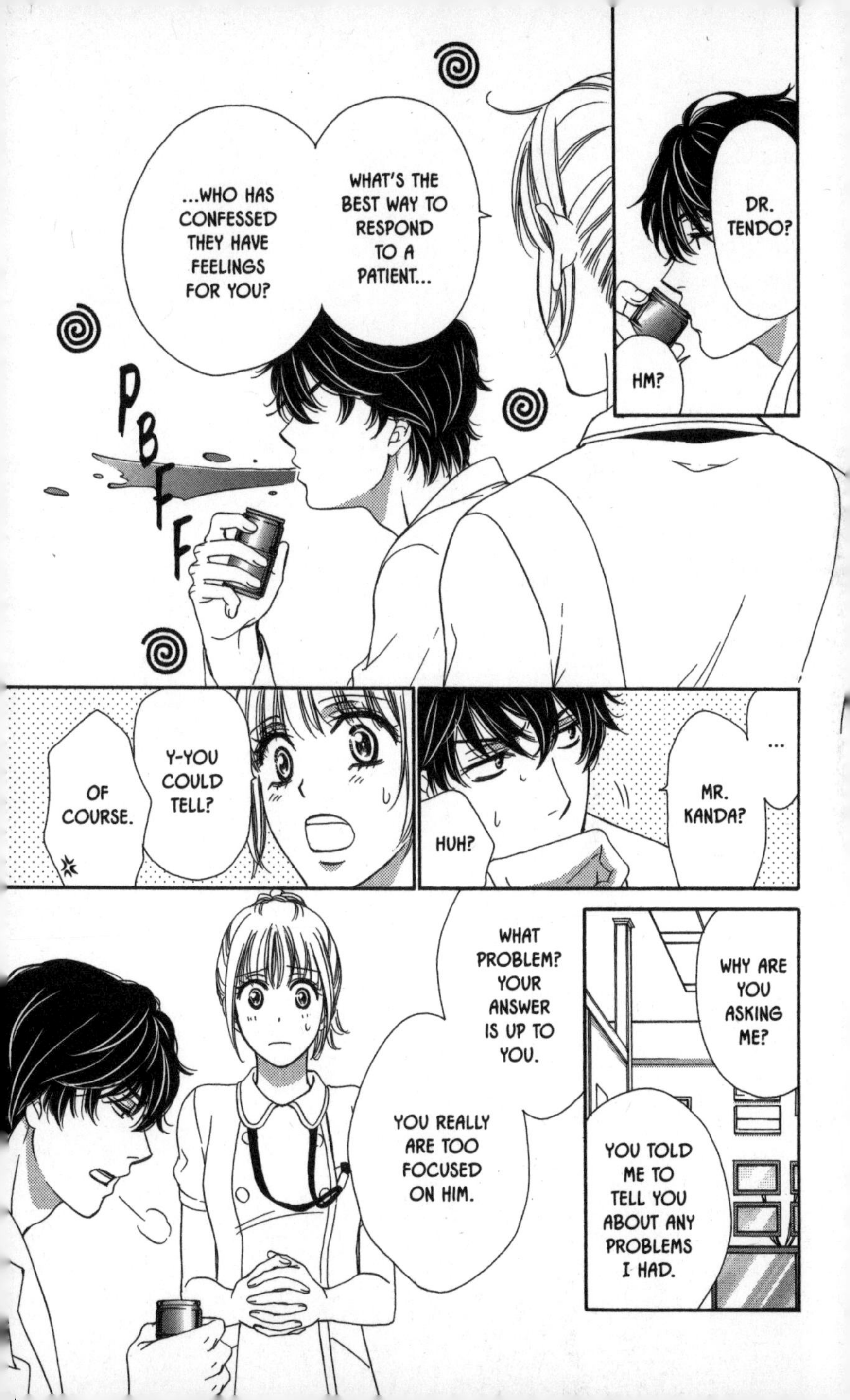
DR. TENDO?
HM?
WHAT'S THE BEST WAY TO RESPOND TO A PATIENT...
...WHO HAS CONFESSED THEY HAVE FEELINGS FOR YOU?
PBFF
...
MR. KANDA?
HUH?
Y-YOU COULD TELL?
OF COURSE.
WHY ARE YOU ASKING ME?
YOU TOLD ME TO TELL YOU ABOUT ANY PROBLEMS I HAD.
WHAT PROBLEM? YOUR ANSWER IS UP TO YOU.
YOU REALLY ARE TOO FOCUSED ON HIM.

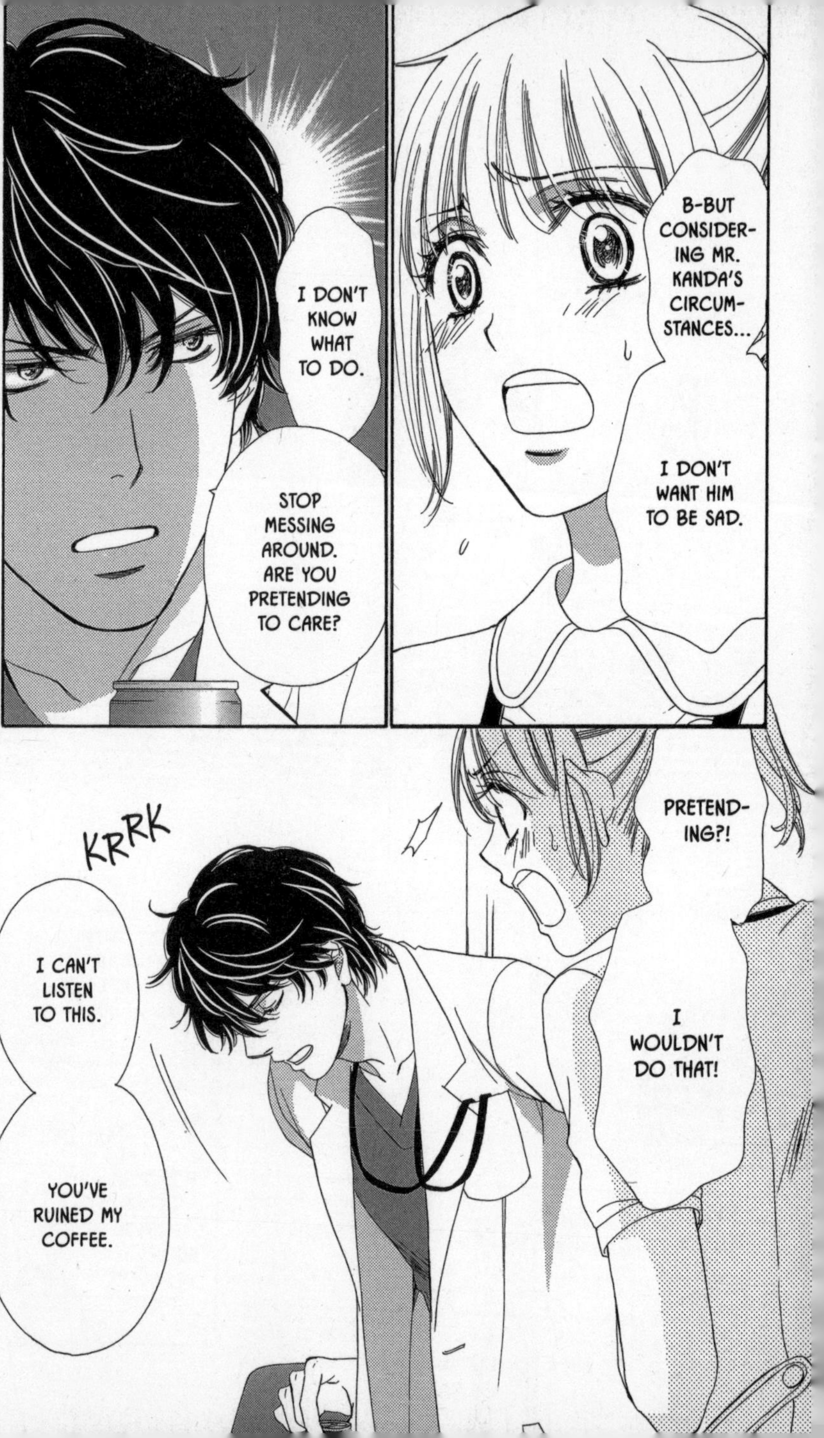
B-BUT CONSIDERING MR. KANDA'S CIRCUMSTANCES...
I DON'T WANT HIM TO BE SAD.
I DON'T KNOW WHAT TO DO.
STOP MESSING AROUND. ARE YOU PRETENDING TO CARE?
PRETENDING?!
I WOULDN'T DO THAT!
KRRK
I CAN'T LISTEN TO THIS.
YOU'VE RUINED MY COFFEE.

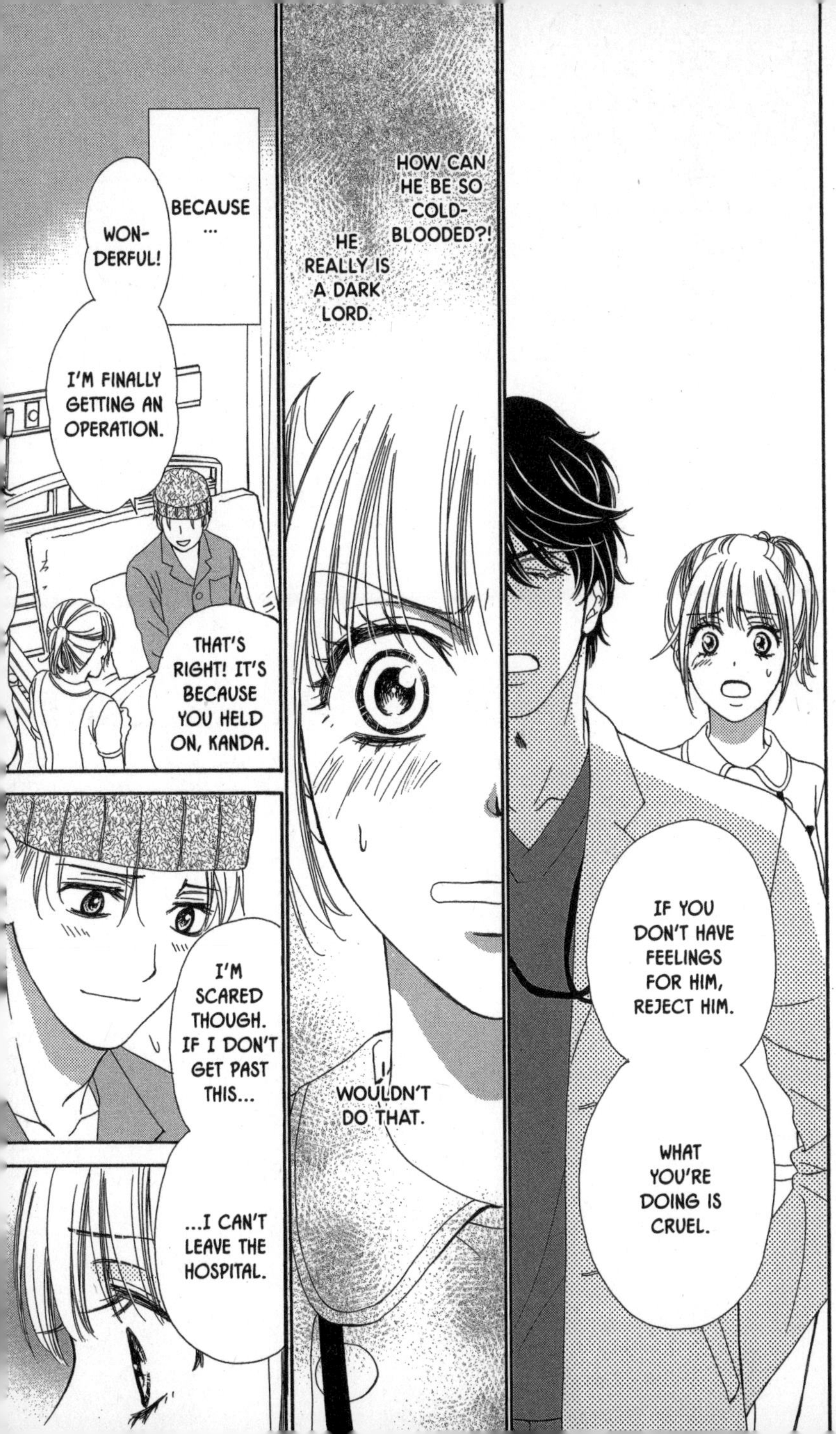
IF YOU DON'T HAVE FEELINGS FOR HIM, REJECT HIM.
WHAT YOU'RE DOING IS CRUEL.
HOW CAN HE BE SO COLD-BLOODED?!
HE REALLY IS A DARK LORD.
I WOULDN'T DO THAT.
BECAUSE ...
WON-DERFUL!
I'M FINALLY GETTING AN OPERATION.
THAT'S RIGHT! IT'S BECAUSE YOU HELD ON, KANDA.
I'M SCARED THOUGH. IF I DON'T GET PAST THIS...
...I CAN'T LEAVE THE HOSPITAL.

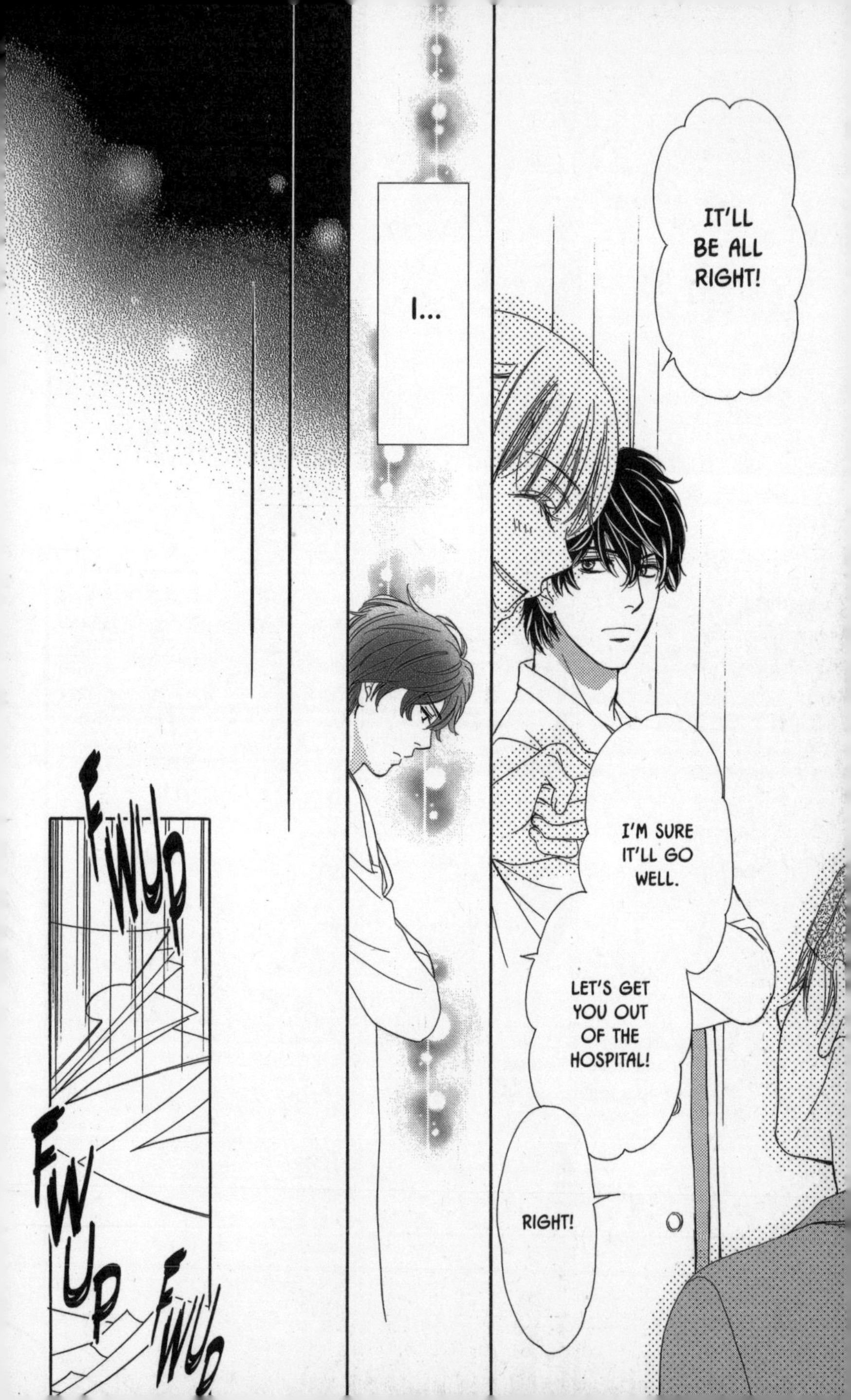
IT'LL BE ALL RIGHT!
I'M SURE IT'LL GO WELL.
LET'S GET YOU OUT OF THE HOSPITAL!
RIGHT!
I...
FWUP
FWUP FWUP

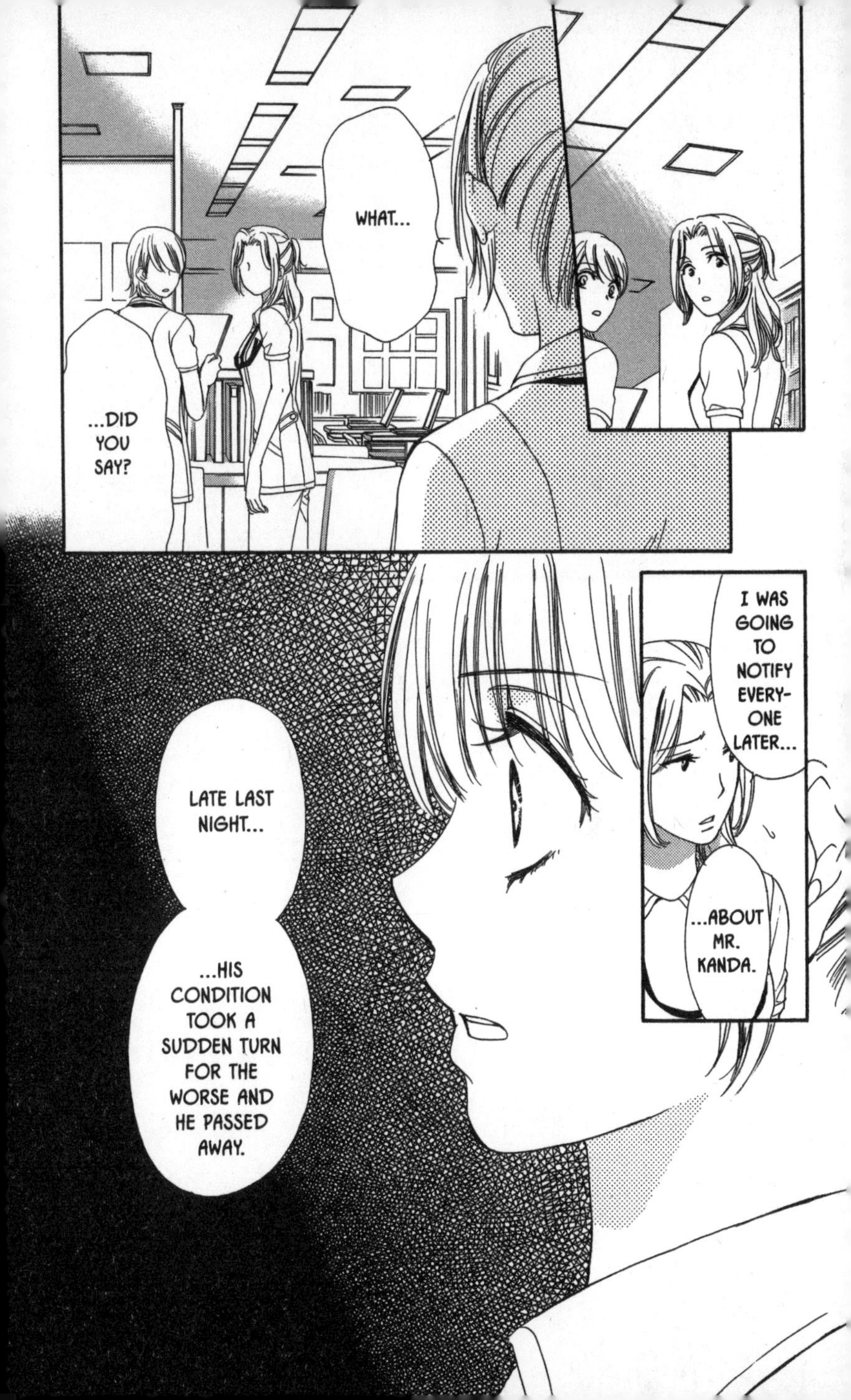
WHAT...
...DID YOU SAY?
I WAS GOING TO NOTIFY EVERY-ONE LATER...
...ABOUT MR. KANDA.
LATE LAST NIGHT...
...HIS CONDITION TOOK A SUDDEN TURN FOR THE WORSE AND HE PASSED AWAY.

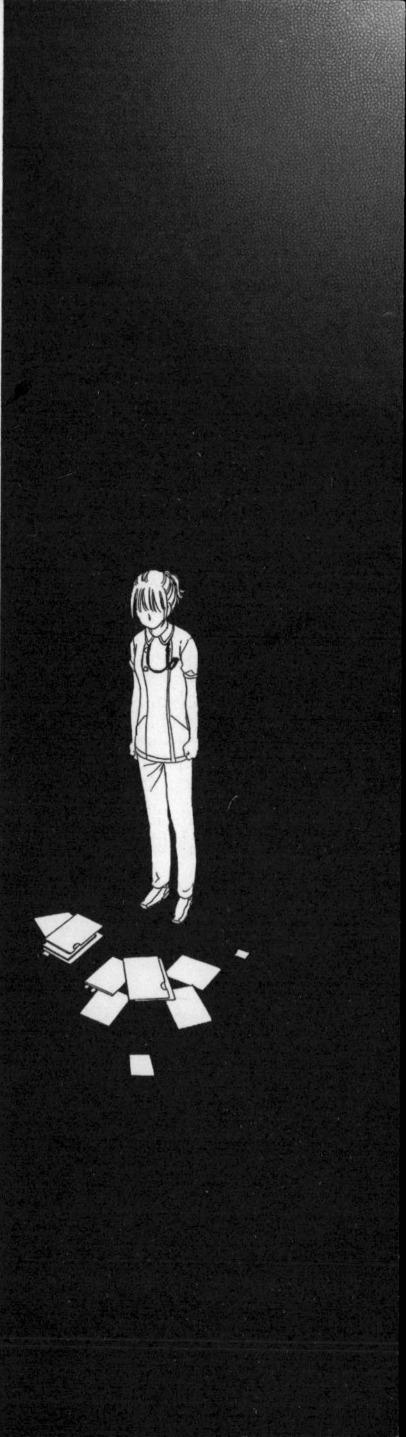

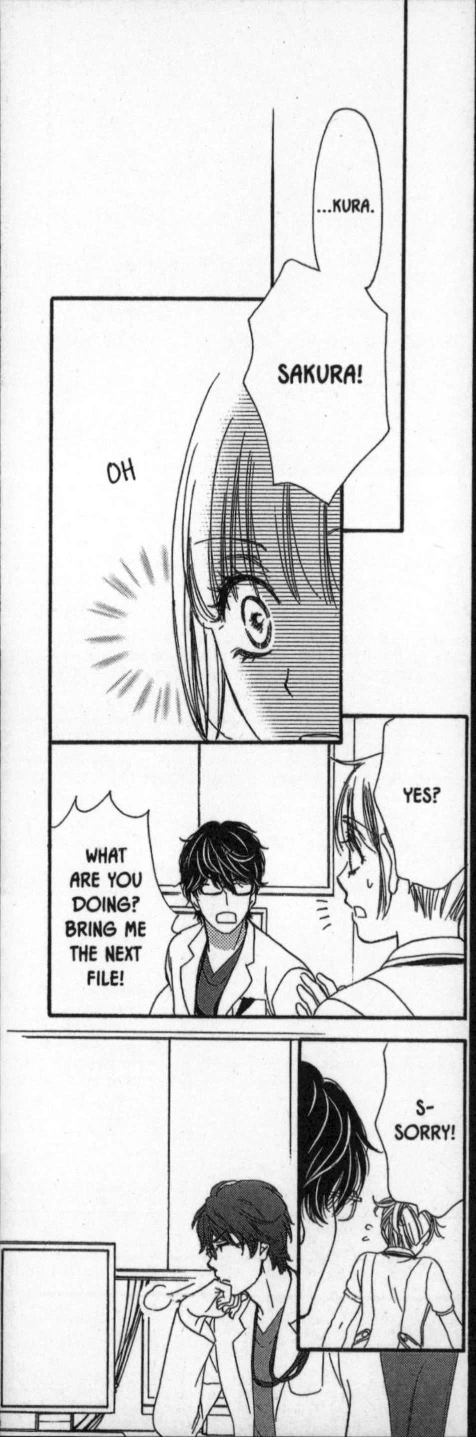
...KURA.
SAKURA!
OH
YES?
WHAT ARE YOU DOING? BRING ME THE NEXT FILE!
S- SORRY!

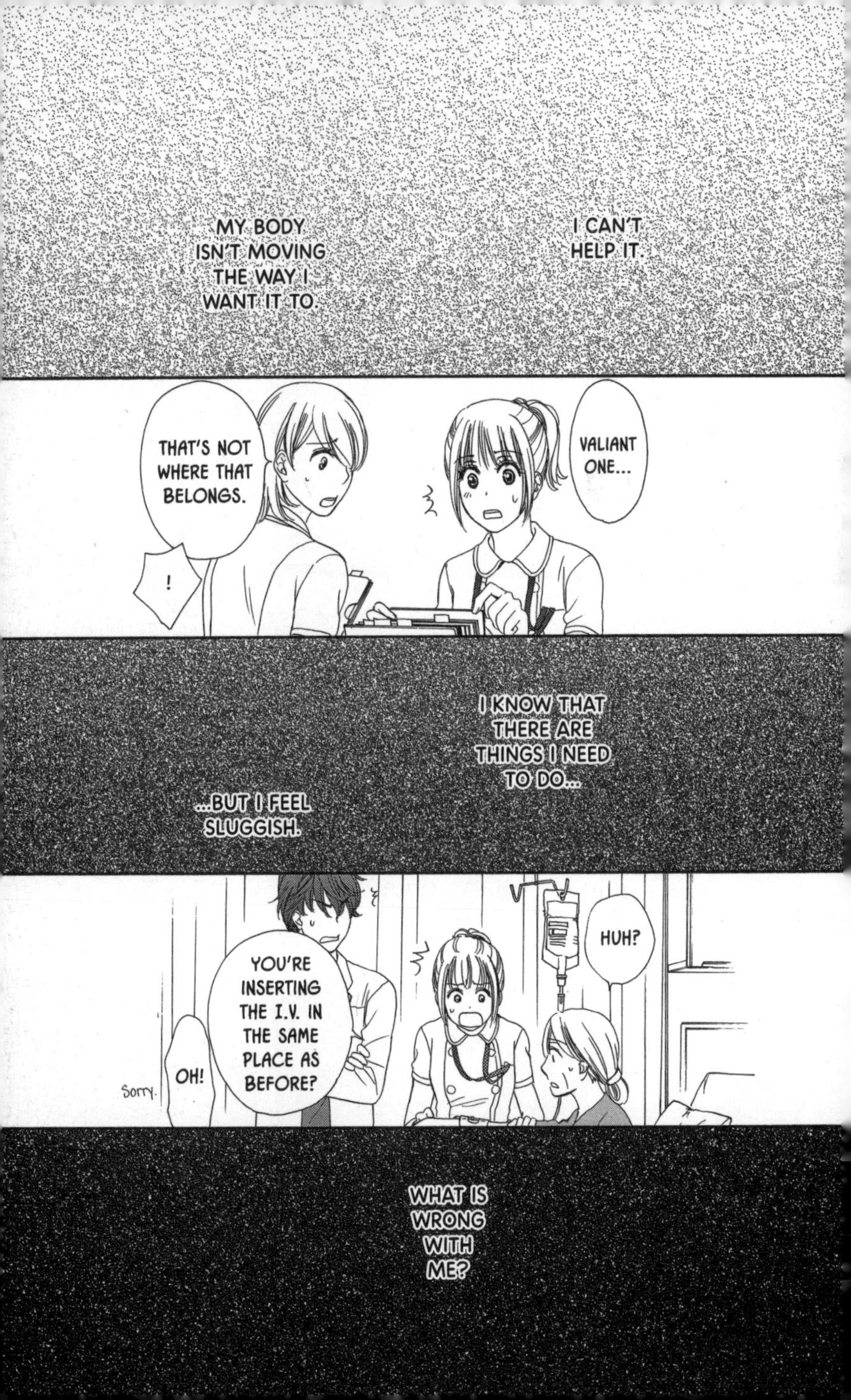
I CAN'T HELP IT.
MY BODY ISN'T MOVING THE WAY I WANT IT TO.
VALIANT ONE...
THAT'S NOT WHERE THAT BELONGS.
!
I KNOW THAT THERE ARE THINGS I NEED TO DO...
...BUT I FEEL SLUGGISH.
HUH?
YOU'RE INSERTING THE I.V. IN THE SAME PLACE AS BEFORE?
OH!
Sorry.
WHAT IS WRONG WITH ME?

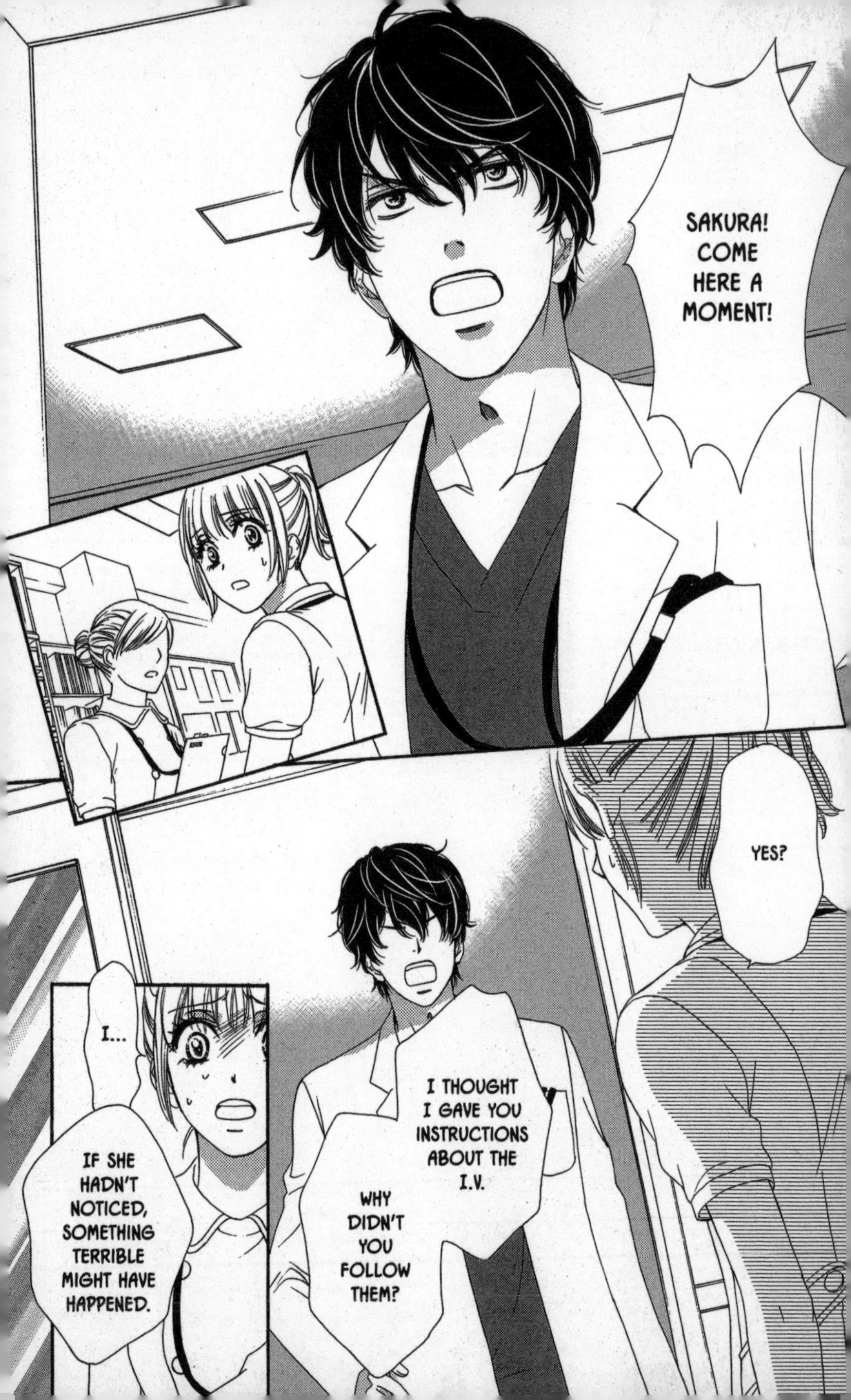
SAKURA! COME HERE A MOMENT!
YES?
I THOUGHT I GAVE YOU INSTRUCTIONS ABOUT THE I.V.
WHY DIDN'T YOU FOLLOW THEM?
I...
IF SHE HADN'T NOTICED, SOMETHING TERRIBLE MIGHT HAVE HAPPENED.

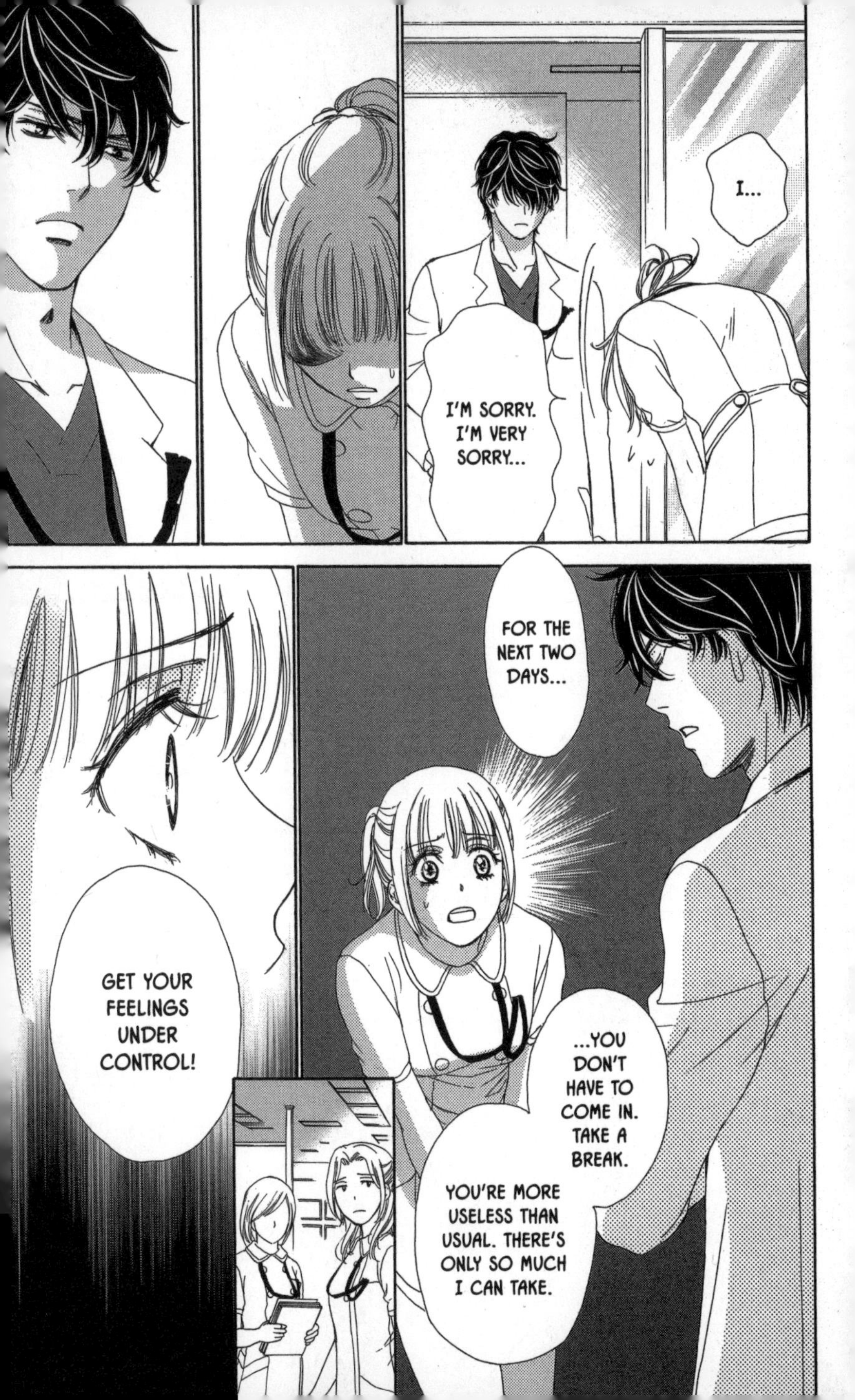
I...
I'M SORRY. I'M VERY SORRY...
FOR THE NEXT TWO DAYS...
...YOU DON'T HAVE TO COME IN. TAKE A BREAK.
YOU'RE MORE USELESS THAN USUAL. THERE'S ONLY SO MUCH I CAN TAKE.
GET YOUR FEELINGS UNDER CONTROL!

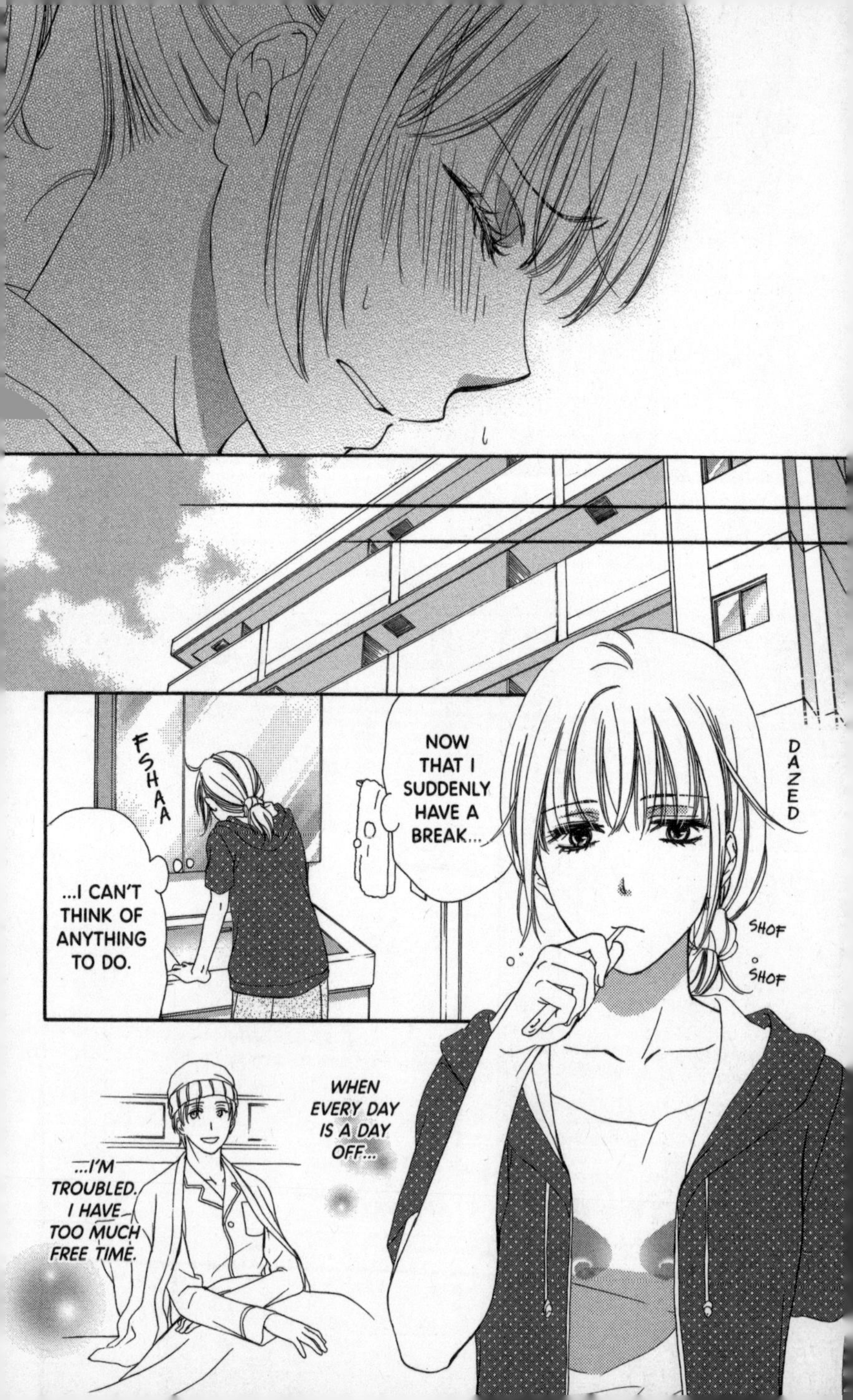
DAZED
NOW THAT I SUDDENLY HAVE A BREAK...
SHOF SHOF
FSHAA
...I CAN'T THINK OF ANYTHING TO DO.
WHEN EVERY DAY IS A DAY OFF...
...I'M TROUBLED. I HAVE TOO MUCH FREE TIME.

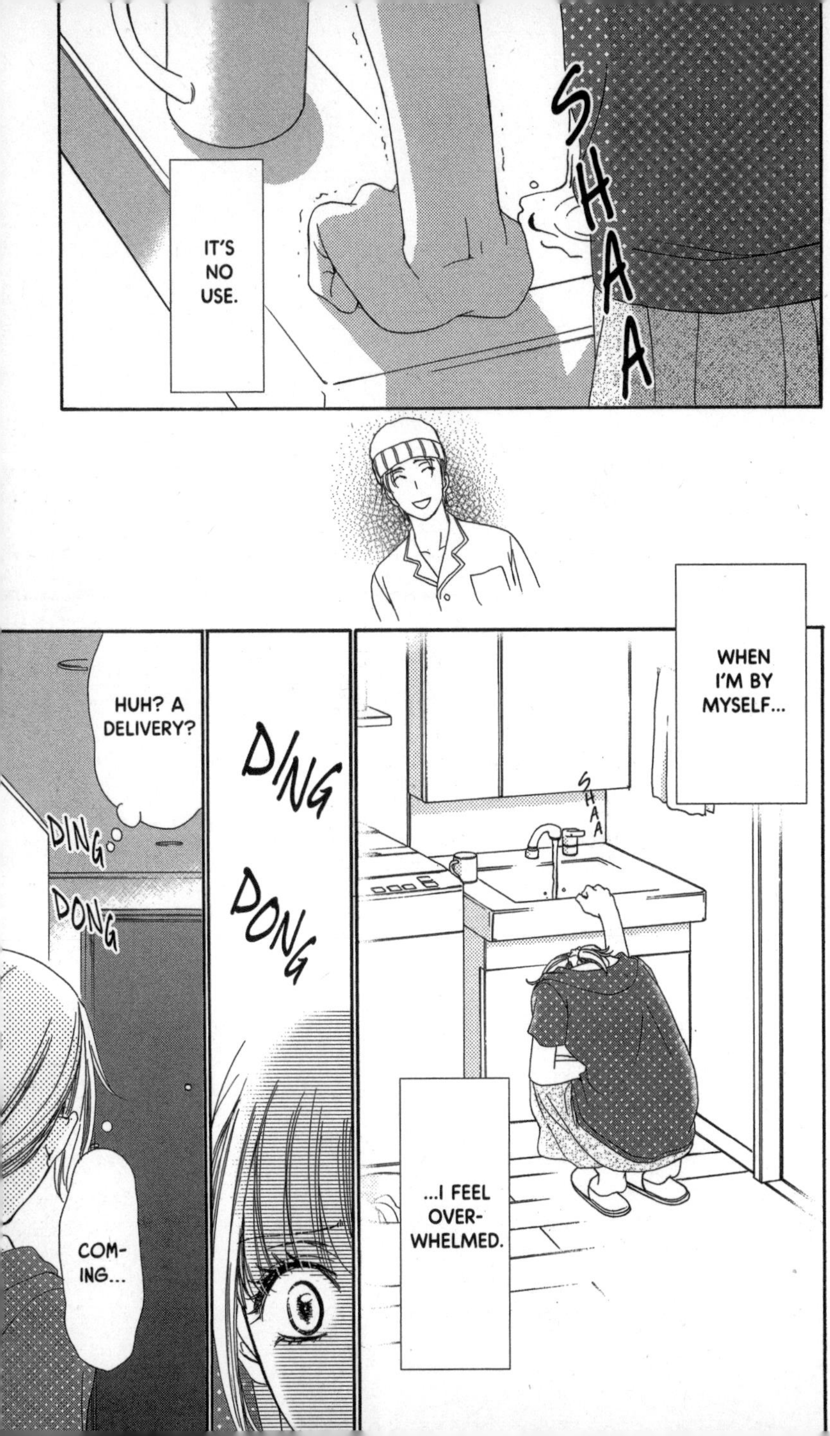
SHAA
IT'S NO USE.
WHEN I'M BY MYSELF...
SHAA
...I FEEL OVER-WHELMED.
DING DONG
HUH? A DELIVERY?
DING DONG
COM-ING...

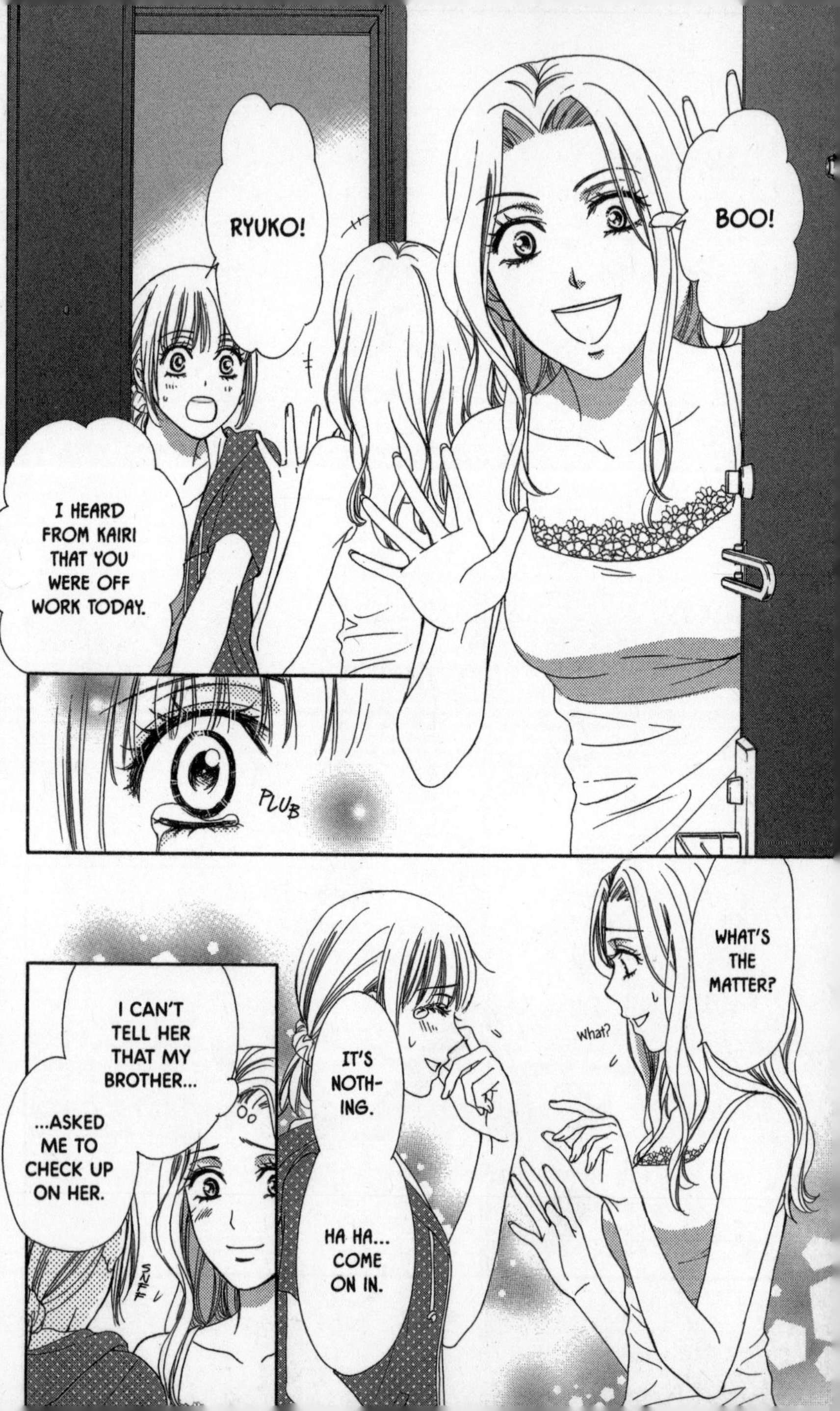
BOO!
RYUKO!
I HEARD FROM KAIRI THAT YOU WERE OFF WORK TODAY.
PLUB
WHAT'S THE MATTER?
What?
IT'S NOTH-ING.
HA HA... COME ON IN.
I CAN'T TELL HER THAT MY BROTHER...
...ASKED ME TO CHECK UP ON HER.
SNFF

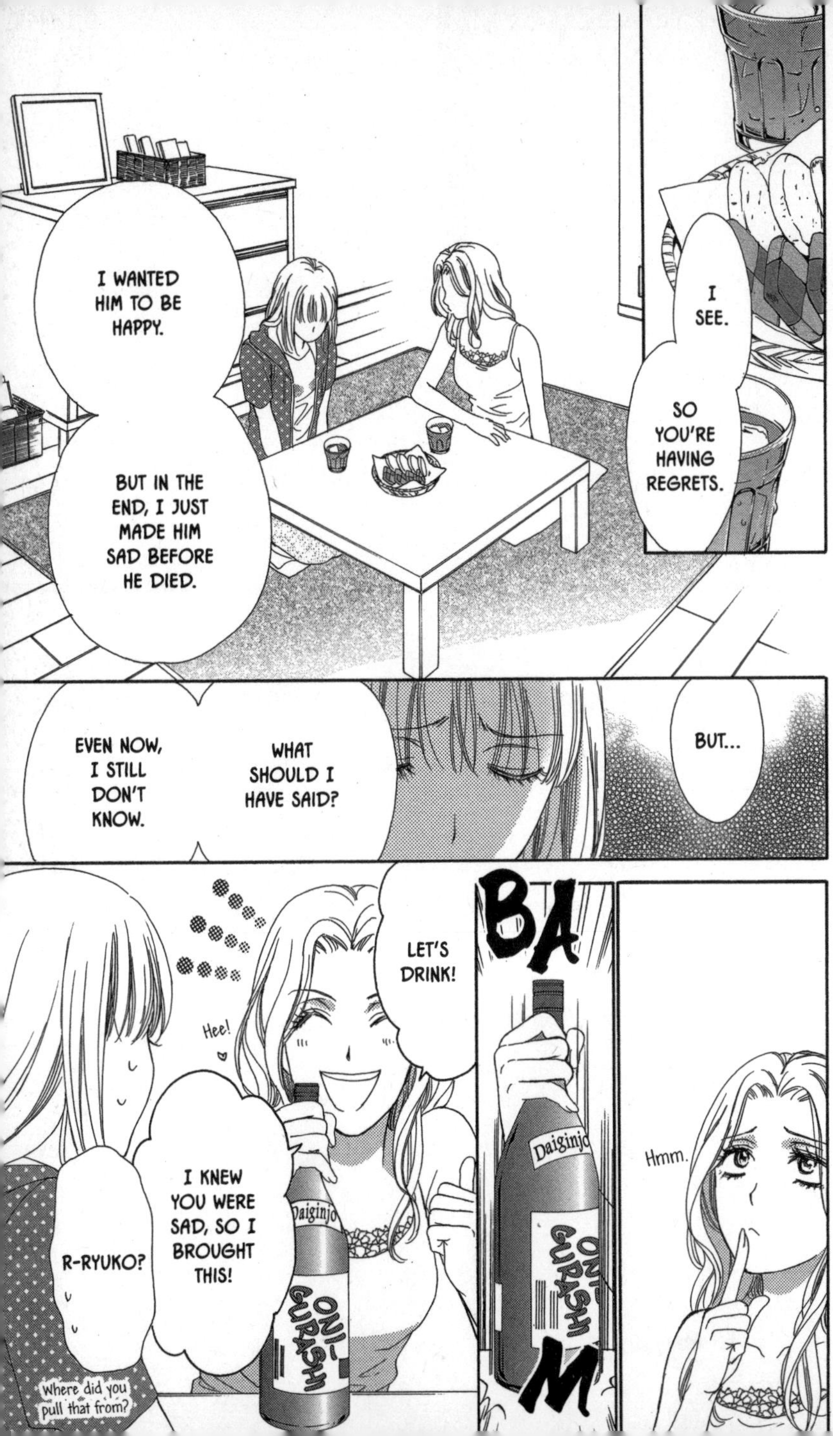
I SEE.
SO YOU'RE HAVING REGRETS.
I WANTED HIM TO BE HAPPY.
BUT IN THE END, I JUST MADE HIM SAD BEFORE HE DIED.
BUT...
WHAT SHOULD I HAVE SAID?
EVEN NOW, I STILL DON'T KNOW.
Hmm.
BAM
Daiginjo
ONI-GURASHI
LET'S DRINK!
Hee!
I KNEW YOU WERE SAD, SO I BROUGHT THIS!
Daiginjo
ONI-GURASHI
R-RYUKO?
Where did you pull that from?

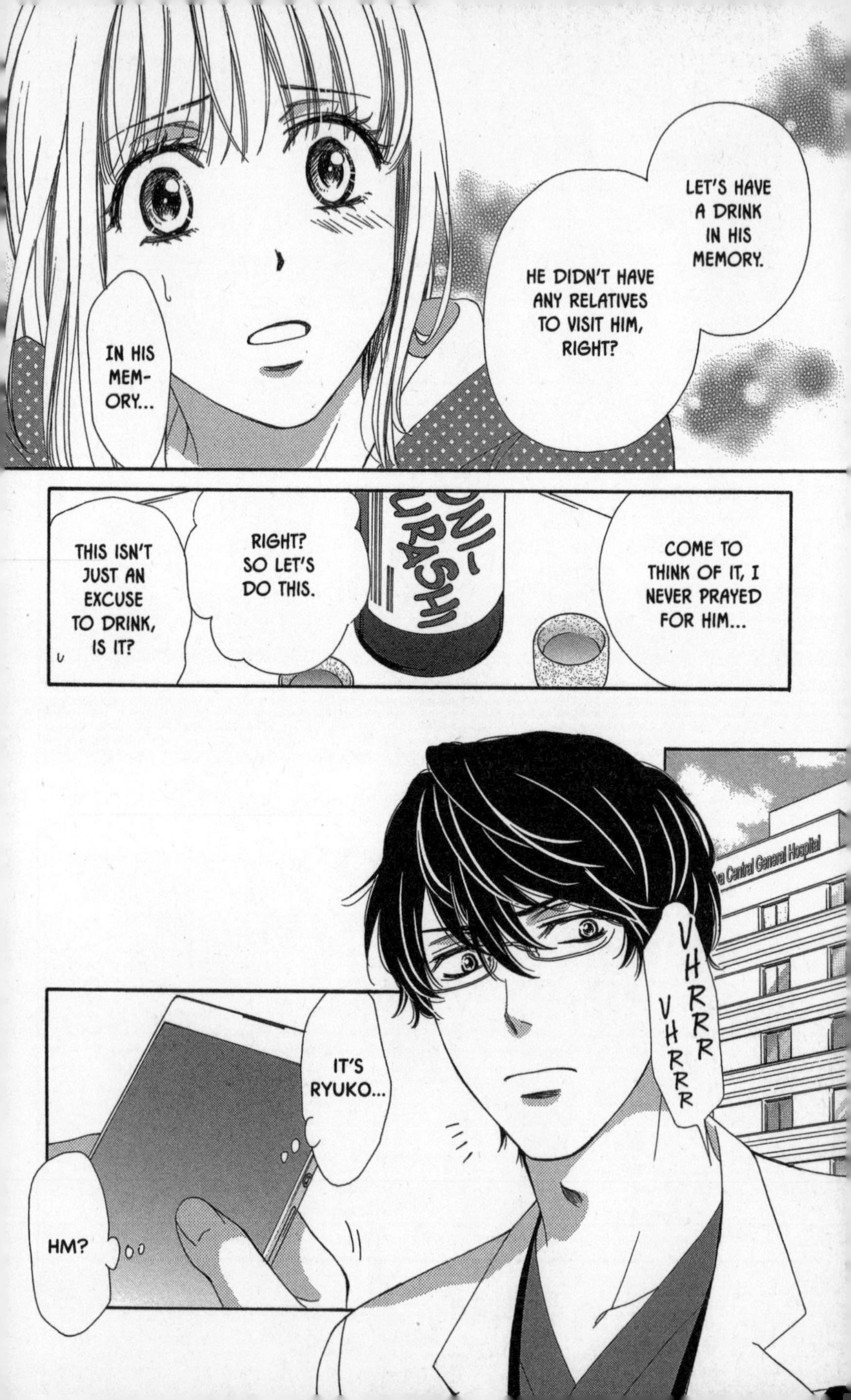
LET'S HAVE A DRINK IN HIS MEMORY.
HE DIDN'T HAVE ANY RELATIVES TO VISIT HIM, RIGHT?
IN HIS MEM-ORY...
COME TO THINK OF IT, I NEVER PRAYED FOR HIM...
RIGHT? SO LET'S DO THIS.
THIS ISN'T JUST AN EXCUSE TO DRINK, IS IT?
VHRRR
VHRRR
IT'S RYUKO...
HM?

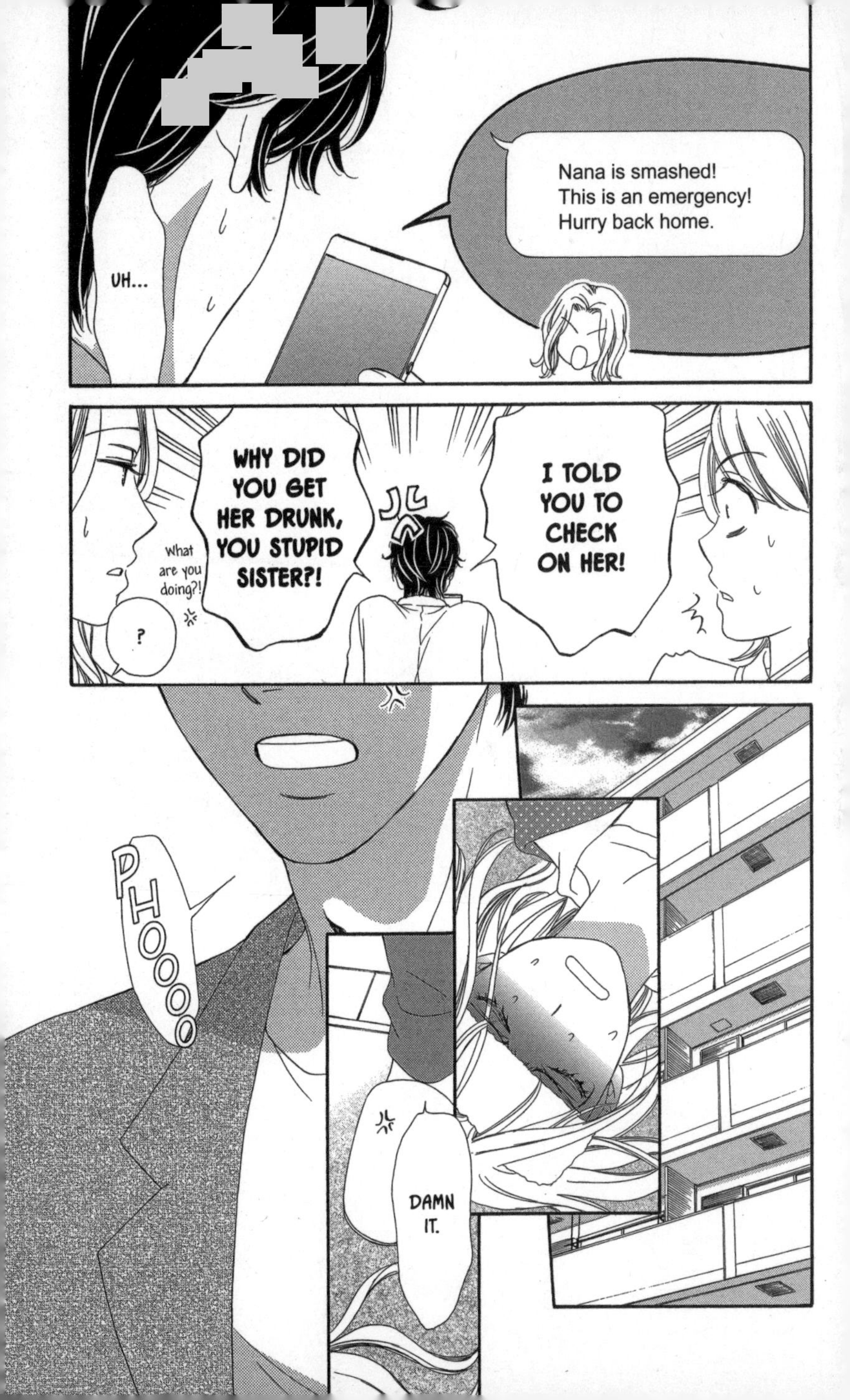
Nana is smashed!
This is an emergency!
Hurry back home.
UH...
I TOLD YOU TO CHECK ON HER!
WHY DID YOU GET HER DRUNK, YOU STUPID SISTER?!
What are you doing?!
?
DAMN IT.
PHOOOO

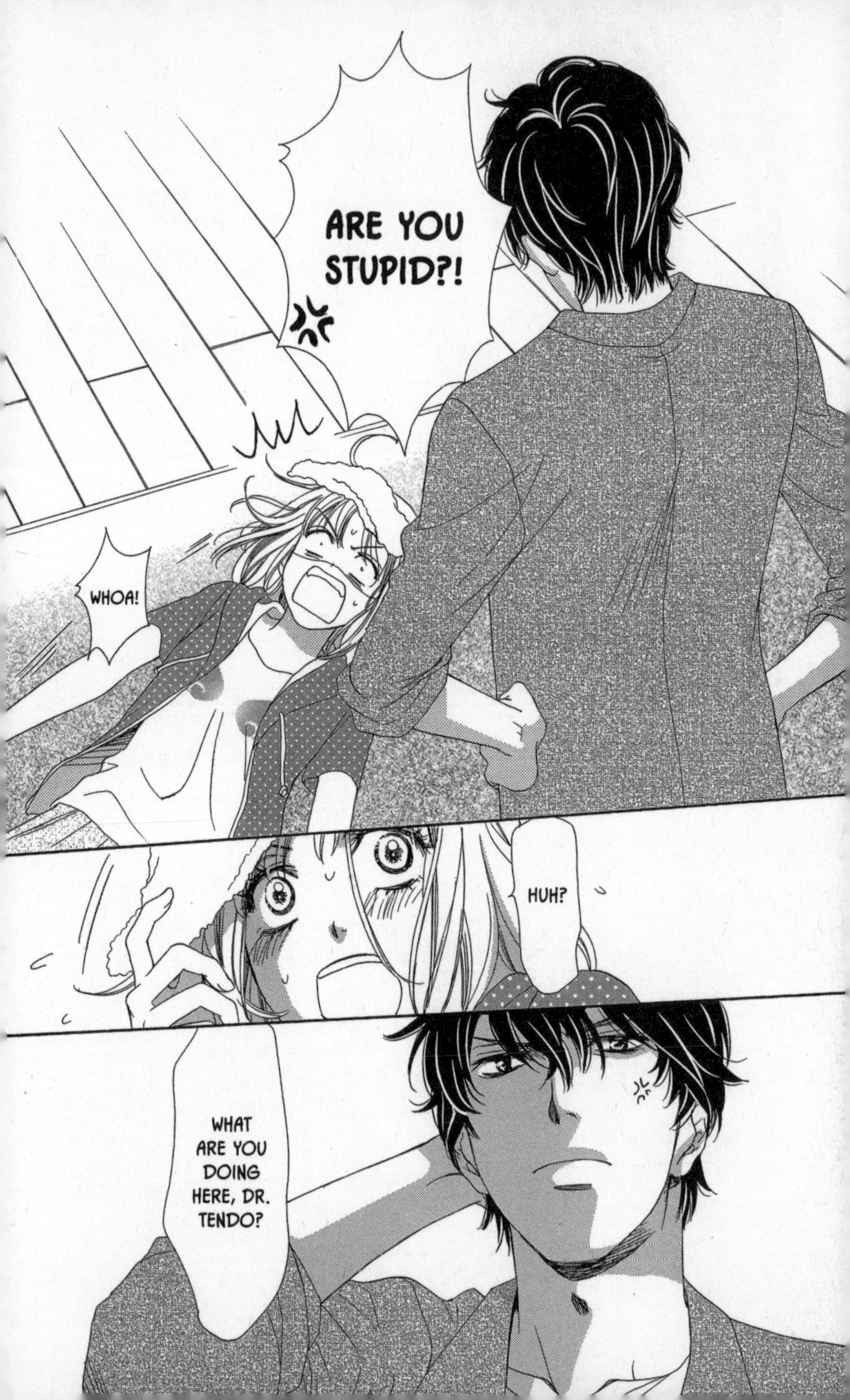
ARE YOU STUPID?!
WHOA!
HUH?
WHAT ARE YOU DOING HERE, DR. TENDO?

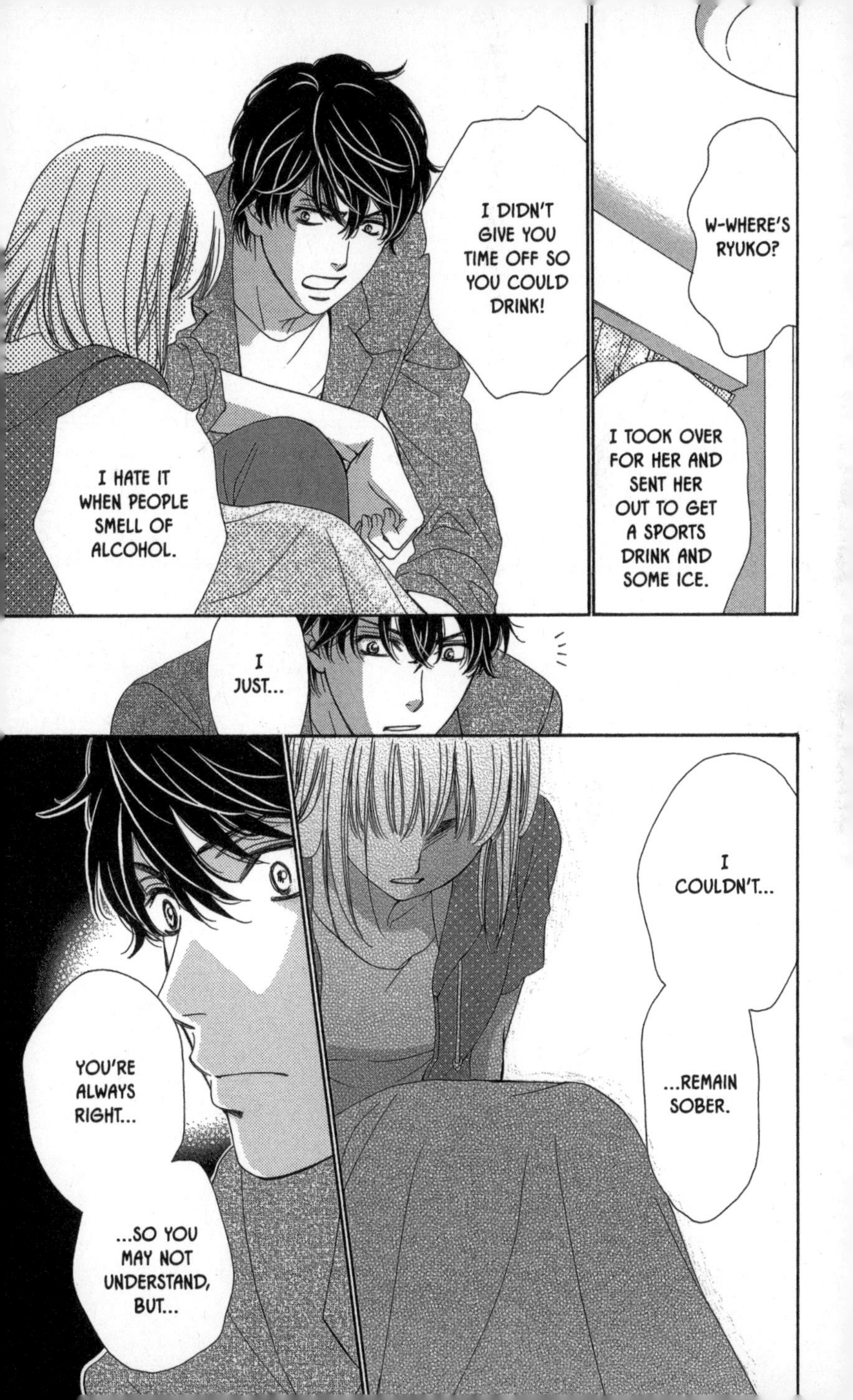
W-WHERE'S RYUKO?
I TOOK OVER FOR HER AND SENT HER OUT TO GET A SPORTS DRINK AND SOME ICE.
I DIDN'T GIVE YOU TIME OFF SO YOU COULD DRINK!
I HATE IT WHEN PEOPLE SMELL OF ALCOHOL.
I JUST...
I COULDN'T...
...REMAIN SOBER.
YOU'RE ALWAYS RIGHT...
...SO YOU MAY NOT UNDERSTAND, BUT...

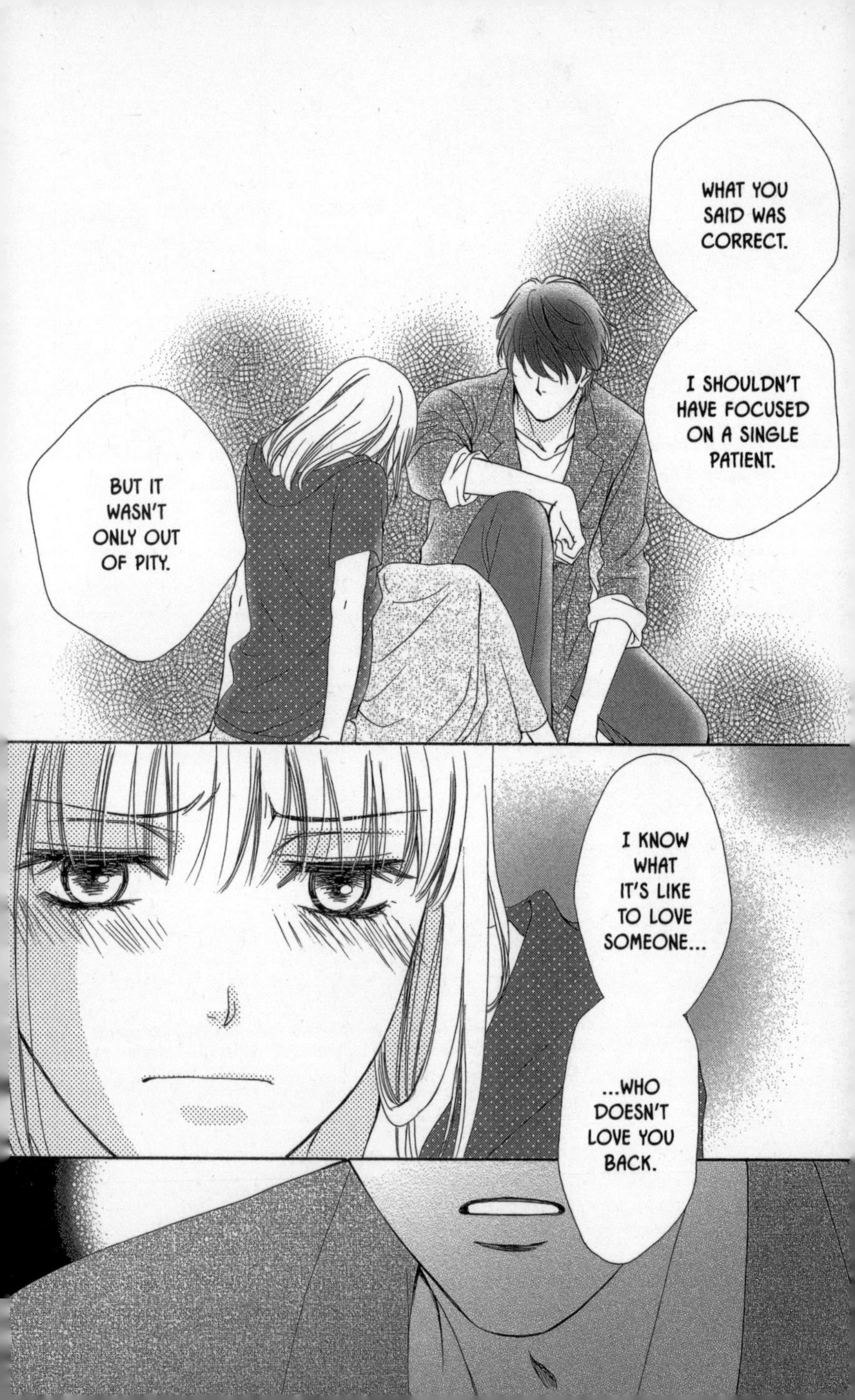
WHAT YOU SAID WAS CORRECT.
I SHOULDN'T HAVE FOCUSED ON A SINGLE PATIENT.
BUT IT WASN'T ONLY OUT OF PITY.
I KNOW WHAT IT'S LIKE TO LOVE SOMEONE...
...WHO DOESN'T LOVE YOU BACK.

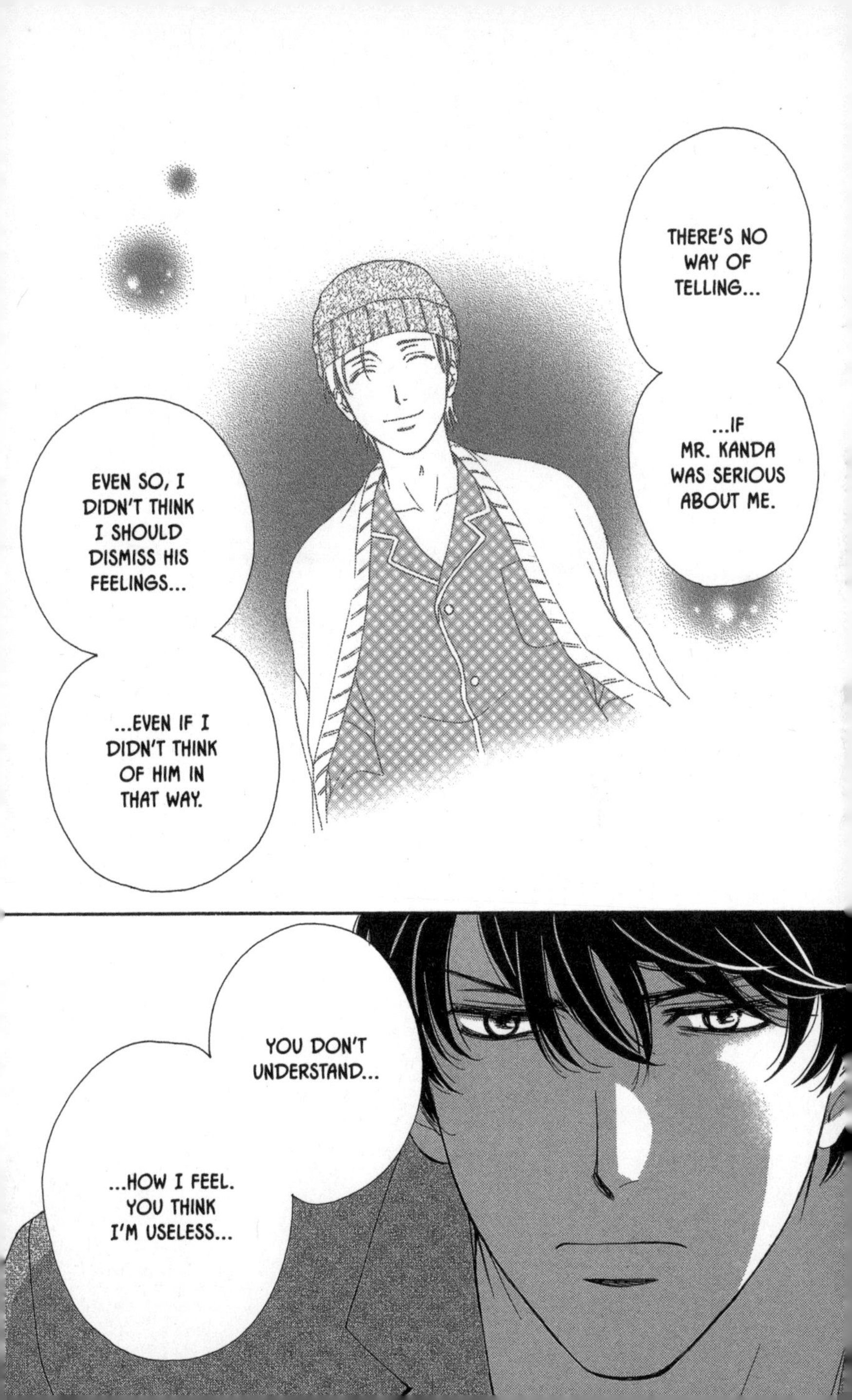
THERE'S NO WAY OF TELLING...
...IF MR. KANDA WAS SERIOUS ABOUT ME.
EVEN SO, I DIDN'T THINK I SHOULD DISMISS HIS FEELINGS...
...EVEN IF I DIDN'T THINK OF HIM IN THAT WAY.
YOU DON'T UNDERSTAND...
...HOW I FEEL. YOU THINK I'M USELESS...

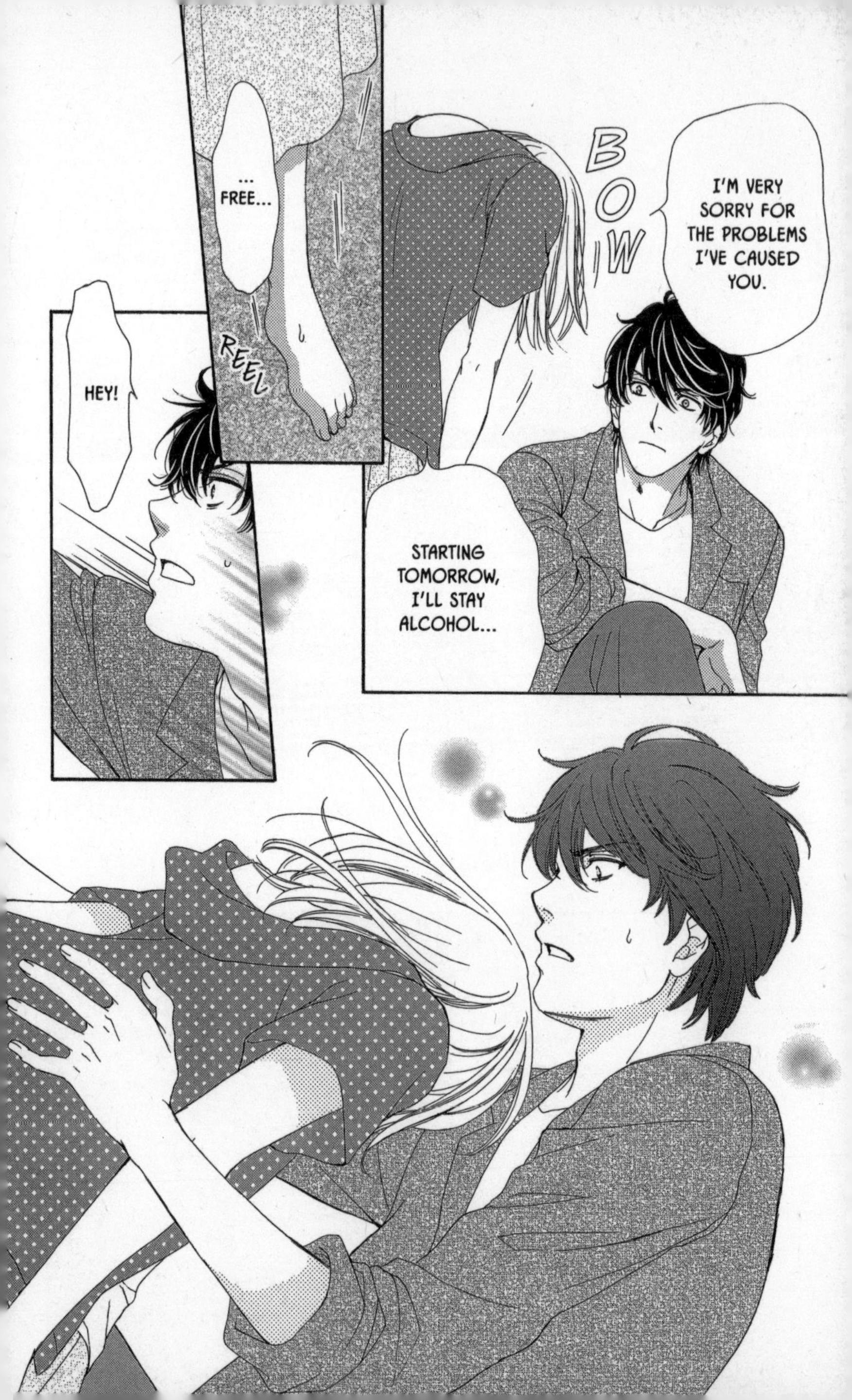
BOW
I'M VERY SORRY FOR THE PROBLEMS I'VE CAUSED YOU.
STARTING TOMORROW, I'LL STAY ALCOHOL...
... FREE...
REEL
HEY!

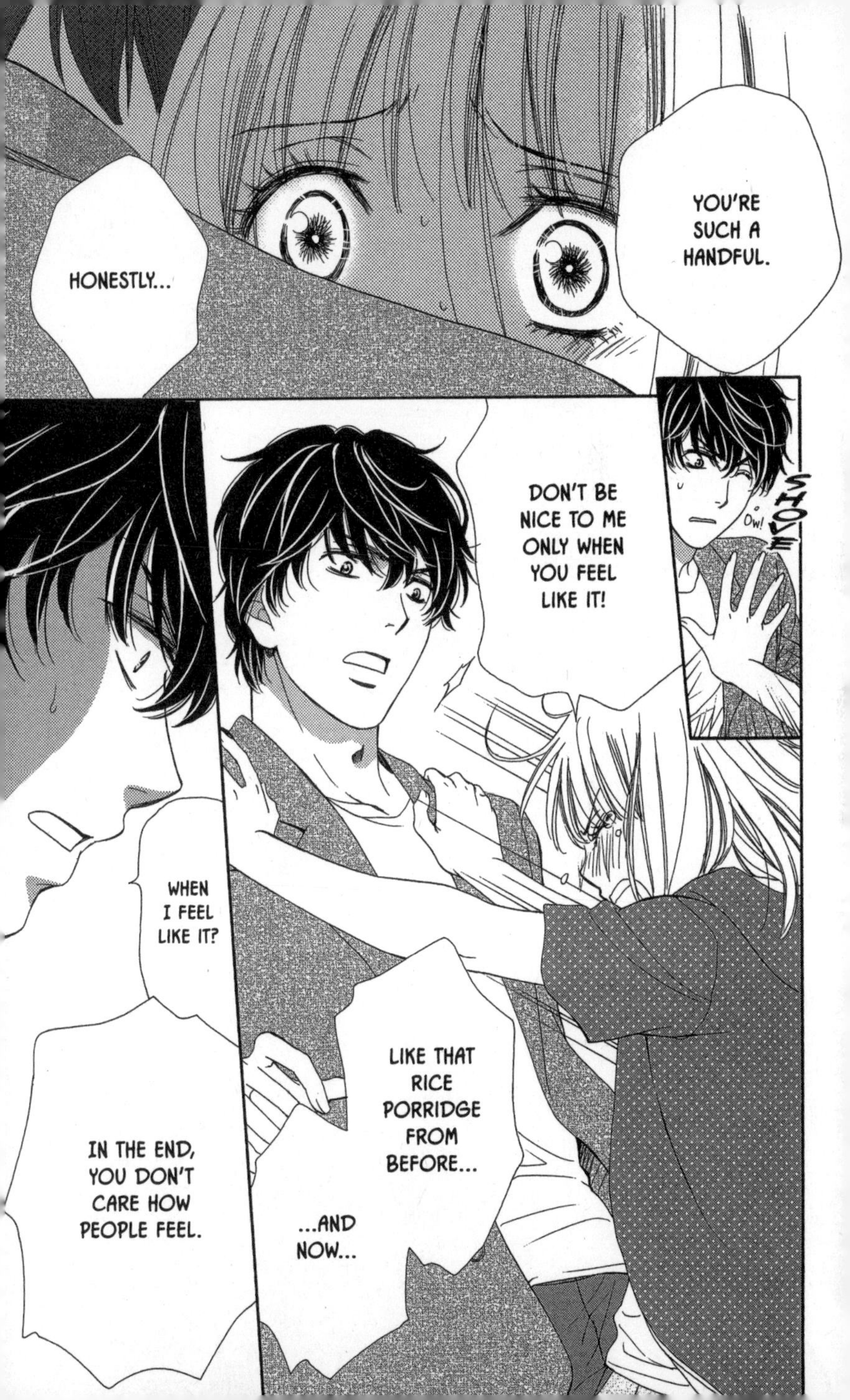
YOU'RE SUCH A HANDFUL.
HONESTLY...
SHOVE
OW!
DON'T BE NICE TO ME ONLY WHEN YOU FEEL LIKE IT!
WHEN I FEEL LIKE IT?
LIKE THAT RICE PORRIDGE FROM BEFORE...
...AND NOW...
IN THE END, YOU DON'T CARE HOW PEOPLE FEEL.

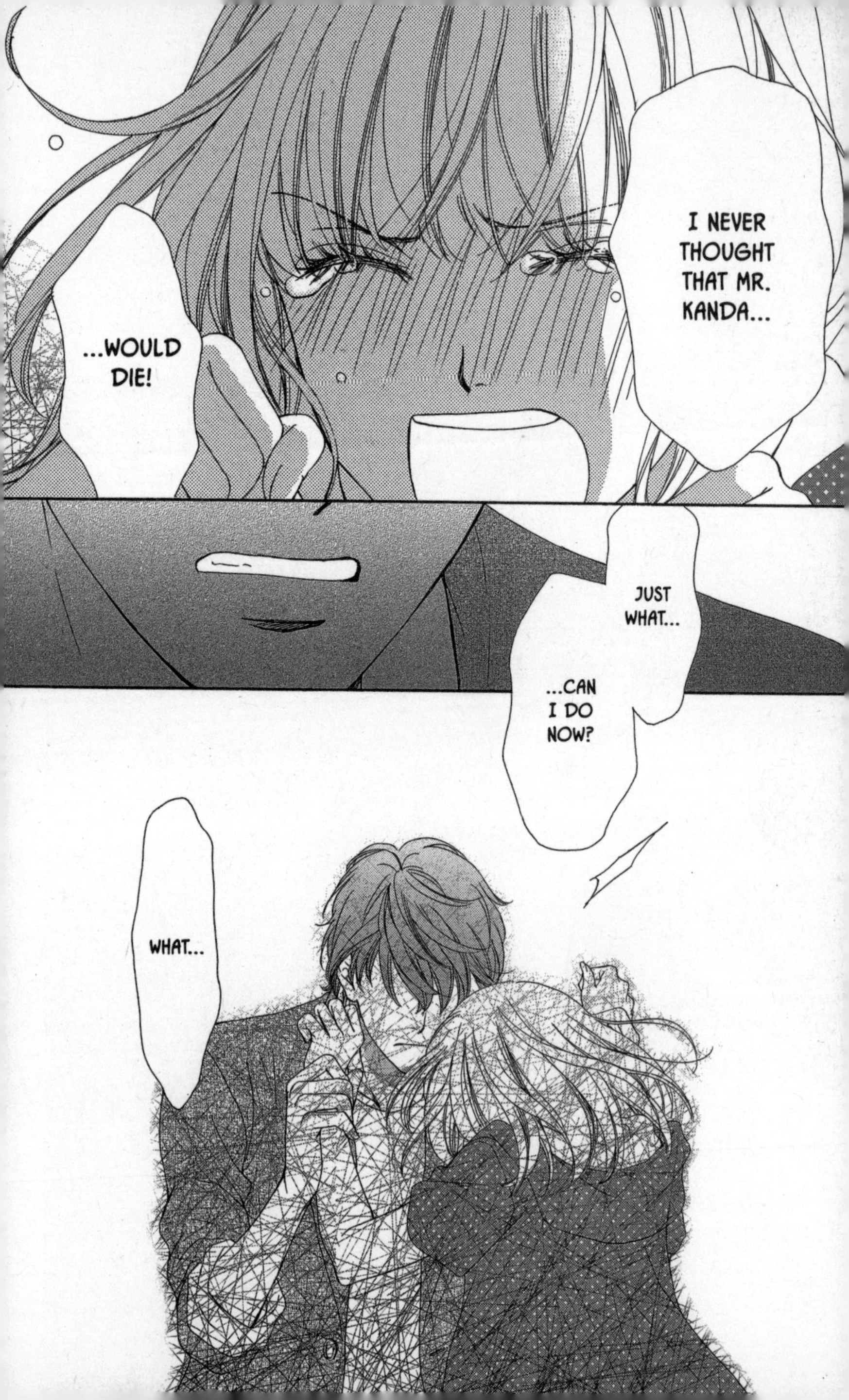
I NEVER THOUGHT THAT MR. KANDA...
...WOULD DIE!
JUST WHAT...
...CAN I DO NOW?
WHAT...

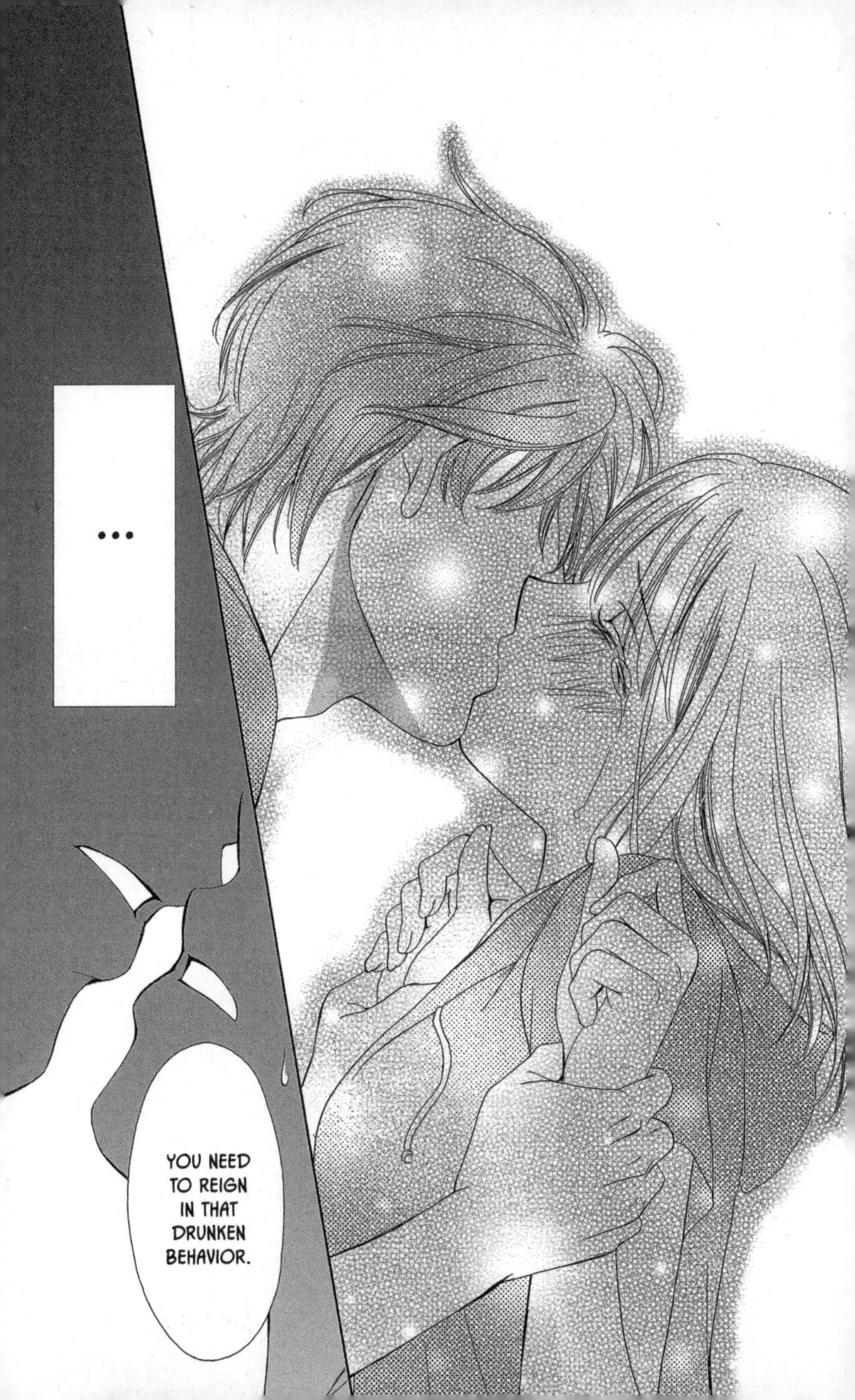
...
YOU NEED TO REIGN IN THAT DRUNKEN BEHAVIOR.

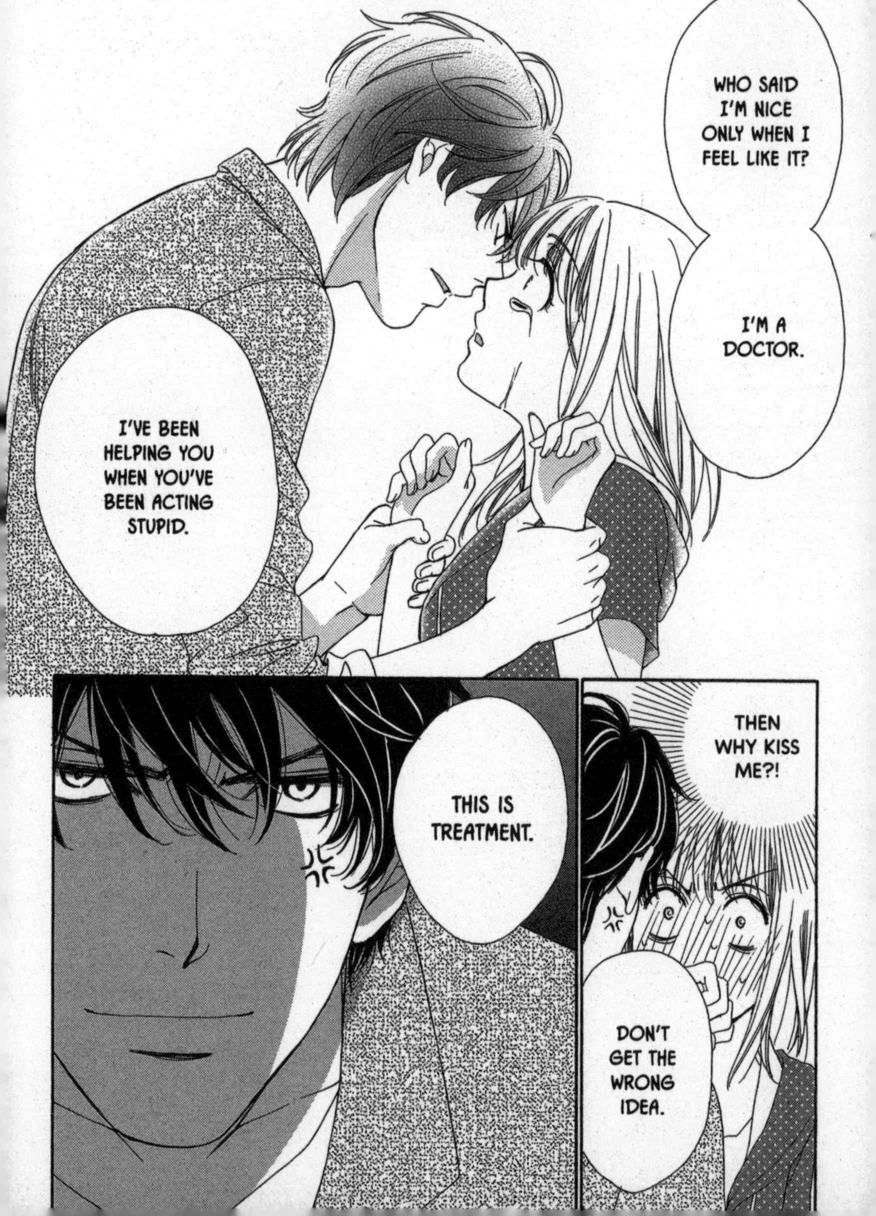
WHO SAID I'M NICE ONLY WHEN I FEEL LIKE IT?
I'M A DOCTOR.
I'VE BEEN HELPING YOU WHEN YOU'VE BEEN ACTING STUPID.
THEN WHY KISS ME?!
DON'T GET THE WRONG IDEA.
THIS IS TREATMENT.

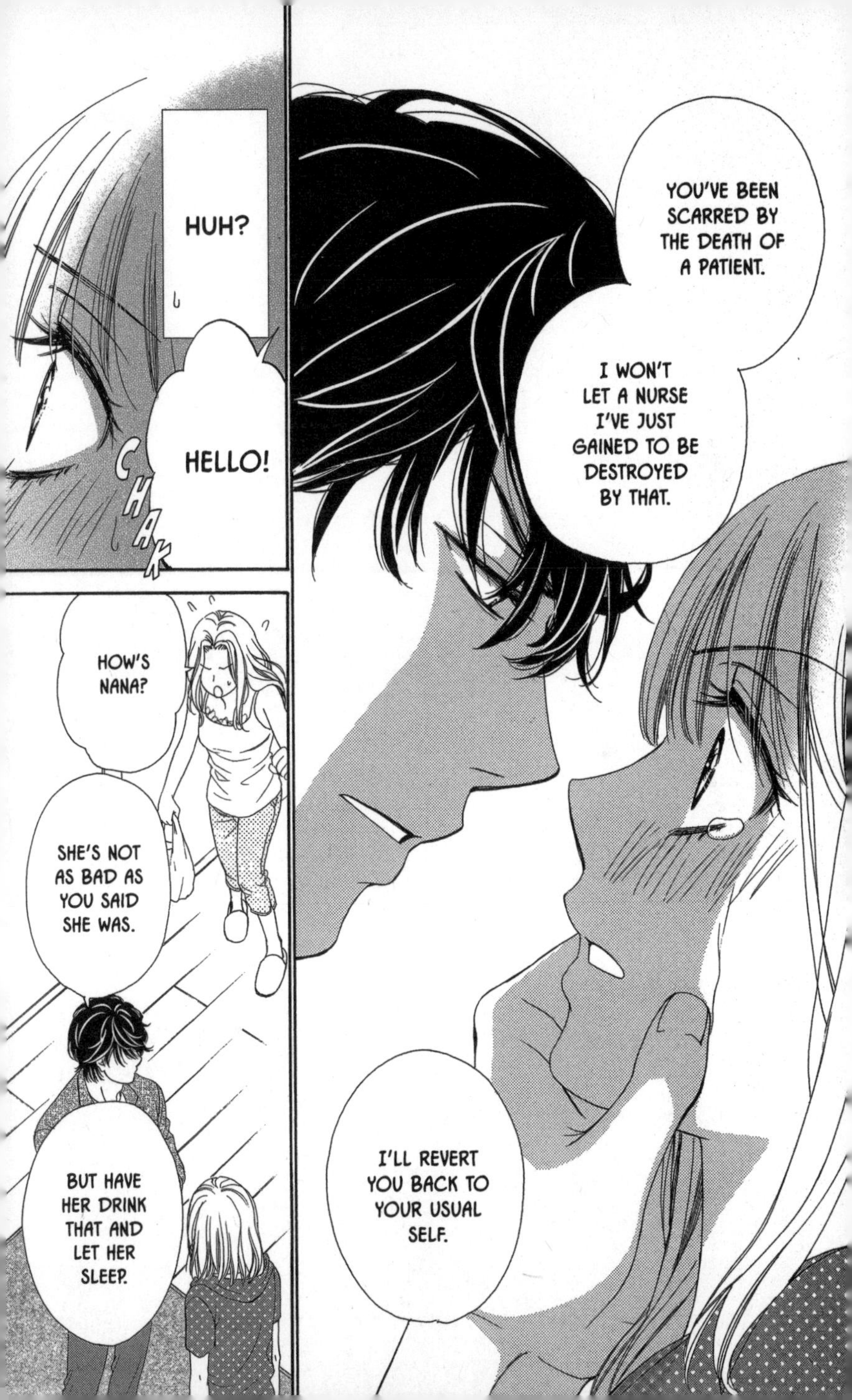
YOU'VE BEEN SCARRED BY THE DEATH OF A PATIENT.
I WON'T LET A NURSE I'VE JUST GAINED TO BE DESTROYED BY THAT.
I'LL REVERT YOU BACK TO YOUR USUAL SELF.
HUH?
HELLO!
CHAK
HOW'S NANA?
SHE'S NOT AS BAD AS YOU SAID SHE WAS.
BUT HAVE HER DRINK THAT AND LET HER SLEEP.

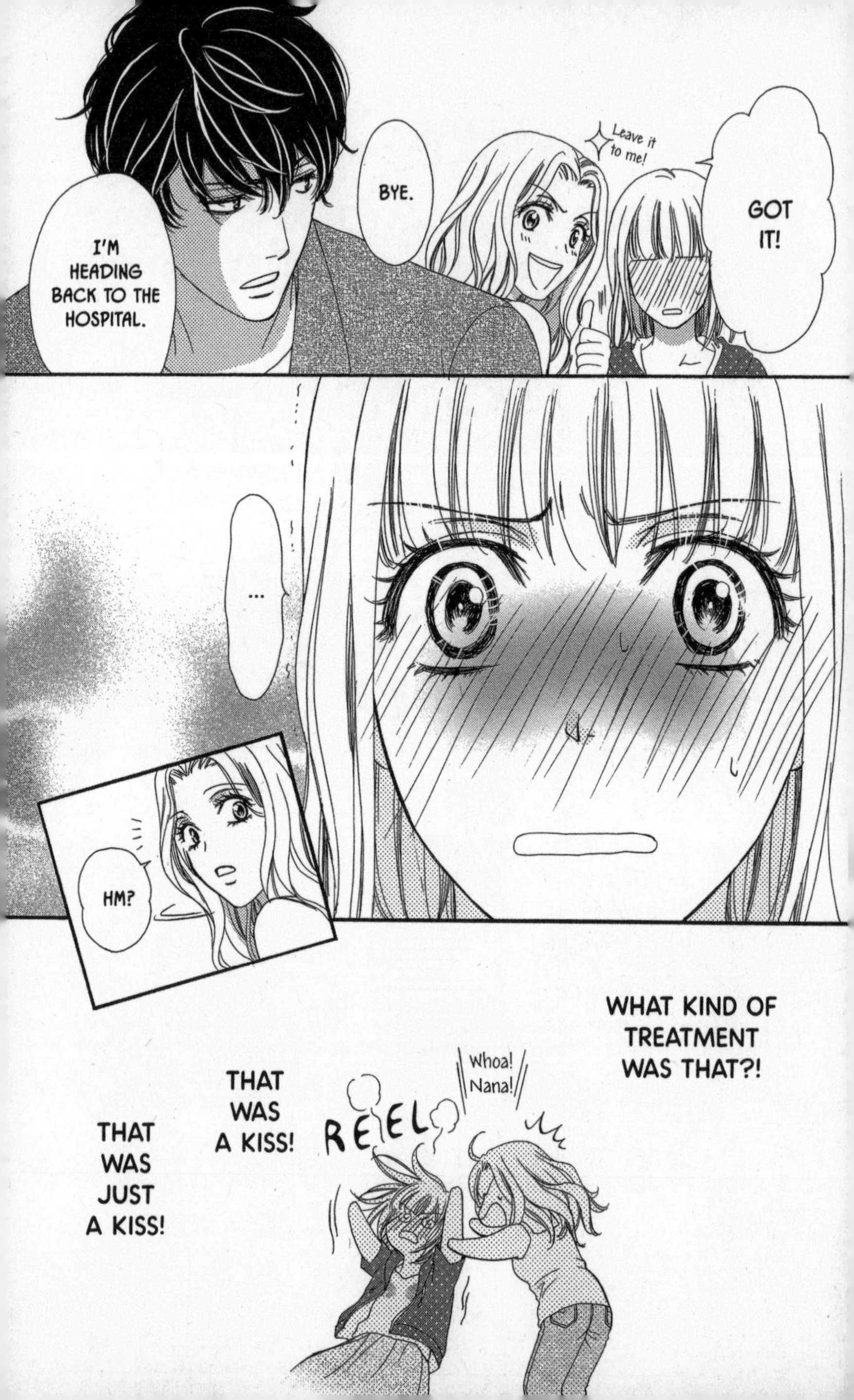
GOT IT!
Leave it to me!
BYE.
I'M HEADING BACK TO THE HOSPITAL.
...
HM?
WHAT KIND OF TREATMENT WAS THAT?!
Whoa! Nana!
REEL
THAT WAS A KISS!
THAT WAS JUST A KISS!

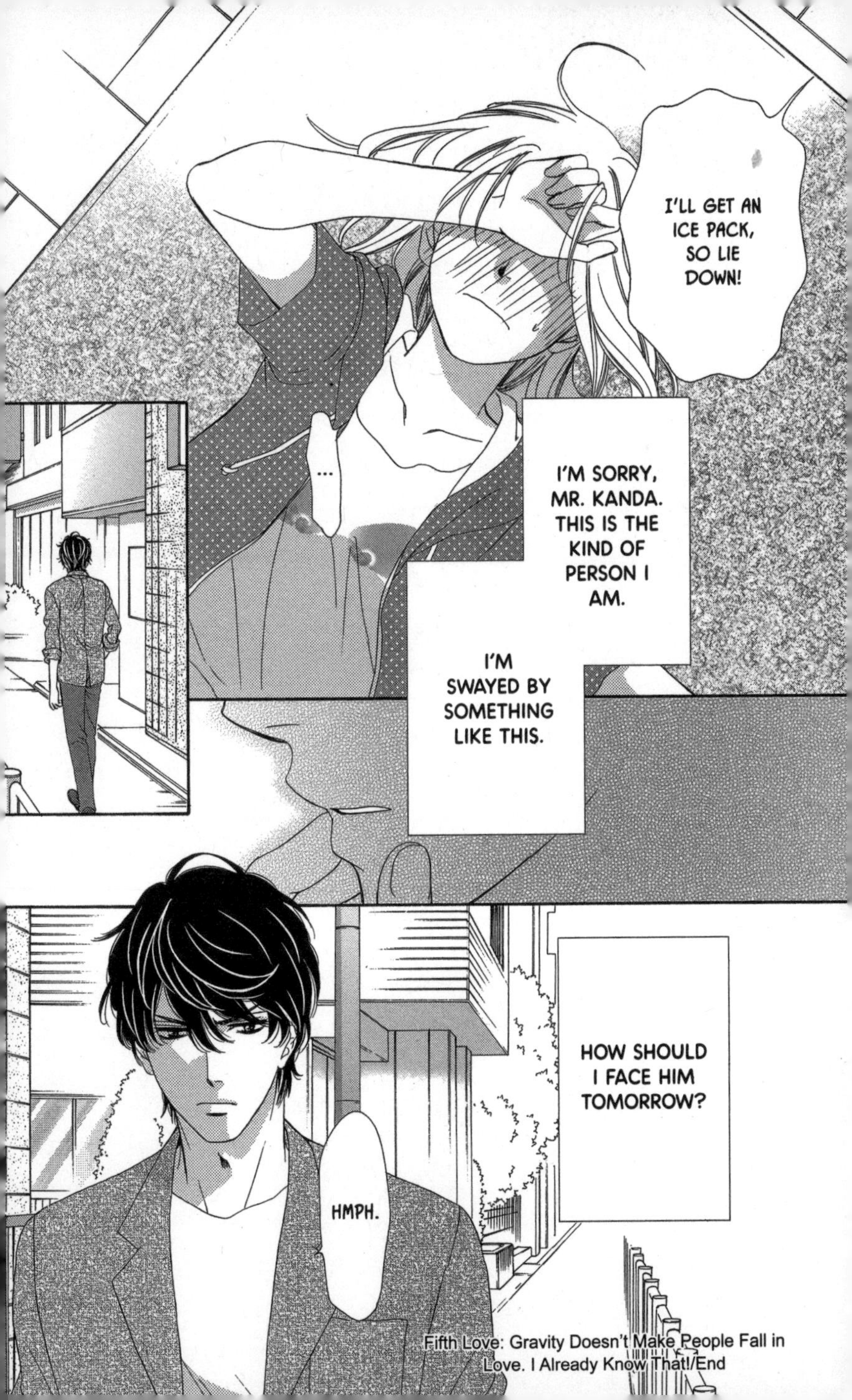
I'LL GET AN ICE PACK, SO LIE DOWN!
...
I'M SORRY, MR. KANDA. THIS IS THE KIND OF PERSON I AM.
I'M SWAYED BY SOMETHING LIKE THIS.
HOW SHOULD I FACE HIM TOMORROW?
HMPH.

Fifth Love: Gravity Doesn't Make People Fall in Love. I Already Know That!/End

They don't wear this nowadays.

A one-sided love for a person you've barely met is something that everyone experiences when they're young. The heroine of this story takes that situation and complicates it even more. On a side note, I was once determined to marry a certain member of a professional baseball team I was a fan of. This was during my first year of high school. When news of his marriage appeared in the sports pages, my friends were worried about me. It was quite painful. (*laugh*)

—Maki Enjoji

Maki Enjoji was born on December 8 in Tokyo. She made her debut with *Fu Junai* (Wicked Pure Love). Her series *Happy Marriage?!*, also published by VIZ Media's Shojo Beat imprint, was made into a live-action drama.

AN INCURABLE CASE OF LOVE

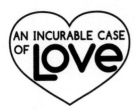

Volume 1

SHOJO BEAT EDITION

STORY & ART BY
Maki Enjoji

TRANSLATION
JN Productions

TOUCH-UP ART & LETTERING
Inori Fukuda Trant

DESIGN
Alice Lewis

EDITOR
Nancy Thistlethwaite

KOI WA TSUZUKU YO DOKOMADEMO Vol. 1
by Maki ENJOJI

Original Japanese edition published by SHOGAKUKAN.
English translation rights in the United States of America, Canada, the United Kingdom, Ireland, Australia and New Zealand arranged with SHOGAKUKAN.

Original Cover Design: Erica ADACHI + Bay Bridge Studio

Printed in the U.S.A.

Published by VIZ Media, LLC
P.O. Box 77010
San Francisco, CA 94107

10 9 8 7 6 5 4 3 2 1
First printing, October 2019

ratings.viz.com RATED M MATURE

PARENTAL ADVISORY
AN INCURABLE CASE OF LOVE is rated M for Mature and is recommended for ages 18 and up. This series contains sexual themes.

VIZ MEDIA
viz.com

Shojo Beat
shojobeat.com

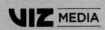

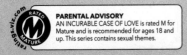

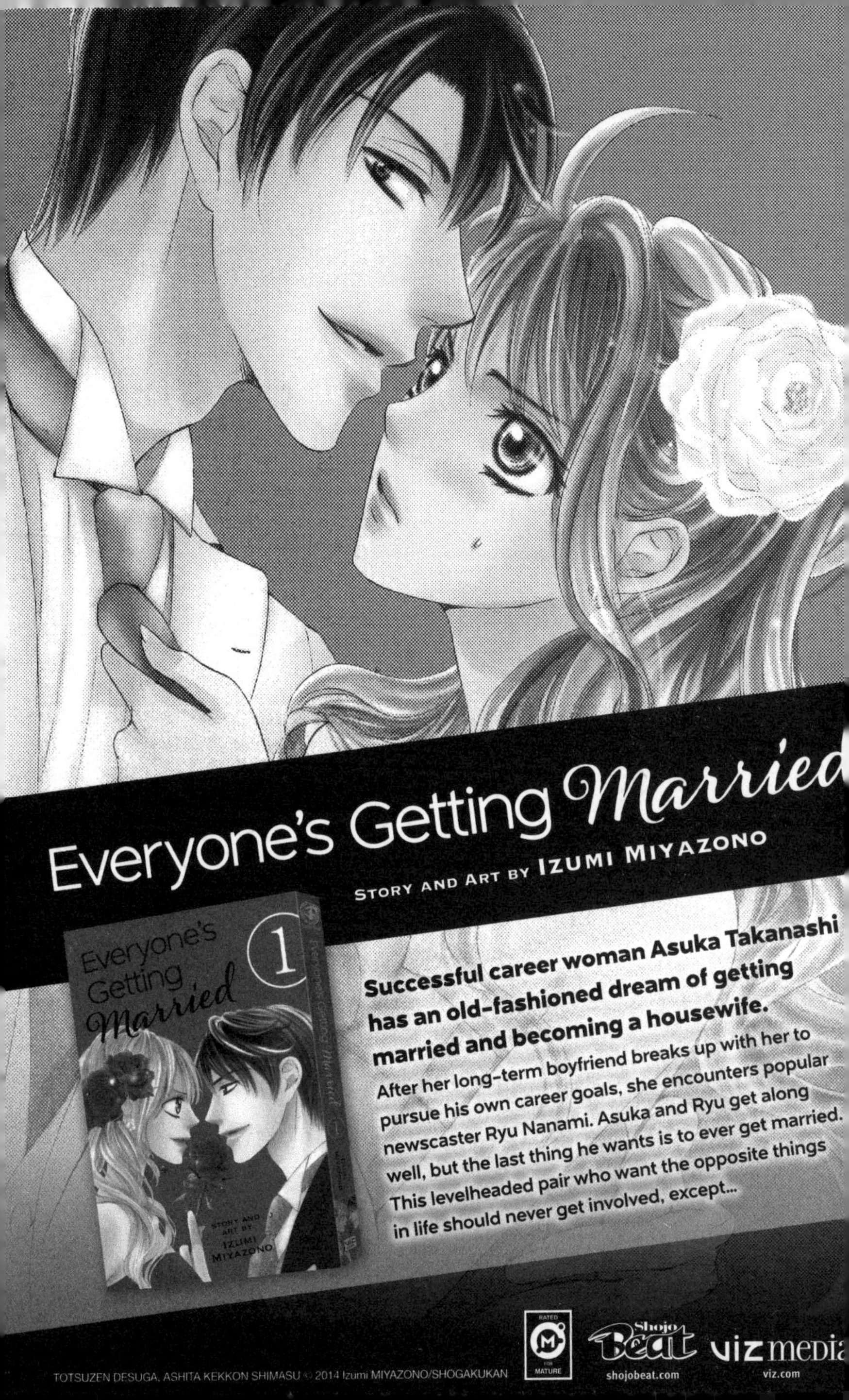
Everyone's Getting Married
Story and Art by Izumi Miyazono
Everyone's Getting Married 1
Story and Art by Izumi Miyazono
Successful career woman Asuka Takanashi has an old-fashioned dream of getting married and becoming a housewife.
After her long-term boyfriend breaks up with her to pursue his own career goals, she encounters popular newscaster Ryu Nanami. Asuka and Ryu get along well, but the last thing he wants is to ever get married. This levelheaded pair who want the opposite things in life should never get involved, except...
Rated M for Mature
Shojo Beat
shojobeat.com
viz media
viz.com
TOTSUZEN DESUGA, ASHITA KEKKON SHIMASU © 2014 Izumi MIYAZONO/SHOGAKUKAN

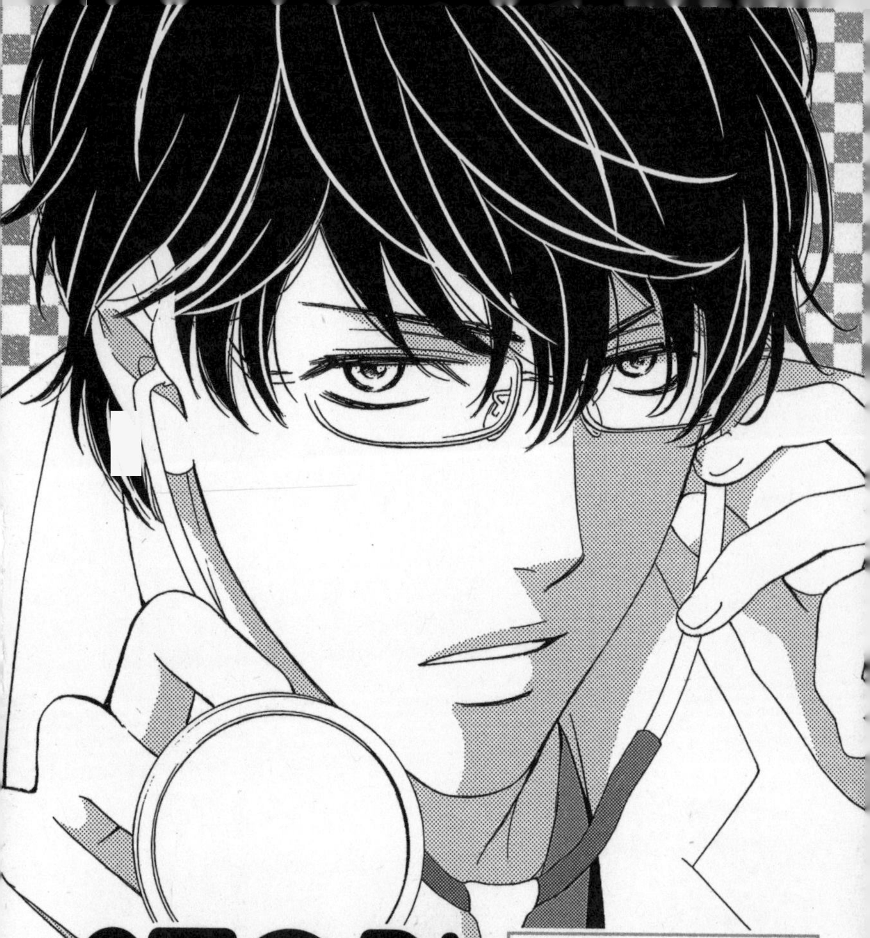

STOP!

You may be reading the wrong way!

In keeping with the original Japanese comic format, this book reads from right to left—so action, sound effects and word balloons are completely reversed to preserve the orientation of the original artwork.

Check out the diagram shown here to get the hang of things, and then turn to the other side of the book to get started!

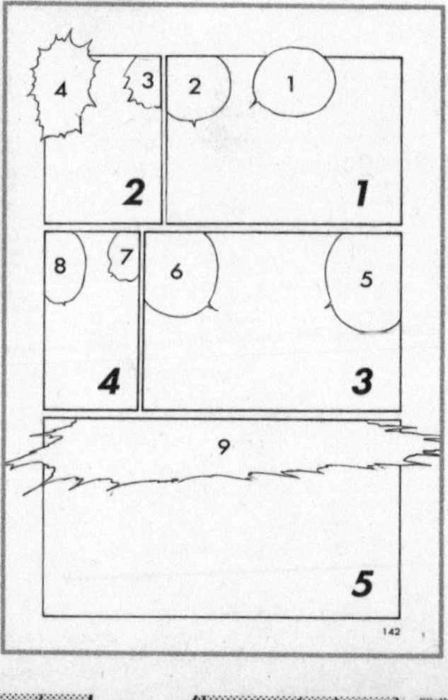
1
2
3
4
1
2
5
6
7
8
3
4
9
5
142